THE NAVARRE BIBLE: STANDARD EDITION

LETTERS TO THE CORINTHIANS

EDITORIAL COMMITTEE

VOLUMES IN THIS SERIES

Standard Edition

NEW TESTAMENT

St Matthew's Gospel
St Mark's Gospel
St Luke's Gospel
St John's Gospel
Acts of the Apostles
Romans and Galatians
Corinthians
Captivity Letters
Thessalonians and Pastoral Letters
Hebrews
Catholic Letters
Revelation

OLD TESTAMENT

The Pentateuch
Joshua–Kings [Historical Books 1]
Chronicles–Maccabees [Historical Books 2]
The Psalms and the Song of Solomon
Wisdom Books
Major Prophets
Minor Prophets

Reader's (Composite) Edition

The Gospels and Acts
The Letters of St Paul

Compact Edition

New Testament

THE NAVARRE BIBLE

Saint Paul's Letters to the Corinthians

in the Revised Standard Version and New Vulgate
with a commentary by members of the
Faculty of Theology of the University of Navarre

FOUR COURTS PRESS • DUBLIN
SCEPTER PUBLISHERS • NEW YORK

Nihil obstat: Stephen J. Greene, *censor deputatus*
Imprimi potest: Desmond, Archbishop of Dublin

Typeset by Carrigboy Typesetting Services for
FOUR COURTS PRESS LTD
7 Malpas Street, Dublin 8, Ireland
e-mail: info@four-courts-press.ie
http://www.four-courts-press.ie
Distributed in North America by
SCEPTER PUBLISHERS, INC.
P.O. Box 211, New York, NY 10018–0004
e-mail: general@scepterpublishers.org
http://www.scepterpublishers.org

The translation of introductions and commentary was made by Michael Adams.

A catalogue record for this title is available from the British Library.
First edition 1991; reprinted many times
Second edition (reset and repaged) 2005

ISBN 1–85182–906–7

Library of Congress Cataloging-in-Publication Data [for first volume in this series]

Bible. O.T. English. Revised Standard. 1999.
The Navarre Bible. – North American ed.
p. cm
"The Books of Genesis, Exodus, Leviticus, Numbers, Deuteronomy in the Revised Standard Version and New Vulgate with a commentary by members of the Faculty of Theology of the University of Navarre."
Includes bibliographical references.
Contents: [1] The Pentateuch.
ISBN 1–889334–21–9 (hardback: alk. paper)
I. Title.
BS891.A1 1999.P75 99–23033
221.7'7—dc21 CIP

ACKNOWLEDGMENTS
Quotation from Vatican II documents are based on the translation in *Vatican Council II: The Conciliar and Post Conciliar Documents*, ed. A. Flannery, OP (Dublin 1981).

The New Vulgate text of the Bible can be accessed via
http://www.vatican.va.archive/bible/index.htm

Printed and bound in Great Britain by MPG Books, Bodmin, Cornwall.

Contents

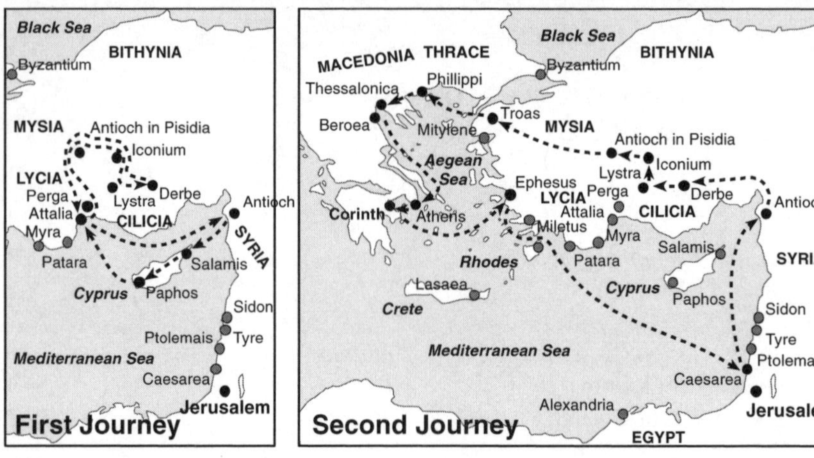

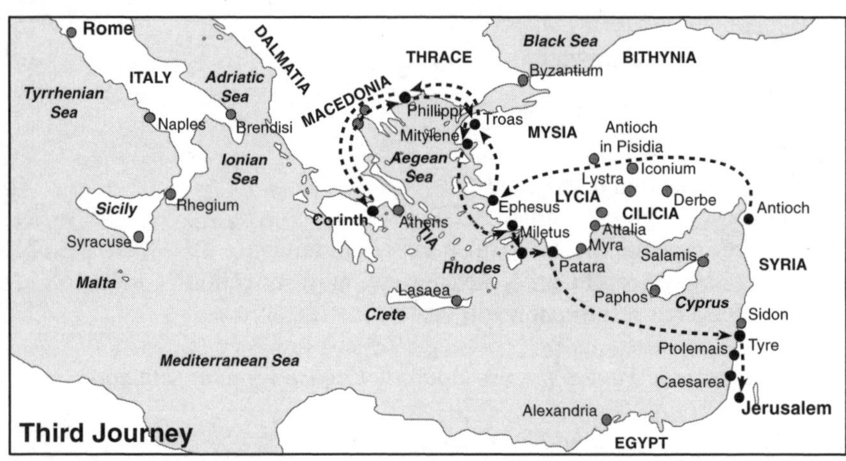

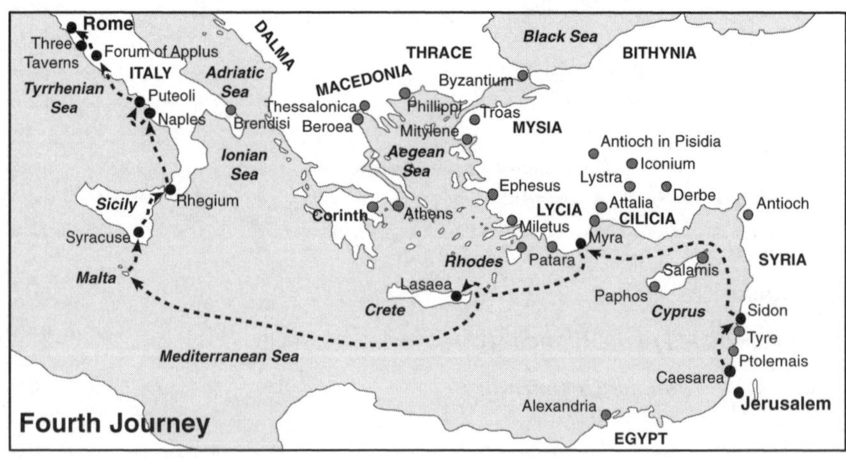

Missionary journeys of St Paul

Preface and Preliminary Notes

The English edition of *The Navarre Bible: New Testament* was published in twelve volumes in 1985–92. These books have been constantly reprinted and have obtained a very wide acceptance.

The project of a new Spanish translation of the Bible, with commentary, was originally entrusted to the faculty of theology at the University of Navarre by St Josemaría Escrivá, the founder of Opus Dei and the university's first chancellor. Because it involved making a new translation of the Bible from the original languages, the project was a much more substantial undertaking than might appear from the English edition.[1] The completion of the project was celebrated in Madrid in February 2005.

The main feature of the English edition, *The Navarre Bible*, is the commentary, that is, the notes and introductions provided by the editors; rarely very technical, these are designed to elucidate the spiritual and theological message of the Bible. Quotations from commentaries by the Fathers, and excerpts from other spiritual writers, not least St Josemaría Escrivá, are provided to show how they read Scripture and made it meaningful in their lives. The Standard Edition also carries the Western Church's official Latin version of the Bible, the *editio typica altera* of the New Vulgate (1986).

For the English edition we consider ourselves fortunate in having the Revised Standard Version as the translation of Scripture and wish to record our appreciation for permission to use that text.[2]

PRELIMINARY NOTES

The headings in the biblical text have been provided by the editors (they are not taken from the RSV); this is true also of the cross references in the marginal notes. These headings are listed in a section at the end of the book, to provide an overview of its content.

References in the margin of the biblical text or its headings point to parallel passages or other passages which deal with the same theme. With the exception of the New Testament and Psalms, the marginal references are to the New Vulgate, that is, they are not normally adjusted (where applicable) to the RSV.

1. *Sagrada Biblia: Antiguo Testamento. Libros poéticas y sapienciales* (Pamplona, 2001) at pp. 7–8 describes the principles governing its translation. **2.** Integral to which are the RSV footnotes, which are indicated by superior letters.

An asterisk in the biblical text refers the reader to the Explanatory Notes that appear in the RSV Catholic Edition of the Bible.

The Navarre Bible: The Letters of Saint Paul and *The Navarre Bible: Romans and Galatians* contain an introductory essay on St Paul's letters which readers of this volume may find useful.

Abbreviations

1. BOOKS OF HOLY SCRIPTURE

Acts	Acts of the Apostles
Amos	Amos
Bar	Baruch
1 Chron	1 Chronicles
2 Chron	2 Chronicles
Col	Colossians
1 Cor	1 Corinthians
2 Cor	2 Corinthians
Dan	Daniel
Deut	Deuteronomy
Eccles	Ecclesiastes (Qoheleth)
Esther	Esther
Eph	Ephesians
Ex	Exodus
Ezek	Ezekiel
Ezra	Ezra
Gal	Galatians
Gen	Genesis
Hab	Habakkuk
Hag	Haggai
Heb	Hebrews
Hos	Hosea
Is	Isaiah
Jas	James
Jer	Jeremiah
Jn	John
1 Jn	1 John
2 Jn	2 John
3 Jn	3 John
Job	Job
Joel	Joel
Jon	Jonah
Josh	Joshua
Jud	Judith
Jude	Jude
Judg	Judges
1 Kings	1 Kings
2 Kings	2 Kings
Lam	Lamentations
Lev	Leviticus
Lk	Luke
1 Mac	1 Maccabees
2 Mac	2 Maccabees
Mal	Malachi
Mic	Micah
Mk	Mark
Mt	Matthew
Nah	Nahum
Neh	Nehemiah
Num	Numbers
Obad	Obadiah
1 Pet	1 Peter
2 Pet	2 Peter
Phil	Philippians
Philem	Philemon
Ps	Psalms
Prov	Proverbs
Rev	Revelation (Apocalypse)
Rom	Romans
Ruth	Ruth
1 Sam	1 Samuel
2 Sam	2 Samuel
Sir	Sirach (Ecclesiasticus)
Song	Song of Solomon
1 Thess	1 Thessalonians
2 Thess	2 Thessalonians
1 Tim	1 Timothy
2 Tim	2 Timothy
Tit	Titus
Wis	Wisdom
Zech	Zechariah
Zeph	Zephaniah

2. OTHER ABBREVIATIONS

ad loc.	*ad locum*, commentary on this passage
AAA	*Acta Apostolicae Sedis*
Apost.	Apostolic
can.	canon
chap.	chapter
cf.	*confer*, compare
Const.	Constitution
Decl.	Declaration
Dz-Sch	Denzinger-Schönmetzer, *Enchiridion Biblicum* (4th edition, Naples-Rome, 1961)
Enc.	Encyclical
Exhort.	Exhortation
f	and following (*pl.* ff)
ibid.	*ibidem*, in the same place
in loc.	*in locum,* commentary on this passage
loc.	*locum*, place or passage
par.	parallel passages
Past.	Pastoral
RSVCE	Revised Standard Version, Catholic Edition
SCDF	Sacred Congregation for the Doctrine of the Faith
sess.	session
v.	verse (*pl.* vv.)

"Sources quoted in the Commentary", which appears at the end of this book, explains other abbreviations used.

Introduction to Paul's Letters to the Corinthians

THE CITY OF CORINTH

Corinth was one of the most important commercial cities in the Roman Empire. Occupying a strategic position on the isthmus of the same name, which linked the Peloponnese peninsula to continental Greece, it had two ports—Cenchreae on the Aegean Sea, and Lechaeum on the Ionian Sea: it was virtually an obligatory stop on the route from Asia to Italy—hence its commercial importance.

Even in St Paul's time Corinth had a long history behind it. According to Homer[1] it had been founded in the ninth century BC; it saw its heyday in the sixth and fifth centuries with its schools of rhetoric and philosophy (the tomb of Diogenes was one of its proudest monuments). In 146 BC it was razed by the Roman general Lucius Mummius Achaicus; a hundred years later Julius Caesar founded a new Roman colony on the ruins of the old city, thereby giving it a new prosperity, which lasted for three centuries.

Corinth was the capital of Achaia (Achaia and Macedonia were the two provinces into which the Romans divided Greece). It was also the residence of the Roman proconsul. In the first century of our era it had a population of some 100,000, making it the largest city in Greece. Up to two-thirds of the population were slaves, the rest being mainly Roman families, who were very much in the ascendancy, as is evident from the many Roman names we find among the first Christians of the city—Crispus, Titius, Justus (cf. Acts 18:7–8); Lucius, Tertius, Gaius, Quartus (cf. Rom 16:21–23); Fortunatus, Stephanas, Achaicus (cf. 1 Cor 16:17). Since it was a key trading centre, it had a cosmopolitan population—including people from Asia Minor, Phoenicians, Egyptians and others. And it had a Jewish community of some size, as can be seen from the fact that there was a synagogue in the city (cf. Acts 18:4).

It was also a city with many different religions and with temples dedicated to all sorts of gods—and it was notorious for its low level of morality.[2] Life "Corinthian-style" was synonymous with depravity. Its aberrations included the cult of Aphrodite, which had a thousand "priestesses" who practised what was euphemistically called "sacred prostitution". St Paul preached the

1. Cf. *The Iliad*, 6, 152, 210 etc. **2.** Cf. Juvenal, *Satires*, 8, 113.

Christian message in this city, and God's help enabled him to found a flourishing Christian community.

THE CHURCH OF CORINTH

From the Acts of the Apostles (cf. 18:1–18) we know that the church of Corinth was founded by St Paul, with the help of Silas and Timothy, during his second missionary journey.[3] The Apostle had arrived in Corinth from Athens, where he had made few converts, despite his brilliant discourse in the Areopagus (cf. Acts 17:16–34). This relative failure in Athens, plus the moral corruption which reigned supreme in Corinth, may explain why he arrived "in much fear and trembling" (1 Cor 2:3). No doubt moved by the Holy Spirit, in this new city the Apostle would leave aside the rhetoric of human wisdom and simply proclaim "nothing except Jesus Christ and him crucified" (1 Cor 2:2).

St Paul spent more than a year and a half teaching in Corinth—in the period 50–52 (cf. Acts 18:11). To begin with he stayed and worked with Aquila and Priscilla, a Christian couple who had been expelled from Rome shortly before because of Claudius' edict against Jews (cf. Acts 18:2). As was his custom, he preached, to begin with, in the synagogue—to Jews and Greeks who believed in the God of Israel (cf. Acts 18:4). Later, because of the opposition he was meeting from Jews, he decided to concentrate on preaching to Gentiles. At that point he changed his lodgings and stayed with Titius Justus, a Gentile who was living close to the synagogue and who may very well have been a convert to Judaism (cf. Acts 18:6–7).

Paul made many converts in Corinth—Crispus, the ruler of the synagogue, being one of the most prominent (cf. Acts 18:8)—but he had his share of setbacks as well. Once, our Lord appeared to him at night in a vision, to raise his spirits (cf. Acts 18:9–10). Increasing opposition from Jews ultimately led to charges being brought against Paul to Gallio, the Roman proconsul; but Gallio gave the matter no importance because he saw it as a complicated Jewish religious squabble (cf. Acts 18:12–17). There is documentary evidence—published in 1902—in the form of an inscription found at Delphi recording that Gallio's term of office in Achaia began in July 51. This allows us to date fairly precisely the Apostle's first stay in Corinth: he would have appeared before Gallio around the start of 52. He left Corinth shortly after this, taking ship with Aquila and Priscilla (cf. Acts 18:18).

During this stay in Corinth St Paul wrote his two letters to the Thessalonians (he had been to Thessalonica shortly before moving to Corinth: cf. Acts 17:1–9), which are chronologically the first New Testament texts.

3. Cf. "Introduction to the Letters of St Paul", in *The Navarre Bible: Romans and Galatians.*

Some time after this, approximately a year later, there arrived in Corinth Apollos, a very eloquent Jew of Alexandrian origin; he carried on the work Paul had begun (cf. Acts 18:26–28; 1 Cor 3:4–6).

The Apostle paid other subsequent visits to the city. During his third missionary journey, when he was founding the church at Ephesus (cf. Acts 19:1–40) it is probable that—after writing 1 Corinthians— he paid a brief visit, in the year 57 (cf. note on 2 Cor 1:15–2:4): on this occasion he himself or one of his assistants must have been the object of some especially serious offence (cf. note on 2 Cor 2:5–11). Later, after writing 2 Corinthians from Macedonia, he spent the winter of 57–58 in the city (cf. Acts 20:1–3).

To judge from the information St Paul provides in his letters, the Christian community at Corinth was one of his largest foundations. Seemingly, Christians of pagan birth were in the majority (cf. 1 Cor 12:2), most of them humble folk, although some of them were educated and even well-to-do (cf. 1 Cor 1:26–29); it was a community of some considerable size, with all walks of life represented (cf. 1 Cor 11:2–6; 14:34–35).

Introduction to the First Letter to the Corinthians

IMMEDIATE BACKGROUND

It is practically certain that the Apostle wrote this first letter towards the end of his sojourn in Ephesus, in the spring of AD 57. He had sent Timothy to Corinth (cf. 1 Cor 4:17; 16:10) and Acts tells us that Paul had been two years and three months in Ephesus prior to Timothy's departure (cf. Acts 19:8, 10, 22), which, it is reasonable to suppose, occurred around Easter, which would explain some of the references the Apostle makes in this letter: for example, he mentions the Azymes (cf. 1 Cor 5:7–8), and he compares Christian self-denial with the athletic training of runners in the stadium (cf. 1 Cor 9:24–27)—perhaps a reference to the Isthmus Games held in Corinth every second spring.[1]

Given the close and frequent commercial ties between Ephesus and Corinth it is not surprising that St Paul was well aware of the situation in Corinth. In fact, we know from 1 Corinthians 5:9 that he had already written a letter to the Corinthians—the so-called "pre-canonical" letter, now lost—in an attempt to put an end to certain abuses.

Leaving aside other possible sources of information available to the Apostle, and looking only at what the letter itself supplies, the following can be inferred. For one thing, the Apostle had been told "by Chloe's people" (1 Cor 1:11) about a number of abuses which had found their way into the church of Corinth: there were various parties in dispute; great laxity as regards unchastity applied (cf. 1 Cor 6:12ff): there was even a case of incest (cf. 1 Cor 5:1ff); some Christians had been bringing cases before pagan courts (cf. 1 Cor 6:1ff); some women behaved without due decorum at liturgical celebrations (cf. 1 Cor 11:2ff; 14:34ff); and there were irregularities in the celebration of the Eucharist (cf. 1 Cor 11:17ff). Also, the community itself had sent a delegation to Paul, made up of Stephanas, Fortunatus and Achaicus (cf. 1 Cor 16:17), bearing a letter in which they sought the Apostle's advice on a number of matters in doubt[2]—things to do with marriage and virginity (cf. 1 Cor 7:1ff), the lawfulness of eating food sacrificed to idols (cf. 1 Cor 8:1ff),

1. Cf. Xenophon, *Hellenica*, 4, 5, 1. **2.** Cf. 1 Cor. 7:1; similar references appear in 7:25; 8:1; 12:1.

charisms and their proper use (cf. 1 Cor 12:1ff), and the resurrection of the dead (cf. 1 Cor 15:1ff).

CONTENT

The specific needs and circumstances of the church of Corinth explain why Paul wrote this letter, why it is structured the way it is and why it deals with so many different subjects and is so clearly pastoral in character. However, the letter is not simply a series of answers to quesions raised; St Paul always solves the problems raised in the light of faith, which means that his replies have a perennial value and throw light on many aspects of Christian dogma and moral teaching.

The letter develops, therefore, not according to a theological-doctrinal structure but rather according to a pastoral one, in which we can distinguish two long parts, with an introduction and an epilogue:

1. In the *introduction* (1:1–9), St Paul begins with the usual greetings and a hymn of thanksgiving.

2. The *first part* deals with various abuses which have arisen (1:10–6:20):
   Divisions among the faithful (1:10–4:21).
   The case of incest (5:1–13).
   Lawsuits between Christians (6:1–11).
   Faults against chastity (6:12–20).

3. In the *second part* the Apostle replies to questions raised by the Corinthians themselves, questions to do with:
   Marriage and celibacy (7:1–40).
   The eating of food sacrificed to idols (8:1–10:33).
   Propriety at liturgical assemblies (11:1–34).
   Gifts and graces (12:1–14:40).
   The resurrection of Christ and the resurrection of the dead (15:1–58).

4. An epilogue (16:1–24) mentions the collection raised for the faithful in Jerusalem and the next journeys the Apostle is planning; it ends with an exhortation and greetings.

The First Letter to the Corinthians is especially important from the doctrinal point of view, due to the wide range of subjects it deals with and the depth of its teaching. Its themes include: divine wisdom and human wisdom; criteria which should govern Christian conduct; diverse aspects of Christian morality; and the next life. So vivid and vital is Paul's writing—which, under the

inspiration of the Holy Spirit, reflects the Apostle's rich personality, deep theology and pastoral generosity of spirit—that we are loath to attempt a systematic analysis here; instead, we will rely on the commentary itself to explain the infrastructure of the letter. However, three great themes deserve special attention—the Church, the Eucharist and the resurrection of the dead.

THE CHURCH

St Paul elaborates his teaching on the Church throughout the entire corpus of his writings. Something only hinted at in one letter is developed in others, with the result that it would not do justice to his thought to try to fit his ecclesiology into only one or two epistles. What we shall say here needs to be filled out with reference to the teaching contained, particularly, in the epistles to the Romans, Ephesians and Colossians.

The basic idea which St Paul teaches is that the Church is a supernatural entity: it has been founded by Christ, Christ is its head, and it is Christ who governs it through his ministers.

The Church's unity derives from the fact that Christians are "Christ's", belong to Christ (cf. 1 Cor 3:23; cf. 2 Cor 10:7). There is no room for factions or divisions (cf. 1 Cor 1:10–11): the source of Christian life is not to be found in Paul, or Apollos, or Cephas; these are merely the servants of one, unique Lord, one God and Father who is "above all and through all and in all" (Eph 4:6). If the Christians in Corinth yield to the temptation to boast about belonging to one grouping or another, the Apostle meets them head on: "Let him who boasts, boast of the Lord" (1 Cor 1:31).

The very simple, yet profound, similes St Paul uses to throw light on the mystery of the Church all hinge on this matter of unity: the Church is a field planted by God (cf. 1 Cor 3:6–9), a building he has erected (cf. 1 Cor 3:9, 11, 16). It is true that none of these metaphors can totally explain the Church, but they do make it plain that the source of unity is God, who gives life to each of the plants in this field;[3] and he it is who causes all the various parts of this unique building to fit together.[4] St Augustine offers a beautiful commentary on this image: "We ourselves are the house of God. In this life we are built up to be the house of God in order to be consecrated as the house of God at the end of life. It takes much effort to build the house, but its consecration brings joy and jubilation [...]. The same happens with the beginning of faith as with the chopping down of trees in the forest or the extraction of rock from the mountain; the neophytes are instructed, baptized and educated in the same way

3. Cf. the allegory of the vine in Jn 15:1–8; of the "olive plant" in Rom 11:17–24. **4.** Many New Testament texts use this metaphor—Mt 16:18; 1 Tim 3:15; Heb 3:1–6, etc.

as stone or wood are worked on and shaped by masons and carpenters. But they come to form a house only when they are brought together by Love."[5]

Of key importance for an understanding of the Church is its description as the "body of Christ." Paul uses this image to explain the Church's connexion with Christ: the Church belongs to him and is joined to him; and since the Church is Christ's people it is also God's people.[6]

St Paul's concept of the Church as a body goes far beyond the human concept of corporate unity, for between Christ and the Church, between Christ and Christians, a unity is established which is not just agreement on goals, or doing certain things together at particular times: it is a living unity; Christ communicates life to the Church and to Christians, thereby making them inseparable. St Augustine writes: "Let us rejoice together and give thanks, for we have become not only Christians but Christ. Do you realize that, brethren? Are you aware of the grace of God that is within you? Rejoice in wonder: we have become Christ. For if he is the head and we the members, the whole man is he and us. The Apostle Paul says as much [...]. The totality of Christ is the head and the members. What does 'head and members' mean? Christ and the Church."[7]

This union between Christ and the Church does not prevent a person being himself. A man or woman's individual personality does not disappear on being united to Christ, nor does the Church lose its personality on being configured to Christ. By separating Christ too much from the Church one is in danger of the heresy of Nestorianism; but if one's notion of the unity that exists between Christ and the Church is such that each is denied its own distinct personality, one is falling into the same error as the Monophysites.

All Christian believers receive from Christ their head the same life of grace. However, according to Pauline teaching, the unity that exists among the members of the mystical body is not only an interior, spiritual unity; it also has a visible structural dimension—with the result that the variety of offices and ministries in the Church in no way detracts from a unity which is both spiritual and hierarchical. Paraphrasing St Paul's teaching, the Second Vatican Council teaches that "as all the members of the human body, though they are many, form one body, so also are the faithful in Christ (cf. 1 Cor 12:12). Also, in the building of Christ's body a diversity of members and functions is involved. There is only one Spirit who, according to his own richness and the needs of the ministries, gives his different gifts for the welfare of the Church (cf. 1 Cor 12:1–11). Among these gifts the primacy belongs to the grace of the Apostles to whose authority the Spirit himself subjects even those who are endowed with charisms (cf. 1 Cor 14). Giving the body unity through himself, both by his own power and by the interior unity of the members, this same Spirit produces and stimulates love among the faithful. From that it follows that if

5. *Sermon*, 136, 1. **6.** Cf Vatican II, *Lumen gentium*, 7 and 9. **7.** *In Ioann. Evang.*, 21, 8.

one member suffers anything, all the members suffer with him, and if one member is honoured, all the members rejoice together (cf. 1 Cor 12:26)."[8]

THE EUCHARIST

At two points in the letter the Apostle deals with doctrine concerning the Eucharist—first as an aside when he is explaining why Christians may not attend banquets at pagan shrines (cf. 1 Cor 10:14–22); and later, in the course of correcting abuses which had arisen in Corinth in the celebration of the Eucharist (cf. 1 Cor 11:17–32).

These two texts spell out certain basic truths about the Eucharist: a) it was instituted by Christ himself; b) it is a sacrifice; c) Christ is really present in the Eucharist under the appearances of bread and wine; d) the relations between our Lord's sacramental body and his mystical body, the Church.

In the first place, St Paul clearly teaches that the Eucharist was instituted by Christ himself (cf. 1 Cor 11:23–25). Of the four New Testament passages which refer to this event (cf. Mt 26:26–29; Mk 14:22–25; Lk 22:14–15), this is the earliest, dating as it does from the year 57. Furthermore, the Apostle is reminding the Corinthians here about a teaching which he handed on to them during his first stay in Corinth, that is, in the period 50–52. In fact, by saying, "I received ... what I also delivered to you" (1 Cor 11:23), St Paul is referring to the fact that his teaching goes right back to the start of the Church.

There is a very close connexion between the account of the institution of the Eucharist given in this letter and that given by St Luke: only these two accounts mention Christ's command to do in his memory what he did at the Last Supper (cf. Lk 22:19; 1 Cor 11:24–25), a commandment which expressly refers to the institution of the Christian priesthood.[9]

Secondly, the epistle clearly shows that the Eucharist is not only a sacrament but also a sacrifice, for it contrasts the Eucharist with pagan sacrifices. The reason why it is unlawful for Christians to take part in the latter stems from the fact that they are idolatrous sacrifices and therefore incompatible with the sacrifice of the Eucharist, which is offered to the true God. This can also be deduced from his comparison of the Eucharist to the victims in Old Testament sacrifices: these victims were a prefiguring of the Eucharist (cf. 1 Cor 10:14–22).

The Mass, which is offered every day in the Church in keeping with Christ's command, perpetuates the unique sacrifice of Christ on the cross, "for as often as you eat this bread and drink the cup, you proclaim the Lord's death until he comes" (1 Cor 11:26). In biblical language this proclamation of the

8. *Lumen gentium*, 7. **9.** Cf Council of Trent, *De SS. Missae sacrificio*, chap. 1; SCDF, *Sacerdotium ministeriale*.

death of our Lord is not just a commemoration of a past event; it also makes present what it proclaims. And so the Church says: "whenever the memorial of this sacrifice is commemorated, the work of our redemption is performed."[10]

Thirdly, St Paul asserts the real presence of Christ under the appearances of bread and wine. Even though Christ's own words about the bread and wine (cf. 1 Cor 11:24–25) leave no room for doubt, St Paul's stern warning—"Whoever eats the bread or drinks the cup of the Lord in an unworthy manner will be guilty of profaning the body and blood of the Lord" (1 Cor 11:27)—implies that Christ is really present under the species of bread and wine; and the same is true of the requirement to examine oneself before Communion "For any one who eats and drinks without discerning the body"—meaning the body *par excellence*, since it is the body of the Lord—"eats and drinks judgment upon himself" (1 Cor 11:29).

Finally, as regards the relations between the Eucharist (the sacramental body of Christ) and the Church (his mystical body), what St Paul says is quite clear: "Because there is one bread, we who are many are one body, for we all partake of the one bread" (1 Cor 10:17). The Second Vatican Council uses these words as its basis when it teaches that "in that body, the life of Christ is communicated to those who believe and who, through the sacraments, are united in a hidden and real way to Christ in his passion and glorification [...]. Really sharing in the body of the Lord in the breaking of the eucharistic bread, we are taken up into communion with him and with one another. 'Because there is one bread, we who are many are one body, for we all partake of the one bread' (1 Cor 10:17). In this way all of us are made members of his body (cf. 1 Cor 12:27), 'and individually members one of another' (Rom 12:5)."[11] The Eucharist, at the same time as it really contains the body and blood of Christ, manifests the unity of the people of God, "which this holy sacrament aptly and admirably brings about."[12]

THE RESURRECTION OF THE DEAD

It should be remembered that the Christians of Corinth found it very difficult to accept the resurrection of the dead (cf. 1 Cor 15:12). Given the environment in which they lived this is not very surprising, for this truth of faith was in conflict with traditional Greek thought—as Paul found out for himself when he spoke in the Areopagus of Athens: "Now when they heard of the resurrection of the dead, some mocked; but others said, 'We will hear you again about this'" (Acts 17:32).

10. *Roman Missal*, 2nd Sunday in ordinary time, prayer over the gifts (literal translation). **11.** *Lumen gentium*, 7. **12.** Ibid., 11.

THE RESURRECTION OF CHRIST

In reply to the doubts which had arisen in Corinth, St Paul first of all discusses the historical fact of the resurrection of Christ. This testimony, written less than thirty years after the event, is of the greatest importance. As is true of his teaching on the Eucharist, this is a teaching which had formed part of apostolic Tradition from the very beginning: "I delivered to you as of first importance what I also received" (1 Cor 15:3).

The death, burial and resurrection of Christ was also the very hinge of St Paul's teaching when he was in Corinth (cf. 1 Cor 15:3–4). The Apostle offers a long list of witnesses of the risen Christ—Peter, James the Less, all the Apostles and five hundred brethren, most of whom at the time of writing were still alive and could testify to what they had seen (cf. 1 Cor 15:5–7). And at the end he adds his own testimony (cf. 1 Cor 15:8).

However, the resurrection of Christ is not only an historical fact; it is also a mystery. This mystery hinges on the glorified condition of the risen Christ, which is witnessed to in all the relevant passages of the New Testament. Thus, St Paul keeps on saying that Christ "appeared" (1 Cor 15:5, 6, 7, 8), thereby giving us to understand that he was seen only by those whom he chose to see him. Paul says the same thing, indirectly, by calling Christ "the first fruits" (cf. 1 Cor 15:20) of those who will rise from the dead. For, even though it is true that some people rose from the dead before Christ—for example, Lazarus, the son of the widow of Nain, the daughter of Jairus—these, however, "were restored to life to die again. But Christ our Lord, having subdued and conquered death, so arose that he could die no more, according to this most clear testimony: 'Christ, being raised from the dead, will never die again; death no longer has dominion over him' (Rom 6:9)."[13]

THE RESURRECTION OF CHRIST, THE BASIS OF OUR FAITH

Christ's resurrection is also the sure ground on which our faith is based. Of all the other miracles worked by our Lord, his own resurrection provides the most conclusive proof of his divinity. "Our Lord very frequently spoke to his disciples of his resurrection (cf. Mt 16:21; 17:22), and seldom or never of his Passion without referring to his resurrection. Thus, when he said, 'The Son of man [...] will be delivered to the Gentiles, and will be mocked and shamefully treated and spit upon; they will scourge him and kill him', he added, 'and on the third day he will rise' (Lk 18:31–33). Also, when the Jews called upon him to give a proof of the truth of his doctrine by some miraculous sign, he said,

13. *Pius V Catechism*, 1, 6, 9.

'No sign shall be given to it except the sign of the prophet Jonah (cf. Mt 12:39–40; Lk 11:29). For as Jonah was three days and three nights in the belly of the whale, so will the Son of man be three days and three nights in the heart of the earth'."[14]

St Paul points out to the Corinthians that "if Christ has not been raised, then our preaching is in vain and your faith is in vain [...]. If Christ has not been raised, your faith is futile, and you are still in your sins" (1 Cor 15:14, 17). As St Augustine comments, "it is no great thing to believe that Christ died, because that is something which pagans and Jews also believe, as do all evil men: all believe that he died. What Christians believe in is the resurrection of Christ: that is what we see as important—our faith in his having risen."[15]

Our faith only makes sense if Christ is alive; only then can he have the power to save us; only then can the sacraments administered in his name have any efficacy. Specifically, our incorporation into Christ by Baptism, whereby we share in his death and resurrection, has value only if Christ has risen. If he had not risen, we would be still in our sins (cf. 1 Cor 15:17).

THE RESURRECTION OF CHRIST, THE CAUSE OF OUR RESURRECTION

Christ's resurrection is not only the basis of our faith; it is also, given our intimate and living union with him through Baptism, the source of our hope that we too will rise: "as Christ rose again, we rest on an assured hope that we too shall rise again; the members must necessarily arrive at the condition of their head."[16]

More specifically, Christ's resurrection is the "efficient cause" of our own. St Paul explains this by his simile of the "first fruits" (cf. 1 Cor 15:20, 23) and by counterposing Christ and Adam: just as death came through a man, so resurrection from the dead comes through a man. For "as in Adam all die, so also in Christ shall all be made alive" (1 Cor 15:22).

Thus, God made Adam the head of the human race. After his sin, he became, for all who are born of him, the cause of their death. Similarly, Christ is the head of the new creation, of redeemed mankind, and he becomes, for all those united to him by generation in Baptism, the cause of their life and resurrection.

THE FORM OUR RESURRECTION WILL TAKE

Finally, the Apostle explains at length our form of existence after rising from the dead (cf. 1 Cor 15:35–53). In other New Testament writings, that is, in the

14. Ibid., 1, 6, 11. **15.** *Enarrationes in Psalmos*, 120. **16.** *St Pius V Catechism*, 1, 6, 12.

Gospels, we are expressly told that all men—sinners as well as the just—shall rise from the dead (cf. Mt 25:31–46; Jn 5:28–29). St Paul expresses this same belief in his speeches before the Sanhedrin (cf. Acts 23:6–8) and the Roman governor Felix (cf. Acts 24:15). However, given his specific purpose in this letter, he concentrates on the glorious resurrection of the elect. This will occur on the last day at the second coming of Christ (cf. 1 Cor 15:23), and it will involve a total transformation of our bodies (cf. 1 Cor 15:51): they will change from a natural to a spiritual mode of existence (cf. 1 Cor 15:44–46). By saying this St Paul is not denying that the risen body is material (that would be a contradiction in terms): what he means is that the spirit will have complete dominion over the body. As a consequence of this dominion, the body will be incorruptible (cf. 1 Cor 15:42), glorious (cf. v. 43), strong (v. 43) and immortal (vv. 53–54).

In this life we shall never be able completely to grasp how the resurrection of the dead will come about, but God has said unambiguously that he is preparing for us "a new dwelling" and "a new earth" (Rev 21:1). "Then with death conquered the sons of God will be raised in Christ and what was sown in weakness and dishonour will put on the imperishable (cf. 1 Cor 15:42, 53); charity and its works will remain (cf. 1 Cor 13:8; 3:14) and all of creation (cf. Rom 8:19–21), which God made for man, will be set free from its bondage to decay."[17]

17. *Gaudium et spes*, 12.

THE FIRST LETTER OF PAUL TO THE CORINTHIANS

The Revised Standard Version, with notes

INTRODUCTION

Greeting

1 [1]Paul, called by the will of God to be an apostle of Christ Jesus,
and our brother Sosthenes,

1:1–9. With slight variations almost all St Paul's letters begin in the same kind of way: there is a greeting (vv. 1–3), which carries the name of the writer, information on the addressee(s), and the conventional phrase; and an act of thanksgiving to God (vv. 4–9), in which the Apostle refers to the main qualities and endowments of the Christians to whom he is writing. By comparing his letters with others that have come down to us from the same period, it is quite apparent that St Paul usually begins his letters in the style of the time. Yet he does not entirely follow this rigid pattern: he changes the usual opening—"Greeting!" (cf. Acts 15:23; 23:26)—to this more personal one, which has a pronounced Christian stamp: "Grace to you and peace." Also, the way in which he introduces himself and describes those he is addressing tells much more than a simple "Paul to the Corinthians: greeting!" Even his words of thanksgiving convey tenderness and warmth—and their tone is not merely human, for he attributes to God the virtues he praises in the faithful.

The Fathers of the Church have drawn attention to this characteristic of Paul's letters—the way he manages to convey a deep doctrinal message in a familiar style, nicely suited to whomever he happens to be addressing: "A doctor", St John Chrysostom explains, "does not treat the patient in the same way at the start of his illness as when he is recovering; nor does a teacher use the same method with children as with those who need more advanced tuition. That is how the Apostle acts: he writes as suits the needs and the times" (*Hom. on Rom*, prologue).

1:1. St Paul attaches to his name three features which identify him—his divine calling; his office as Apostle of Jesus Christ; and the will of God, the source of his apostolic vocation.

"Called": this is a carefully chosen word designed to convey the vigorous and personal way God called him. He calls all men to faith, to grace, to holiness, and to heaven (cf., e.g., Rom 1:7; 1 Cor 1:2; 1:26; 7:20; Eph 1:18). By defining himself as "called" (cf. Rom 1:1), St Paul is very probably referring to the episode on the road to Damascus (cf. Acts 9:1–19), when Christ changed his life, as he had earlier changed the lives of the Twelve.

"Apostle of Christ Jesus": Paul can find no stronger expression than this to describe his mission: he is forever applying this title to himself—thirty-five times by our reckoning. This fact of his apostleship is the basis of his authority—authority to praise, teach, admonish and correct orally and in writing. He is so totally identified with this mission that he has no other purpose than to pursue it; his life is dedicated to this end; all his thoughts, words and actions are aimed at achieving it. Humbly (because he once persecuted the Church: 1 Cor 15:9) and yet forthrightly (cf. 1 Cor 9:1–2) he puts himself on the same level as the Twelve as far as vocation and apostleship are concerned.

"By the will of God": the Apostle's energy and vitality are attributable not to himself but to God, who had plans for Paul ever since he was in his mother's womb (Gal 1:15); so much so that later in

Acts 9:14 [2]To the church of God which is at Corinth, to those sanctified in Christ Jesus, called to be saints* together with all those who in every place call on the name of our Lord Jesus Christ, both their Lord and ours:

---

this letter he actually says, "If I preach the Gospel, that gives me no ground for boasting. For necessity is laid upon me. Woe to me if I do not preach the Gospel" (1 Cor 9:16).

"Our brother, Sosthenes": it is uncertain whether this was the same person as the ruler of the synagogue in Corinth mentioned in Acts (18:17). The prominent position given him here suggests that he was someone well-known to the community at Corinth, either for his ministry among them or because he often accompanied St Paul; he may have been the secretary, or scribe, who actually wrote the letter down (cf. 16:21).

1:2. "The church of God at Corinth": the addressee of the letter. The very grammar of the phrase emphasizes the fact that the Church is not the totality of the local communities: rather, each local community—here, the Christians of Corinth—represents the whole Church, which is one and indivisible: "The Apostle calls it [the community] 'the church of God' in order to show that unity is one of its essential and necessary characteristics. The Church of God is one in its members and forms nothing but a single Church with all the communities spread throughout the world, for the word 'church' does not mean schism: it means unity, harmony, concord" (St John Chrysostom, *Hom on 1 Cor*, 1, ad loc.).

In another three brush-strokes St Paul here describes those who make up the Church—those sanctified in Jesus Christ, those called to be saints, those who invoke the name of our Lord Jesus Christ.

"Those sanctified in Christ Jesus": the faithful receive at Baptism the grace which makes them a holy people (cf. Ex 19:6; 1 Pet 2:9); the participle "sanctified" implies something stable, such as is the intimate union between the individual Christian and Jesus. The formula "in Christ Jesus" here refers to the fact that the baptized are grafted on to Christ like branches attached to a vine (cf. Jn 15:1ff); this link with Christ is what makes them saints, that is, sharers in God's own holiness; and it involves a duty to strive for moral perfection. "As those who profess any art, even though they depart from its rules, are still called artists, so in like manner the faithful, although offending in many things and violating the engagements to which they had pledged themselves, are still called holy, because they have been made the people of God and have consecrated themselves to Christ by faith and Baptism. Hence, St Paul calls the Corinthians sanctified and holy, although it is certain that among them there were some whom he severely rebuked as carnal, and charged with grosser crimes" (*St Pius V Catechism*, 1, 10, 15).

"Called to be saints": through faith and Baptism "all Christians in any state or walk of life are called to the fullness of Christian life and to the perfection of love" (Vatican II, *Lumen gentium*, 40).

"Those who in every place call on the name of our Lord Jesus Christ": this circumlocution describes Christian believers (cf. Acts 9:14, 21; 22:16; Rom 10:12); what makes them different from others is that they worship Jesus Christ as Lord and God, in the same way as the faithful of the Old Covenant invoked the name of Yahweh. To be a member of the Church of God, therefore, it is essential that a person believe that Christ is God. "We believe in our Lord Jesus Christ, who is

[3]Grace to you and peace from God our Father and the Lord Jesus Christ. Ps 103:13 Rom 1:7

Thanksgiving

[4]I give thanks to God[a] always for you because of the grace of God Rom 3:24
which was given you in Christ Jesus, [5]that in every way you were 2 Cor 12:8
enriched in him with all speech and all knowledge—[6]even as the
testimony to Christ was confirmed among you—[7]so that you are
not lacking in any spiritual gift, as you wait for the revealing of
our Lord Jesus Christ; [8]who will sustain you to the end, guiltless
in the day of our Lord Jesus Christ. [9]God is faithful, by whom you 1 Jn 1:3
were called into the fellowship of his Son, Jesus Christ our Lord.

---

the Son of God. He is the eternal Word of the Father before time began, one in substance with the Father, *homoousios tō Patri*, through whom all things were made. He was incarnate of the Virgin Mary by the power of the Holy Spirit and was made man. 'Equal, therefore, to the Father according to his divinity, less than the Father according to his humanity, his unity deriving not from some impossible confusion of substance but from his Person'" (Paul VI, *Creed of the People of God*, 11).

1:3. Peace of soul, that "serenity of mind, tranquillity of soul, simplicity of heart, bond of love, union of charity" of which St Augustine spoke (*De verb. Dom. serm.*, 58), originates in the friendship with God which grace brings with it; it is one of the fruits of the Holy Spirit (cf. Gal 5:22–23). This is the only true kind of peace: "There is no true peace, just as there is no true grace, other than the grace and peace which come from God," St John Chrysostom teaches. "Possess this divine peace and you will have nothing to fear, even if you be threatened by the direst danger, whether from men or even from the demons themselves; whereas see how everything is a cause of fear for the man who is at war with God through sin" (*Hom. on 1 Cor*, 1, ad loc.).

1:4–9. After the greeting, words of thanksgiving conclude the introduction to the letter, before St Paul begins the doctrinal part. He reminds the Corinthians that they owe their privileged position to God. They, like all Christians, received God's grace in Christ, and that grace has enriched them in every way, for it causes man to share in God's very nature (cf. 2 Pet 1:4), raising him to an entirely new level of existence. This transfiguration enables a person, even here, to know the perfections of God's inner life and to partake of that life—albeit in a limited, imperfect way—through the theological virtues of faith, hope and charity, which grace brings and which elevate the mind and will to know and love God, One and Three.

St Paul teaches the need to give thanks to God and he sets us an example in this regard. Obdurate sinners fail to acknowledge the benefits God gives them (cf. Rom 1:21), but Christians should always base their prayer on gratitude to God (cf. Phil 4:6). "Nothing charms God

a. Other ancient authorities read *my God*

PART ONE

Correction of abuses

1. DIVISIONS AMONG THE CORINTHIANS

An appeal for unity

Phil 2:2 10 I appeal to you, brethren, by the name of our Lord Jesus Christ,
that all of you agree and that there be no dissensions among you,
but that you be united in the same mind and the same judgment.

---

more than a heart that is grateful either on its own account or on account of others" (Chrysostom, *Hom. on 1 Cor*, 2, ad loc.).

1:5–6. The grace of God, mentioned in the previous verse, embraces gifts, including those to do with eloquence and knowledge. So richly does God endow the Christian that St Alphonsus exclaims: "Our wretchedness should not make us uneasy, for in Jesus crucified we shall find all richness and all grace (cf. 1 Cor 1:5, 7). The merits of Jesus Christ have enriched us with all the wealth of God and there is no grace we might desire that we cannot obtain by asking for it" (*The Love of God*, chap. 3). The Fathers interpret these gifts as meaning that the Corinthians had such a good grasp of Christian teaching that they were able to expound it: "There are those who have the gift of knowledge but not that of speech; and there are others who have the gift of speech but not knowledge. The faithful in general, who are uneducated, know these truths, but they cannot clearly explain what they have in their soul. You on the other hand, St Paul says, are different; you know these truths and you can speak about them; you are rich in the gift of speech and in that of knowledge" (Chrysostom, *Hom. on 1 Cor*, 2, ad loc.).

1:8–9. "The day of our Lord": in St Paul's writings and in the New Testament generally, this refers to the day of the General Judgment when Christ will appear as Judge, clothed in glory (cf. 2 Cor 1:14; 1 Thess 5:2).

Christians actively hope that that Day will find them "blameless" (cf. Phil 1:10; 1 Thess 3:13; 5:23); the basis for this hope is God's faithfulness—an attitude frequently applied to him in the Old Testament (cf. Deut 7:9; Is 49:7) and in St Paul's letters (cf. 1 Cor 10:13; 2 Cor 1:18; 1 Thess 5:24; 2 Thess 3:3; Heb 10:23): the Covenant which God made with the chosen people was primarily a gift and a grace, but it also was a legal commitment. The Covenant was grounded on God's fidelity, which was not merely a matter of legal obligation: it involved faithful, constant love. God's fidelity will find its fullest expression in the Redemption brought about by Jesus Christ: "If, in fact, the reality of the Redemption," Pope John Paul II says, "in its human dimension, reveals the unheard-of greatness of man, *qui talem ac tantum meruit habere Redemptorem*, at the same time *the divine dimension of the Redemption* enables us [...] to uncover the depth of that love which does not recoil before the extraordinary sacrifice of the Son, in order to

11 For it has been reported to me by Chloe's people that there is Jn 1:42
quarrelling among you, my brethren. 12 What I mean is that each Acts 18:24ff
one of you says, "I belong to Paul," or "I belong to Apollos," or "I 1 Cor 3:4; 3:22f

---

satisfy the fidelity of the Creator and Father towards human beings, created in his image" (*Dives in misericordia*, 7).

1:10–17. St Paul takes the Corinthians to task for the strife in their community—not, it seems, quarrels over matters of doctrine, but minor disagreements due to preferences for certain teachers. Even so, the Apostle is very much against factions, and he starts his letter by stressing that unity is essential to the Church.

He makes four points, as it were—an appeal (v. 10); a description of the state of affairs in Corinth (vv. 11–12); a doctrinal reflection: Christ cannot be divided (v. 13); and a summary of his (Paul's) ministry (vv. 14–17).

His appeal is virtually a warning: "I appeal to you by the name of our Lord Jesus Christ." The Apostle only calls on the name of our Lord when he has very serious counsel to offer (cf. 1 Thess 4:1; 2 Thess 3:6); he makes it clear that it is a very grave matter to put the unity of the Church at risk. Each of these groups in Corinth is appealing to whichever authority it prefers—without Paul, Apollos or Cephas having any say in the matter. Christ cannot be divided and therefore neither can the Church, Christ's body (cf. 1 Cor 12:12–31).

Finally, St Paul points out their feeble grounds for basing divisions on personal relationships: very few of them can claim to have been baptized by him, because his concentration has been on evangelization.

This entire passage is a defence of Church unity. Throughout the centuries the Church has confessed this truth of faith—from the Apostles' Creed ("I believe in the Holy Catholic Church") right down to the *Creed of the People of God* of Paul VI: "We believe that the Church which Christ founded and for which he prayed is indefectibly one in faith and in worship, and one in the communion of a single hierarchy" (no. 21).

1:10. "That you all agree … in the same mind and the same judgment": St Paul is not calling for mere external unity or just living peaceably or being sure to come together for certain liturgical ceremonies. He wants something that goes much deeper than that: the concord that should reign among them should stem from their being of one mind, from feeling the same way about things. In saying this he obviously does not mean to restrict the freedom every Christian enjoys as far as earthly affairs are concerned: it is the unity *of the Church* that Paul is discussing, and in that area there is no room for factions among Christians (cf. v. 11). Differences, diversity, which do not affect the unity of the Church are something lawful and positively good.

One basic dimension of Church unity is unity of faith. That is why the Fathers and the Magisterium have borrowed from what St Paul says here, to show that genuine progress in understanding the content of truths of faith must always keep in line with earlier understanding of the same: "any meaning of the sacred dogmas that has once been declared by holy Mother Church must always be retained; and there must never be any deviation from that meaning on the specious grounds of a more profound understanding. 'Therefore, let there be growth […] and all possible progress in

Eph 4:5 belong to Cephas,"* or "I belong to Christ." 13Is Christ divided?
Was Paul crucified for you? Or were you baptized in the name of
Acts 18:8
Rom 16:23 Paul? 14I am thankful[b] that I baptized none of you except Crispus

---

understanding, knowledge, and wisdom whether in single individuals or in the whole body, in each man as well as in the entire Church, according to the stage of their development but only within proper limits, that is, in the same doctrine, in the same meaning, and in the same purport [*eodem sensu eademque sententia*]' (St Vincent of Lerins, *Commonitorium*, 28)" (Vatican I, *Dei Filius*, chap. 4).

1:11–12. St Paul now goes on to discuss the dissensions (v.10) which "Chloe's people" have told him about. We must presume that Chloe was a woman well known in the church at Corinth; and obviously there is no question of secret denunciations but of a well-intentioned effort to bring to Paul's attention a problem requiring solution. Chloe's people might have been members of her family or servants of hers who had visited the Apostle in Ephesus (cf. 1 Cor 16:15–17).

Although St Paul does not go into much detail, we can see that a number of groupings had grown up among the Corinthians. They each claimed to follow a prominent Christian (clearly without any encouragement from their "heroes"), and a certain rivalry had developed which could easily undermine the unity of faith. The group who claimed Apollos—a Jewish convert from Alexandria (Egypt), a man of eloquence, well versed in the Scriptures (cf. Acts 18:24–28)—would have emerged after Apollos spent some time preaching in Corinth shortly after Paul left there (cf. Acts 19:1).

"I belong to Cephas": the Peter group may have consisted of people who knew him to be the leader of the Apostles (cf. 3:21–23; 9:4–5; 15:5); St Peter may have passed through Corinth at some point, but there is no evidence of a visit and it is more likely that some of his disciples or converts had come to the city.

"I belong to Christ": this can be interpreted as a reference either to a fourth group very attached to certain preachers from Jerusalem, of a Judaizing tendency —and therefore very attached to Jewish traditions and very disinclined to acknowledge the newness of Christ's message; or else to some Christians who were disgusted at the petty quarrelling of the other groups and, therefore, would naturally claim to belong to Christ and only to Christ. It is possible, however, that this is a personal statement of St Paul's, designed to show how foolish these groups are: You may say that you belong to Paul, to Apollos or to Peter: but I belong to Christ.

What the Apostle says here should lead us to avoid narrow-mindedness: each of us has his own job to do, where God put him, but he should also make his own the sentiments and concerns of the universal Church.

1:13–16. Crispus was, or had been, the ruler of the synagogue at Corinth and had become a Christian through Paul's preaching (cf. Acts 18:8). Gaius was another convert of Paul's and the Apostle had stayed with him when he was in Corinth (cf. Rom 16:2). Stephanas' family had been the first to be converted in the province of Achaia; and Stephanas himself was now with St Paul in Ephesus (cf. 1 Cor 16:15–17).

b. Other ancient authorities read *I thank God*

and Gaius; 15 lest any one should say that you were baptized in my
name. 16(I did baptize also the household of Stephanas. Beyond that, 1 Cor 16:15–17
I do not know whether I baptized any one else.) 17For Christ did not 1 Cor 2:4
send me to baptize but to preach the gospel, and not with eloquent
wisdom, lest the cross of Christ be emptied of its power.

There is no excuse for divisions, the Apostle tells them: unity is not dependent on which teacher you had or who baptized you; it is something based on Christ—whom all the preachers preach; Christ was the one who was crucified for everyone, and his is the name they were baptized in. And there is only one Christ; therefore, they all belong to him.

It is through Baptism, the door of the Christian life, that a Christian becomes part of the one body of Christ; there the merits gained by Christ on the cross are applied to him, and the baptized person is configured to his dead and risen Lord: "Do you not know that all of us who have been baptized into Christ Jesus were baptized into his death? We were buried therefore with him by baptism into death, so that as Christ was raised from the dead by the glory of the Father we too might walk in newness of life" (Rom 6:3–4). And the Second Vatican Council states that: "by the sacrament of Baptism [...] man becomes truly incorporated into the crucified and glorified Christ and is reborn to a sharing of the divine life, as the Apostle says: 'for you were buried with him in baptism, in which you were also raised with him through faith in the working of God, who raised him from the dead' (Col 2:12)" (*Unitatis redintegratio*, 22).

1:16. "When we read that an entire family was baptized by Paul (cf. 1 Cor 1:16), it is sufficiently obvious that the children of the family must also have been cleansed in the saving font" (*St Pius V Catechism*, 2, 2, 32). The practice of baptizing small children is a tradition received from the Apostles; "Three passages of the Acts of the Apostles (16:15; 16:33; 18:8) speak of the baptism of a whole household or family" (SCDF, *Instruction on Infant Baptism*, note 2). The Magisterium of the Church has often reminded Christians of their duty to baptize their children in the first weeks after birth (cf. *Code of Canon Law*, 867, 1), because Baptism is absolutely necessary for salvation.

1:17. In the first part of this verse St Paul is giving the reasons for his actions as described in the preceding verses. The second part he uses to broach a new subject—the huge difference between this world's wisdom and the wisdom of God.

"Christ did not send me to baptize but to preach the Gospel": this is a reminder that preaching is St Paul's main task, as it is of the other apostles (cf. Mk 3:14). This does not imply a belittling of Baptism: in his mandate to the apostles to go out into the whole world (cf. Mt 28:19–20), our Lord charged them to baptize as well as to preach, and we know that St Paul did administer Baptism. But Baptism—the sacrament of faith—presupposes preaching: "faith comes from what is heard" (Rom 10:17). St Paul concentrates on preaching, leaving it to others to baptize and gather the fruit—a further sign of his detachment and upright intention.

In Christian catechesis, evangelization and the sacraments are interdependent. Preaching can help people to receive the sacraments with better dispositions, and it can make them more aware of what the

The wisdom of the cross

Rom 1:16 [18]For the word of the cross is folly to those who are perishing, but
Is 29:14 to us who are being saved it is the power of God. [19]For it is written,
"I will destroy the wisdom of the wise,
and the cleverness of the clever I will thwart."

---

sacraments are; and the graces which the sacraments bring help them to understand the preaching they hear and to be more docile to it. "Evangelization thus exercises its full capacity when it achieves the most intimate relationship, or better still a permanent and unbroken intercommunication, between the Word and the Sacraments. In a certain sense it is a mistake to make a contrast between evangelization and sacramentalization, as is sometimes done. It is indeed true that a certain way of administering the Sacraments, without the solid support of catechesis regarding these same Sacraments and a global catechesis, could end up by depriving them of their effectiveness to a great extent. The role of evangelization is precisely to educate people in the faith so as to lead each individual Christian to live the Sacraments as true Sacraments of faith—and not to receive them passively or apathetically" (Paul VI, *Evangelii nuntiandi*, 47).

1:18–4:21. St Paul's writings are not an academic study of particular doctrinal subjects, one after the other, logically arranged. The Apostle's lively mind and the letter-form he uses create an interweaving of profound theological ideas, practical applications of teaching and expressions of warm, apostolic affection. In this section of the letter St Paul discusses the causes of divisions among the Corinthian Christians: they have failed to discover where true wisdom lies (1:18–3:3), or what the true mission of Church ministers is (3:4–4:13). He ends this part of the letter with some words of warning (4:14–21).

Human wisdom ought to be in line with the wisdom of God. But it has gone off course and become "wisdom of the world", relying only on miracles or on logic; only grace can make a person truly wise: therefore, no Christian can boast of obtaining wisdom by his own efforts (1:18–31). Even St Paul relied only on the wisdom of the cross (2:1–5).

Divine wisdom, which men are called to have a share in, is the plan of salvation revealed by God and taught by the Holy Spirit (2:6–16); the Corinthians have not yet attained it (3:1–3).

The Corinthians' second shortcoming is that they fail to understand the role of Church ministers: these are not working for themselves but for the building-up of the whole Church; every Christian—and the entire Church—belongs to God and Christ alone (3:4–23); Christians are not to sit in judgment over God's ministers: God is their judge (4:1–7). Therefore, the important thing is for Christians to be faithful and to abound in the grace of God, even if the holders of Church office are not very impressive (4:8–13).

1:18–19. The cross of Christ leads the way to true wisdom and prudence. No one may remain indifferent to it. Some people see the message of the cross, "the word of the cross", as folly: these are on the road to perdition. Others—those who are on the road to salvation—are discovering that the cross is "the power of God", because it has conquered the devil and sin. The Church has always seen the cross in this light: "This is the wood of the cross, on which hung the Saviour of

[20]Where is the wise man? Where is the scribe? Where is the Is 19:12
debater of this age? Has not God made foolish the wisdom of the
world? [21]For since, in the wisdom of God, the world did not know Rom 1:19f
God through wisdom, it pleased God through the folly of what we
preach to save those who believe. [22]For Jews demand signs and Mt 12:38
Greeks seek wisdom, [23]but we preach Christ crucified, a stum- Acts 17:18ff
bling block to Jews and folly to Gentiles, [24]but to those who are
called, both Jews and Greeks, Christ the power of God and the
wisdom of God. [25]For the foolishness of God is wiser than men, 2 Cor 13:4
and the weakness of God is stronger than men.

---

the world" (*Roman Missal*, Good Friday liturgy).

The saints have rejoiced in this truth: "O most precious gift of the Cross! How splendid it looks! [...] It is a tree which begets life, without causing death; which sheds light, without casting shadows; which leads to Paradise and does not expel anyone therefrom; it is the wood which Christ ascended, as a king mounting his chariot, to defeat the devil who had usurped the power of death, and to set mankind free from the thrall in which the devil held it. This wood, on which the Lord, valiant fighter in the combat, was wounded in his divine hands and feet and side, healed the effects of sins and the wounds which the pernicious dragon had inflicted on our nature [...]. That supreme wisdom, which, so to speak, burgeoned on the cross, exposed the boasts and the foolish arrogance of the wisdom of the world" (St Theodore the Studite, *Oratio in adorationem crucis*).

In the cross the words of Isaiah (29:14) quoted by St Paul are fulfilled. Simplicity and humility are needed if one is to discover the divine wisdom of the cross. "The message of Christ's cross", St Thomas says, "contains something which to human wisdom seems impossible—that God should die, or that the Almighty should give himself up into the power of violent men. It also contains things which seem to be contrary to worldly prudence—for instance, someone being able to flee from contradictions and yet not doing so" (*Commentary on 1 Cor* ad loc.)

1:20–25. After stressing the importance of the message of the cross, St Paul now contrasts the wisdom of God and the wisdom of the world.

By "wisdom of the world" he means the attitude of man when he is not pursuing his proper goal: this term "world", which has various meanings in Sacred Scripture (cf. note on Jn 17:14–16), in St Paul has the pejorative meaning of "all sinful men", people estranged from God (cf. 1 Cor 1:27; 2:12; 3:19; 5:10; 11:32). This human wisdom cannot attain knowledge of God (cf. Rom 1:19–25), either because it demands external signs or because it accepts only rational arguments.

For the Jews only signs will do—miracles which prove God's presence (cf. Mt 12:38ff; Lk 11:29); they want to base their faith on things the senses can perceive. For people with this attitude, the cross of Christ is a scandal, that is, a stumbling block, which makes it impossible for them to gain access to divine things, because they have in some way imposed limits as to how God may reveal himself and how he may not.

Mt 11:25
Jn 7:48

Jas 2:5
1 Sam 16:7

26For consider your call, brethren; not many of you were wise
according to worldly standards, not many were powerful, not
many were of noble birth; 27but God chose what is foolish in the

---

The Greeks—St Paul is referring to the Rationalists of his time—think that they are the arbiters of truth, and that anything which cannot be proved by logical argument is nonsense. "For the world, that is, for the prudent of the world, their wisdom turned into blindness; it could not lead them to see God [...]. Therefore, since the world had become puffed up by the vanity of its dogmas, the Lord set in place the faith whereby believers would be saved by what seemed unworthy and foolish, so that, all human conjecture being of no avail, only the grace of God might reveal what the human mind cannot take in" (St Leo the Great, *Fifth Nativity Sermon*).

Christians, whom God has called out from among the Jews and the Gentiles, do attain the wisdom of God, which consists in faith, "a supernatural virtue. By that faith, with the inspiration and help of God's grace, we believe that what he has revealed is true—not because its intrinsic truth is seen by the natural light of reason, but because of the authority of God who reveals it, who can neither deceive nor be deceived" (Vatican I, *Dei Filius*, chap. 3). The same council goes on to teach that faith is in conformity with reason (cf. Rom 12:1) and that, in addition to God's help, external signs—miracles and prophecies—and rational argument do act as supports of faith.

1:21. "In the wisdom of God ...": this has been interpreted in two ways, which complement one another. Roughly, the first interpretation is this: according to God's most wise designs, since the world could not attain knowledge of God by its own efforts, through philosophy, through those elaborate systems of thought the Greeks were so proud of, God decided to save believers through the preaching of the Cross, which to human eyes seemed foolishness, a stumbling block (v. 22).

The second interpretation, favoured by many Fathers and by St Thomas Aquinas, contrasts divine wisdom—as manifested in creation and in the Old Testament—with human wisdom. It runs on these lines: since the world, because of its distorted view of things, failed to attain knowledge of God, despite the way he manifested himself in creation (cf. Rom 1:19–20) and Holy Scripture, God has decided to save man in a remarkable, paradoxical way which better reflects divine wisdom—the preaching of the Cross.

In both interpretations it is clear that the Apostle is trying to squeeze into one expression a number of truths—that God's salvific plans are eternal; that human wisdom, which is capable, on its own, of discovering God through his works, has become darkened; that the cross is the climax of the all-wise plans of God; that man cannot be truly wise unless he accepts "the wisdom of the cross", no matter how paradoxical it may seem.

1:25. In his plan of salvation God our Lord wants to use things which to man's mind seem foolish and weak, so that his wisdom and power will shine out all the more. "All that Jesus Christ did for us has been meritorious for us; it has all been necessary and advantageous to our salvation; his very weakness has been for us no less useful than his majesty. For, if by the power of his divinity he has released us from the captivity of sin, he has also, through the weakness of his flesh,

world to shame the wise, God chose what is weak in the world to
shame the strong, [28]God chose what is low and despised in the
world, even things that are not, to bring to nothing things that are,

---

destroyed death's rights. As the Apostle so beautifully said, 'the weakness of God is stronger than men'; indeed, by this folly he has been pleased to save the world by combating the wisdom of the world and confounding the wise; for, possessing the nature of God and being equal to God, he abased himself, taking the form of a servant; being rich, he became poor for love of us; being great, he became little; being exalted, humble; he became weak, who was powerful; he suffered hunger and thirst, he wore himself out on the roads and suffered of his own free will and not by necessity. This type of folly, I repeat: has it not meant for us a way of wisdom, a model of justice and an example of holiness, as the same Apostle says: 'The foolishness of God is wiser than men'? So true is this, that death has freed us from death, life has freed us from error, and grace from sin" (St Bernard, *De laudibus novae militiae*, 11, 27).

1:26–29. As in the case of the Apostles —"You did not choose me, but I chose you" (Jn 15:16)—it is the Lord who chooses, who gives each Christian his vocation. St Paul emphasizes that the initiative lies with God by saying three times that it was God who chose those Corinthians to be Christians, and he did not base his choice on human criteria. Human wisdom, power, nobility, these were not what brought them to the faith —nor the inspirations which God later gives. "God is no respecter of persons (cf. 2 Chron 19:7; Rom 2:1; Eph 6:9; Col 3:25; etc.)", St Josemaría Escrivá reminds us. "When he invites a soul to live a life fully in accordance with the faith, he does not set store by merits of fortune, nobility, blood or learning. God's call precedes all merits [...]. Vocation comes first. God loves us before we even know how to go toward him, and he places in us the love with which we can respond to his call" (*Christ Is Passing By*, 33).

Thus, God chooses whomever he wants to, and these first Christians—uneducated, unimportant, even despised people, in the world's eyes—will be what he uses to spread his Church and convert the wise, the strong and the "important": this disproportion between resources and results will make it quite clear that God is responsible for the increase.

However, this does not mean that none of the first Christians was educated or influential, humanly speaking. The Acts of the Apostles, for example, tell us about early converts who were out of the ordinary—a minister of the court of the Kandake of Ethiopia; a centurion, Cornelius; Apollos; Dionysius the Areopagite; etc. "It would appear that worldly excellence is not godly unless God uses it for his honour. And therefore, although at the beginning they were indeed few, later God chose many humanly outstanding people for the ministry of preaching. Hence the gloss which says, 'If the fisherman had not faithfully led the way, the orator would not have humbly followed'" (St Thomas Aquinas, *Commentary on 1 Cor,* ad loc.).

1:27. St Paul's words remind us that supernatural resources are the thing an apostle must rely on. It is true that human resources are necessary, and God counts on them (cf. 1 Cor 3:5–10); but the task God has commended to Christians exceeds

Rom 3:27 Eph 2:9 [29]so that no human being might boast in the presence of God. [30]He
Deut 8:17f is the source of your life in Christ Jesus, whom God made our
Jer 9:22f wisdom, our righteousness and sanctification and redemption;
2 Cor 10:17 [31]therefore, as it is written, "Let him who boasts, boast of the Lord."

Paul's preaching in Corinth

1 Cor 1:17 **2** [1]When I came to you, brethren, I did not come proclaiming to
Gal 6:14 you the testimony[c] of God in lofty words or wisdom. [2]For I

---

their abilities and can be carried out only with his help. The Second Vatican Council reminded priests of this verse, when stressing the need for humility; and what it says can be useful to all Christians: "The divine task for the fulfilment of which they have been set apart by the Holy Spirit (cf. Acts 13:2) transcends all human strength and human wisdom; for 'God chose what is weak in the world to shame the strong' (1 Cor 1:27). Therefore the true minister of Christ is conscious of his own weakness and labours in humility. He tries to discover what is well-pleasing to God (cf. Eph 5:10) and, bound as it were in the Spirit (cf. Acts 20:22), he is guided in all things by the will of him who wishes all men to be saved. He is able to discover and carry out that will in the course of his daily routine by humbly placing himself at the service of all those who are entrusted to his care by God in the office that has been committed to him and the variety of events that make up his life" (*Presbyterorum ordinis*, 15).

1:30–31. God's call makes a person a member of Christ Jesus, through Baptism; and if a Christian is docile to grace he or she will gradually become so like Christ as to be able to say with St Paul, "It is no longer I who live, but Christ who lives in me" (Gal 2:20). This "being in Christ Jesus" enables a person to share in the wisdom, righteousness, sanctification and redemption which Jesus is for the Christian.

Jesus Christ indeed is the "wisdom" of God (cf. Col 1:15f; Heb 1:2f), and knowing him is true wisdom, the highest form of wisdom. He is for us our "righteousness", because through the merits obtained by his incarnation, death and resurrection he has made us truly righteous (= just, holy) in God's sight. He is also the source of all holiness, which consists in fact in identification with Christ. Through him, who has become "redemption" for us, we have been redeemed from the slavery of sin. "How well the Apostle orders his ideas: God has made us wise by rescuing us from error; and then he has made us just and holy by giving us his spirit" (Chrysostom, *Hom. on 1 Cor*, 5, ad loc.).

In view of the complete gratuitousness of God's choice (vv. 25–28) and the immense benefits it brings with it, the conclusion is obvious: "'*Deo omnis gloria.* All glory to God.' It is an emphatic conclusion of our nothingness. He, Jesus, is everything. We, without him, are worth nothing: nothing. Our vainglory would be just that: vain glory; it would be sacrilegious robbery. There should be no room for that 'I' anywhere" (St Josemaría Escrivá, *The Way*, 780).

2:1–3. The Apostle had come to Corinth from Athens, as we know from the Acts of the Apostles (17:16–34); in that city he

c. Other ancient authorities read *mystery* (or *secret*)

decided to know nothing among you except Jesus Christ and him
crucified.* [3]And I was with you in weakness and in much fear and Acts 18:9 2 Cor 7:15
trembling; [4]and my speech and my message were not in plausible
words of wisdom, but in demonstration of the Spirit and of power,
[5]that your faith might not rest in the wisdom of men but in the 2 Cor 12:12
power of God.

---

had not made many converts, despite his brilliant discourse in the Areopagus. This fact, and the moral corruption of Corinthian society, may explain his arriving "in much fear and trembling" (v. 3); he must have felt that he had a difficult task ahead of him. As it turned out, he must have met many difficulties: our Lord appeared to him at night in a vision to comfort and encourage him: "Do not be afraid, but speak and do not be silent; for I am with you" (Acts 18:9–10). St Paul, therefore, putting no reliance on carefully argued speeches, proclaims Christ crucified, to make sure that faith is grounded on God alone.

St Paul sums up his entire message here—"Jesus Christ and him crucified". The Church, on whom it devolves to continue the mission of the apostles, does nothing but make Jesus Christ known: "Our spirit is set in one direction," Pope John Paul II points out; "the only direction for our intellect, will and heart is towards Christ our Redeemer, towards Christ, the Redeemer of man. We wish to look towards him—because there is salvation in no one else but him, the Son of God—repeating what Peter said, 'Lord, to whom shall we go? You have the words of eternal life' (Jn 6:68) […]. The Church lives his mystery, draws unwearyingly from it and continually seeks ways of bringing this mystery of her Master and Lord to mankind—to the peoples, the nations, the succeeding generations, and every individual human being—as if she were ever repeating, as the Apostle did, 'For I decided to know nothing among you except Jesus Christ and him crucified' (1 Cor 2:2). The Church stays within the sphere of the mystery of the Redemption, which has become the fundamental principle of her life and mission" (*Redemptor hominis*, 7).

Every Christian, for his part, should try to see that those around him "desire to know Jesus Christ and him crucified and that they be firmly convinced and with the most heartfelt piety and devotion believe that no other name under heaven has been given to men by which we may be saved (cf. Acts 4:12), since he is the expiation for our sins (cf. 1 Jn 2:2)" (*St Pius V Catechism*, introduction, 10).

2:4–5. Just as Paul's preaching did not rely on eloquence, faith must not be based on human wisdom (cf. note on 1 Cor 1:20–25). He says that he based his message on "demonstration of the Spirit and power"—probably a reference to the powerful action of divine grace on those who listened to his preaching, with grace manifesting itself in conversions and extraordinary charisms. This power of God explains how they came to believe.

God continues to act through the Christian message, which "is unique. It cannot be replaced. It does not permit either indifference, syncretism or accommodation. It is a question of people's salvation. It is the beauty of the Revelation that it represents. It brings with it a wisdom that is not of this world. It is able to stir up by itself faith—faith that rests on the power of God (cf. 1 Cor 2:5). It is truth. It merits having the

Divine wisdom

[6]Yet among the mature we do impart wisdom, although it is not a
wisdom of this age or of the rulers of this age, who are doomed to
Rom 16:25 pass away. [7]But we impart a secret and hidden wisdom of God,
which God decreed before the ages for our glorification. [8]None of
Is 64:3 the rulers of this age understood this; for if they had, they would
not have crucified the Lord of glory. [9]But, as it is written,

> "What no eye has seen, nor ear heard,
> nor the heart of man conceived,
> what God has prepared for those who love him,"

---

apostle consecrate to it all his time and all his energies, and to sacrifice for it, if necessary, his own life" (Paul VI, *Evangelii nuntiandi*, 5).

2:6–8. After showing that the wisdom of the world serves no purpose and that people need to submit to the cross of Christ, the Apostle teaches that the Gospel is not contrary to reason; only, the wisdom it holds is much more profound, it is divine wisdom. This is the wisdom he spreads "among the mature", the *perfecti*, that is, those Christians who are well established in the faith, as distinct from the "babes" referred to in 3:1, who still have need of brilliant arguments. These mature Christians St Paul is referring to are not an inner core of privileged people, for all the baptized are called to attain full knowledge of the Son of God (cf. Eph 4:11–16).

This wisdom is completely foreign to this world, this age, and its rulers, that is, those who are responsible for the evil in the world: there is a reference here both to those who directly caused our Lord's death (the Sanhedrin, Herod, Pilate: cf. v. 8), and to the devil and the fallen angels, as can be seen from similar New Testament references (cf. Lk 4:6; Jn 12:31; Eph 2:2).

"Secret and hidden": a reference to the content of divine wisdom and to its revelation. It means the same as God's plan of salvation, which extends to all men—including the Gentiles (cf. Eph 3:6–8) and, in some way, to all creation (Eph 1:10); man can never completely grasp its meaning, just as he can never totally understand God; however, this secret and hidden wisdom can be known by means of Revelation (cf. Lk 8:10; Col 1:26), which we are given in Christ (cf. Rom 16:25–26; Eph 1:8–10; 3:3–7; Col 1:26–27), even though we can only fully grasp it in heaven. There are, therefore, three ways of looking at this wisdom-mystery-salvation: it is part of God's plans from all eternity; it is manifested in Revelation and especially in Jesus Christ, who died and is risen; we attain it partially in this life and fully in heaven.

"Lord of glory": here St Paul attributes to Christ on the cross a title which the Old Testament reserved for God alone (cf. Ex 24:15; 40:34; Is 42:8), thereby making it clear that Jesus Christ is God, equal to the Father.

2:9. These words of Isaiah 64:2–3 sum up the content of God's plan—all those gifts which man's mind cannot grasp (cf. Eph 3:19) and which God has had ready from all eternity for those who love him. These gifts are nothing less than God's love for men.

Because these gifts are only fully attained in the next life, Christian tradition sees in these words a description of heaven: "How blessed, how marvellous, are

[10]God has revealed to us through the Spirit. For the Spirit searches Mt 13:11
everything, even the depths of God. [11]For what person knows a
man's thoughts except the spirit of the man which is in him? So
also no one comprehends the thoughts of God except the Spirit of
God. [12]Now we have received not the spirit of the world, but the Jn 16:13f
Spirit which is from God, that we might understand the gifts
bestowed on us by God. [13]And we impart this in words not taught
by human wisdom but taught by the Spirit, interpreting spiritual
truths to those who possess the Spirit.[d]

---

the gifts of God. Some of them, indeed, already lie within our comprehension—the life that knows no death, the shining splendour of righteousness, truth in freedom, trusting faith, the holiness of chastity. But what of the things that God has prepared for those who hope in him? Only the Creator and Father of eternity knows them. Let us strive earnestly to be counted among those who wait patiently in order to earn a share in his promised gifts" (St Clement of Rome, *First Letter to the Corinthians*, 35).

And the *Pius V Catechism*, for its part, teaches that "With this truth, the minds of the faithful should be deeply impressed—that the happiness of the saints is full to overflowing of all those pleasures which can be enjoyed or even desired in this life, whether they have to do with the powers of the mind or of the perfection of the body; although this must be in a manner more exalted than, to use the Apostle's words, eye has seen, ear heard, or the heart of man conceived" (1, 13, 12).

2:10–12. "God has revealed to us through the Spirit": meaning the Holy Spirit, the third person of the Blessed Trinity, "which is from God" (v. 12) and knows the very depths of God (vv. 10–11). These words reveal to us the divinity of the Holy Spirit; knowing a person implies having intimacy with him; the Holy Spirit knows the depths of God because by nature he is God, equal to the Father and the Son (cf. Mt 11:25). "The Holy Spirit is equally God with the Father and the Son, equally omnipotent and eternal, infinitely perfect, the supreme good, infinitely wise, and of the same nature as the Father and the Son [...]. Scripture also attributes to him the power to sanctify, to vivify, to search the depths of God, to speak through the Prophets, and to be present in all places—all of which can be attributed to God alone" (*St Pius V Catechism*, 1, 9, 4).

Jesus had told his Apostles that "when the Spirit of truth comes, he will guide you into all truth" (Jn 16:13); and on the day of Pentecost the Holy Spirit did open their minds to understand the truth revealed by Jesus Christ. The Holy Spirit also acted in St Paul, so that he had the same knowledge of Revelation as the other Apostles (cf. Gal 2:1–10). The same Spirit continues to act in the Church: "The Holy Spirit, who is the spirit of truth, because he proceeds from the Father, eternal Truth, and the Son, substantial truth, receives from each of them, along with his essence, all truth, which he then communicates to the Church, helping never to err" (Leo XIII, *Divinum illud munus*, 7).

2:13. The handing on of the faith calls for great care in the terminology used:

d. Or *interpreting spiritual truths in spiritual language*; or *comparing spiritual things with spiritual*

1 Cor 2:6 14 The unspiritual[e] man does not receive the gifts of the Spirit of
God, for they are folly to him, and he is not able to understand
them because they are spiritually discerned. 15 The spiritual man
Is 40:13 judges all things, but is himself to be judged by no one. 16 "For
Rom 11:34 who has known the mind of the Lord so as to instruct him?" But
we have the mind of Christ.

"The Church, with the long labour of centuries and not without the help of the Holy Spirit, has established a rule of language and confirmed it with the authority of the Councils. This rule, which has more than once been the watchword and banner of orthodox faith, must be religiously preserved, and let no one presume to change it at his own pleasure or under the pretext of new science" (Paul VI, *Mysterium fidei*, 3).

The Church has always been concerned about this need to explain the deposit of faith accurately: "You have received gold," St Vincent of Lerins comments, "let you therefore give gold. I do not want you to give one thing instead of another. I do not want you to be so shameless and deceptive that you give me lead or bronze in place of gold; I do not want something that looks like gold: I want pure gold" (*Commonitorium*, 22).

The last part of this verse is unclear and can be translated in various ways as the RSV text and note show.

2:14–16. The original text (v. 14) says "*psychikos*". This is not easy to translate. Some versions say "natural man", others "animal man", which is literally what the New Vulgate says. What it means is the person who acts only by using his or her human faculties (intelligence and will) and who therefore can be wise only in the things of this world. The spiritual man is the Christian reborn by the grace of God; grace elevates his faculties to enable him to perform actions which have a supernatural value—acts of faith, hope and charity. A person who is in the state of grace is able to perceive the things of God, because he carries with him the Spirit in his soul in grace, and he has Christ's mind, Christ's attitude. "We have no alternative", St Josemaría Escrivá teaches. "There are only two possible ways of living on this earth: either we live a supernatural life, or we live an animal life. And you and I can only live the life of God, a supernatural life" (*Friends of God*, 200).

St John Chrysostom very graphically contrasts the capacity of the spiritual man and that of the unspiritual man as far as understanding God's plan of salvation is concerned: "He who has sight sees everything, including the person who has no sight; but the sightless person cannot see the things of the person who has sight. We Christians know what our own situation is, and we also know the situation of unbelievers; the unbelievers, however, do not understand ours. Like them we know —and we know better than they do—the nature of things present; unbelievers do not know the sublimity of things to come, whereas we already see what will some day become of the world, and what sinners will suffer, and the righteous enjoy" (*Hom. on 1 Cor*, 7, ad loc.). And St Thomas Aquinas: "A conscious person rightly perceives both that he is awake and that the other person is asleep; but the person who is asleep cannot form a

e. Or *natural*

The Corinthians are still unspiritual

3 1But I, brethren, could not address you as spiritual men, but as Jn 16:12
men of the flesh, as babes in Christ. 2I fed you with milk, not Heb 5:12f
solid food; for you were not ready for it; and even yet you are not 1 Pet 2:2
ready, 3for you are still of the flesh. For while there is jealousy and 1 Cor 1:10f
strife among you, are you not of the flesh, and behaving like
ordinary men?

Apostolic ministry

4For when one says, "I belong to Paul," and another, "I belong to 1 Cor 1:12
Apollos," are you not merely men?

---

correct judgment concerning either himself or the one who is awake. Therefore, things are not the way they are seen by someone asleep: they are as they appear to be to a conscious person [...]. And so the Apostle says that 'the spiritual man judges all things': for a person whose understanding is enlightened and whose affections are regulated by the Holy Spirit forms correct judgments on particular matters to do with salvation. He who is unspiritual has a darkened understanding and disordered affection as far as spiritual things are concerned, and therefore the spiritual man cannot be judged by the unspiritual man, just as the sleeping person cannot judge the one who is awake" (*Commentary on 1 Cor,* ad loc.).

3:1–3. The Christians of Corinth have themselves to blame for their inability to grasp everything they have been taught. The counterposing of spirit and flesh does not mean that there are two kinds of people in the Church; it is, rather, a fatherly reproach on the Apostle's part: through Baptism they are called to a full (intellectual and practical) grasp of spiritual truths; but because they are letting themselves be led by human principles they are still in a state of lethargy. As St John Chrysostom comments, the reason is that "unclean living makes it difficult for a person to know the truth. Just as a man who is blinded by error cannot for long keep to the right road, so too is it very difficult for someone who is leading a bad life to accept the demands our sublime mysteries make on us. To embrace truth one needs to be detached from all one's passions [...]. This freedom of soul must be total, if one is to attain truth" (*Hom. on 1 Cor*, 8, ad loc.).

"As babes in Christ": St Paul is not referring to the spiritual childhood taught by Jesus Christ (cf. Mt 18:1–6; 1 Pet 2:2). The Apostle uses this comparison to show that one needs to make progress in the Christian life: a Christian has a duty to develop the infused virtues he received in Baptism. To be more specific, the Apostle mentions "jealousy and strife" (v. 3) as two great sins which are paralysing the Corinthians: they leave a Christian in a lamentable, unspiritual state and prevent him from attaining the spiritual things to which he has been called (cf. Heb 5:12–17).

3:4–17. Using the dissension at Corinth (cf. 1:11–13), which clearly shows that the Corinthians are still acting in a very unspiritual way (v. 4), St Paul describes the true nature of apostolic office. He stresses that God is the source of all apostolic work: it is he "who gives the growth" (v. 7); man is God's instrument—a servant or minister (v. 5), a fellow

5What then is Apollos? What is Paul? Servants through whom
Acts 18:24, 27 you believed, as the Lord assigned to each. 6I planted, Apollos
watered, but God gave the growth. 7So neither he who plants nor
he who waters is anything, but only God who gives the growth.
8He who plants and he who waters are equal, and each shall
Mt 13:3–9 receive his wages according to his labour. 9For we are God's
Eph 2:20–22 fellow workers;[f] you are God's field, God's building.

---

worker (v. 9)—in this task, which can only be carried out if Jesus Christ is its foundation (v. 11). St Paul develops these ideas using two effective similes—a field (vv. 6–9) and a building (vv. 9–17).

3:5–7. Using a comparison with farm work, St Paul shows the instrumental role men and women play in the apostolate. Only God, through his grace, can make the seed of faith take root and bear fruit in souls: "It may be that going and weeping they [God's workers] cast their seeds; it may be with anxious care they nourished it; but to make it sprout and bring forth the cherished fruit, this is the work of God alone and his powerful assistance. This, also, is to be well considered, that men are nothing more than instruments which God uses for the saving of souls and that these instruments must be fit, therefore, to be handled by God" (St Pius X, *Haerent animo*, 9).

In this sense, every effort man makes is to no avail (cf. v. 7); yet God chooses to use man's input to produce supernatural fruit which is totally disproportionate: "We must remember that we are only instruments," St Josemaría Escrivá points out. "'What is Apollos? What is Paul? Servants through whom you have believed, as the Lord assigned to each. I planted, Apollos watered, but only God gives the growth' (1 Cor 3:4–6). The teaching, the message which we have to communicate, has in its own right an infinite effectiveness which comes not from us but from Christ. It is God himself who is bent on bringing about salvation, on redeeming the world" (*Christ Is Passing By*, 159).

3:8. The recompense God gives someone who works in the building up of the Church has not so much to do with his particular mission (the various jobs are "equal"), or with the kind of harvest, as with the work itself, the effort one puts into the God-given job. "Since Christians have different gifts (cf. Rom 12:6) they should collaborate in the work of the Gospel, each according to his opportunity, ability, charism and ministry (cf. 1 Cor 3:10); all who sow and reap (cf. Jn 4:37), plant and water, should be one (cf. 1 Cor 3:8) so that 'working together for the same end in a free and orderly manner' (*Lumen gentium*, 18) they might together devote their powers to the building up of the Church" (Vatican II, *Ad gentes*, 28). Therefore, what really matters is that one does whatever job one has been given with the maximum love possible, without losing heart: "[my chosen ones] shall not labour in vain", the Lord assures them, through the prophet Isaiah (65:23).

3:9. "God's field, God's building". The Second Vatican Council uses these images to describe the inner nature of the Church: "The Church is a cultivated field, the tillage of God (cf. 1 Cor 3:9). On that land the ancient olive tree grows whose holy roots were the prophets and in

f. Or *fellow workers for God*

[10]According to the grace of God given to me, like a skilled
master builder I laid a foundation, and another man is building
upon it. Let each man take care how he builds upon it. [11]For no Is 28:16

---

which the reconciliation of Jews and Gentiles has been brought about and will be brought about again (Rom 11:13–26). That land, like a choice vineyard, has been planted by the heavenly cultivator (Mt 21:33–43; cf. Is 5:1f). Yet the true vine is Christ who gives life and fruitfullness to the branches, that is, to us, who through the Church remain in Christ without whom we can do nothing (Jn 15:1–5).

"Often, too, the Church is called the building of God (1 Cor 3:9). The Lord compared himself to the stone which the builders rejected, but which was made into the cornerstone (Mt 21:42; cf. Acts 4:11; 1 Pet 2:7; Ps 117:22). On this foundation the Church is built by the Apostles (cf. 1 Cor 3:11) and from it the Church receives solidity and unity. This edifice has many names to describe it—the house of God in which his family dwells; the household of God in the Spirit (Eph 2:19:22); the dwelling-place of God among men (Rev 21:3); and, especially, the holy temple. This temple, symbolized in places of worship built out of stone, is praised by the Fathers and, not without reason, is compared in the liturgy to the Holy City, the New Jerusalem. As living stones we here on earth are built into it (1 Pet 2:5). It is this holy city that is seen by John as it comes down out of heaven from God when the world is made anew, prepared like a bride adorned for her husband (Rev 21:1f)" (*Lumen gentium*, 6).

The Lord wants Christians to be living stones in this building and has associated them in the redemptive task of saving all mankind, so that in the course of their own redemption they might also be co-redeemers with him, completing "what is lacking in Christ's afflictions for the sake of his body, that is, the church" (Col 1:24): "Jesus has wanted every person to cooperate freely in the work of redemption [...]. The work of salvation is still going on, and each one of us has a part in it [...]. It is worth while putting our lives on the line, giving ourselves completely, so as to answer to the love and the confidence that God has placed in us. It is worth while, above all, to decide to take our Christian faith seriously" (St Josemaría Escrivá, *Christ Is Passing By*, 129).

3:10–11. With a solemn introduction ("According to the commission of God given to me", which equipped him for his ministry), St Paul identifies what holds together the community at Corinth and its individual members—Jesus Christ, the essential basis for every spiritual building. Christ, as St Peter reminds us, is "the stone which was rejected by you builders, but which has become the head of the corner. And there is salvation in no one else, for there is no other name under heaven given among men by which we must be saved" (Acts 4:11–12).

Therefore, all genuine catechesis must be Christ-centred; it must all be focussed on Jesus Christ, perfect God and perfect man, and on his teachings. Catechesis, says John Paul II, means "to reveal in the Person of Christ the whole of God's eternal design reaching fulfilment in that Person. It is to seek to understand the meaning of Christ's actions and words and of the signs worked by him, for they simultaneously hide and reveal his mystery. Accordingly, the definitive aim of catechesis is to put people not only in touch but in communion, in intimacy,

Acts 4:11f other foundation can any one lay than that which is laid, which is
1 Pet 2:4 Jesus Christ. 12Now if any one builds on the foundation with gold,
1 Pet 1:7 silver, precious stones, wood, hay, straw—13each man's work will
become manifest; for the Day* will disclose it, because it will be

---

with Jesus Christ; only he can lead us to the love of the Father in the Spirit and make us share in the life of the Holy Trinity [...]. We must therefore say that in catechesis it is Christ, the Incarnate Word and Son of God, who is taught—everything else is taught with reference to him—and it is Christ alone who teaches —anyone else teaches to the extent that he is Christ's spokesman, enabling Christ to teach with his lips" (*Catechesi tradendae*, 5–6).

Also, reflection on the fact that Jesus Christ is the foundation of the spiritual building, leads to the conclusion that a Christian "needs to be not only linked to Jesus Christ," St John Chrysostom points out, "but to adhere to him, to be firmly attached to him: to be separated from him to the least degree is to be lost [...]. Notice all the comparisons the Apostle makes to explain this intimate unity: Jesus Christ is the head, we the body, for there can be no gap between head and body. He is the foundation, we the building; he is the vine, we the branches; he the spouse, we the bride; he is the shepherd, we the flock; he is the way along which we are to travel; we are the temple, and God dwells therein; he is the first-born, we his brethren; he is the heir and we co-heirs; he is life and we have life through him; he is the resurrection and we men are raised up; he is the light by which our darkness is dispelled" (*Hom. on 1 Cor*, 8, ad loc.).

3:12–13. Developing the simile of the building, St Paul appeals to Church ministers to act responsibly, reminding them that a day of judgment will come.

Further on (v. 17), he refers to those who positively destroy the Church; here he addresses ministers dedicated to the service of the faithful; the various materials, some valuable (gold, silver), others not worth much (hay, straw) stand for the intentions—good, not so good—of preachers, and whether they preach the full message in all its richness, or only a cheap version of it. The Fathers and Doctors of the Church see here a reference to the gravity of venial sins: some people inordinately seek material things, which hinder them from drawing closer to God; others try to use spiritual things for their selfish advancement; or else their teachings, while not being erroneous, contain things which are useless or unclear or at least unproven (cf. *Commentary on 1 Cor,* ad loc.).

"The Day": the Apostle is referring to the Last Day, when Christ will come as Judge; sometimes he actually says "the day of our Lord Jesus Christ" (cf. 1 Cor 1:8; 1 Thess 5:2). Although St Paul does not make explicit mention of any judgment but this Last Judgment when Jesus "shall come to judge the living and the dead" (*Apostle's Creed*), obviously—as the Church has always believed—there is also a judgment "immediately after death" (Benedict XII, *Benedictus Deus, Dz–Sch*, 1000). It is described as the "particular" or individual judgment because "when each one of us departs this life, he is instantly placed before the judgment seat of God, where all that he has ever done or spoken or thought during life shall be subjected to the most rigid scrutiny" (*St Pius V Catechism*, 1, 8, 3).

revealed with fire, and the fire will test what sort of work each one
has done. 14If the work which any man has built on the foundation
survives, he will receive a reward. 15If any man's work is burned
up, he will suffer loss, though he himself will be saved, but only
as through fire.
16Do you not know that you are God's temple* and that God's 1 Cor 6:19
Spirit dwells in you? 17If any one destroys God's temple, God will 2 Cor 6:16
destroy him. For God's temple is holy, and that temple you are.

The fire which the Apostle mentions here should be understood in the context of his metaphor of the building; it means that God's judgment is final; there is no appeal against it, because just as fire reveals the solidity of the construction, so God's judgment show up the actions of each person in their true light. Also, it should not be forgotten that fire usually accompanies the theophanies (special appearances of God) mentioned in the Bible (cf. Ex 3:2; 19:18; 2 Thess 1:8); it is, therefore, a way of showing that only God—not men—can judge. Furthermore, it is significant that St Paul, when speaking of retribution, mentions fire; some Fathers have seen this as a reference to the severity of the punishment meted out in hell and purgatory.

3:14–15. In describing the reward given to those who work at the building of the Church, St Paul writes in the same figurative style as in the rest of the passage. One thing comes across very clearly: everyone will be paid according to his works; if good materials have been used, that is, if he was upright and held on to the correct teaching, the reward is assured. But if he used defective materials, that is, if he did not have the right intention or if he did not hold on to the faith of the Church, he will not earn a reward.

We cannot be sure that St Paul is here referring to purgatory; but it is quite in order to interpret "he will be saved, but only as through fire" in that sense. Catholic teaching on purgatory is based on many passages of the Bible (2 Mac 12:39–46; Mt 12:31–32; 5:25–26; 1 Cor 15:29; etc.) and on the uninterrupted tradition of prayer for the dead. "The Catholic Church, by the teaching of the Holy Spirit, in accordance with Sacred Scripture and the ancient tradition of the Fathers (teaches) that there is a purgatory and that the souls detained there are helped by the prayers of the faithful and especially by the acceptable sacrifice of the altar" (Council of Trent, *De Purgatorio*).

Many Fathers, particularly from St Augustine on, have connected this verse with purgatory: "Some will be saved through a purifying fire; for a long or short period depending on the extent to which they were attached to things which do not endure" (*Enchiridion*, 1, chap. 68).

3:16–17. These words apply to the individual Christian, and to the Church as a whole (cf. note on 1 Cor 3:9). The simile of the Church as God's temple, often used by St Paul (cf. 1 Cor 6:19–20; 2 Cor 6:16), shows that the Holy Trinity dwells in the soul in grace. As Leo XIII reminds us, "by means of grace God dwells in the just soul as in a temple, in a special and intimate manner" (*Divinum illud munus*, 10). Although this indwelling is attributed to the Holy Spirit (cf. Jn 14:17; 1 Cor 6:19), it really comes about through the presence of the three persons of the Blessed Trinity, because all actions of God which terminate outside God himself

Rev 3:17 18Let no one deceive himself. If any one among you thinks that
he is wise in this age, let him become a fool that he may become
Job 5:12f wise. 19For the wisdom of this world is folly with God. For it is
Ps 94:11 written, "He catches the wise in their craftiness," 20and again,
"The Lord knows that the thoughts of the wise are futile." 21So let

---

(activities "*ad extra*") are to be seen as actions of the one, unique divine nature.

This sublime mystery, which we could never have suspected, was revealed by Jesus Christ himself: "The Spirit of truth [...] dwells with you, and will be in you [...]. If a man loves me, he will keep my word and my Father will love him, and we will come to him and make our home with him" (Jn 14:17–23). Although this is a matter which we can never plumb in this life, some light is thrown on it if we remember that "the divine persons are said to inhabit inasmuch as they are present to intellectual creatures in a way that transcends human comprehension, and are known and loved (cf. *Summa theologiae*, 1, 43, 3) by them, yet in a way that is unique, purely supernatural, and in the deepest sanctuary of the soul" (Pius XII, *Mystici Corporis*, *Dz–Sch*, 35).

Reflection on this wonderful fact will help us to realize how extremely important it is to live in the grace of God, and to have a horror of mortal sin, which "destroys God's temple," depriving the soul of God's grace and friendship.

Moreover, through this indwelling a human being begins to receive an inkling of what the beatific vision—heaven—will be like, for "this admirable union [of indwelling] differs only by virtue of man's [present] condition and state from that union whereby God fills the blessed [in heaven]" (*Divinum illud munus*, 11).

The presence of the Trinity in the soul in grace invites the Christian to try to have a more personal and direct relationship with God, whom we can seek at every moment in the depths of our souls: "Get to know the Holy Spirit, the Great Stranger, on whom depends your sanctification. Don't forget that you are God's temple. The Advocate is in the centre of your soul: listen to him and be docile to his inspirations" (St Josemaría Escrivá, *The Way*, 57).

3:18–20. As an application of his teaching about true wisdom, St Paul shows Christians that the worst kind of foolishness is that of thinking one is wise when one in fact is not. He uses two biblical quotations (Job 5:13; Ps 94:11) as a gloss to prove that an exclusively human approach is always doomed to failure.

Christians, therefore, are wiser the more they identify their desires with the plan God has for each; that is, the more supernatural their outlook on life is: "We must learn to acquire the divine measure of things, never losing our supernatural outlook, and realizing that Jesus makes use also of our weaknesses to reveal his glory. So, whenever your conscience feels the stirrings of self-love, of weariness, of discouragement, or the weight of your passions, you must react immediately and listen to the Master, without letting the sad truth about our lives frighten us, because as long as we live our personal failings will always be with us" (St Josemaría Escrivá, *Friends of God*, 194).

3:21–23. One consequence of the defective wisdom which St Paul spoke about in the preceding verses is the Corinthians'

no one boast of men. For all things are yours, 22whether Paul or
Apollos or Cephas or the world or life or death or the present or the
future, all are yours; 23and you are Christ's; and Christ is God's. 1 Cor 11:3

Servants of Christ

4 1This is how one should regard us, as servants of Christ and
stewards of the mysteries of God. 2Moreover it is required of Lk 12:42

---

desire to seize on one particular teacher. They have forgotten that all ministers are there to serve the faithful (v. 5). In fact, the Apostle tells them, it is not only the teachers that are theirs: "all things are yours." This clearly emphasizes the great dignity involved in being a Christian: by being an adoptive son of God, a brother of Jesus Christ, the Christian has a share in Christ's lordship over the universe (cf. 1 Cor 15:24–28), and is the master of all creation (cf. 2 Cor 6:10), through which he should move with a certain proprietorial feeling, called as he is to live in the freedom of the glory of the sons of God (cf. Rom 8:21), a freedom which God has won for him (cf. Gal 4:31). Human factions and dissensions of the type that have arisen among the Corinthians show that they have forgotten all this and therefore their sense of vocation has become impoverished. The Christian belongs to Christ alone: he has only one master, Christ. "Mine are the heavens and mine is the earth", St John of the Cross explains; "mine are the people, the righteous are mine and the Mother of God, and all things are mine; and God himself is mine and for me, for Christ is mine and all for me. What, then, do you ask for and seek, my soul? All this is yours, and it is all for you. Do not despise yourself, do not despise the crumbs that fall from your Father's table" (*A Prayer of the Soul enkindled by Love*).

The Apostle's words also remind us of the love and respect that man should have for created things, which God has entrusted to him (cf. Vatican II, *Gaudium et spes*, 37). "The world is not evil," St J. Escrivá reminds us, "for it has come from God's hands; it is his creation; Yahweh looked upon it and saw that it was good (cf. Gen 1:7ff). We ourselves, mankind, make it evil and ugly with our sins and infidelities [...] our age needs to give back to matter and to the most trivial occurrences and situations their noble and original meaning. It needs to restore them to the service of the Kingdom of God, to spiritualize them, turning them into a means and an opportunity for a continuous meeting with Jesus Christ [...]. It is understandable that the Apostle should write: 'all things are yours, you are Christ's and Christ is God's' (1 Cor 3:22–23). We have here an ascending movement which the Holy Spirit, infused in our hearts, wants to call forth from this world, upwards from the earth to the glory of the Lord" (*Conversations*, 114–115).

4:1–2. The features of every apostle, as outlined here by St Paul—"servants of Christ", "stewards of God's mysteries"—put this ministry beyond the reach of grudges and petty squabbles. "Servants of Christ", that is, ministers of Christ, are people to whom he has entrusted his property—his teaching and his sacraments—for them to protect it faithfully and, acting as his agents, to manage it, pass it on and "disperse" it to others (cf. *Commentary on 1 Cor,* ad loc.). As Paul stresses, a basic qualification for being a

stewards that they be found trustworthy. [3]But with me it is a very
small thing that I should be judged by you or by any human court.
Mt 7:1 I do not even judge myself. [4]I am not aware of anything against
Lk 12:2f myself, but I am not thereby acquitted. It is the Lord who judges
Rom 2:16 me. [5]Therefore do not pronounce judgment before the time, before
the Lord comes, who will bring to light the things now hidden in
darkness and will disclose the purposes of the heart. Then every
man will receive his commendation from God.

---

servant or steward is trustworthiness: "Those are untrustworthy stewards who when it comes to dispensing the divine mysteries do not seek the welfare of the people, the honour of Christ or the advantage of his members [...]. Trustworthy stewards are those who always seek the honour of God and the welfare of his members" (ibid., ad loc.).

The Magisterium of the Church has often applied these words to the Christian priesthood: "The Apostle of the Gentiles thus perfectly sums up what may be said of the greatness, the dignity and the duty of the Christian priesthood: 'This is how one should regard us, as servants of Christ and stewards of the mysteries of God' (1 Cor 4:1). The priest is the minister of Christ, an instrument, that is to say, in the hands of the divine Redeemer. He continues the work of the redemption in all its universality and divine efficacy, that work that wrought so marvellous a transformation in the world. Thus the priest, as is said with good reason, is indeed 'another Christ', for, in some way, he is himself a continuation of Christ: 'As the Father has sent me, even so I send you' (Jn 20:21), is spoken to the priest, and hence the priest, like Christ, continues to give 'glory to God in the highest; and on earth peace among men with whom he is pleased' (Lk 2:14). A priest is appointed 'steward of the mysteries of God' (cf. 1 Cor 4:1) for the benefit of the members of the mystical body of Christ, since he is the ordinary minister of nearly all the sacraments—those channels through which the grace of the Saviour flows for the good of humanity. The Christian, at almost every important stage of his mortal career, finds at his side the priest with power received from God, for the purpose of communicating or increasing that grace which is the supernatural life of his soul" (Pius XI, *Ad catholici sacerdotii*).

4:3–5. A servant, an employee, is obviously answerable for his actions—but he is answerable only to his master; only his master can judge him. Therefore, referring to the minister of Christ, St Paul declares that only our Lord can be his judge, because it is to him his service is owed. This teaching applies in the first place to Church ministers; but it also applies to all the faithful, for all should serve God by putting their talents to good use. Therefore, it is not for us to judge others, unless we have some special position which obliges us to do so. And certainly any judgment we do make is valid only if it accords with the will of God; any type of rash judgment would lead to very unfortunate results. Even that judgment we make about ourselves—examination of conscience, which St Paul seems to be hinting at when he says that he is not aware of anything against himself—should be made with the help of grace. It is not a matter of subjective introspection, but rather a sincere review made in the presence of God. It is not

6I have applied all this to myself and Apollos for your benefit,
brethren, that you may learn by us not to go beyond what is
written, that none of you may be puffed up in favour of one
against another. 7For who sees anything different in you? What Jn 3:27
have you that you did not receive? If then you received it, why do
you boast as if it were not a gift?

---

meant to be a reply to the question, What do I think of my behaviour?; but rather to a different question, What does God think of it? Thus, a Christian should not be trying to meticulously measure his conduct, but to have recourse to God, who is rich in mercy. If so, the end-product of his examination will never be like that of the Pharisee, "God, I thank thee that I am not like other men", but, instead, like the publican's "God, be merciful to me, a sinner" (Lk 18:11, 13).

The Apostle, as we can see, is speaking of his own experience, and speaking from a heart full of pastoral solicitude: he is not merely giving advice or taking people to task.

4:6. "Not to go beyond what is written": this is open to various interpretations. It may be a proverb with which the Corinthians were familar, meaning that one should stay on safe ground (in this case, Paul's guidelines for the infant Church at Corinth). "What is written" could also refer to all scripture or just to the quotations which Paul has used (cf. 1:19, 31; 3:19). In any event he makes it clear to the Corinthians that it is they themselves who, due to their immaturity and pride, have caused the dissensions in their community through exalting one preacher at the expense of others. Paul and Apollos have behaved quite properly and therefore cannot be held responsible for these divisions.

4:7. The Apostle comes back again to insist on what he said earlier (cf. 1:26–31): they have no cause to boast about the calling they have received. God called them without any merit on their part. "To be humble is to walk in the truth, for it is absolutely true to say that we have no good thing in ourselves, but only misery and nothingness; and anyone who fails to understand this is walking in falsehood" (St Teresa of Avila, *Interior Castle*, 6, chap. 10). Therefore, the attitude of a humble soul, reflecting on the graces he or she has received, should be one of gratitude to God, the giver. Here is what St John of Avila has to say about this verse: "If you have the grace of God and want to please him and do excellent things, do not glory in yourself, but rather in him who made it possible—God. And if you boast of having used your free will well, or freely consented to God's inspirations, do not boast even on that account: boast rather of God who made you consent, inspiring you and gently influencing you—and who in fact gave you that free will whereby you were able to give your free consent. And if you are inclined to boast about the fact that you could have resisted God's inspiration and good influence and yet did not resist it, you should not boast about that either, for that is a matter not of doing something but of not doing something; and even that you owe to God, because he who helped you to consent in doing good also helped you not to reject that help. Any good use you make of your free will, in things to do with your salvation, is a gift from God [...]. So, always boast only in God, from whom all the good you have comes; and

Trials experienced by apostles

Rev 3:17 [8]Already you are filled! Already you have become rich! Without
us you have become kings! And would that you did reign, so that
2 Cor 4:8–12; we might share the rule with you! [9]For I think that God has
6:4–10; 11:23–33 exhibited us apostles as last of all, like men sentenced to death;
2 Tim 3:10–12 because we have become a spectacle to the world, to angels and to
men. [10]We are fools for Christ's sake, but you are wise in Christ.
We are weak, but you are strong. You are held in honour , but we
2 Cor 11:23–27 in disrepute. [11]To the present hour we hunger and thirst, we are ill-
Acts 18:3 clad and buffeted and homeless, [12]and we labour, working with our
own hands. When reviled, we bless; when persecuted, we endure;
[13]when slandered, we try to conciliate; we have become, and are
now, as the refuse of the world, the offscouring of all things.

---

remember that without him the only harvest you reap is nothing, and vanity and evil" (*Audi, filia,* chap. 66).

4:8. Verse 8 sums up a series of ironic remarks about the conceitedness of these Corinthians whom St Paul is taking to task. St Thomas Aquinas comments as follows: "The Apostle here considers four types of pride: the first, when one thinks that what one has does not come from God [...]; the second, which is similar, when one thinks that one has done everything on one's own merit; the third, when one boasts of having something which one does not in fact have [...]; the fourth, when one despises others and is concerned only about oneself" (*Commentary on 1 Cor,* ad loc.).

The Apostle dramatically describes the disabilities which followers of Christ are happy to bear; like people sentenced to death in the arena they are a spectacle for everyone to watch. In other letters he again tells of the suffering an apostle must expect (cf. 2 Cor 6:3–10; 11:23–33; 2 Tim 3:11).

The last words in the passage—"the refuse of the world, the offscouring of all things"—may refer to a barbaric custom that obtained in some Greek cities: in the face of some public calamity, a citizen, in exchange for being treated royally for a period, agreed to be sacrificed to the gods; on the day of his sacrifice the people had the right to heap every kind of insult and filth upon him; he was "the offscouring of everyone". This sacrifice was offered to free the city of evil spells. Even if they do refer to this custom, these words have also a much deeper meaning: Christ by dying on the cross has redeemed the world; the apostle must follow in the footsteps of his Master, knowing that suffering completes "what is lacking in Christ's afflictions for the sake of his body, that is, the Church" (Col 1:24). Therefore, there is no trace of protest in what St Paul is saying here: he is pointing to the value of suffering, which the cross of Christ, helps us to recognize. "I will tell you which are man's treasures on earth," St Josemaría Escrivá writes, "so that you won't let them go to waste: hunger, thirst, heat, cold, pain, dishonour, poverty, loneliness, betrayal, slander, prison ..." (*The Way*, 194).

Admonishment

[14]I do not write this to make you ashamed, but to admonish you as
my beloved children. [15]For though you have countless guides in Gal 4:19
Christ, you do not have many fathers. For I became your father in
Christ Jesus through the gospel. [16]I urge you, then, be imitators of
me. [17]Therefore I sent[g] to you Timothy, my beloved and faithful 1 Cor 11:1
child in the Lord, to remind you of my ways in Christ, as I teach Acts 19:22
them everywhere in every church. [18]Some are arrogant, as though

---

4:14–16. St Paul brings up the subject of the spiritual paternity of the Corinthians, because it was he who begot them in the faith. In view of this fact, his reproaches take on a special seriousness; his purpose is not to make them feel ashamed but to encourage them to acquire the virtues they need and to have them build up the Church, which has been established as "a communion of life, love and truth" (Vatican II, *Lumen gentium*, 9).

"Be imitators of me": whenever the Apostle puts himself forward as a model for the faithful (cf. 1 Cor 11:1; 2 Thess 3:7; Phil 3:17; Gal 4:12) he refers to the sufferings which his apostolate has brought upon him. All Christians should act in like manner (1 Thess 1:6–7; 2:14). If they do, they will be a support for one another, they will come to have the same sentiments as Christ Jesus, (Phil 2:5), and will be keeping his commandment that each carry his own cross (Mt 16:24).

The saints understood all this and taught others to face up to suffering, even severe suffering. "We always find that those who walked closest to Christ our Lord were those who had to bear the greatest trials. Consider the trials suffered by his glorious Mother and by the glorious Apostles. How do you suppose St Paul could endure such terrible trials? [...] You know very well that, so far as we can learn, he took not a day's rest, nor can he have rested by night, since it was then that he had to earn his living" (St Teresa, *Interior Castle*, 7, chaps. 4, 5).

4:17. Timothy was one of St Paul's most faithful and zealous co-workers; Paul often described him as his beloved son (cf. 1 Tim 1:2; 2 Tim 1:2; 2:1). From his second missionary journey onwards, Timothy had been his faithful companion (cf. Acts 16:1ff), working with him to build up the Christian churches the Apostle was founding. Later he was with St Paul during his first imprisonment in Rome, after which Paul put him in charge of the community at Ephesus (cf. 1 Tim 1:3). During his second imprisonment in Rome, Paul sent for him urgently, to have him at his side during the last stage of his life (cf. 2 Tim 4:9, 12).

At this point—we are on the third missionary journey—just as he had previously been been sent to Thessalonica to strengthen the faith of the Christians in that city and to report back to St Paul (cf. 1 Thess 3:1–5), Timothy is being sent to Corinth, where he had earlier helped in Paul's preaching (cf. Acts 18:5ff; 2 Cor 1:19). His commission is to remind them of St Paul's teaching—which is the teaching of Christ—as it is taught in "every church" by the Apostles and their co-workers. This is a clear indication of the unity of doctrine that was to be found from the very beginning in the various Christian communities which were springing up.

4:18–20. St Paul prefers to send Timothy rather than go in person (v. 18); further on, he speaks in detail about his next journey and the reason why he does not

g. Or *am sending*

I were not coming to you. 19But I will come to you soon, if the
Lord wills, and I will find out not the talk of these arrogant people
1 Cor 2:4 but their power. 20For the kingdom of God does not consist in talk
but in power. 21What do you wish? Shall I come to you with a rod,
or with love in a spirit of gentleness?

2. A CASE OF INCEST

Punishment of the sinner

Lev 18:8; 20:11 5 1It is actually reported that there is immorality among you, and
of a kind that is not found even among pagans; for a man is

---

go at this point: "I do not want to see you now just in passing" (16:5–9). When he does go, his preaching will be in sharp contrast to all the talk of the worldly-wise which he has been referring to (cf. 1:18–3:4); it will prove truly effective in spreading the Kingdom of God (vv. 19–20).

4:21. The Apostle is conscious of being the shepherd of this Christian community which has sprung up in Corinth as a result of his preaching—and conscious, also, of his responsibility before God for the salvation of their souls. He desires always to act "in a spirit of gentleness", without confronting anyone or distressing anyone. However, he is quite ready to go against his inclinations and brandish the "rod", that is, to speak out boldly, if that is what the good of the faithful calls for—energetically admonishing them or even distancing from ecclesial communion those who constitute a danger to other Christians (cf., e.g., the next chapter of the letter).

St Augustine will later remind pastors of their duty in this regard: "Do you realize the dangers that could result from your keeping quiet? The godless man dies, and rightly so; he dies in his sin and in his godlessness: it is his own negligence that kills him [this negligence, according to St Augustine in the following passage, lies in the fact that he could have contacted the pastor but he did not. There is also negligence on the pastor's side if he remains silent]. However, because he was negligent and at the same time the one whose responsibility it was to admonish him failed to do so, the man himself rightly dies and the pastor too is rightly condemned. On the other hand, as the sacred text says, if he warns the godless man [...] 'You are going to die', and if the man fails to avoid the threatening sword, and the sword falls and kills him, he will die in his sin; but you, on the other hand, will have saved your soul (cf. Ezek 33:2–9). So, we [pastors] must need not remain silent: but you, if it should happen that we do in fact remain silent, should be sure to listen to the words of the Pastor in the Holy Scriptures" (*Sermon,* 46, 20).

5:1–6:20. These chapters cover the same general subject: after taking the Corinthians to task for their disunity (a sin which is the cause of other evils), and before replying to questions they themselves have raised (chaps. 7ff), St Paul deals with two matters which are inhibiting the Christian life of that community—sins

living with his father's wife.* 2And you are arrogant! Ought you Lev 18:29
not rather to mourn? Let him who has done this be removed from Deut 27:20
among you.
3For though absent in body I am present in spirit, and as if Col 2:5
present, I have already pronounced judgment 4in the name of the
Lord Jesus on the man who has done such a thing. When you are
assembled, and my spirit is present, with the power of our Lord

---

of unchastity, and recourse to pagan courts.

He begins with the case of incest and the punishment of the man in question (5:1–8), and uses this incident to tell the Corinthians how obstinate sinners should be treated: they should be excluded from the Christian community (5:9–13).

The other matters—sins of impurity and recourse to pagan courts—provide him with an opportunity to give more general practical advice in an elevated tone: firstly, he deals with lawsuits between Christians and how disputes should be solved (6:1–8); human injustice leads him, by association, to describe those sins which prevent people from inheriting the Kingdom of heaven (6:9–11). And then, in a lyrical passage, he extols the dignity of the human body and the need to keep it for God: this is a beautiful hymn in praise of the virtue of holy purity (6:12–20).

5:1–2. With sadness in his heart Paul admonishes these Christians for their passive attitude to behaviour so scandalous that even pagans would not tolerate it: a Christian was co-habiting with his step-mother—something which even Roman law forbade. Clearly it could not have been his own mother, for no society would tolerate that; the woman would have been his father's second wife, and probably his father was dead; and the woman must have been a pagan, because the Apostle's references are to the man.

It is possible that some self-opinionated Corinthians were arguing in favour of what the man was doing; it may be that they were misinterpreting the idea of conversion being a kind of new birth (cf. Jn 3:5), and using this as a pretext for saying that previous family ties were no longer binding (as some Jewish rabbis taught converts to Judaism).

The Apostle accepts no excuse for this type of behaviour: he stresses the gravity of the sin and moves quickly and boldly to see that action is taken.

If the incestuous man is guilty of grave sin, also are those Christians who condone his behaviour. Jesus' teaching is that one should correct an erring person (cf. Mt 18:15–17). "Therefore, when in our own life or in that of others we notice that 'something is wrong', something that requires the spiritual and human help which, as children of God, we can and ought to provide, the prudent thing to do is to apply the appropriate remedy by going to the root of the trouble, resolutely, lovingly and sincerely. There is no room here for inhibition, for it is a great mistake to think that problems can be solved by omissions or procrastination" (St Josemaría Escrivá, *Friends of God*, 157).

5:3–5. In addition to giving his personal decision on the case of the incestuous man (v. 3), St Paul also supplies a solemn formula of excommunication (vv. 4–5). This contains four key elements: "in the name of the Lord Jesus", showing that the Church's judgment is on a higher than human plane; "with the power of our Lord Jesus", showing that the

1 Tim 1:20 Jesus, [5]you are to deliver this man to Satan* for the destruction of the
flesh, that his spirit may be saved in the day of the Lord Jesus.[h]
Gal 5:9 [6]Your boasting is not good. Do you not know that a little leaven
Is 53:7 leavens the whole lump? [7]Cleanse out the old leaven that you may

Church's authority derives from Christ himself: "Whatever you bind on earth shall be bound in heaven" (Mt 18:18; cf. Mt 16:19; 28:28); "when you are assembled and my spirit is present": although this is not technical language—which would be out of place in a letter—it is easy to see here a reference to collegiality of decisions taken under the hierarchical authority of the Apostle.

And then the sentence is described: "you are to deliver this man to Satan." The erring man should be kept away from the Church, unable to draw on its spiritual resources and exposed to the hostile power of the devil. "The excommunicated, because they are outside the Church, lose some of the benefits it contains. There is an additional danger: the Church's prayer renders the devil less able to tempt us; therefore, when someone is excluded from the Church, he can be easily overcome by him. So it was that in the early Church when someone was excommunicated it was common for him to be physically tormented by the devil" (St Thomas Aquinas, *Super Symbolum Apostolorum*, 10). However, this punishment is a temporary one, imposed "that his spirit may be saved in the day of the Lord Jesus", that is, imposed in order to bring him to correct his behaviour.

Throughout history the Church has used its power to impose sanctions (even severe ones such as excommunication) when other means of persuasion have failed. "If on account of the gravity of the sin [public] punishment be necessary, they [bishops] must use rigour with meekness, justice with mercy, and severity with gentleness, so as to maintain without asperity that discipline which is good and necessary for people, and which leads those who are corrected to mend their ways; or, if they do not wish to change, so that their punishment may serve as a salutary warning to others and lead them away from vice" (Council of Trent, *De reformatione*, chap. 1).

5:6. Jesus used the example of leaven in dough to describe the growth of goodness (cf. Mt 13:31–33 and par.) and also of evil (cf. Mk 8:15–16 and par.): in both cases a small amount can produce a very large result. Here St Paul uses the simile to show the Corinthians the harm the incestuous man's behaviour can do to the whole community through the bad example and scandal he gives and also through others' consenting to his sin and not doing what they can to get him to reform (cf. St Thomas, *Commentary on 1 Cor,* ad loc.).

St Paul draws attention to the gravity of the sin of scandal—"anything said, done or omitted which leads another to commit sins" (*St Pius X Catechism*, 417): "For, all other sins, no matter how grave they be, do injury only to the person who commits them; but this sin harms those others whom it steers off God's path. How can satisfaction be made for this injury, which involves killing a soul whom Christ has bought with his blood? For if gold is what gold is worth, the blood of Christ is what cost blood. Whence it follows that, if these people be

h. Other ancient authorities omit *Jesus*

be a new lump, as you really are unleavened. For Christ, our
paschal lamb, has been sacrificed. 8Let us, therefore, celebrate the Ex 12:3–20
festival, not with the old leaven, the leaven of malice and evil, but
with the unleavened bread of sincerity and truth.

Obstinate sinners are to be shunned

9I wrote to you in my letter not to associate with immoral men;* 2 Cor 6:17
10not at all meaning the immoral* of this world, or the greedy and 1 Jn 5:19

---

condemned, not only will they undergo punishment for their faults but also for the faults of those whom they led into evil. Therefore, every Christian realizes how justly Christ spoke when he said (Mt 18:7), 'Woe to the world for temptations to sin'" (Fray Luis de Granada, *Sermon on Public Sins*).

5:7–8. The Apostle is here using examples taken from the Jewish celebration of the Passover and the Azymes, to draw spiritual lessons for the Corinthians. The Passover was the principal Jewish feast, and its central rite the eating of the passover lamb. At the passover meal, as also on the seven days following, which were also feast-days, the eating of leavened bread was forbidden, which was why they were described as the days of the Azymes (*a-zyme* = without leaven). Thus, in the Book of Exodus God laid it down that during these days no leaven should be kept in Jewish homes (cf. Ex 12:15, 19).

Jesus Christ, our Passover, our paschal lamb, "has been sacrificed". The paschal lamb was a promise and prefigurement of the true Lamb, Jesus Christ (cf. Jn 1:29), who was the victim of the sacrifice on Calvary, offered on behalf of all mankind: "He is the true lamb who took away the sins of the world; by dying he destroyed our death; by rising he restored our life" (*Roman Missal*, first Easter Preface). The perennial value of the sacrifice of Christ on the cross (cf. Heb 10:11–14), renewed every time Mass is said, means that Christians are always celebrating a festival. Therefore, the Apostle concludes, Christians should eliminate—from community life and personal life—the old leaven, which in the context of the festival symbolizes impurity and sinfulness; and they should always live a genuinely Christian life, with azymes, the symbol of cleanness and purity, "of sincerity and truth".

"The present time is, then, a festival day," St John Chrysostom comments, "for when he says 'let us celebrate the festival', Paul does not add: 'for Passover or Pentecost is imminent.' No, he is pointing out that all this life is a festival for Christians by virtue of the ineffable benefits they have received. Indeed, Christians, what wonders have you not received from God? For your sakes Jesus Christ has become man; he has freed you from eternal damnation, to call you to take possession of his kingdom. With this thought in mind, how can you not be in continuous festival right through your life on earth? Poverty, sickness or the persecution which oppresses us—these should not discourage us: this present life, the Apostle tells us, is a life of rejoicing" (*Hom. on 1 Cor,* ad loc.).

5:9–10. This is all we know about the letter he mentions, which must have been lost at some later stage. Obviously it could not have contained any substantial

robbers, or idolaters, since then you would need to go out of the
2 Thess 3:6 world. 11But rather I wrote[i] to you not to associate with any one
2 Jn 10 who bears the name of brother if he is guilty of immorality* or
greed, or is an idolater, reviler, drunkard, or robber—not even to

---

revelation not to be found in other passages of Scripture: God would not have allowed something to be lost which was necessary to the universal Church. St Paul is clarifying something he said in the earlier letter—about not associating with sexually immoral people—which, in view of the current behaviour of the Corinthians, they do not seem to have understood very well; it is not a matter of not mixing with sinful pagans, but rather of shunning those who call themselves Christians but are taking no steps to give up sinning.

Corinth was an exceptionally loose-living city. To avoid contact with non-Christian sinners, the faithful would have had to "go out of the world" and St Paul would never have given such advice; as we shall see, he later writes: "I have become all things to all men, that I might by all means save some" (1 Cor 9:22). A Christian should do whatever he can to save all, using every supernatural and human resource available to him: only when someone constitutes a danger to a Christian's own soul should he avoid that person. But it would be cowardice to cut oneself off from the world (cf. notes on 3:21–23; 2 Cor 5:6) and from healthy involvement in this life, just because of the difficulties one might encounter, difficulties arising from a dechristianized or unchristian environment: "we children of God ought not to remain aloof from earthly endeavours, for God has placed us here to sanctify them and make them fruitful with our blessed faith, which alone is capable of bringing true peace and joy to all men wherever they may be [...]. We urgently need to christianize society. We must imbue all levels of mankind with a supernatural outlook, and each of us must strive to raise his daily duties, his job or profession, to the order of grace. In this way all human occupations will be lit up by a new hope that transcends time and the inherent transience of earthly realities" (St Josemaría Escrivá, *Friends of God*, 210).

5:11–13. The Apostle returns to the central theme of this chapter—what to do about the incestuous man—with some directives of more general application: the same policy should be followed in regard to those who commit the sins mentioned in v. 11: "not even to eat with such a one", that is, not to let them take part in liturgical gatherings (cf. 1 Cor 11), or have close personal relationships with them (cf. 2 Jn 10). At the end of the chapter he repeats this condemnation, using words often found in the Old Testament (cf. Deut 17:7): "Drive out the wicked person from among you" (v. 13). Although he is directly referring to the man guilty of incest, this can be translated, as the New Vulgate does, in a more general way: "Drive out evil from among you."

The list of sins in v. 11 is very similar to that which appears in the following chapter (1 Cor 6:9–10); in St Paul's letters we can find up to thirteen lists of grave sins. In devout, educated circles at that time, it was quite common for lists of sins to be circulated, the Jewish lists having different sins from the Greek. St

i. Or *now I write*

eat with such a one. [12]For what have I to do with judging outsiders? Is it not those inside the church whom you are to judge?
[13]God judges those outside. "Drive out the wicked person from among you." Deut 13:6

Paul, who may have been acquainted with both types of list, is not transcribing them literally; he gives a profoundly Christian character to both the form and the content of the lists he provides.

He is not devising an exhaustive list of sins but rather reminding the actual addressees of his letters about the sins they are in most danger of committing. He begans by condemning the sin which has led to what he has just been saying—in this case, incest; in chapter 6, injustice; etc. Also the gravity of the sins can be deduced from what they lead to—not so much the havoc they can wreak on society as the punishment which they merit: people who sin in this way will not inherit the Kingdom (1 Cor 6:9; Gal 5:19–21; Eph 5:5); they provoke God's anger (Col 3:5–8); sinners will be asked to account for themselves on the Last Day (2 Tim 3:2–5; 1 Cor 5:5); they are deserving of death (Rom 1:29–31); etc.

As far as the content of these sins is concerned, it is easy to see that they involved breaking one or other of the ten commandments. Although St Paul is not writing a systematic treatise on moral theology, he does make a point of always referring to three sins—greed, idolatry and impurity.

Greed, which goes beyond merely desiring to possess wealth, involves using others—and if necessary using even God—to obtain personal advantage or pleasure. It is, therefore, the sin most opposed to charity, which implies serving God and serving other people for God's sake.

Hence the Apostle mentions idolatry in the same context; in fact, idolatry, which consists in not giving God the glory that he is due as the only God, always, like greed, ends up in man's thinking that he needs nothing from God (cf. Rom 1:21). "The origin of every sin", St Augustine comments, "is pride; if they had thanked God for the wisdom he gives them, they would never have attributed it to their own reasoning" (*Expositio quorumdam propositionum ex Epistola ad Romanos*, prop. 4). St Thomas Aquinas is even more explicit about the blindness of the proud: "He who turns his back on God, relying on himself and not on God, enters spiritual darkness" (*Commentary on Rom*, 1, 21).

Also, impurity, that is, every disorder against the sixth and ninth commandments, is a grave sin, similar to idolatry (cf. Rom 1: 24–27; 1 Cor 10:6–8): since the body belongs to God and is a member of Christ (cf. 1 Cor 6:14), every disordered use of the generative faculty involves a certain misdirection of the worship that is owed to God: the body, which ought to give glory to God, is trying to glory in itself. That is why throughout his letters the Apostle puts special emphasis on the real reason why these sins are so serious—the fact that they all offend directly against the glory due to God.

3. RECOURSE TO PAGAN COURTS

6 1When one of you has a grievance against a brother, does he
Dan 7:22 dare go to law before the unrighteous* instead of the saints?
Wis 3:8 Rev 20:4 2Do you not know that the saints will judge the world? And if the
world is to be judged by you, are you incompetent to try trivial

---

6:1–6. As usually happens in his letters, in the course of dealing with some more or less important event in the Christian community, the Apostle moves on to a much higher plane, and from there focuses light onto the particular problem.

In this case, the scandal is that Christians are involved in lawsuits against one another (v. 7) and are bringing these cases before pagan courts instead of trying to settle them within the sphere of the Church; Paul, as we can see, is quite incensed: "How dare any of your members ..."

Through Baptism, Christians become holy, justified; that is, they have obtained a share in the life and virtues of Christ and are called to follow his example. Furthermore, like the Apostles (cf. Mt 19:28; Lk 22:30), Christians will judge men and angels on the Last Day. They are, therefore, instruments of and witnesses to divine justice. So, they really should not go to law against each other; and if they do have grievances the Christian community itself should provide people who are equipped to act as arbitrators and have the grace of state to solve the problems that arise. St Paul is not down-playing civil authority and its autonomy, for all authority comes from God (Rom 13: 1–5); he himself submitted to Roman tribunals, and he even appealed to Caesar (cf. Acts 25:11–12). The specific advice he gives here—that Christians should not bring cases before pagan courts—ties in with Jewish practice. Primarily, the Apostle is recommending to Christians to practise fraternity and solve disagreements without going to pagan courts. Moreover, going to law would be a great disservice to the Gospel: what attraction could a community hold which was divided within itself? It is this grave scandal that he particularly wants to avoid.

6:3. The only Judge of the living and the dead, of angels and men, is Jesus Christ. Christians are so intimately linked to Christ that St Paul sees no objections to attributing the actions of the head to all the members. Therefore, he does not attempt to speculate on the particular form the Last Judgment will take—whether, for example, men will judge angels or at least the fallen angels. His aim here may be simply to emphasize the intimate union of the Christian with Christ, which ought to be reflected in just dealings with one another.

6:7–8. This is the reason why St Paul is so hard on the Corinthians. They have failed to understand and to apply what our Lord said in the Sermon on the Mount about bearing injuries (Mt 5:39–42). Worse still, they have gone to law against each other in contravention of the standard set by those early Christians, who had one heart and soul (cf. Acts 4:32). And they have tried to solve their disagreements in pagan courts which know nothing of Christian brotherhood. St John Chrysostom points out the transgressions the Corinthians are guilty of: "For one thing, not bearing injuries patiently; for another, offending others; then looking

cases? [3]Do you not know that we are to judge angels? How much
more, matters pertaining to this life! [4]If then you have such cases,
why do you lay them before those who are least esteemed by the
church? [5]I say this to your shame. Can it be that there is no man
among you wise enough to decide between members of the
brotherhood, [6]but brother goes to law against brother, and that
before unbelievers?

[7]To have lawsuits at all with one another is defeat for you. Why
not rather suffer wrong? Why not rather be defrauded? [8]But you
yourselves wrong and defraud, and that even your own brethren.

Mt 5:39
Lk 6:29
1 Thess 5:15
1 Pet 3:9

[9]Do you not know that the unrighteous will not inherit the
kingdom of God? Do not be deceived; neither the immoral,* nor

---

for abitrators to decide on the matter; finally, using this procedure in a dispute with a Christian, a brother in the faith" (*Hom. on 1 Cor,* ad loc.).

St Paul's advice about money can usefully be read in the light of Romans 12:17–21: this shows us that he is not saying that a passive and weak attitude to difficulties is the right one: difficulties should be faced and an effort made to do positive good, at all times, to everyone.

"Let us especially resolve not to judge others, not to doubt their good will, to drown evil in an abundance of good, sowing loyal friendship, justice and peace all around us. And let us resolve never to become sad if our upright conduct is misunderstood by others; if the good which, with the continuous help of our Lord, we try to accomplish is misinterpreted by people who delight in unjustly guessing at our motives and who accuse us of wicked designs and deceitful behaviour. Let us forgive always, with a smile on our lips. Let us speak clearly, without hard feelings, when in conscience we think we ought to speak. And let us leave everything in the hands of our Father God, with a divine silence—'Jesus was silent' (Mt 26:63)—if we are confronted with personal attacks, no matter how brutal and shameful they might be. Let us concern ourselves only with doing good deeds: God will see to it that they 'shine before men' (Mt 5:16)" (St J. Escrivá, *Christ Is Passing By*, 72).

6:9–10. In this list of sins, similar to that given in the previous chapter (cf. 1 Cor 5:10–11), St Paul explicitly teaches that those who commit these sins will not inherit the Kingdom, that is, will not attain eternal salvation. The whole list is a kind of explanation of what "unrighteousness" means. Thus, not only those go against righteousness who wrongly go to law or defraud others: righteousness, justice, in the language of the Bible is equivalent to holiness and therefore is opposed to every kind of sin.

"Do not be deceived": the Greek can also be translated as "Do not let yourselves be deceived" (cf. Eph 5:5–6). Certainly, to make out that such actions are good is worse than to commit them. And yet in Corinth, and in other places at other times, there have been and are false ideologies which interpret sinfullness as virtue. To combat tendencies that seek to tone down or deny the reality of grave sin, the Church points out that "a person sins mortally not only when his action comes from direct contempt for love of God and neighbour, but also when he

Gal 5:19ff Eph 5:5 idolaters, nor adulterers, nor homosexuals,[j]* [10]nor thieves, nor the
Rev 21:8; 22:15 greedy, nor drunkards, nor revilers, nor robbers will inherit the
Jn 3:5 kingdom of God. [11]And such were some of you. But you were
Eph 2:1–6 Tit 3:3–7 washed, you were sanctified, you were justified in the name of the
1 Jn 2:12 Lord Jesus Christ and in the Spirit of our God.

4. FORNICATION, A GRAVE SIN

Respect for the body

1 Cor 10:23 [12]"All things are lawful for me," but not all things are helpful. "All
things are lawful for me," *but I will not be enslaved by anything.

---

consciously and freely, for whatever reason, chooses something which is seriously disordered [...]. Pastors of souls must exercise patience and generosity; but they are not allowed to render God's commandments null, nor to reduce unreasonably people's responsibility" (SCDF, *Declaration concerning Sexual Ethics*, 10). Like Christ, pastors should be uncompromising with evil and merciful to evildoers.

6:11. This reminder about the dignity of Christians brings to an end this series of warnings. It reminds the Corinthians of their Baptism, its effects and their need to return to their initial holiness.

These last words clearly contain a reference to the Trinitarian formula used at Baptism (cf. Mt 28:19). The inclusion of the name of the three persons of the Blessed Trinity implies an act of faith in God, One and Three, and recognition that grace and justification are given us by the Father, have been merited by his Son Jesus Christ, and are applied to us through the action of the Holy Spirit.

Three words sum up the effects of Baptism—"washed", "sanctified", and "justified" (cf. Acts 22:16; Eph 5:16; Tit 3:5); in addition to erasing original sin, and any personal sin, Baptism gives us sanctifying grace and the infused virtues: "The followers of Christ, called by God not in virtue of their works but by his design and grace, and justified in the Lord Jesus, have been made sons of God in baptism, the sacrament of faith, and partakers of the divine nature, and so are truly sanctified. They must therefore hold on to and perfect in their lives that sanctification which they have received from God" (*Lumen gentium,* 40).

Reminding them of baptismal innocence, St Paul encourages the Corinthians to return to that state by a new conversion. After Baptism, the sacrament of Penance received with the right dispositions restores sanctifying grace and is, moreover, a means Christ chooses to conserve men in grace and bring them growth in grace: "The sacrament of Penance contributes [much] to the development of the Christian life" (Vatican II, *Christus Dominus*, 30).

6:12–20. In the second part of this chapter, the Apostle deals with the gravity of the sin of impurity. The moral degradation into which mankind had fallen prior to

j. Two Greek words are rendered by this expression

13"Food is meant for the stomach and the stomach for food"—and 1 Thess 4:3–5
God will destroy both one and the other. The body is not meant for
immorality,* but for the Lord, and the Lord for the body. 14And God
raised the Lord and will also raise us up by his power.

---

the coming of Jesus Christ (cf. Rom 1:18–22) had led some pagan societies to lose all sense of sexual sin—which was why the Apostle had sometimes to remind Christians of pagan birth of the gravity of that sin (cf., e.g., Acts 15:29; 1 Thess 4: 3–5).

The situation in Corinth was particularly serious: the worship of Aphrodite, for example, had led people to see prostitution as a kind of consecration to that goddess. This is why St Paul has to point out to these recent converts that impurity is a serious sin; he rejects the kind of argument used to justify it (vv. 12–14) and explains why it offends Jesus Christ (vv. 15–18) and the Holy Spirit (vv. 19–20). "The Apostle points out the specifically Christian motive for practising chastity, when he condemns the sin of fornication not only in the measure that this action is injurious to one's neighbour or to the social order but because the fornicator offends against Christ who has redeemed him with his blood and of whom he is a member, and against the Holy Spirit of whom he is the temple" (SCDF, *Declaration concerning Sexual Ethics*, 11).

6:12–14. "All things are lawful for me": the Apostle may have used this expression himself to explain Christian freedom as opposed to the prescriptions of the Jewish law on matters of legal impurity, food, sabbath observance, etc.; and to stress the freedom which Jesus Christ won for men by dying on the cross (cf. Gal 4:31); this freedom means that the Christian is no longer a slave of the devil or of sin, and—by sharing through Baptism in Christ's kingship—has obtained dominion over all the things of the earth. But some people were misinterpreting this and were using their freedom as an excuse for living without reference to the commandments of God. St Paul makes it clear that everything which is not opposed to God's law is permissible, and that everything which goes counter to that law means falling again into the old slavery: "It cannot happen that the soul should go its way without anyone to direct it; that is why it has been redeemed in such a way that it has Christ as its King—his yoke is easy and his burden light (cf. Mt 11:30)—and not the devil, whose rule is oppressive" (Origen, *In Rom. Comm.*, 5, 6).

Another sophism was to present impurity as a natural need of the body, in the same way as food is natural. St Paul rejects this argument by showing that the relationship between food and the stomach is not parallel to that of the body and fornication: the body is not even necessarily orientated to marriage, for although marriage is necessary for the spread of the human race, it is not a necessity for every individual (cf. *St Pius V Catechism*, 2, 8, 12). The Apostle places the body on a much higher plane: "the body is for the Lord, and the Lord for the body", and it is God's will to raise it up to live again in heaven (cf. Rom 8:11), where there will be no longer any need for bodily nourishment.

From this orientation of the whole person—body and soul—to God arises the eminently positive character of the virtue of purity, which tends to fill the heart with love of God, who "has not called us for uncleanness but [to live] in

Offence to Christ and the Holy Spirit

1 Cor 12:27 [15]Do you not know that your bodies are members of Christ? Shall
I therefore take the members of Christ and make them members
Gen 2:24 of a prostitute? Never! [16]Do you not know that he who joins

---

holiness" (1 Thess 4:7). "We belong to God completely," St Josemaría Escrivá reminds us, "soul and body, flesh and bones, all our senses and faculties [...]. If one has the spirit of God, chastity is not a troublesome and humiliating burden, but a joyful affirmation. Will-power, dominion, self-mastery do not come from the flesh or from instinct. They come from the will, especially if it is united to the Will of God. In order to be chaste (and not merely continent or decent) we must subject our passions to reason, but for a noble motive, namely, the promptings of Love.

"I think of this virtue as the wings which enable us to carry God's teaching, his commandments, to every environment on this earth, without fear of becoming contaminated in the process. Wings, even in the case of those majestic birds which soar higher than the clouds, are a burden and a heavy one. But without wings, there is no way of flying. I want you to grasp this idea clearly, and to decide not to give in when you feel the sting of temptation, with its suggestion that purity is an unbearable burden. Take heart! Fly upwards, up to the sun, in pursuit of Love" (*Friends of God*, 177).

6:15–18. St Paul here explains how gravely offensive this sin is to Jesus Christ. The Christian has become a member of Christ's body through Baptism; he is meant to live in an intimate relationship with him, sharing his very life (cf. Gal 2:20, to be "one spirit with him" (cf. Rom 12:5; 1 Cor 12:27). Sexual immorality is as terrible as to hack oneself off from the body of Christ, to become one body with a prostitute. Hence the gravity of this sin, a sin against one's own body, which is part of the mystical body of Christ.

"Shun [sexual] immorality": this is the route one must take when tempted against chastity. Temptations against other virtues can be overcome by putting up resistance, but in this case "one does not win by putting up resistance, because the more one thinks about the thing, the more influenced one becomes; one wins by fleeing—that is, by avoiding unclean thoughts completely and by avoiding all occasions of sin" (St Thomas Aquinas, *Commentary on 1 Cor,* ad loc.). A Christian has all kinds of resources he can use to practise chastity in a very refined way: "The first is to be very vigilant about what we look at, and what we think and say and do; second, to have recourse to prayer; third, to frequent the sacraments worthily; fourth, to fly from anything which might tempt us to sin; fifth, to have great devotion to the Blessed Virgin. If we do all that, then, no matter what our enemies do, no matter how frail this virtue be, we can be quite sure of holding on to it" (St John Mary Vianney, *Sermon on the 17th Sunday after Pentecost*, 2); see also the note on Mt 5: 27–30.

6:19–20. Fornication is not only a profanation of the body of Christ but also of the temple of the Holy Spirit—for God dwells in the soul, through grace, as in a temple (cf. note on 1 Cor 3:16–17).

"Contemplative prayer will rise within you whenever you meditate on this impressive reality: something as material as my body has been chosen by the Holy Spirit as his dwelling place ... I no longer

himself to a prostitute becomes one body with her? For, as it is
written, "The two shall become one flesh."[k] 17But he who is united — Jn 17:21ff
to the Lord becomes one spirit with him. 18Shun immorality.*
Every other sin which a man commits is outside the body; but the
immoral man sins against his own body. 19Do you not know that — 1 Cor 3:16f
your body is a temple of the Holy Spirit within you, which you — 1 Cor 7:23
have from God? You are not your own; 20you were bought with a — Phil 1:20
price. So glorify God in your body. — 1 Pet 1:18

---

belong to myself ... My body and soul, my whole being, belong to God ... And this prayer will be rich in practical consequences, drawn from the great consequence which the Apostle himself proposes: 'glorify God in your body' (1 Cor 6:20)" (St Josemaría Escrivá, *Conversations*, 121).

"You were bought with a price": the Redemption wrought by Christ, culminating with his death on the cross, is the price paid to set mankind free from slavery to the devil, to sin and to death. "You know that you were ransomed from the futile ways inherited from your fathers, not with perishable things such as silver and gold, but with the precious blood of Christ, like that of a lamb without blemish or spot" (1 Pet 1:18–19; cf. Eph 1:7). That is why "you are not your own": you now belong to God; the Christian is part of Christ's body, and a temple of the Holy Spirit. Reflection on this wonderful truth should lead the Christian always to live in accordance with his new status. "Christian, remember who you are; you have been given a share in God's very nature; do not, therefore, even think of reverting by unworthy conduct to your earlier evil ways. Remember who your head is and whose body you are part of. Do not forget that you were set free from the power of darkness and brought into the light, to the Kingdom of God. Thanks to the sacrament of Baptism, you have become a temple of the Holy Spirit: do not think of turning out so noble a guest by evil deeds; do not think of subjecting yourself to the slavery of the devil: for the price paid for you was the blood of Christ" (St Leo the Great, *First Nativity Sermon*).

6:20. "So, glorify God in your body": this follows logically from what the Apostle has been saying. "Purity as a virtue, that is, an ability to 'control (one's) own body in holiness and honour' (cf. 1 Thess 4:4), allied to the gift of purity as the fruit of the indwelling of the Holy Spirit in the 'temple' of the body, makes for such dignity in interpersonal relationships that *God himself is glorified in the body*. Purity is the glory of the human body in God's sight. It is the glory of God in the human body" (John Paul II, *General Audience*, 18 March 1981).

In commenting on this passage, St John Chrysostom recalls what our Lord says in Matthew 5:16—"that they may see your good works and give glory to your Father who is in heaven"—to show that a Christian's chaste life should lead those around him to God. "When they see a holy man practising the highest virtues, they feel obliged to reflect and they blush to see the difference between their life and that of a Christian. For, when they see someone who shares their own nature being so much above them (a great deal more than heaven is above earth) do they not feel obliged to believe that a divine power is at work [to produce such sanctity]?" (*Hom. on 1 Cor*, 18, ad loc.).

k. Greek *one flesh*

PART TWO

Answers to various questions

5. MARRIAGE AND VIRGINITY

Relations between husband and wife

Eph 5:22ff 7 [1]Now concerning the matters about which you wrote. It is well
for a man not to touch a woman. [2]But because of the temptation to immorality, each man should have his own wife and each

---

This chapter marks the beginning of the second part of the letter, in which St Paul replies to various questions raised by the faithful of Corinth; he opens his remarks with the phrase "Now concerning ..." (cf. 7:1, 25; 8:1; 12:1). The question which he now takes up may have been put by some Corinthians who, in view of the corrupt pagan environment of the city, were inclined to view virginity as a way all should follow, and to see marriage as something bad. In his reply St Paul deals with marriage and its indissolubility (vv. 1–16), celibacy (vv. 25–38) and widowhood (vv. 39–40). Verses 17–24 are a digression in which he explains that conversion to Christianity does not necessarily involve a change in a person's state of life or a change in external circumstances.

7:1–9. The Apostle explains briefly that marriage is something quite lawful. For a proper understanding of what he says, both here and in vv. 25–35, it should be remembered that he is replying to a query which was apparently arguing that celibacy is the only possible state of life for a Christian; and therefore he is making only two basic points—that, absolutely speaking, celibacy is on a higher plane than marriage; but marriage is something good and holy for those who are called to it. He is not writing a full dissertation on marriage, which God instituted at the start of creation (cf. Gen 1:27–28) and which Jesus Christ raised to the dignity of a sacrament (cf. Mt 19:4–6; Jn 2:2). Although in this letter he does have some things to say about the grandeur of marriage (cf., e.g., 7:7, 14, 17; 11:3), it will be in the Letter to the Ephesians that he elaborates on this subject, comparing the union between husband and wife to that between Christ and the Church. "Whoever condemns marriage also deprives virginity of its glory; whereas whoever praises it makes virginity more attractive and luminous. Something which seems good only when compared with something bad, is not very valuable; but when it is greater than things which everyone gives great value to, then indeed it is good to a superlative degree" (St John Chrysostom, *De virginitate*, 10, 1).

So, in reply to the question raised, St Paul says here that it is good to be celibate, but in order to be so one needs a special gift from God (v. 7). Bearing in mind also the moral climate of Corinth—which so actively prompted impurity and could give rise to so many temptations of the devil (vv. 2, 5, 9)—it is better for those who do not have this gift to be

woman her own husband.* 3The husband should give to his wife
her conjugal rights, and likewise the wife to her husband. 4For the
wife does not rule over her own body, but the husband does;
likewise the husband does not rule over his own body, but the wife
does. 5Do not refuse one another except perhaps by agreement for Ex 19:15
a season, that you may devote yourselves to prayer; but then come
together again, lest Satan tempt you through lack of self-control.
6I say this by way of concession, not of command. 7I wish that all Mt 19:12

---

married; the calling to marriage is, like virginity, a gift of God. Clearly he does not mean that the basic purpose of marriage is to free people from temptation: he simply wants those whom God is not calling to celibacy, not to try to be celibate and run the risk of being unable to cope with temptation.

Without underestimating its other purposes, marriage is ordained by its very nature to the begetting and rearing of children (cf. *Gaudium et spes*, 50). "According to the plan of God, marriage is the foundation of the wider community of the family, since the very institution of marriage and conjugal love is ordained to the procreation and education of children, in whom they find their crown [...]. Thus, the fundamental task of the family is to serve life, to actualize in history the original blessing of the Creator—that of transmitting by procreation the divine image from person to person" (John Paul II, *Familiaris consortio*, 14 and 28).

7:3–6. From what St Paul says, it would seem that some people were arguing that virginity is necessary for all and therefore those who are already married should live as celibates. That is not the case, the Apostle tells them, and if in a particular case husband and wife want to practise complete continence, then they should do so by mutual agreement and only for a period, in order not to put themselves unnecessarily in the way of being tempted by Satan. He makes it clear that he is not laying this down as a commandment, but "by way of concession"; as he goes on to say (v. 7), he would like everyone to be celibate like himself, but he knows that God gives different gifts to different people.

At the same time, the Apostle does provide beautiful teaching about the duties of married couples: husband and wife are no longer the owners of their own bodies; each has a right over the other's body: they form one flesh (cf. Gen 2:24) in such a way that, belonging to one another, they owe themselves to each other in strict justice.

7:7. St Paul lived a celibate life; God had called him to be fully dedicated to his service. Paul would like everyone to be like himself: in vv. 25–35 he will say that celibacy is a higher state than marriage; but he shows that, as Jesus Christ taught (cf. Mt 19:11–12), celibacy is a special gift from God. "The response to the divine call is an answer of love to the love which Christ has shown us so sublimely (Jn 15:13; 3:16). This response is included in the mystery of that special love for those souls who have accepted his most urgent appeals (cf. Mk 10:21). Grace with a divine force increases the longings of love. And love, when it is genuine, is total, exclusive, stable and lasting, an irresistible spur to all forms of heroism. And so, the free choice of sacred celibacy has always been considered by the Church 'as something that signifies

were as I myself am. But each has his own special gift from God,
one of one kind and one of another.
8To the unmarried and the widows I say that it is well for them
1 Tim 5:14 to remain single as I do. 9But if they cannot exercise self-control,
they should marry. For it is better to marry than to be aflame with
passion.

Indissolubility of marriage

Mt 5:32 Mk 10:11f 10To the married I give charge, not I but the Lord, that the wife
Lk 16:18 should not separate from her husband 11(but if she does, let her
1 Cor 7:12; 25:40 remain single or else be reconciled to her husband)—and that the
husband should not divorce his wife.

---

and stimulates charity' (*Lumen gentium*, 42). It signifies a love without reservations, it stimulates to a charity which is open to all" (Paul VI, *Sacerdotalis caelibatus*, 24; cf. note on Mt 19:11–12).

From what the Apostle says—"each has his own special gift from God"—it is clear that the vocation to marriage is also a gift of God (cf. *Lumen gentium*, 11) and therefore family life, conjugal duties, education of children, the effort to maintain and improve the family's standard of living, are things which husband and wife should supernaturalize, things which should help them live a life of dedication to God. "Marriage is a divine path on earth", St Josemaría Escrivá explains. "The purpose of marriage is to help married people sanctify themselves and others. For this reason they receive a special grace in the sacrament instituted by Jesus Christ. Those who are called to the married state will, with the grace of God, find within their state everything they need to be holy, to identify themselves each day more with Jesus Christ, and to lead those with whom they live to God" (*Conversations*, 91).

7:10–11. When speaking of celibacy St Paul says that it is not something he commands but only something he recommends (cf. v. 25); however, when referring to the indissolubility of marriage, he makes it quite clear that it is a matter of God's teaching and not just his own. Jesus in fact was unequivocal about the unity and indissolubility of marriage: neither the husband (cf. Mt 5:21–32; 19:3–12) nor the wife (cf. Mk 10:12) is to attempt to break up a marriage. No authority on earth may dissolve "what God has joined together" (Mt 19:6); only the death of one or other of the partners breaks the marriage bond (cf. 1 Cor 7:39). Even if the couple separate, the bond between them is not dissolved, and therefore neither can contract a new, genuine marriage. This indissolubility affects not only a Christian marriage, but every genuine marriage.

The Church, which is the authoritative interpreter of Holy Scripture and of the natural law, has always taught that marriage is one and indissoluble (cf. note on Mt 5:31–32). "It is a fundamental duty of the Church to reaffirm strongly [...] the doctrine of the indissolubility of marriage. To all those who, in our times, consider it too difficult, or indeed impossible, to be bound to one person for the whole of life, and to those caught up in a culture that rejects the indissolubility of marriage and openly mocks the commitment of spouses to fidelity, it is necessary to reconfirm the good news of the definitive nature of that conjugal love that has in

The Pauline privilege

[12]To the rest I say, not the Lord, that if any brother has a wife who is
an unbeliever, and she consents to live with him, he should not
divorce her. [13]If any woman has a husband who is an unbeliever, and
he consents to live with her, she should not divorce him. [14]For the
unbelieving husband is consecrated through his wife, and the
unbelieving wife is consecrated through her husband. Otherwise, your
children would be unclean, but as it is they are holy. [15]But if the Rom 14:19
unbelieving partner desires to separate, let it be so; in such a case the
brother or sister is not bound. For God has called us[1] to peace. [16]Wife,
how do you know whether you will save your husband? Husband,
how do you know whether you will save your wife?

Christ its foundation and strength (cf. Eph 5:25).

"Being rooted in the personal and total self-giving of the couple, and being required by the good of the children, the indissolubility of marriage finds its ultimate truth in the plan that God has manifested in his revelation: he wills and he communicates the indissolubility of marriage as a fruit, a sign and a requirement of the absolutely faithful love which God has for man and which the Lord Jesus has for the Church. [...]

"To bear witness to the inestimable value of the indissolubility and fidelity of marriage is one of the most precious and most urgent tasks of Christian couples in our time" (*Familiaris consortio*, 20).

7:12–16. After reminding the Corinthians of one of the essential properties of marriage—indissolubility—the Apostle now discusses the special case—frequently found at this time—of a marriage between pagans, one of whom later becomes a Christian.

In the pagan world, civil law tended to be very lax as far as divorce was concerned. According to Jewish custom of the time, when a pagan became a Jew and was circumcised, he was obliged to keep all the precepts of the Mosaic Law, including that of avoiding social intercourse with Gentiles, because that would involve legal uncleanness. To resolve this situation, Jewish law laid it down that all previous commitments, including the marriage bond, were dissolved when a person became a Jew.

However, St Paul adopts a different solution. Even in this situation he maintains that the marriage bond remains in place; the Old Law regulations about legal uncleanness have been set aside by Christ: they are not applicable in the situation described. Only in the case where the pagan party does not wish to live peaceably is the baptized party free to separate and marry again.

In the light of this teaching three things should be noted:

(a) Jesus Christ never spoke about this kind of situation: therefore, the Apostle says that what he has to say comes from him, not from the Lord (v. 12): he does not mean that he is contradicting the clear teaching of Christ on indissolubility, which he has just explained (cf. vv. 10–11; Mt 5:19, etc.); what he is doing is applying—under the inspiration of the Holy Spirit—general teaching to a particular situation.

(b) The other members of a family (spouse, children) are sanctified by the

l. Other ancient authorities read *you*

Leading the life God has assigned

Rom 12:3 — 17 Only, let every one lead the life which the Lord has assigned to
1 Cor 7:20, 24 — him, and in which God has called him. This is my rule in all the
1 Mac 1:4ff — churches. 18 Was any one at the time of his call already circumcised? Let him not seek to remove the marks of circumcision. Was
any one at the time of his call uncircumcised? Let him not seek
Rom 2:25ff, Gal 5:6; 6:15 — circumcision. 19 For neither circumcision counts for anything nor
uncircumcision, but keeping the commandments of God.

---

partner who has received Baptism (vv. 13–14). That is, the conversion of one of the spouses, far from being to the detriment of the family, is something very good and a benefit to all; Baptism is not in any way a cause of division; rather it reinforces and sanctifies marriage and family. Conversion, therefore, does not make for dissolution but for indissolubility.

(c) Only when the unbelieving partner disrupts family life or does not allow the Christian partner to live in accordance with his or her faith, does the Christian become free to contract a new marriage.

The Church has followed the solution outlined by St Paul; this is usually called the "Pauline privilege" (cf. *Code of Canon Law*, can. 1143–1147).

St Paul is not referring to that marriage which one party who is *already* a Catholic may contract with an unbeliever or with a non-Catholic Christian (a "mixed marriage"). In these cases, which arose much later on, the Church requires certain commitments from the non-Catholic party, and the marriage contracted is valid and indissoluble (cf. *Code of Canon Law*, can. 1124–1128).

7:17–24. "Let each one lead the life which the Lord has assigned to him": St Paul repeats this idea in vv. 20 and 24. Some Corinthians may have been misapplying the consequences of being "reborn" through Baptism, making out that this involved a total change, not only internal but external as well, in a person's life. The Apostle explains by giving two examples—circumcision (vv. 18–20) and slavery—which show that external circumstances cannot inhibit Christian life; in fact, God designs these circumstances as a positive help towards Christian living.

The Christian calling does not take anyone out of his or her place, nor is there any reason why it should entail changing the external circumstances of one's life. What it does involve is interior conversion, such that the ordinary, everyday situation in which a person lives out his life—work, family, recreation, social relationships—now helps towards holiness, becoming a way to holiness, a setting in which one can find God, and a context and opportunity for apostolate.

"Our calling discloses to us the meaning of our existence. It means being convinced, through faith, of the reason for our life on earth. Our life, present, past and future, acquires a new dimension, a depth we did not perceive before. All happenings and events now fall into proper perspective: we understand where God is leading us, and we feel ourselves borne along by this task entrusted to us" (St Josemaría Escrivá, *Christ Is Passing By*, 45).

7:19. "What counts is ... keeping the commandments of God", living in accordance with the will of God in the place he has allocated. Neither circumcision nor the lack of it matters: "In Christ Jesus neither circumcision nor uncircumcision

20 Every one should remain in the state in which he was called.
21 Were you a slave when called? Never mind. But if you can gain Eph 6:6
your freedom, avail yourself of the opportunity.[x] 22 For he who was Rom 6:18ff
called in the Lord as a slave is a freedman of the Lord. Likewise
he who was free when called is a slave of Christ. 23 You were 1 Cor 6:20
bought with a price; do not become slaves of men. 24 So, brethren, 1 Cor 7:17–20
in whatever state each was called, there let him remain with God.

Excellence of virginity

25 Now concerning the unmarried,[x2] I have no command of the 1 Cor 7:10, 40
Lord, but I give my opinion as one who by the Lord's mercy is

---

is of any avail, but faith working through love" (Gal 5:6; cf. Gal 6:15). Jews and Gentiles, slaves and free man, have all received the same faith and the same calling: "By one spirit we were all baptized into one body—Jews or Greeks, slaves or free" (1 Cor 12:13).

7:21–23. "Avail yourself of the opportunity": although the original text can be interpreted as meaning "avail of the opportunity to gain your freedom", St Paul's words best fit the context if he is taken to say, "If you are set free, use it as an opportunity to live out your Christian vocation." At that time, the question of abolition of slavery had not yet arisen; however, it should be noted that St Paul is constantly declaring that all men are equal before God (cf. Gal 3:28–29; and Philem); when Christian teaching began to imbue all levels of society, slavery began to disappear.

Besides, St Paul explains that we are all free in the Lord: "How is the slave a freeman while continuing a slave?" St John Chrysostom asks. "When he is freed from passions and from diseases of the mind; when he looks down upon riches and wrath and all like passions [...]. It is possible for one who is a slave not to be a slave; and for one who is a free man to be a slave" (*Hom. on 1 Cor*, 19, ad loc.).

It is also true that we are all servants and slaves of the Lord: the Christian should never forget the example set by Jesus Christ, who came "not to be served but to serve" (20:28) and by St Paul, who though he was free "made myself a slave to all, that I might win the more" (1 Cor 9:19). Far from being a source of humiliation, serving others for love of God is something honourable and a source of justifiable pride. "We will be slaves either way. Since we must serve anyway, for whether we like it or not this is our lot as men, then there is nothing better than recognizing that Love has made us slaves of God. From the moment we recognize this we cease being slaves and become friends, sons. Then we see the difference: we find ourselves tackling the honest occupations of the world just as passionately and just as enthusiastically as others do, but with peace in the depth of our hearts. We are happy and calm, even in the midst of difficulties, for we are not putting our trust in passing things, but in what lasts forever" (St Josemaría Escrivá, *Friends of God*, 35).

7:25–35. The Apostle now explains the excellence of virginity or celibacy (vv. 26ff) for love of God as compared with marriage. The Magisterium of the Church

x. Or *make use of your present condition instead* **x2** Greek *virgins*

trustworthy. 26I think that in view of the present[m] distress it is well
for a person to remain as he is. 27Are you bound to a wife? Do not
seek to be free. Are you free from a wife? Do not seek marriage.
28But if you marry, you do not sin, and if a girl[m2] marries she does

---

has explicitly spoken on the same lines (cf. Council of Trent, *De Sacrum matrimonio*, can. 10; Pius XII, *Sacra virginitas*, 11).

He begins by saying that he has no commandment from the Lord on this matter (cf. note on 7:12–16; Mt 19–12) but he for his part recommends celibacy, and his advice carries weight because he is an Apostle chosen by the Lord in his mercy. The reasons why he makes this recommendation reduce to one, basically—the love of God: the unmarried person can dedicate himself or herself to God more fully than a married person can, who has to look after the family and is "divided" (v. 34). "This is the main purpose and primary reason for Christian virginity—to dedicate oneself exclusively to divine things, giving them all one's attention and love, thinking of Him constantly and consecrating oneself to Him completely, body and soul" (Pius XII, *Sacra virginitas*, 5). This exclusive dedication to God will lead to a full and productive life because it enables a person to love others and devote himself or herself to them with great freedom and availability. Also, celibacy has an eschatological dimension: it is a special sign of heavenly delights (cf. Vatican II, *Perfectae caritatis*, 12), and points to the fact that the blessed in heaven live as angels (cf. Mt 22:30).

St Paul's references to marriage should be understood in the context in which he is writing (cf. note on 7:1–9). All he wants to make clear here is that, although celibacy is a higher state, marriage is not something bad: those who marry are not doing anything wrong (v. 28), nor is there any need for married people to live as celibates (vv. 3–5) or to separate (v. 27). However, only someone who acknowledges the great value that marriage has is in a position to appreciate celibacy as a gift of God. "Virginity or celibacy for the sake of the Kingdom of God not only does not contradict the dignity of marriage but presupposes it and confirms it. Marriage and virginity or celibacy are two ways of expressing and living the one mystery of the covenant of God with his people. When marriage is not esteemed, neither can consecrated virginity or celibacy exist; when human sexuality is not regarded as a great value given by the Creator, the renunciation of it for the sake of the Kingdom of heaven loses its meaning" (John Paul II, *Familiaris consortio*, 16)

7:28. "Worldly troubles" (tribulation of the flesh): this is not in any way perjorative of marriage: "Married love is uniquely expressed and perfected by the exercise of the acts proper to marriage. Hence the acts in marriage by which the intimate and chaste union of the spouses takes place are noble and honourable: the truly human performance of these acts fosters the self-giving they signify and enriches the spouses in joy and gratitude" (Vatican II, *Gaudium et spes*, 49).

The phrase is very like that used in v. 33 ("worldly affairs"): that is, married people cannot ignore the material needs of their family. This is also what the Apostle means when he says that the married man's interests are "divided"

m. Or *present* **m2** Greek *virgin*

not sin. Yet those who marry will have worldly troubles, and I
would spare you that. [29]I mean, brethren, the appointed time has Lk 14:26
grown very short; from now on, let those who have wives live as Rom 13:11
though they had none, [30]and those who mourn as though they
were not mourning, and those who rejoice as though they were not
rejoicing, and those who buy as though they had no goods, [31]and 1 Jn 2:15ff
those who deal with the world as though they had no dealings
with it. For the form of this world is passing away.
[32]I want you to be free from anxieties. The unmarried man is
anxious about the affairs of the Lord, how to please the Lord;
[33]but the married man is anxious about worldly affairs, how to Lk 14:20
please his wife, [34]and his interests are divided. And the unmarried
woman or girl[m2] is anxious about the affairs of the Lord, how to be

---

(v. 34), that is, he cannot please God unless he attend to the needs—including material needs—of his family. Married people have to turn these circumstances—inherent in their state of life—into a means of sanctification. "Husband and wife are called to sancify their married life", St Josemaría Escrivá writes, "and to sanctify themselves in it. It would be a serious mistake if they were to exclude family life from their spiritual development. The marriage union, the care and education of children, the effort to provide for the needs of the family as well as for its security and development, the relationships with other persons who make up the community—all these are among the ordinary human situations that Christian couples are called upon to sanctify" (*Christ Is Passing By*, 23).

7:29–31. In their letters, St Paul and the other Apostles frequently remind us that life is short (cf. Rom 13:11–14; 2 Pet 3:8; 1 Jn 2:15–17), in order to encourage us to make the very best use of our time to serve God, and others for his sake. "When I reflect on this, how well I understand St Paul's exclamation when he writes to the Corinthians, '*tempus breve est*' (1 Cor 7:29). How short indeed is the time of our passing through this world! For the true Christian these words ring deep down in his heart as a reproach to his lack of generosity, and as a constant invitation to be loyal. Brief indeed is our time for loving, for giving, for making atonement. It would be very wrong, therefore, for us to waste it, or to cast this treasure irresponsibly overboard. We must not squander this period of the world's history which God has entrusted to each one of us" (St Josemaría Escrivá, *Friends of God*, 39).

A Christian, therefore, should always be detached from worldly things, and never let himself become the slave of anything or anyone (cf. 1 Cor 7:23; *Lumen gentium*, 42) but, instead, always have his sights on eternal life. "It is a great help towards this", St Teresa of Avila teaches, "if we keep a very constant care of the vanity of all things, and the rapidity with which they pass away, so that we may withdraw our affections from everything and fix them on what will last forever. This may seem to be a poor kind of help but it will have the effect of greatly fortifying the soul. With regard to little things, we must be very careful, as

m² Greek *virgin*

holy in body and spirit; but the married woman is anxious about
worldly affairs, how to please her husband. 35I say this for your
own benefit, not to lay any restraint upon you, but to promote
good order and to secure your undivided devotion to the Lord.
36If any one thinks that he is not behaving properly toward his
betrothed,[m2] if his passions are strong, and it has to be, let him do as
he wishes: let them marry—it is no sin. 37But whoever is firmly established in his heart, being under no necessity but having his desire
under control, and has determined this in his heart, to keep her as his
betrothed,[m2] he will do well. 38So that he who marries his betrothed[m2]
does well; and he who refrains from marriage will do better.

Advice to widows

Rom 7:2 39A wife is bound to her husband as long as he lives. If the husband
dies, she is free to be married to whom she wishes, only in the Lord.

---

soon as we begin to be fond of them, to think no more about them and to turn our thoughts to God. His majesty will help us to do this" (*Way of Perfection*, chap. 10).

7:35. There is clearly no question of trying to deceive anyone by encouraging him to dedicate himself to a way of life in which he cannot persevere. St Paul is merely pointing out that the unmarried person is more available to the service of the Lord.

7:36–38. Two main theories have been put forward to explain this obscure passage. The first is that the Apostle was referring to a custom which obtained in the early times of the Church, whereby a Christian would receive a young female Christian into his house to protect her virginity or prevent her pagan family forcing her to marry. We know of this custom from second- and third-century documents; but there is no reference to it in first-century documents, except for this reference, if indeed it be one. The other theory is that the Apostle is addressing the father or guardian who, according to the custom of the time, had to make the final decision about whether his daughter or ward should marry. In this case, instead of translating it as "let them marry", it should be "he can decide that she marry."

"And it has to be": it is not clear what this means. One interpretation is that "it is desirable that they marry" because otherwise they would not be acting with propriety, nor would they feel strong enough to stay unmarried; the second is that "it is desirable that she be given in marriage", because this would mean that the father saw that it was not good for him to oblige his daughter to remain celibate.

Despite the obscurity of this passage, St Paul's general meaning is clear and he expresses it from different angles: marriage is something good and holy; but no one in particular is obliged to marry; those who by divine vocation—"he who has determined this in his heart"—are called to celibacy and virginity are doing an even better thing (cf. v. 38).

7:39–40. Following what St Paul says here, the Church has always taught that

m2 Greek *virgin*

40But in my judgment she is happier if she remains as she is. And I think that I have the Spirit of God. 1 Cor 2:16; 7:25f

6. FOOD OFFERED TO IDOLS

Idols have no real existence

8 1Now concerning food offered to idols:* we know that "all of us Acts 15:29
possess knowledge." "Knowledge" puffs up, but love builds up.

---

the marriage bond is broken by the death of one of the spouses and the other is then free to marry again. It is not quite clear what is meant by "only in the Lord". The most probable meaning is that the Apostle is recommending that the person marry a Christian, given the danger of apostasy resulting from mixed marriages in those early days.

In any event, as in the case of unmarried persons, he recommends, as the most perfect thing to do, to stay unmarried, consecrated to the service of God, if that is the divine will.

Later, writing to Timothy, the Apostle gives more explicit directions about widows; some widows should be supported by their families; others should dedicate themselves to the service of the Church in a permanent way; and all should behave with the decorum proper to their state (cf. 1 Tim 5:9–16).

8:1–10:31. In these chapters St Paul deals with food offered to idols. In pagan religions a portion of the sacrificial food went to the donors, who could consume it in the temple itself (cf. 1 Cor 8:10), or take it home. The meat could also be sold in the market. For some Christians this posed no problem; but for others—who were afraid that by eating this meat they were in some way taking part in the idolatrous worship from which it came (cf. 8:7)—various practical questions arose: when buying meat, ought they to ask where it came from? (cf. 10:25–26); could they accept invitations to meals at which food of this type might be served? (cf. 10:27ff). The Council of Jerusalem, which took place around 48–50, had written to the Christians of Antioch, Syria and Cilicia telling them to abstain from food which had been sacrificed to idols (cf. Acts 15:23–29). When St Paul was preaching in Corinth two years later, he probably did not say anything on this subject, given the very pagan environment of that city—very different from the experience of the communities the Council had been addressing: if the faithful at Corinth had to avoid meat of this kind, they should have had to isolate themselves from their fellow-citizens.

In replying to the questions put to him, the Apostle first explains the general principles that apply: they may eat meat of this type, for idols have no real existence (8:1–6), but sometimes charity requires that they do abstain from it (8:7–13); he illustrates what he says by quoting what he himself does (9:1–27) and lessons drawn from the history of Israel (10:1–13); and, finally, he deals with particular queries the Corinthians have raised (10:14–33).

8:1–6. Clearly, idols are mere things and therefore food sacrificed to them can be eaten without any qualms (10:25–27). But some Christians did not yet grasp this, and they were being shocked to see

Gal 6:3 — [2]If any one imagines that he knows something, he does not yet know
Gal 4:9 — as he ought to know. [3]But if one loves God, one is known by him.
Deut 6:4; 1 Cor 10:19 — [4]Hence, as to the eating of food offered to idols, we know that
Ps 81:6 — "an idol has no real existence," and that "there is no God but one."
Jn 10:34 — [5]For although there may be so-called gods in heaven or on earth—
Mal 2:10; Rom 11:36; Eph 4:5 — as indeed there are many "gods" and many "lords"—[6]yet for us

---

other Christians eating this food (cf. 8:7–13). So, St Paul again reminds the Corinthians (cf. 1:18–34) that they must not rely on their "knowledge" unless it be accompanied by charity. "The source of all the Corinthians' problems", St John Chrysostom comments, "was not their lack of knowledge but their lack of charity and lack of concern for their neighbour. This was the cause of the divisions in that church, the cause of the vanity which was blinding them and of all the disorder for which the Apostle has censured them and will censure them. He will often speak to them about charity, and try to clarify, so to speak, the fount of all good things [...]. Have love: that way your knowledge will not lead you astray. I should like your knowledge to outstrip that of your brethren. If you love them, far from being aloof and looking down on them, you will strive to have them share your insights" (*Hom. on 1 Cor*, 20, ad loc.).

8:3. "One is known by him [God]": that is, God has recognized him as one of his own, God is pleased with him: it is almost the same as "God has called him", "God has chosen him".

8:4–6. St Paul reminds the Corinthians, who were living in a pagan and polytheistic environment, of the first and basic truth of the Christian creed: there is only one true God. Even though the idols which pagans worship were called "gods" (as in Greek mythology) or "lords" (as heroes or divinized emperors were described), they were such only in the imagination of men. The only one who really merits these titles is the living and true God who is revealed to us in Holy Scripture as One and Three.

8:6. Both the Father and the Son are God and Lord: "Just as St Paul does not take from the Father the rank of Lord, when he says that the Son is the only Lord, so he is not denying the Son the rank of God, when he says that the Father is the one and only God" (St John Chrysostom, *Hom. on 1 Cor,* 20, ad loc.) In fact the title "Lord" is used with reference to God; so, calling Jesus Christ "Lord" is the same as calling him "God"; besides, what the Apostle here says of the Father, he attributes elsewhere to the Son; and vice versa (cf., e.g., Rom 11:36; Eph 4:5–6; Col 16–17; Heb 2:10). Creation is something that is done by all three divine persons of the Blessed Trinity, and the Blessed Trinity is also the end or goal of all created things (cf. Fourth Council of the Lateran, *De fide catholica*, chap. 1).

Although St Paul does not mention the Holy Spirit in this passage, he does speak of him elsewhere in the letter (cf. 2:10ff; 6:19–20.)

8:7–13. Charity requires that one abstain from food sacrificed to idols, if eating can cause scandal to others, can be "a stumbling block to the weak" (v. 9). The Apostle's teaching is clear: if there is any danger of scandalizing someone for whom Christ has died, "I will never eat meat" (v. 13; cf. similar teaching in Rom 14:14–23).

there is one God, the Father, from whom are all things and for
whom we exist, and one Lord, Jesus Christ, through whom are all
things and through whom we exist.

Not scandalizing the weak

7However, not all possess this knowledge. But some, through 1 Cor 10:27
being hitherto accustomed to idols, eat food as really offered to an
idol; and their conscience, being weak, is defiled. 8Food will not Rom 14:17
commend us to God. We are no worse off if we do not eat, and no Heb 13:9
better off if we do. 9Only take care lest this liberty of yours some- Gal 5:13
how become a stumbling block to the weak. 10For if any one sees
you, a man of knowledge, at table in an idol's temple, might he
not be encouraged, if his conscience is weak, to eat food offered
to idols? 11And so by your knowledge this weak man is destroyed, Rom 14:15
the brother for whom Christ died. 12Thus, sinning against your
brethren and wounding their conscience when it is weak, you sin
against Christ. 13Therefore, if food is a cause of my brother's Rom 14:21
falling, I will never eat meat, lest I cause my brother to fall.

The scandal caused to those Christians is an example of what is called giving "scandal to the weak", whereby an action in itself good or indifferent can lead others into sin because of their ignorance, weakness or poor understanding of the faith. In such cases also one should, out of charity, try to avoid giving scandal (cf. note on Rom 14:13–21).

8:11–13. St Paul emphasizes the gravity of the scandal given by those Corinthians who in the blindness of their pride failed to realize the harm they were doing to other brothers in the faith: they might lead into perdition someone "for whom Christ died"; our Lord sacrificed himself on the cross for each and every person in every generation. "How precious must man be in the eyes of the Creator; if he 'gained so great a Redeemer' (*Exsultet* at the Easter Vigil), and if God 'gave us his only son' in order that man 'should not perish but have eternal life' (cf. Jn 3:16)" (John Paul II, *Redemptor hominis*, 10). One should never lose sight of the immense value of every individual, a value which can be deduced especially from the price paid for him—the death of Christ. "For every soul is a wonderful treasure; every person is unique and irreplaceable. Every single person is worth all the blood of Christ" (St Josemaría Escrivá, *Christ Is Passing By*, 80).

The Apostle also points out that by giving scandal "you sin against Christ": our Lord himself said this: "as you did it to one of the least of these my brethren, you did it to me" (Mt 25:40; cf. 25:45); this was something deeply engraved on Paul's soul ever since the time, when he was persecuting Christians, he heard Jesus say to him, "Why do you persecute me?" (Acts 9:4). The Christian should always see Christ in others.

From this it follows logically that, if necessary, as he says, "I will never eat meat." One must be ready for any sacrifice if the salvation of a soul is at stake.

The right of apostles to receive maintenance from the faithful

Acts 9:17 Rom 1:1 **9** 1 Am I not free? Am I not an apostle? Have I not seen Jesus our
2 Cor 3:2f Lord? Are not you my workmanship in the Lord? 2 If to others
I am not an apostle, at least I am to you; for you are the seal of my
apostleship in the Lord.
3 This is my defence to those who would examine me.* 4 Do we
Lk 8:1–3 not have the right to our food and drink? 5 Do we not have the right

---

9:1–27. In chapter 8 St Paul explained how charity requires that in some situations one should not exercise certain rights in order not to harm one's neighbour. Now he illustrates this principle by referring to his own case: he is an apostle and therefore he could claim certain rights (vv. 1–14), but out of love for the vocation God has given him and out of love for all souls, he has completely renounced these rights (vv. 15–27). The entire chapter, particularly vv. 19–23, shows the true greatness of St Paul who, dedicating himself fully to his God-given mission, made himself "all things to all men" (v. 22) to save as many as possible.

9:1–2. Before describing the rights he could claim (vv. 4–14), Paul defends his apostleship. In other passages of his letters he makes a more detailed apologia (cf. Gal 1:16 2:21; 2 Cor 10:1 12:21). Here he simply points to two things which justify his title of "Apostle": he has seen Jesus (cf. Acts 9:1–19; 1 Cor 15:8) and is the founder of the church at Corinth (cf. Acts 18:1–18).

9:4–14. The Apostle lists some rights he might claim—that of being accompanied by a Christian woman to look after him (cf. note on vv. 5–6), and the right to be maintained by the faithful. He makes his point first by reference to common sense, by comparing himself to a soldier—who has a right to be supported by those he serves—and to a vineyard worker and a shepherd, who earn their living by their work; the Apostle also, who works to serve others, by preaching and administering the sacraments, should be supported by the faithful, who are as it were the produce of his work. Also, he cites Deuteronomy 25:4—what the Law of Moses says about the ox that grinds corn—and recalls our Lord's commandment: "the labourer deserves his wages" (Lk 10:7; cf. Mt 10:10; in 1 Timothy 5:18 St Paul will also use the same quotations).

The fifth commandment of the Church—"To support the Church"—and the *Pius X Catechism* (504) remind the people of their duty to provide for the adequate upkeep of the clergy.

The Second Vatican Council pointed out that "completely devoted as they are to the service of God in the fulfilment of the office entrusted to them, priests are entitled to receive a just remuneration. For 'the labourer deserves his wages' (Lk 10:7), and 'the Lord commanded that they who proclaim the Gospel should get their living by the Gospel' (1 Cor 9:14). For this reason, insofar as provision is not made from some other source for the just remuneration of priests, the faithful are bound by a real obligation to see to it that the necessary provision for a decent and fitting livelihood for the priests is available" (*Presbyterorum ordinis*, 20).

9:5–6. "Wife": Greek, "a woman, a sister." It cannot be deduced from this text that the Apostles were married, although we do know that St Peter, for one, was married (cf. Mk 1:29–31; Mt 8:14–15;

to be accompanied by a wife,[n]* as the other apostles and the
brethren of the Lord and Cephas? [6]Or is it only Barnabas and I
who have no right to refrain from working for a living? [7]Who 2 Tim 2:6
serves as a soldier at his own expense? Who plants a vineyard
without eating any of its fruit? Who tends a flock without getting
some of the milk?

[8]Do I say this on human authority? Does not the law say the Deut 25:4
same? [9]For it is written in the law of Moses, "You shall not Lk 12:24
muzzle an ox when it is treading out the grain." Is it for oxen that
God is concerned? [10]Does he not speak entirely for our sake? It was
written for our sake, because the ploughman should plough in hope
and the thresher thresh in hope of a share in the crop. [11]If we have Rom 15:27
sown spiritual good among you, is it too much if we reap your
material benefits? [12]If others share this rightful claim upon you, do 2 Cor 11:9
not we still more?

Nevertheless, we have not made use of this right, but we endure
anything rather than put an obstacle in the way of the gospel of
Christ. [13]Do you not know that those who are employed in the Num 18:8, 31 Deut 18:1–3
temple service get their food from the temple, and those who
serve at the altar share in the sacrificial offerings? [14]In the same
way, the Lord commanded that those who proclaim the gospel
should get their living by the gospel.

St Paul does not exercise that right

[15]But I have made no use of any of these rights, nor am I writing Acts 18:3
this to secure any such provision. For I would rather die than have

---

Lk 4:38–39). The Gospels mention certain women as accompanying our Lord and his disciples, providing for them out of their resources and ministering to them (cf. Lk 8:1–3; 23:55). To meet their material needs some Apostles counted on the help of women, but Paul and Barnabas did not avail of this right.

As explained at length in notes on Mt 12:46–47 and Mk 6:1–3, the expression "the brethren of the Lord" refers to various kinds of relatives of Jesus, because Hebrew and Aramaic did not have separate words for brothers, cousins etc. We know that Jesus was Mary's only child and that she was ever-virgin (cf. Paul IV, Const. *Cum quorumdam*). In these "brethren" St Paul may have included St James the Less, Judas the son of James and Simon the Zealot.

On St Barnabas see the note on Acts 4:36–37.

9:15–18. As he already said in v. 12, St Paul makes it clear that he has not exercised so far, nor does he envisage doing so, his right to be supported by the faithful. Conscious that his God-given calling obliges him to preach the Gospel, he prefers to carry out that mission without receiving anything in exchange. His attitude shows both his greatness and

n. Greek *a woman, a sister*

Jer 20:9 any one deprive me of my ground for boasting. 16For if I preach
the gospel, that gives me no ground for boasting. For necessity is
Acts 9:15f laid upon me. Woe to me if I do not preach the gospel! 17For if I
do this of my own will, I have a reward; but if not of my own will,
2 Cor 11:7 I am entrusted with a commission. 18What then is my reward? Just
this: that in my preaching I may make the gospel free of charge,
not making full use of my right in the gospel.

---

his humility: he faces every kind of suffering, privation and danger for the sake of the Gospel (cf. 2 Cor 11:23–33), and yet he considers that he is doing no more than his duty. His policy recalls our Lord's teaching: "When you have done all that is commanded you, say, 'We are unworthy servants; we have only done what was our duty'" (Lk 17:10; cf. Mt 10:8).

To keep to this self-imposed policy, St Paul had to add to all his work of evangelization the additional effort to earn his own living. In the Acts of the Apostles, for example, we learn of his manual work in Corinth (18:3) and Ephesus (20:34); and he himself tells the Thessalonians that "we worked night and day, that we would not burden any of you, while we preached to you the gospel of God" (1 Thess 2:9; 2 Thess 3:9). Only in the case of the Philippians, for whom he had very particular affection, did he allow any exception to this rule (cf. Phil 4:15–16). However, at no time did he feel that others were doing wrong in acting differently, "for the Lord had disposed that those who proclaim the Gospel be supported by it [...]. But he [Paul] went further and chose not even to take what was his due" (St Augustine, *Sermon,* 46, 4).

9:16. The Church has often used these words of St Paul to remind the faithful that our Lord has called them to the apostolate through the sacraments of Baptism and Confirmation. The Second Vatican Council explains what this apostolate involves: "The witness of life, however, is not the sole element in the apostolate; the true apostle is on the lookout for occasions of announcing Christ by word, either to unbelievers to draw them towards the faith, or to the faithful to instruct them, strengthen them, incite them to a more fervent life; 'for Christ's love urges us on' (2 Cor 5:14), and in the hearts of all should the Apostle's words find echo: 'Woe to me if I do not preach the Gospel' (1 Cor 9:16)" (*Apostolicam actuositatem*, 6).

St John Chrysostom anticipates the kinds of excuse people might offer to avoid this duty: "There is nothing colder than a Christian who is not concerned about the salvation of others [...]. Do not say, I cannot help others: for, if you are truly a Christian it is impossible not to. Natural objects have properties that cannot be denied; the same is true of what I have just said, because it is the nature of a Christian to act in that way. Do not offend God by deception. If you said that the sun cannot shine, you would be committing an offence against God and making a liar of him. It is easier for the sinner to shine or give warmth than for a Christian to cease to give light: it is easier for that to happen than for light to become darkness. Do not say that that is impossible: what is impossible is the contrary [...]. If we behave in the correct way, everything else will follow as a natural consequence. The light of Christians cannot be hidden, a lamp shining so brightly cannot be hidden" (*Hom. on Acts*, 20).

[19]For though I am free from all men, I have made myself a Mt 20:26f
slave to all, that I might win the more. [20]To the Jews I became as a Acts 16:3
Jew, in order to win Jews; to those under the law I became as one
under the law—though not being myself under the law—that I might
win those under the law. [21]To those outside the law I became as one
outside the law—not being without law toward God but under the
law of Christ—that I might win those outside the law. [22]To the weak 2 Cor 11:29
I became weak, that I might win the weak. I have become all things
to all men, that I might by all means save some. [23]I do it all for the
sake of the gospel, that I may share in its blessings.

The need for asceticism

[24]Do you not know that in a race all the runners compete, but only Gal 5:7; 2 Tim 4:7
one receives the prize? So run that you may obtain it. [25]Every

---

9:19–23. Because he is one with Christ (cf. Gal 2:20), who "came not to be served but to serve, and to give us his life as a ransom for many" (Mt 20:28), the Apostle makes himself "all things to all men", so generous is he and so eager to save as many souls as possible, at the cost of whatever sacrifice and humilation might be involved. "A Christian has to be ready to share his life with everyone at all times, giving to everyone the chance to come nearer to Christ Jesus. He has to sacrifice his own desires willingly for the sake of others, without separating people into watertight compartments, without pigeonholing them or putting tags on them as though they were merchandise or insect specimens. A Christian cannot afford to separate himself from others, because, if he did that, his life would be miserably selfish. He must become 'all things to all men, in order to save all men' (1 Cor 9:22)" (St Josemaría Escrivá, *Christ Is Passing By*, 124).

Obviously this concern for others should not lead to diluting the truths of faith. Referring to this point, Pope Paul VI wrote: "The apostle's art is a risky one. The desire to come together as brothers must not lead to a watering-down or subtracting from the truth. Our dialogue must not weaken our attachment to our faith. In our apostolate we cannot make vague compromises about the principles of faith and action on which our profession of Christianity is based. An immoderate desire to make peace and sink differences at all costs is, fundamentally, a kind of scepticism about the power and content of the Word of God which we desire to preach. Only one who is completely faithful to the teaching of Christ can be an apostle. And only he who lives his Christian life to the full can remain uncontaminated by the errors with which he comes into contact" (*Ecclesiam suam*, 33).

9:24–27. These similes taken from athletics would have been appropriate for the Corinthians, for their city hosted the biennial Isthmus games. Often, when speaking about the Christian life, the Apostle uses metaphors taken from sport—races (cf. Gal 5:7; Phil 3:12–14; 2 Tim 4:7), combats (1 Tim 6:12; 2 Tim 4:7) and laurel crowns (2 Tim 4:8).

A Christian's life on earth must involve interior striving; he should approach this with a competitive, sportive

Phil 3:14; 2 Tim 4:7f; 1 Pet 5:4 Jas 1:12

athlete exercises self-control in all things. They do it to receive a
perishable wreath, but we an imperishable. [26]Well, I do not run
aimlessly, I do not box as one beating the air; [27]but I pommel my
body and subdue it, lest after preaching to others I myself should
be disqualified.

The lesson of Israel's history

Ex 13:21; 14:22

10 [1]I want you to know, brethren, that our fathers were all
under the cloud, and all passed through the sea, and all were
baptized into Moses in the cloud and in the sea, [2]and all ate the

---

spirit, facing up to any sacrifices that prove necessary, and not letting obstacles, failures or personal limitations get him down: "We should not be surprised to find, in our body and soul, the needle of pride, sensuality, envy, laziness and the desire to dominate others. This is a fact of life, proven by our personal experience. It is the point of departure and the normal context for winning in this intimate sport, this race toward our Father's house. St Paul says: 'I do not run aimlessly, I do not box as one beating the air; but I pommel my body and subdue it, lest after preaching to others I myself should be disqualified' (1 Cor 9:26) [...]. In this adventure of love we should not be depressed by our falls, not even by serious falls, if we go to God in the sacrament of Penance contrite and resolved to improve. A Christian is not a neurotic collector of good behaviour reports. Jesus Christ our Lord was moved as much by Peter's repentance after his fall as by John's innocence and faithfullness. Jesus understands our weakness and draws us to himself on an inclined plane. He wants us to make an effort to climb a little each day" (*Christ Is Passing By*, 75).

9:27. While we are in this present life, our perseverance can never be taken for granted: "Let no one feel assured of this gift with an absolute certainty, although all ought to have most secure hope in the help of God. For unless we are unfaithful to his grace, God will bring the good work to perfection, just as he began it, working both the will and the performance (cf. Phil 2:13)" (Council of Trent, *De iustificatione*, chap. 13). Therefore, the Apostle points out, the ascetical effort which every person must keep on making in this life includes physical mortification and self-control. Helped by God's grace and confident of his mercy, a Christian who makes this effort will be able to say as St Paul did at the end of his life, "there is laid up for me a crown of righteousness which the Lord, the righteous judge, will award to me on that day" (2 Tim 4:8).

10:1–33. St Paul now points to the lessons which the self-assured and proud Corinthians might draw from certain events in the history of Israel (vv. 1–13). He focuses mainly on the Exodus from Egypt to the Promised Land: during this journey God worked many wonders (vv. 1–4), but because of their frequent infidelity most of the Israelites died before the journey was over (vv. 5–10); this, the Apostle concludes, should serve as a lesson to us: if we rely too much on ourselves we run the risk of being unfaithful to God and deserving rejection, like those Israelites (vv. 1113). St John Chrysostom says that "God's gifts to the Hebrews were figures of the gifts of Baptism and the Eucharist which we were

same supernatural[o] food 3and all drank the same supernatural[o] Ex 16:4, 35 Deut 8:3
drink. 4For they drank from the supernatural[o] Rock which fol- Ex 17:5f
lowed them, and the Rock was Christ. 5Nevertheless with most of Num 14:16, 23, 30
them God was not pleased; for they were overthrown in the
wilderness.

---

to be given. And the punishments meted out to them are figures of the punishment which our ingratitude will deserve; hence his reminder to be watchful" (cf. *Hom. on 1 Cor*, 23).

In the second part of the chapter (vv. 14–33), St Paul gives the final part of his reply to the question about food offered to idols, with advice as to how to act in certain situations.

10:1–4. The Exodus of the Israelites was marked by many prodigies. St Paul recalls some of these—God leading the way by day in the form of a pillar of cloud (cf. Ex 13;21–22), the crossing of the Red Sea (cf. Ex 14:15–31); the feeding with manna (cf. Ex 16:13–15) and the drinking water which Moses caused to flow out of a rock (cf. Ex 17:1–7; Num 20:2–13).

St Paul sees the land and the sea as symbolizing two basic elements in Christian Baptism—the Holy Spirit and the water (cf. *St Pius V Catechism*, 2, 2,9). By following Moses in the cloud and through the sea, the Israelites were somehow linked to him, into anticipating the way the Christian is fully incorporated into Jesus through Baptism (cf. Rom 6:3–11),

St Paul calls the manna and the water from the rock "supernatural" food and drink because these are symbols of the Eucharist (cf. Jn 6:48–51). The Fathers, in commenting on these verses, stress the superiority of the Eucharist over what prefigures it: "Consider now which of the two foods is the more sublime [...]. The manna came down from heaven, it [the Eucharist] is to be found higher than heaven; the manna belonged to heaven, (the Eucharist) to the Lord of heaven; the manna rotted away if it was kept for another day, (the Eucharist) knows no corruption because whoever tastes it with the right dispositions will never experience corruption. For them [the Israelites] the water sprang up from the rock; for you blood flows from Christ. The water quenched the (Israelites') thirst for a short while; the blood cleanses you forever. The Jews drank and were thirsty; you, once you have drunk, can no longer feel thirst. In their case everything that happened was symbolic; in yours it is real. If you are amazed by it and yet it was no more than a shadow, how much more awesome must that reality be whose mere shadow amazes you" (St Ambrose, *Treatise on the Mysteries*, 1, 8, 48).

"The rock was Christ": in the Old Testament Yahweh was at times described as the rock (cf. Deut 32:4, 15, 18, 2 Sam 22:32; 23:3; Is 17:10; etc.); as he does elsewhere (cf., e.g., Rom 9:33; 10:11–13; Eph 4:8), St Paul here applies to Jesus Christ the prerogatives of Yahweh, thereby showing his divinity. Elsewhere in the New Testament our Lord is spoken of as the cornerstone (cf. Mt 21:42; Acts 4:11; Eph 2:20). By referring to the rock as "following them" St Paul may be citing—without accepting it—a rabbinical legend which claimed that the rock from which the water gushed

o. Greek *spiritual*

Num 11:4, 34 6Now these things are warnings for us, not to desire evil as they
Ex 32:6 did. 7Do not be idolaters as some of them were; as it is written, "The
Num 25:1, 9 people sat down to eat and drink and rose up to dance." 8We must not
indulge in immorality as some of them did, and twenty-three
Num 21:5f thousand fell in a single day. 9We must not put the Lord[p] to the test,
Num 14:2, 36; 17:6 as some of them did and were destroyed by serpents; 10nor grumble,
as some of them did and were destroyed by the Destroyer. 11Now
these things happened to them as a warning, but they were written
down for our instruction, upon whom the end of the ages has come.
Gal 6:1 12Therefore let any one who thinks that he stands take heed lest he
Mt 6:13 fall. 13No temptation has overtaken you that is not common to man.
God is faithful, and he will not let you be tempted beyond your
strength, but with the temptation will also provide the way of escape,
that you may be able to endure it.

---

continued to stay with the Israelites in the desert.

10:5–10. In spite of all the marvels God kept doing for the Israelites during the Exodus, only a few of those who left Egypt managed to enter the Promised Land (cf. Num 26:65). St Paul lists some of the repeated infidelites of the people of Israel which brought God's punishment upon them—idolatry (cf. Ex 32), sexual immorality (cf. Num 25), grumbling against God and Moses (cf., for example, Ex 15:23–25; 16:2–3; 17:2–7; Num 21:4–9; 17:6–15).

10:11–13. The events in the history of Israel mentioned in the Old Testament foretell things which will happen when Christ comes (cf. note on 1 Cor 10:1–4); they are also instructive for us. Here St Paul emphasizes that however many benefits God showers on us, no one should think that his eternal salvation is assured. "The greater you are, the more you must humble yourself; so you will find favour in the sight of the Lord" (Sir 3:20); one must continually implore God's help and not rely on one's own strength.

At the same time St Paul recalls God's faithfulness (cf. also Phil 1:6; 1 Thess 5:24; 2 Thess 3:3): God never allows us to be tempted beyond our strength, and he always gives us the graces we need to win out. "If anyone plead human weakness to excuse himself for not loving God, it should be explained that he who demands our love pours into our hearts by the Holy Spirit the fervour of his love (cf. Rom 5:5); and this good spirit our heavenly Father gives to those that ask him (cf. Lk 9:13). With reason, therefore, did St Augustine pray: 'Give what thou commandest, and command what thou pleasest' (*Confessions*, 10, 29, 31 and 37). As, then, God is ever ready to help us, especially since the death of Christ the Lord, by which the prince of this world was cast out, there is no reason why anyone should be disheartened by the difficulty of the undertaking. To him who loves, nothing is difficult" (*St Pius V Catechism*, 3, 1, 7).

p. Other ancient authorities read *Christ*

Idolatry and the Eucharist, incompatible

[14]Therefore, my beloved, shun the worship of idols. [15]I speak as to 1 Jn 5:21
sensible men; judge for yourselves what I say. [16]The cup of Mt 26:26ff
blessing which we bless, is it not a participation[q] in the blood of Acts 2:42 1 Cor 11:23ff
Christ? The bread which we break, is it not a participation in the
body of Christ? [17]Because there is one bread, we who are many 1 Cor 12:12, 27
are one body, for we all partake of the one bread. [18]Consider the Lev 7:6, 15

10:14–22. After illustrating the general principles by reference to what he himself does and the lessons of the history of Israel (cf. note on chaps. 8–10), St Paul returns to the subject of food sacrificed to idols. Christians may not attend the banquets which take place at pagan shrines, for that would amount to idolatry. By eating the meat of animals offered to Yahweh, Jews participated in the sacrifice and worship in his honour; and, by receiving the body and blood of the Lord, Christians unite themselves to Christ; similarly, those who take part in idolatrous banquets are associating themselves not with false gods—which have no existence—but with demons. In the Old Testament it is pointed out that things sacrificed to idols are in fact being offered to demons, who are enemies of the worship of God (cf. Deut 32:17; Ps 106:36–38; Bar 4:7).

St Paul's words confirm two basic truths of faith connected with the sublime mystery of the Eucharist—its sacrificial character, adverted to here by drawing a parallel between it and pagan sacrifices (cf. v. 21; Council of Trent, *De SS. Missae sacrificio*, chap. 1), and the real presence of Christ, as can be seen by the reference to the body and blood of Christ (v. 16). The Church's faith has always maintained that the holy sacrifice of the Mass is the renewal of the divine sacrifice of Calvary; in every Mass Christ once again offers God the Father his body and blood, as a sacrifice for all men, with the difference that what was offered on the cross in a bloody manner is offered on the altar in an unbloody manner. "In the divine sacrifice that is offered in the Mass, the same Christ who offered himself once in a bloody manner on the altar of the cross is present and is offered in an unbloody manner (cf. Heb 9:27). [...] For it is one and the same victim—he who now makes the offering through the ministry of priests and he who then offered himself on the cross; the only difference is in the manner of the offering" (*De SS. Missae sacrificio*, chap. 2). "The Eucharist is above all a sacrifice—the sacrifice of Redemption and at the same time the sacrifice of the New Covenant" (John Paul II, *Letter to all bishops*, 24 February 1980). See also the notes on Mt 26:26–29 and par.

On the real presence of Jesus Christ in the Eucharist, see the note on 1 Cor 11:27–32.

10:16–17. The principal effect of the Blessed Eucharist is intimate union with Jesus. The very name "communion"—taken from this passage of St Paul (cf. *St Pius V Catechism*, 2, 4, 4)—points to becoming one with our Lord by receiving his body and blood. "What in fact is the bread? The body of Christ. What do they become who receive Communion? The body of Christ" (Chrysostom, *Hom. on 1 Cor*, 24, ad loc.).

q. Or *communion*

people of Israel; are not those who eat the sacrifices partners in the
1 Cor 8:4 Ps 106:37 altar? [19]What do I imply then? That food offered to idols is
2 Cor 6:15f Rev 9:20 anything, or that an idol is anything? [20]No, I imply that what
pagans sacrifice they offer to demons and not to God. I do not
want you to be partners with demons.* [21]You cannot drink the cup
of the Lord and the cup of demons. You cannot partake of the table
of the Lord and the table of demons. [22]Shall we provoke the Lord
Deut 4:24; 32:21 to jealousy? Are we stronger than he?

Practical solutions to certain questions

1 Cor 6:12 [23]"All things are lawful," but not all things are helpful. "All things are
Rom 15:2 1 Cor 10:33 lawful," but not all things build up. [24]Let no one seek his own good,
but the good of his neighbour. [25]Eat whatever is sold in the meat
market without raising any question on the ground of conscience.

St Augustine places these words on Jesus' lips to describe what happens at Holy Communion: "You will not change me into you as happens with bodily food; rather, you will be changed into me" (*Confessions*, 7, 10, 16).

Due to this intimate union with Christ, the Eucharist is at one and the same time the sacrament where the entire Church demonstrates and achieves its unity, and where a very special kind of solidarity is developed among Christians. That is why it is called a "symbol of unity" and a "bond of love;" (Council of Trent, *De SS. Eucharistia*, chap. 8; cf. *Lumen gentium*, 7; *Unitatis redintegratio*, 2). The Fathers of the Church have seen a symbol of this union in the very materials—bread and wine—used to make the Eucharist. The *St Pius V Catechism* sums up this as follows: "the body of Christ, which is one, consists of many members (cf. Rom 12:4–5; 1 Cor 10:17; 12:12), and of this union nothing is more strikingly illustrative than the elements of bread and wine; for bread is made from many grains and wine is pressed from many clusters of grapes. Thus they signify that we, though many, are most closely bound together by the bond of the divine mystery and made, as it were, one body" (2, 4, 18).

"We who are many ...": the literal translation would be "We the many". The text derives from a Hebrew expression indicating plurality or even totality as distinct from a single entity or a minority; the RSV catches this idea. The same turn of phrase is found, for example, in Mt 20:28; Mk 10:45; Is 53:11.

10:23–33. St Paul concludes by dealing with some particular cases: there is no objection to eating at home meat bought in the market, no need to worry where it comes from; nor is there any need to check on the source of meat served when one eats out with unbelievers. Food deriving from sacrifices should be avoided only if there is a need to avoid giving scandal and if it is possible to do so.

Each person is morally responsible not only for his own actions, considered in themselves, but also for any influence his behaviour has on the good or bad actions of others. Therefore, one must try not only to do the right thing but also to avoid one's good actions leading others to commit sin. This obligation to cooperate in good actions should lead

[26]For "the earth is the Lord's, and everything in it." [27]If one of the Ps 24:1
unbelievers invites you to dinner and you are disposed to go, eat Lk 10:8
whatever is set before you without raising any question on the
ground of conscience. [28](But if some one says to you, "This has been 1 Cor 8:7
offered in sacrifice," then out of consideration for the man who
informed you, and for conscience' sake—[29]I mean his conscience,
not yours—do not eat it.) For why should my liberty be determined
by another man's scruples? [30]If I partake with thankfulness, why am 1 Tim 4:4
I denounced because of that for which I give thanks?

[31]So, whether you eat or drink, or whatever you do, do all to the Col 3:17
glory of God. [32]Give no offence to Jews or to Greeks or to the church Rom 14:13
of God, [33]just as I try to please all men in everything I do, not 1 Cor 9:19ff 1 Cor 10:24
seeking my own advantage, but that of many, that they may be saved.

7. THE CELEBRATION OF THE EUCHARIST

Women in church 1 Cor 4:16 Phil 3:17

11 [1]Be imitators of me, as I am of Christ. [2]I commend you 2 Thess 3:7
because you remember me in everything and maintain the 1 Thess 2:13ff 2 Thess 2:15
traditions even as I have delivered them to you. [3]But I want you to Gen 3:16 1 Cor 3:23 Eph 5:23

Christians to bring the good influence of Christ's message to bear on all fields of human activity (cf. Vatican II, *Apostolicam actuositatem*, 16), and to avoid a policy restricted to not oneself doing anything wrong.

10:31. In everything he does—even in apparently unimportant things, like eating and drinking—a Christian should seek the glory of God, by always acting with the best of intentions. In the case of meals, the practice of saying grace before and after helps us to be mindful of God in that situation.

"When you sit down to eat," St Basil says, commenting on this verse, "pray. When you eat bread, do so thanking him for being so generous to you. If you drink wine, be mindful of him who has given it to you for your pleasure and as a relief in sickness. When you dress, thank him for his kindness in providing you with clothes. When you look at the sky and the beauty of the stars, throw yourself at God's feet and adore him who in his wisdom has arranged things in this way. Similarly, when the sun goes down and when it rises, when you are asleep or awake, give thanks to God, who created and arranged all things for your benefit, to have you know, love and praise their Creator" (*Hom. in Julittam martyrem*).

11:1–14:40. In this section St Paul deals with certain matters connected with public worship: first, he teaches that women should wear a head covering (vv. 1–16); he goes on to indicate the respect, order and decorum which should mark the celebration of the Eucharist (vv. 17–34); and he ends with a long passage about

understand that the head of every man is Christ, the head of a
woman is her husband, and the head of Christ is God. 4Any man
who prays or prophesies with his head covered dishonours his
2 Cor 3:18 head, 5but any woman who prays or prophesies with her head
unveiled dishonours her head—it is the same as if her head were
shaven. 6For if a woman will not veil herself, then she should cut off

---

the gifts of the Holy Spirit and their use in liturgical assemblies (chaps. 12–14).

When reading this section it is important to notice the specific instructions the Apostle gives, especially his teaching on men and women, the Eucharist, and the gifts of the Holy Spirit.

11:1–16. Christianity has much to say about the dignity of women and their role in the family and in society; women also have an important role in the Church, but one distinct from that of men. St Paul gives three reasons why women, by keeping their heads covered, should be externally different from men: man and woman should honour God but each in their own way (vv. 2–6); they have been created different but they are mutually orientated to each other (vv. 7–12); Christian practice and profane custom both show that women's mode of dress is not unimportant (vv. 13–16).

11:1. This piece of advice forms a conclusion to the previous chapter. St Paul proposes himself as a model not because he is the exemplar of all virtues but because by imitating his life and following in his footsteps we are following those of Christ, who is our only proper model. The same applies to all other saints: their lives teach us to practise the Christian virtues. "To look on the lives of those who have faithfully followed Christ is to be inspired with a new reason for seeking the city which is to come (cf. Heb 13:14 and 11:10), while at the same time we are taught to know a most safe path by which, despite the vicissitudes of the world, and in keeping with the state of life and condition proper to each of us, we will be able to arrive at perfect union with Christ, that is, holiness. God shows to men, in a vivid way, his presence and his face in the lives of those companions of ours in the human condition who are more perfectly transformed into the image of Christ (cf. 2 Cor 3:18)" (Vatican II, *Lumen gentium*, 50).

11:2–6. It may well be that the Apostle sensed that behind the matter of the veil lay other questions that went deeper than that of women's attire. In fact, he refers rather formally to "traditions", that is, transmitted customs which are expressions of a way of thinking. One thing at least can be clearly deduced from what he says here: external comportment at public worship is a matter of some importance because it reflects people's inner dispositions.

He begins in fact by establishing a theological principle which throws light on this matter of the veil: "the head of every man is Christ, the head of every woman is her husband, and the head of Christ is God" (v. 3). He is not in any way undervaluing the dignity of women; they have the same rights and the same calling to holiness as men have, but they have a special mission of their own. It must be remembered that all mankind, woman and man, is ordained to Christ, the head, and through him to God himself.

This teaching, which is repeated in v. 11, runs right through everything the Apostle has to say: "There is neither

her hair; but if it is disgraceful for a woman to be shorn or shaven, let
her wear a veil. 7For a man ought not to cover his head, since he is Gen 1:26f; 5:1
the image and glory of God; but woman is the glory of man. 8(For Gen 2:21–23
man was not made from woman, but woman from man. 9Neither 1 Tim 2:13 Gen 2:18
was man created for woman, but woman for man.) 10That is why a Gen 3:16
woman ought to have a veil[r] on her head, because of the angels. 1 Cor 14:34
11(Nevertheless, in the Lord woman is not independent of man nor
man of woman; 12for as woman was made from man, so man is
now born of woman. And all things are from God.) 13Judge for
yourselves; is it proper for a woman to pray to God with her head
uncovered? 14Does not nature itself teach you that for a man to
wear long hair is degrading to him, 15but if a woman has long hair,
it is her pride? For her hair is given to her for a covering. 16If any 1 Cor 14:33
one is disposed to be contentious, we recognize no other practise,
nor do the churches of God.

Abuses in the celebration of the Eucharist

17But in the following instructions I do not commend you, because
when you come together it is not for the better but for the worse.
18For, in the first place, when you assemble as a church, I hear that 1 Cor 1:10–12; 3:3
there are divisions among you; and I partly believe it, 19for there

---

male nor female; for you are all one in Christ Jesus" (Gal 3:28). What matters is that there be a structured solidarity in mankind which allows all to be built into an ordered unity with Christ Jesus.

11:7–12. This alludes to the accounts of the creation of man contained in the first two chapters of Genesis. There it is revealed that man—that is, man and woman—is the likeness of God not only individually but also in their relationship to one another, for each was created for the other.

Angels are present in every human activity, especially in acts of worship (v. 10), in which the members of the Church on earth join with those in heaven to render due worship to God. The presence of the angels is an added incentive to the maintenance of due decorum by women.

11:13–16. Lastly, St Paul appeals to custom. Given that in both the Jewish and the Greek worlds it was customary for women to appear in public in special attire, with all the more reason should Christian women dress in a special way at public worship. The Apostle must have in mind the danger—more proximate in the case of women—of acting with a certain vanity or frivolity. He is arguing in favour of that good taste, even in matters of external deportment, which so dignifies women.

11:17–22. Here St Paul discusses a much more serious abuse. These Christians used to combine the celebration of the Eucharist with a meal in common. In principle, this meal was intended to be a sign of charity and solidarity among those present: hence the fact that it was sometimes called an *agape* or fraternal

r. Greek *authority* (the veil being a symbol of this)

must be factions among you in order that those who are genuine
among you may be recognized. [20]When you meet together, it is
not the Lord's supper that you eat.* [21]For in eating, each one goes
ahead with his own meal, and one is hungry and another is drunk.
[22]What! Do you not have houses to eat and drink in? Or do you
despise the church of God and humiliate those who have nothing?
What shall I say to you? Shall I commend you in this? No, I will not.

Mt 26:26–29 Mk 14:22–25 Lk 22:14ff Ex 12:14 Deut 16:3

The institution of the Eucharist and its worthy reception

[23]For I received from the Lord what I also delivered to you, that
the Lord Jesus on the night when he was betrayed took bread,
[24]and when he had given thanks, he broke it, and said, "This is my
body which is for[s] you. Do this in remembrance of me." [25]In the
same way also the cup, after supper, saying, "This cup is the new
covenant in my blood. Do this, as often as you drink it, in
remembrance of me." [26]For as often as you eat this bread and
drink the cup, you proclaim the Lord's death until he comes.

Ex 24:8 Jer 31:31ff

---

banquet; these meals also provided an opportunity to help those most in need. However, certain abuses had arisen: instead of a meal in which all shared equally, they had been eating in groups, each group eating the food they had brought, which meant that some ate and drank too much, while others did not have enough or had nothing at all. The net effect was that this meal—giving rise as it did to discontent and discord—was in sharp contrast with the Eucharist, the source of charity and unity. Very early on in the Church the Eucharist was separated from these meals, which then became simple fraternal meals with no liturgical significance.

11:23–26. These verses clearly bear witness to the early Christians' faith in the eucharistic mystery. St Paul is writing around the year 57—only twenty–seven years since the institution of the Eucharist—, reminding the Corinthians of what they had been taught some years earlier (*c.* the year 51). The words "received" and "delivered" are technical terms used to indicate that a teaching is part of apostolic Tradition; cf. also 1 Cor 15:3. These two passages highlight the importance of that apostolic Tradition. The words "I received from the Lord" are a technical expression which means "I received through that Tradition which goes back to the Lord himself."

There are three other New Testament accounts of the institution of the Eucharist (Mt 26:26-29; Mk 14:22–25; Lk 22:16–20). This account, which is most like St Luke's, is the earliest of the four.

The text contains the fundamental elements of Christian faith in the mystery of the Eucharist: 1) the institution of this sacrament by Jesus Christ and his real presence in it; 2) the institution of the Christian priesthood; 3) the Eucharist is the sacrifice of the New Testament (cf. notes on Mt 26:26–29; Mk 14:22–25; Lk 22:16–20; 1 Cor 10:14–22).

"Do this in remembrance of me": in instituting the Eucharist, our Lord charged that it be re-enacted until the end of time

s. Other ancient authorities read *broken for*

[27]Whoever, therefore, eats the bread or drinks the cup of the Heb 10:29
Lord in an unworthy manner will be guilty of profaning the body
and blood of the Lord. [28]Let a man examine himself, and so eat of 2 Cor 13:5

(cf. Lk 22:19), thereby instituting the priesthood. The Council of Trent teaches that Jesus Christ our Lord, at the Last Supper, "offered his body and blood under the species of bread and wine to God the Father and he gave his body and blood under the same species to the apostles to receive, making them priests of the New Testament at that time. [. . .] He ordered the apostles and their successors in the priesthood to offer this sacrament when he said, 'Do this in remembrance of me', as the Catholic Church has always understood and taught" (*De SS. Missae sacrificio*, chap. 1; cf. can. 2). And so, Pope John Paul II teaches, the Eucharist is "the principal and central reason-of-being of the sacrament of the priesthood, which effectively came into being at the moment of the institution of the Eucharist, and together with it" (*Letter to all bishops*, 24 February 1980).

The word "remembrance" is charged with the meaning of a Hebrew word which was used to convey the essence of the feast of the Passover—commemoration of the exodus from Egypt. For the Israelites the passover rite not only reminded them of a bygone event: they were conscious of making that event present, reviving it, in order to participate in it, in some way, generation after generation (cf. Ex 12:26–27; Deut 6:20–25). So, when our Lord commands his Apostles to "do this in remembrance of me", it is not a matter of merely recalling his supper but of renewing his own passover sacrifice of Calvary, which already, at the Last Supper, was present in an anticipated way.

11:27–32. These words are an unambiguous assertion of the real presence of Jesus in the eucharistic species. There Jesus is present, really, truly and substantially, whole and entire—with his body, blood, soul and divinity—in each and every part of the consecrated species. "The Church of God has always believed that immediately after the consecration the true body and blood of our Lord, together with his soul and divinity, exist under the species of bread and wine. His body exists under the species of bread and his blood under the species of wine according to the import of the words. But the body exists under the species of wine, his blood under the species of bread, and his soul under both species in virtue of the natural connexion and concomitance which unite the parts of Christ our Lord, who has risen from the dead and dies now no more (cf. Rom 6:9). Moreover, Christ's divinity is present because of its admirable hypostatic union with his body and soul. It is, therefore, perfectly true that just as much is present under either species as is present under both. For Christ, whole and entire, exists under the species of bread and under any part of that species, and similarly the whole Christ exists under the species of wine and under its parts" (Council of Trent, *De SS. Eucharistia*, chap. 3).

This real presence of our Lord in the Eucharist explains why one needs to be prepared in body and soul to receive it, and why receiving it unworthily has such grave consequences (vv. 27–29). The Council of Trent, recalling what St Paul says in vv. 27–28, teaches that "no one who has a mortal sin on his conscience shall dare to receive the Holy Eucharist before making a sacramental confession, regardless of how contrite he may think

the bread and drink of the cup. 29For any one who eats and drinks
without discerning the body eats and drinks judgment upon
himself. 30That is why many of you are weak and ill, and some
have died.[t] 31But if we judged ourselves truly, we should not be
Deut 8:5ff Heb 12:5f judged. 32But when we are judged by the Lord, we are chastened[u]
so that we may not be condemned along with the world.

---

he is. This holy Council declares that this custom is to be kept forever" (*De SS. Eucharistia*, chap. 7; cf. *Code of Canon Law*, can. 916).

The Church also recommends careful preparation for Holy Communion, by acts of faith, hope and charity, contrition, adoration and humility, made with a fervent desire to receive Jesus Christ (cf. *St Pius X Catechism*, 639), and also that communicants spend some time in thanksgiving after Communion (cf. ibid., 640).

As regards the eucharistic fast, a practice designed to foster reverence for the Sacrament, the current discipline of the Church prescribes that "Whoever is to receive the blessed Eucharist is to abstain for at least one hour before holy communion from all food and drink, with the sole exception of water and medicine" (*Code of Canon Law*, can. 919, 1).

11:28. Apropos of these words, Pope John Paul II writes: "This call by the Apostle indicates at least indirectly the close link between the Eucharist and Penance. Indeed, if the first word of Christ's teaching, the first phrase of the Gospel Good News, was 'Repent, and believe in the gospel' (*metanoeite*: Mk 1:15), the Sacrament of the Passion, Cross and Resurrection seems to strengthen and consolidate in an altogether special way this call in our souls. The Eucharist and Penance thus become in a sense two closely connected dimensions of authentic life in accordance with the spirit of the Gospel, of truly Christian life. The Christ who calls to the eucharistic banquet is always the same Christ who exhorts us to penance and repeats his 'Repent'" (*Redemptor hominis*, 20).

11:30–32. "That is why": the Apostle seems to be saying that the cause of many illnesses and even deaths among the Corinthians is their irreverence towards the Eucharist—which would suggest that they were guilty of many abuses, and serious ones at that.

From Christ's teaching (cf. Jn 9:3; 11:4) we know that not all evils can be taken to be punishment for personal sin; in fact, they may be a means of purification and growth in virtue, and, if borne in solidarity with Christ's sufferings, they have a salvific value and can do us great good (cf. Rom 8:8). But it is also true that God can punish grave sins even in this life; by saying that the Corinthians' misfortunes are a punishment from God, the Apostle is emphasizing that sacrilege and any other irreverence towards the Eucharist is a very serious offence.

11:33–34. These precise instructions show how keen the Apostle is to surround the mystery of the Eucharist with due adoration, respect and reverence, which are a logical consequence of the sublimity of this sacrament. The Church is tireless in making this point: "when celebrating the Sacrament of the body and blood of the Lord, the full magnitude of the divine

t. Greek *have fallen asleep* (as in 15:6, 20) **u.** Or *when we are judged we are being chastened by the Lord*

[33]So then, my brethren, when you come together to eat, wait
for one another—[34]if any one is hungry, let him eat at home—lest
you come together to be condemned. About the other things I will
give directions when I come.

8. GIFTS AND GRACES

Kinds of spiritual gifts

12 [1]Now concerning spiritual gifts, brethren, I do not want you
to be uninformed.* [2]You know that when you were heathen,
you were led astray to dumb idols, however you may have been

---

mystery must be respected, as must the full meaning of this sacramental sign in which Christ is really present and is received, the soul is filled with grace and the pledge of future glory is given (cf. Vatican II, *Sacrosanctum Concilium*, 47).

"This is the source of the duty to carry out rigorously the liturgical rules and everything that is a manifestation of community worship offered to God himself, all the more so because in this sacramental sign he entrusts himself to us with limitless trust, as if not taking into consideration our human weakness, our unworthiness, the force of habit, or even the possibility of insult. Every member of the Church, especially bishops and priests, must be vigilant in seeing that this Sacrament of love shall be at the centre of the life of the people of God, so that through all the manifestations of worship due to it Christ shall be given back 'love for love' and truly become 'the life of our souls' (cf. Jn 6:51–57; 14:6; Gal 2:20)" (John Paul II, *Redemptor hominis*, 20).

12:1–14:40. St Paul here takes up a new theme—the gifts of the Holy Spirit, which were being used in an unsatisfactory way in public worship, as we know from the previous chapter. Firstly he explains what these gifts are and the close connexion between them and the doctrine of the mystical body (chap. 12); he then speaks lyrically about charity, the greatest of all the gifts (chap. 13); and he ends with some directives about how those with special gifts should behave at liturgical assemblies.

He begins by remarking on how uninformed the Corinthians seem to be on this subject—the same point as he made in connexion with food offered to idols (cf. 10:1–13); he realizes that moral deviations often originate in poor knowledge of Church teaching.

Spiritual gifts, also called "charisms" (cf. 1 Cor 12:4, 9, 28, 30, 31), are exceptional graces usually bestowed for the benefit of the whole Christian community to build up the Church. Theologians usually distinguish them from sanctifying grace, which directly perfects the individual who has it, even though all benefit from it through the communion of saints. The spiritual gifts dealt with here also benefit the individual who has them, even though they are bestowed for the benefit of others, for they are a visible manifestation of the Holy Spirit and help the Church to operate at its best.

The Second Vatican Council puts this clearly and concisely: "It is not only through the sacraments and the

1 Jn 4:1–3 moved. [3]Therefore I want you to understand that no one speaking
by the Spirit of God ever says "Jesus be cursed!" and no one can
say "Jesus is Lord" except by the Holy Spirit.
Rom 12:6 [4]Now there are varieties of gifts, but the same Spirit; [5]and there
are varieties of service, but the same Lord; [6]and there are varieties
of working, but it is the same God who inspires them all in every
one. [7]To each is given the manifestation of the Spirit for the
common good. [8]To one is given through the Spirit the utterance of

---

ministrations of the Church that the Holy Spirit makes holy the people, leads them and enriches them with his virtues. Allotting his gifts according as he wills (cf. Cor 12:11), he also distributes special graces among the faithful of every rank. By these gifts he makes them fit and ready to undertake various tasks and offices for the renewal and building up of the Church, as it is written, 'the manifestation of the Spirit for the common good' (1 Cor 12:7). Whether these charisms be very remarkable or more simple and widely diffused, they are to be received with thanksgiving and consolation since they are fitting and useful for the needs of the Church. Extraordinary gifts are not to be rashly desired, nor is it from them that the fruits of apostolic labours are to be presumptuously expected" (*Lumen gentium*, 12).

12:3. This provides a general principle for discerning signs of the Holy Spirit—recognition of Christ as Lord. It follows that the gifts of the Spirit can never go against the teaching of the Church. "Those who have charge over the Church should judge the genuineness and proper use of these gifts [...], not indeed to extinguish the Spirit, but to test all things and hold fast to what is good (cf. Thess 5:12 and 19–21)" (*Lumen gentium*, 12).

12:4–7. God is the origin of spiritual gifts. Probably when St Paul speaks of gifts, service (ministries), "varieties of working", he is not referring to graces which are essentially distinct from one another, but to different perspectives from which these gifts can be viewed, and to their attribution to the three divine persons. Insofar as they are gratuitously bestowed they are attributed to the Holy Spirit, as he confirms in v. 11; insofar as they are granted for the benefit and service of the other members of the Church, they are attributed to Christ the Lord, who came "not to be served but to serve" (Mk 10:45); and insofar as they are operative and produce a good effect, they are attributed to God the Father. In this way the various graces which the members of the Church receive are a living reflection of God who, being essentially one, in so is a trinity of persons. "The whole Church has the appearance of a people gathered together by virtue of the unity of the Father and of the Son and of the Holy Spirit" (St Cyprian, *De dominica oratione*, 23). Therefore, diversity of gifts and graces is as important as their basic unity, because all have the same divine origin and the same purpose—the common good (v. 7): "It is the Holy Spirit, dwelling in those who believe and pervading and ruling over the entire Church, who brings about that wonderful communion of the faithful and joins them together so intimately in Christ that he is the principle of the Church's unity. By distributing various kinds of spiritual gifts and ministries he enriches the Church of Jesus Christ with different functions 'in order to equip the

wisdom, and to another the utterance of knowledge according to
the same Spirit, 9to another faith by the same Spirit, to another
gifts of healing by the one Spirit, 10to another the working of Acts 2:4
miracles, to another prophecy, to another the ability to distinguish 1 Jn 4:1–3
between spirits, to another various kinds of tongues, to another the
interpretation of tongues. 11All these are inspired by one and the Eph 4:7
same Spirit, who apportions to each one individually as he wills.

Unity and variety in the mystical body of Christ

12For just as the body is one and has many members, and all the Rom 12:4–5
members of the body, though many, are one body, so it is with 1 Cor 10:17;
Christ. 13For by one Spirit we were all baptized into one body—Jews 12:27 Gal 3:28; Eph
or Greeks, slaves or free—and all were made to drink of one Spirit. 4:4–6; Col 3:11

---

saints for the work of service, so as to build up the body of Christ' (Eph 4:12)" (Vatican II, *Unitatis redintegratio*, 2).

12:8–11. The list of special gifts which St Paul gives here is not meant to be exhaustive, as is also true of the list in vv. 28–30, and those in other letters (cf., e.g., Rom 12:6–9 and Eph 4:11). It is in fact quite difficult to identify exactly what each gift involves. What is clear is that the action of the Holy Spirit is enormously fruitful and that in the Corinthian community of the time it took all kinds of forms, some of them quite exceptional.

Over the centuries and in our own time also, the Holy Spirit can bestow exceptional gifts on the faithful, gifts which manifest themselves in dramatic ways, for God's power is quite unlimited (cf. Is 59:1); however, these extraordinary gifts are not the only things that promote the spread of the Church: "*Renewal in the Spirit*", John Paul II teaches, "will be authentic and will have real fruitfulness in the Church, not so much according as it gives rise to extraordinary charisms, but according as it leads the greatest possible number of the faithful, as they travel their daily paths, to make a humble, patient and persevering effort to know the mystery of Christ better and better, and to bear witness to it" (*Catechesi tradendae,* 72). It is important, therefore, to realize that the Holy Spirit continues to act in the Church: "The action of the Holy Spirit can pass unnoticed, because God does not reveal to us his plans, and because man's sin clouds over the divine gifts. But faith reminds us that God is always acting. He has created us and maintains us in existence, and he leads all creation by his grace toward the glorious freedom of the children of God (cf. Rom 8:21)" (St Josemaría Escrivá, *Christ Is Passing By*, 130).

12:12–13. In Greek and Latin literature, society is often compared to a body; even today we talk of "corporations", a term which conveys the idea that all the citizens of a particular city are responsible for the common good. St Paul, starting with this metaphor, adds two important features: 1) he identifies the Church with Christ: "so it is with Christ" (v. 12); and 2) he says that the Holy Spirit is its life-principle: "by one Spirit we were all baptized … , and all made to drink of the Spirit" (v. 13). The Magisterium summarizes this teaching by defining the Church as the "mystical body of Christ",

1 Cor 12:20 [14]For the body does not consist of one member but of many.
[15]If the foot should say, "Because I am not a hand, I do not belong
to the body," that would not make it any less a part of the body.

---

an expression which "is derived from and is, as it were, the fair flower of the repeated teaching of Sacred Scripture and the holy Fathers" (Pius XII, *Mystici Corporis*).

"So it is with Christ": "One would have expected him to say, So it is with the Church, but he does not say that [...]. For, just as the body and the head are one man, so too Christ and the Church are one, and therefore instead of 'the Church' he says 'Christ'" (Chrysostom, *Hom. on 1 Cor*, 30, ad loc.). This identification of the Church with Christ is much more than a mere metaphor; it makes a Church a society which is radically different from any other society: "The complete Christ is made up of the head and the body, as I am sure you know well. The head is our Saviour himself, who suffered under Pontius Pilate and now, after rising from the dead, is seated at the right hand of the Father. And his body is the Church. Not this or that church, but the Church which is to be found all over the world. Nor is it only that which exists among us today, for also belonging to it are those who lived before us and those who will live in the future, right up to the end of the world. All this Church, made up of the assembly of the faithful—for all the faithful are members of Christ—has Christ as its head, governing his body from heaven. And although this head is located out of sight of the body, he is, however, joined to it by love" (St Augustine, *Enarrationes in Psalmos*, 56, 1).

The Church's remarkable unity derives from the Holy Spirit who not only assembles the faithful into a society but also imbues and vivifies its members, exercising the same function as the soul does in a physical body: "In order that we might be unceasingly renewed in him (cf. Eph 4:23), he has shared with us his Spirit who, being one and the same in head and members, gives life to, unifies and moves the whole body. Consequently, his work could be compared by the Fathers to the function that the principle of life, the soul, fulfils in the human body" (Vatican II, *Lumen gentium*, 7).

"All were made to drink of one Spirit": given that the Apostle says this immediately after mentioning Baptism, he seems to be referring to a further outpouring of the Holy Spirit, possibly in the sacrament of Confirmation. It is not uncommon for Holy Scripture to compare the outpouring of the Spirit to drink, indicating that the effects of his presence are to revive the parched soul; in the Old Testament the coming of the Holy Spirit is already compared to dew, rain etc.; and St John repeats what our Lord said about "living water" (Jn 7:38; cf. 4:13–14).

Together with the sacraments of Christian initiation, the Eucharist plays a special role in building up the unity of the body of Christ. "Really sharing in the body of the Lord in the breaking of the eucharistic bread, we are taken up into communion with him and with one another. 'Because the bread is one, we, who are many, are one body, for we all partake of the one bread' (1 Cor 10:17). In this way all of us are made members of his body (cf. 1 Cor 12:27), 'and individual members of one another' (Rom 12:5)" (*Lumen gentium*, 7).

12:14–27. The unity of the mystical body, which derives from a single life-principle, the Holy Spirit, and tends

16And if the ear should say, "Because I am not an eye, I do not
belong to the body," that would not make it any less a part of the
body. 17If the whole body were an eye, where would be the
hearing? If the whole body were an ear, where would be the sense
of smell? 18But as it is, God arranged the organs in the body, each
one of them, as he chose. 19If all were a single organ, where would
the body be? 20As it is, there are many parts, yet one body. 21The 1 Cor 12:14
eye cannot say to the hand, "I have no need of you," nor again the
head to the feet, "I have no need of you." 22On the contrary, the
parts of the body which seem to be weaker are indispensable,
23and those parts of the body which we think less honourable we
invest with the greater honour, and our unpresentable parts are
treated with greater modesty, 24which our more presentable parts

---

towards a common same goal, that is, the building up of the Church, means that all its members, whatever their position, have the same basic dignity and the same importance. St Paul develops this thinking by a very effective literary device: he personifies the members of the human body and imagines the nobler members looking down on the lesser ones (vv. 21–24). This serves to reaffirm the truth of v. 25: "that the members may have the same care for one another". The responsibility of each Christian derives from the very essence of the vocation he or she receives at Baptism and Confirmation: "In the Church there is a diversity of ministries," St Josemaría Escrivá explains, "but there is only one aim—the sanctification of men. And in this task all Christians participate in some way, through the character imprinted by the sacraments of Baptism and Confirmation. We must all feel responsible for the mission of the Church, which is the mission of Christ. He who does not have zeal for the salvation of souls, he who does not strive with all his strength to make the name and the teaching of Christ known and loved, will not understand the apostolicity of the Church.

"A passive Christian has failed to understand what Christ wants from all of us. A Christian who 'goes his own way', unconcerned about the salvation of others, does not love with the heart of Jesus. Apostolate is not a mission exclusive to the hierarchy, or to priests and religious. The Lord calls all of us to be, by our example and word, instruments of the stream of grace which springs up to eternal life" (*In Love with the Church*, 15).

12:22–23. St Paul points to what happens in the human body and shows that those parts which seem least attractive are often the most valuable. Christians do need to be resourceful and to act with a sense of personal responsibility, but they need to combine this with humility: "Don't be a fool! It's true that at most you play the part of a little bolt in that great undertaking of Christ's. But do you know what happens when a bolt is not tight enough or when it works itself out of place? Bigger parts also work loose or the gearwheels get damaged and broken. The work is slowed up. Perhaps the whole machine will be rendered useless. What a big thing it is to be a little bolt!" (St Josemaría Escrivá, *The Way*, 830).

do not require. But God has so composed the body, giving the
greater honour to the inferior part, 25that there may be no discord
in the body, but that the members may have the same care for one
Rom 12:15 another. 26If one member suffers, all suffer together; if one
member is honoured, all rejoice together.
Rom 12:5ff 27Now you are the body of Christ and individually members of
Rom 1:1 it. 28And God has appointed in the church first apostles, second
Eph 4:11f prophets, third teachers, then workers of miracles, then healers,

---

12:26. This mutual dependence, the fact that Christians are in living union with one another, is something which the Church has always taught. Pope Paul VI stated this dogma of faith as follows: "We believe in the communion of all the faithful of Christ, whether these still make their pilgrim way on earth, whether, their life over, they undergo purification or they enjoy the happiness of heaven. One and all they go to form the one Church. We likewise believe that in this communion we are surrounded by the love of a compassionate God and his saints, who always listen to our prayers, even as Jesus told us, 'Ask and you shall receive' (Lk 11:9–10; Jn 16:24)" (*Creed of the People of God,* 30).

This sublime truth gives us a sense of solidarity with one another and makes us continually feel revitalized—like a sick person who has been given a blood transfusion (cf. St Josemaría Escrivá, *The Way*, 544)—through the merits of all the members of the Church and especially those of Jesus Christ: "It should be noted", St Thomas Aquinas points out, "that not only are the effects of Christ's passion communicated to us but also the merits of his life. Moreover, the good done by all the saints is communicated to those who live in charity, for all form one single thing [...]. So, a person who lives in charity shares in all the good done throughout the world [...]. Thus, we obtain two things through the communion of saints; one is that the merits of Christ are communicated to all of us; the other, that the good done by one redounds to the benefit of all" (*Super Symbolum Apostolorum*, 10).

12:28–30. St Paul concludes this description of the different parts of the body by applying it to the Church, where variety of functions does not detract from unity. It would be a serious mistake not to recognize in the visible structure of the Church, which is so multifaceted, the fact that the Church founded by Christ is *one*, visible at the same time as it is spiritual. The Second Vatican Council puts this very clearly: "But the society structured with hierarchical organs and the mystical body of Christ, the visible society and the spiritual community, the earthly Church and the Church endowed with heavenly riches, are not to be thought of as two realities. On the contrary, they form one complex reality which comes together from a human element and a divine element. For this reason the Church is compared, not without significance, to the mystery of the incarnate Word. As the assumed nature, inseparably united to him, serves the divine Word as a living organ of salvation, so, in a somewhat similar way, does the social structure of the Church serve the Spirit of Christ who vivifies it, in the building up of the body (cf. Eph 4:15)" (*Lumen gentium*, 8).

The Church is this way because that is the will of its founder, Jesus Christ: "The Church is by divine will a hierarchical institution. The Second Vatican

helpers, administrators, speakers in various kinds of tongues.
[29]Are all apostles? Are all prophets? Are all teachers? Do all work
miracles? [30]Do all possess gifts of healing? Do all speak with
tongues? Do all interpret? [31]But earnestly desire the higher gifts. 1 Cor 14:1
And I will show you a still more excellent way.*

Hymn to charity

13 [1]If I speak in the tongues of men and of angels, but have not
love, I am a noisy gong or a clanging cymbal. [2]And if I Mt 7:22; 17:20

Council describes it as a 'society structured with hierarchical organs' (*Lumen gentium*, 8) in which 'the ministers are invested with a sacred power' (ibid., 18). The hierarchy is not only compatible with freedom; it is at the service of the freedom of the children of God (cf. Rom 8:21). [...] 'Hierarchy' means holy government and sacred order. In no way does it imply a merely human arbitrary order or a subhuman despotism. Our Lord established in the Church a hierarchical order which should not degenerate into tyranny, because authority is as much a call to serve as is obedience.

"In the Church there is equality, because once baptized we are all equal, all children of the same God, our Father. There is no difference as Christians between the Pope and someone who has just joined the Church. But this radical equality does not mean that we can change the constitution of the Church in those things that were established by Christ. By expressed divine will there are different functions which imply different capacities, an indelible 'character' conferred on the sacred ministers by the sacrament of Order. At the summit of this order is Peter's successor and with him, and under him, all the bishops with the triple mission of sanctifying, governing and teaching" (St Josemaría Escrivá, *In Love with the Church*, 30).

12:31. "Earnestly desire the higher gifts": according to some Greek manuscripts this can be translated "earnestly seek the greater gifts." St Paul is encouraging his Christians to put greater value on those gifts of the Holy Spirit which contribute most to the goal of the Church than on those which are spectacular. He probably has in mind the teaching he will develop (chap. 14) about the superiority of graces and charisms to do with teaching and catechesis.

"A still more excellent way": this undoubtedly refers to charity, which he goes on to describe and praise (chap. 13). Therefore, what is called his "hymn to charity" is not a digression, much less a later addition, but an outpouring of the Apostle's soul, which perfectly explains why charity is the greatest of all gifts, a sure route to holiness and salvation, and the identifying mark of the Christian: "the first and most necessary gift is charity, by which we love God above all things and our neighbour because of him. [...] This is because love, as the bond of perfection and fullness of the law (cf. Col 3:14, Rom. 13:10), governs, gives meaning to, and perfects all the means of sanctification. Hence the true disciple of Christ is marked by love both of God and of his neighbour" (Vatican II, *Lumen gentium*, 42).

13:1–13. This wonderful hymn to charity is one of the most beautiful pages in Pauline writing. The literary style of the chapter is designed to present charity in

have prophetic powers, and understand all mysteries and all
knowledge, and if I have all faith, so as to remove mountains, but
Mt 6:22 have not love, I am nothing. 3If I give away all I have, and if I
deliver my body to be burned,[v] but have not love, I gain nothing.

---

all its splendour. St Paul sings the praises of love as seen from three points of view—the superiority and absolute need of this gift (vv. 1–3); its features and practical expression (vv. 4–7); and the fact it endures for ever (vv. 8–13).

Love, the charity of which St Paul is speaking, has nothing to do with selfish desire for physical passionate possession; nor is it restricted to mere philantrophy, whose motivation is purely humanitarian: charity is a love which is to be found in the new order of things established by Christ; its origin, content and purpose are radically new; it is born of the love of God for men, a love so intense that he sacrificed his only-begotten Son (Jn 3:16). The Christian is enabled to respond to this love of God by this gift of the Holy Spirit, charity (cf. Gal 5:22; Rom 15:30), and by virtue of this divine love he discovers God in his neighbour: he recognizes that all are children of the one Father and brothers and sisters of Jesus Christ: "Our love is not to be confused with sentimentality or mere good fellowship, nor with that somewhat questionable zeal to help others in order to convince ourselves of our superiority. Rather, it means living in peace with our neighbour, venerating the image of God that is found in each and every person and doing all we can to get them in their turn to contemplate that image and learn to turn to Christ" (St Josemaría Escrivá, *Friends of God*, 230).

13:1–3. Charity is so excellent a gift that without it all other gifts make no sense. To make this clear St Paul mentions those gifts which appear to be most exceptional—the gift of tongues; knowledge; and heroic actions.

Firstly, the gift of tongues. St Thomas Aquinas comments that the Apostle "rightly compares words lacking in charity to the sound of lifeless instruments, to the sound of a bell or cymbals, whose sound though clear is a dead sound. The same occurs in the speech of someone who has no charity; no matter how brilliant it be, it comes across as something dead, because it is of no help as far as meriting eternal life is concerned" (*Commentary on 1 Cor,* ad loc.). By way of emphasis St Paul speaks of the tongues of angels as the highest degree of the gift of tongues.

"I am nothing": this conclusion could not be more emphatic. A little further on (1 Cor 15:10), St Paul will himself say that "by the grace of God I am what I am", to make us see that from God's love for man (grace) derives man's love for God and for his neighbour for God's sake (charity).

Knowledge and faith, which need not ever be separated, also acquire their full meaning in the Christian who lives by love: "Each one according to his own gifts and duties must steadfastly advance along the way of a living faith, which arouses hope and works through love" (Vatican II, *Lumen gentium*, 41).

Strictly speaking, martyrdom is the supreme act of love. St Paul is referring here as in the previous points to hypothetical cases or merely external gestures, which seem to betoken detachment and generosity, but are in fact mere

v. Other ancient authorities read *body that I may glory*

[4]Love is patient and kind; love is not jealous or boastful; [5]it is not arrogant or rude. Love does not insist on its own way; it is not irritable or resentful; [6]it does not rejoice at wrong, but rejoices in

Rom 13:8–10
1 Thess 5:14f
Rom 12:9f

---

appearances: "If someone does not have charity", St Augustine says, "even though he may have these gifts at the moment, they will be taken away from him. What he has will be taken away because he is missing the main thing, that whereby he will have everything and which will keep him safe [...]. He has the power to possess, but he has no charity in what he does; and because he lacks charity, what he has in his possession will be taken from him" (*Enarrationes in Psalmos*, 146, 10).

13:4–7. In his listing of the qualities of charity, St Paul, under the inspiration of the Holy Spirit, begins with two general features—patience and kindness—which the Bible attributes to God. Both of these lead on to thirteen particular ways in which love expresses itself.

Patience is a quality often praised in the Bible: in the Psalms God is said to be slow to anger (Ps 145:8); patience means great serenity in the face of injury; kindness has to do with being inclined to do good to others. St Thomas Aquinas explains this by starting with the etymology of the word: "Kindness [*benignitas,* benignity] is like good fuel [*bona igneitas*]: just as fire causes solid substances to become liquid and start to melt, charity sees to it that a person does not keep his things for himself but distributes them to others" (*Commentary on 1 Cor,* ad loc.). Since to charity are attributed qualities which in the first instance apply to God, we can see the excellence of this virtue: "Charity towards our neighbour is an expression of our love of God. Accordingly, when we strive to grow in this virtue, we cannot fix any limits to our growth. The only possible measure for the love of God is to love without measure: on the one hand, because we will never be able to thank him enough for what he has done for us; and on the other, because this is exactly what God's own love for us, his creatures, is like: it overflows without calculation or limit" (St Josemaría Escrivá, *Friends of God*, 232).

"Love is patient", St Gregory the Great comments, "because it bears serenely the injury it suffers. It is kind, because it repays evil with good. It is not jealous, because it covets nothing in this world: it does not know what it is to envy worldly prosperity. It is not boastful, because it yearns only for spiritual reward, and it is not carried away by external things. It is not arrogant, because it thrives only on the love of God and neighbour and avoids whatever would take it from the path of righteousness. It is not covetous, because although it ardently pursues its own spiritual goals, it does not desire the goods of others. It does not insist on its own way, because it scorns as alien those things it temporarily possesses here below: it seeks to hold on only to what is enduring. It is not irritable, and even though injuries seek to provoke it, it does not let itself have any desire for vengeance, for no matter how difficult a time it may have in this life, it hopes for greater rewards in the next. It is not resentful, because it has invested its thought in the love of purity, and having rooted out all hatred it is incapable of harbouring in its heart any type of aversion. It does not rejoice at wrong, because it feels affection for others and does not rejoice at seeing the ruin of its enemies. It rejoices in the right, because by loving

Prov 10:12 the right. 7Love bears all things, believes all things, hopes all
things, endures all things.
1 Pet 4:8 8Love never ends; as for prophecies, they will pass away; as for
tongues, they will cease; as for knowledge, it will pass away. 9For our
knowledge is imperfect and our prophecy is imperfect; 10but when
the perfect comes, the imperfect will pass away. 11When I was a
child, I spoke like a child, I thought like a child, I reasoned like a

---

others as it loves itself, it is as pleased to see goodness in them as if it were indeed something to its own personal advantage" (*Moralia*, 10, 7–8, 10).

13:7. The repetition of the word "all" reinforces the absolute, essential, value of charity. This is not hyperbole, much less a depiction of utopia: it is recognition of the fact, as the Word of God confirms, that love lies at the very source of all Christian virtue. "Since we are all children of God," the founder of Opus Dei reminds us, "our fraternity is not a cliché or an empty dream; it beckons as a goal which, though difficult, is really ours to achieve.

"As Christians we must show that affection of this kind is in fact possible, whatever cynics, sceptics, those disappointed in love or those with a cowardly outlook on life might say. It may be quite difficult to be truly affectionate, for man was created free and he can rebel against God in a useless and bitter way. But it is possible and people can attain it, because it flows as a necessary consequence of God's love for us and our love for God. If you and I want it, Jesus also wants it. Then we will obtain a full and fruitful understanding of the meaning of suffering, sacrifice and unselfish dedication in ordinary life" (*Friends of God*, 233).

13:8–13. Love is enduring; it will never disappear. In this sense it is greater than all God's other gifts to man; each of those gifts is designed to help man reach perfection and eternal beatitude; charity, on the other hand, is beatitude, blessedness, itself. A thing is imperfect, St Thomas comments, for one of two reasons —either because it contains certain defects, or because it will later be superseded. In this second sense knowledge of God and prophecy are overtaken by seeing God face to face. "Charity, on the other hand, which is love of God, does not disappear but, rather, increases; the more perfect one's knowledge of God, the more perfectly does one love him" (St Thomas Aquinas, *Commentary on 1 Cor,* ad loc.).

St Paul is constantly reminding us to pursue the goal of charity, the bond of perfection (cf. Col. 3:14). Following his example the saints teach the same message; St Teresa of Avila puts it in this way: "I only want you to be warned that, if you would progress a long way on this road and ascend to the mansions that we desire, it is not a matter of thinking much, but of loving much; do, then, whatever most arouses you to love. Perhaps we do not know what it is to love; that would not greatly surprise me; for love consists, not in what most pleases us, but in the strength of our determination to desire to please God in everything and to endeavour to do everything we can not to offend him, and to pray him ever to advance the honour and glory of his Son and the growth of the catholic Church" (*Interior Castle*, 4, 1, 7).

13:11–12. "Then I shall understand fully, even as I have been fully understood": the Old Testament usually avoids mentioning God by name; these words in

child; when I became a man, I gave up childish ways. [12]For now we 2 Cor 5:7 Jas 1:23 1 Jn 3:2
see in a mirror dimly, but then face to face. Now I know in part; then
I shall understand fully, even as I have been fully understood. [13]So 1 Thess 1:3 1 Jn 4:16
faith, hope, love abide, these three; but the greatest of these is love.

Prophecy, the gift of tongues, and interpretation of tongues

14 [1]Make love your aim, and earnestly desire the spiritual 1 Cor 12:10, 31 1 Thess 5:20
gifts, especially that you may prophesy. [2]For one who

---

effect mean "Then I will know God as he knows me."

The knowledge which God has of men is not merely speculative: it involves an intimate, personal union which embraces a person's mind and will and all his or her noble aspirations. Thus in Holy Scripture God is said to know someone when he shows a preferential love for him (1 Cor 8:3), particularly when he choses him out to be a Christian (Gal 4:8).

Happiness in heaven consists in this direct knowledge of God. To explain this better St Paul uses the simile of the mirror: in those times mirrors were made of metal and produced a reflection which was blurred and dark; but it is still easy for us to understand what St Paul means; as St Thomas explains, in heaven "we shall see God face to face, because we shall see him directly, just as we see a man face to face. And by seeing in this way we become very like God, becoming sharers in his beatitude: for God has knowledge of his own substance in its very essence and therein his happiness lies. Therefore does St John (1 Jn 3:2) write: 'When he appears we shall be like him, for we shall see him as he is'" (*Summa contra gentiles*, 3, 51).

In this connexion the Church's Magisterium teaches that "in the usual providence of God, the souls of all the saints who departed this world [...] see the divine essence with an intuitive and even face-to-face vision, without the interposition of any creature in the function of object seen; rather, the divine essence immediately manifests itself to them plainly, clearly, openly [...]. We also define that those who see the divine essence in this way take great joy from it, and that because of this vision and enjoyment the souls of those who have already died are truly blessed and possess life and eternal rest" (Benedict XII, *Benedictus Deus*, *Dz–Sch*, 1000f).

13:13. Faith, hope and charity are the most important virtues in the Christian life. They are called "theological" virtues, "because they have God as their direct and principal object" (*St Pius X Catechism*, 859), and it is he himself who infuses them into the soul together with sanctifying grace (cf. ibid., 861).

When discussing the superiority of charity over faith and hope, St Thomas Aquinas says that the greatest of these virtues is that which most directly unites one to good: "Faith and hope attain God in so far as we derive from him the knowledge of truth or the acquisition of good; whereas charity attains God himself that it may rest in him, not that something else should come to us from him" (*Summa theologiae*, 2–2, 23, 6).

14:1. St Paul here reaffirms the value of charity in relation to the other spiritual gifts—which are good and which it is right to desire: "earnestly desire the spiritual gifts." But charity is absolutely essential and one must do what one can

speaks in a tongue speaks not to men but to God; for no one
understands him, but he utters mysteries in the Spirit.
3On the
other hand, he who prophesies speaks to men for their upbuilding

---

to obtain it. The Fathers have commented that love not only implies a gift of the Holy Spirit; it involves first and foremost his active presence in the soul of the Christian: "The Holy Spirit can confer every kind of gift without being himself present; however, when he grants the gift of charity he proves that he himself is present by means of grace" (St Fulgentius, *Contra Fabianum*, 8).

The Apostle urges Christians by telling them to "make love your aim". He has made it quite clear that charity is a gift, the greatest gift of all, but it is also a commandment, the first commandment and the one whose fulfilment is the distinguishing mark of Christians: "Our Lord Jesus Christ became incarnate and took on our nature to reveal himself to mankind as the model of all virtues, 'Learn from me', he says to us, 'for I am gentle and lowly in heart' (Mt 11:29).

"Later, when he explains to the Apostles the mark by which they will be known as Christians, he does not say, 'Because you are humble.' He himself is purity most sublime, the immaculate Lamb. Nothing could stain his perfect, unspotted holiness. Yet he does not say, 'You will be known as my disciples because you are chaste and pure.'

"He passed through this world completely detached from earthly goods. Though he is the Creator and Lord of the whole universe, he did not even have a place to lay his head (cf. Mt 8:20). Nevertheless he does not say, 'They will know that you are mine because you are not attached to wealth.' Before setting out to preach the Gospel he spent forty days and forty nights in the desert keeping a strict fast (cf. Mt 4:2). But once again, he does not tell his disciples, 'Men will recognize you as God's servants because you are not gluttons or drunkards.'

"No, the distinguishing mark of apostles, of true Christians in every age, is, as we have heard: 'By this', precisely by this, 'all men will know that you are my disciples, if you have love for one another' (Jn 13:35)" (St Josemaría Escrivá, *Friends of God*, 224).

14:2–5. Throughout this chapter St Paul is teaching the value of the various gifts of the Holy Spirit (vv. 2–25) and giving some specific directives about deportment at public worship (vv. 26–40).

He stresses one gift—that of prophecy—without undervaluing the other, the gift of tongues. The gift of prophecy here means the faculty of speaking in the name of God and by divine inspiration for the consolation and edification of the hearers; it does not necessarily include the ability to foretell future events or reveal hidden things. The gift of tongues is a supernatural gift, because this form of speech and its effects are beyond the natural capacity of man.

The criterion to be used to discern the gifts of the Holy Spirit is service of the Church: "so that the Church may be edified" (v. 5). This is why the gift of prophecy is preferable to other gifts, after charity: "This is the rule", St John Chrysostom comments, "constantly followed by St Paul—to give preference to the gifts that make for the edifying of the Church. Someone will ask, 'Is it possible for someone to speak in tongues without speaking to the benefit of his brethren?' Listen: those Christians do speak [in tongues], but what they say is

and encouragement and consolation. 4He who speaks in a tongue
edifies himself, but he who prophesies edifies the church. 5Now I Num 11:29
want you all to speak in tongues, but even more to prophesy. He
who prophesies is greater than he who speaks in tongues, unless
some one interprets, so that the church may be edified.

6Now, brethren, if I come to you speaking in tongues, how shall 1 Cor 12:8
I benefit you unless I bring you some revelation or knowledge or
prophecy or teaching? 7If even lifeless instruments, such as the
flute or the harp, do not give distinct notes, how will any one know
what is played? 8And if the bugle gives an indistinct sound, who
will get ready for battle? 9So with yourselves; if you in a tongue
utter speech that is not intelligible, how will any one know what is
said? For you will be speaking into the air. 10There are doubtless
many different languages in the world, and none is without
meaning; 11but if I do not know the meaning of the language, I
shall be a foreigner to the speaker and the speaker a foreigner to
me. 12So with yourselves; since you are eager for manifestations
of the Spirit, strive to excel in building up the church.

13Therefore, he who speaks in a tongue should pray for the 1 Cor 12:10
power to interpret. 14For if I pray in a tongue, my spirit prays but

---

less helpful to the edification, exhortation and consolation of souls than the gift of prophecy. Both [prophets and those who speak in tongues] are acting as the voice of the Holy Spirit who moves and inspires them; but what the prophet says is useful to those faithful who hear him, whereas the gift of tongues does not lead to understanding unless the hearers themselves have received the same supernatural gift" (*Hom. on 1 Cor*, 35, ad loc.).

14:6–11. St Paul uses the example of musical instruments to show how important it is to make oneself understood. In music, clarity and harmony are called for. If an instrument does not produce clear notes, it is not very useful; however, when the notes are clear they need to be in harmony to produce acceptable music. If one is trying to help the faithful to know God better, one's exposition needs to be clear and harmonious, that is, the words one uses should be easy to understand and should be in keeping with the teaching of the faith.

14:12–20. These verses, in the context of the whole chapter, help to show the nature of the gift of tongues. Apparently the gift was a supernatural faculty to pray or sing the praises of God with great enthusiasm, using strange words: often an interpreter—who had the gift to interpret what was said (cf. 1 Cor 12:10)—explained the meaning. These extraordinary signs witnessed to the presence of the Holy Spirit in the Church; St Paul himself had this gift of tongues (v. 18); but those who possess this gift do not preach and make no claim to teach. Their actions may help others to pray; but what is more important is the education of Christians' faith, to make them "mature in thinking" (v. 20).

Eph 5:19 my mind is unfruitful. 15What am I to do? I will pray with the
2 Cor 1:20 spirit and I will pray with the mind also; I will sing with the spirit
and I will sing with the mind. 16Otherwise, if you bless[w] with the
spirit, how can any one in the position of an outsider[x] say the
"Amen" to your thanksgiving when he does not know what you
are saying? 17For you may give thanks well enough, but the other
man is not edified. 18I thank God that I speak in tongues more than
you all; 19nevertheless, in church I would rather speak five words
Rom 16:19 with my mind, in order to instruct others, than ten thousand words
Eph 4:14 in a tongue.
Phil 3:12, 15 20Brethren, do not be children in your thinking; be babes in
Deut 28:49 Is 28:11f evil, but in thinking be mature. 21In the law it is written, "By men
of strange tongues and by the lips of foreigners will I speak to this
people, and even then they will not listen to me, says the Lord."
22Thus, tongues are a sign not for believers but for unbelievers,
Acts 2:13 while prophecy is not for unbelievers but for believers. 23If,
therefore, the whole church assembles and all speak in tongues,
and outsiders or unbelievers enter, will they not say that you are

---

14:15–17. The terms St Paul uses here—"spirit", "mind"—are not distinct parts of the human soul (the soul is spiritual and therefore does not have parts). Praying "with the spirit" means praying effectively, with the emotions; praying "with the mind" means understanding what one is saying. One application of this is that vocal prayer should be devout and attentive: "Slowly. Consider what you are saying, to whom it is being said and by whom. For that hurried talk, without time for reflection, is noise, empty clatter. And with Saint Teresa, I will tell you that, however much you work your lips, I do not call it prayer" (St Josemaría Escrivá, *The Way,* 85).

The "thanksgiving" referred to in vv. 16 and 17 seems to be prayers in praise of God, not specifically the eucharistic sacrifice.

From this and other passages we can see how St Paul uses his apostolic authority to regulate the use of "charisms", these special graces so abundant in the early Church.

14:23–25. Another reason for giving preference to the gift of prophecy is apostolate with unbelievers and simple folk. In v. 22 we were told that the gift of speaking in strange tongues can be of help to unbelievers: it attracts because it is spectacular; now the Apostle goes further, to say that even for these people it involves certain possible dangers: hearers may even think that those who speak in strange tongues are demented; whereas, if someone has the gift of prophecy and uses it to communicate the Christian message, his hearers can hear the Word of God and may be converted. The Second Vatican Council has re-stated this teaching: "Extraordinary gifts are not to be rashly desired, nor is it from them that the fruits of apostolic labours are to be presumptuously expected" (*Lumen gentium*, 12).

w. That is, *give thanks to God* **x.** Or *him that is without gifts*

mad? [24]But if all prophesy, and an unbeliever or outsider enters, Acts 4:13
he is convicted by all, he is called to account by all, [25]the secrets Is 45:14
of his heart are disclosed; and so, falling on his face, he will Dan 2:47 Zech 8:23
worship God and declare that God is really among you. Jn 4:19; 16:8

Regulation of liturgical assemblies

[26]What then, brethren? When you come together, each one has a Eph 4:12
hymn, a lesson, a revelation, a tongue, or an interpretation. Let all
things be done for edification. [27]If any speak in a tongue, let there be

---

The apostolic effects mentioned here are important ones: *conviction*, that is, drawing a person to the faith; *being called to account*, or helped to realize the seriousness of bad conduct, which was the effect Jesus had on the Samaritan woman (Jn 4:17–18); *worshipping God*, that is, committing oneself to a life that is consistent with the faith one has received; and, finally, declaring that "God is really among you", that is, recognizing the supernatural character of the Church. "The true apostle", Vatican II says, "is on the lookout for occasions of announcing Christ by word, either to unbelievers to draw them towards the faith, or to the faithful to instruct them, strengthen them, incite them to a more fervent life" (*Apostolicam actuositatem*, 6).

14:26–40. St Paul concludes by giving some guidelines on how the faithful should conduct themselves at public worship: he first addresses those who speak in tongues (vv. 27–28); then those who prophesy (vv. 29–33); then women (vv. 34–35); and finally he summarizes what he has been saying (vv. 36–40).

He uses the word "church" three times here (vv. 28, 33, 34), referring to local communities and liturgical assemblies. In every local church the universal Church is present. The Fathers developed this teaching and the Second Vatican Council has come back to it: the Church is not the totality of isolated particular churches, forming a multicoloured mosaic, as it were: rather, "the one, holy, catholic and apostolic Church of Christ is truly present and active in the particular church" (*Christus Dominus*, 11).

This explains why the Christian communities of Jerusalem, Antioch, Caesarea, Ephesus, Corinth and other cities are called "churches", and why St Paul describes them as "the churches of the saints" (v. 33).

The universal Church is also present in gatherings of the faithful, most especially at celebrations of the Eucharist: "This Church of Christ is really present in all legitimately organized groups of the faithful, which, in so far as they are united to their pastors, are also quite appropriately called churches in the New Testament" (*Lumen gentium*, 26). This explains why St Paul is particularly keen on ensuring that at liturgical gatherings everything should make for the edification of the faithful (v. 26) and be done "decently and in order" (v. 40).

14:27–28. These are very specific directives applying to those endowed with the gift of tongues. Although they have to do with those particular charisms, the point comes across clearly that from the beginning liturgical ceremonies were to be so regulated as to encourage active and fruitful participation by the laity: "Pastors of souls should be watchful", Vatican II says, "to ensure that when the

only two or at most three, and each in turn; and let one interpret.
28But if there is no one to interpret, let each of them keep silence in
Acts 17:11 1 Thess 5:21 church and speak to himself and to God. 29Let two or three prophets
speak, and let the others weigh what is said. 30If a revelation is made
to another sitting by, let the first be silent. 31For you can all prophesy
one by one, so that all may learn and all be encouraged; 32and the
spirits of prophets are subject to prophets. 33For God is not a God of
confusion but of peace.

Gen 3:16 1 Cor 11:3 Eph 5:22 1 Thess 2:12 Tit 2:5 As in all the churches of the saints, 34the women should keep
silence in the churches. For they are not permitted to speak, but
should be subordinate, as even the law says. 35If there is anything

---

liturgy is celebrated, not only are the laws governing valid and lawful celebration observed, but that the faithful are fully aware of what they are doing, actively engaged in the rite and enriched by it" (*Sacrosanctum Concilium*, 11).

14:32. "The spirits of prophets are subject to prophets": this is a further directive about the use to be made of spiritual gifts: those who speak as prophets must submit to the authority of other Christians, who have the gift of being able to adjudicate on the genuineness of what is said in prophecy. This will ensure that no one arrogantly claims to have a spiritual gift and deceives himself or others. The functions of the Church Magisterium include identifying whether the spiritual gifts of certain people have a divine origin and are contributing to the renewal of the Church. It exercises this function, for example, when it gives its approval to particular teachings and apostolic activities which arise in the course of its history.

14:33–35. From the Acts of the Apostles, as also other letters of St Paul, we know that some women cooperated with him in the ministry of evangelization; sometimes he thanked them by name (cf. e.g., Rom 16:1–12; Phil 4:2–3). "Some of them often exercised an important influence on conversions—Priscilla, Lydia and others; [...] Phoebe, in the service of the church of Cenchreae (cf. Rom 16:1). All these facts manifest within the Apostolic Church a considerable development *vis-à-vis* the customs of Judaism" (SCDF, *Inter insigniores*, 3).

The Apostle now gives a very clear ruling (which he repeats in 1 Timothy 2:11–14): "women should keep silence in the churches." He is not opposed to women prophesying (cf. 1 Cor 11:5): "the prohibition solely concerns the official function of teaching in the Christian assembly. For St Paul this prescription is bound up with the divine plan of creation (cf. 1 Cor 11:7; Gen 2:18–24). [...] Nor should it be forgotten that we owe to St Paul one of the most vigorous texts in the New Testament on the fundamental equality of men and women, as children of God in Christ (cf. Gal 3:28)" (ibid., 4).

The variety of roles to be found in the Church—including the fact that the ministerial priesthood is restricted to men chosen by God—is compatible with the essential equality of men and women: "the priesthood does not form part of the rights of the individual, but stems from the economy of the mystery of Christ and the Church. [...] It therefore remains for us to meditate more deeply on the nature of the real equality of the baptized, which is one of the great affirmations of Christianity: equality is in no way identity,

they desire to know, let them ask their husbands at home. For it is
shameful for a woman to speak in church. [36]What! Did the word of
God originate with you, or are you the only ones it has reached?
[37]If any one thinks that he is a prophet, or spiritual, he should 1 Jn 4:6
acknowledge that what I am writing to you is a command of the
Lord. [38]If any one does not recognize this, he is not recognized. [39]So,
my brethren, earnestly desire to prophesy, and do not forbid speaking
in tongues; [40]but all things should be done decently and in order. Col 2:5

9. THE RESURRECTION OF THE DEAD

Christ's resurrection and his appearances

15 [1]Now I would remind you, brethren, in what terms I 1 Thess 2:13
preached to you the gospel, which you received, in which
you stand, [2]by which you are saved, if you hold it fast—unless
you believed in vain.

---

for the Church is a differentiated body, in which each individual has his or her role. The roles are distinct and must not be confused; they do not favour the superiority of some *vis-à-vis* the others, nor do they provide an excuse for jealousy; the only better gift, which can and must be desired, is love (cf. 1 Cor 12–13). The greatest in the Kingdom of heaven are not the ministers but the saints" (ibid., 6).

15:1–58. Some of the Corinthian Christians were objecting to the doctrine of the resurrection of the dead, because this was a belief with which Greeks were unfamiliar, even those Greeks who held that the soul was immortal. Given the great importance of this doctrine, St Paul replies at length, pointing first to the historical fact of Christ's resurrection (vv. 1–11) and how it necessarily connects up with the resurrection of the dead in general (vv. 12–34). He then goes on to discuss what form this resurrection will take (vv. 35–58). This letter, which began with an exposition on Jesus Christ crucified, the power and wisdom of God (cf. 1:18 2:5), ends with a development of doctrine on the resurrection of Christ and the consequent resurrection of the members of his mystical body.

To understand what St Paul is saying it is useful to bear in mind that here he is referring only to the glorious resurrection of the just. Elsewhere in Scripture it is clearly stated that all men will rise from the dead (cf., e.g., Jn 5:28–29; Acts 24:15).

15:1–11. The resurrection of Jesus Christ is one of the essential doctrines of the Catholic faith, explicitly stated in the first creeds or symbols of the faith. It is in fact the supreme argument in favour of the divinity of Jesus and his divine mission: our Lord proclaimed it many times (cf., e.g., Mt 16:21–28; 17:22–27; 20:17–19), and by rising from the dead he provided the sign which he had promised those who did not believe him (cf. Mt 12:38–40).

This point is so important that the primary role of the Apostles is to bear witness to Christ's resurrection (cf. Acts 1:22; 2:32; 3:15; etc.); the proclamation

Is 53:8f [3]For I delivered to you as of first importance what I also
Mt 28:10 received, that Christ died for our sins in accordance with the
scriptures, [4]that he was buried, that he was raised on the third day
Is 54:7 in accordance with the scriptures, [5]and that he appeared to
Lk 24:34 Cephas, then to the twelve. [6]Then he appeared to more than five

---

of the resurrection of the Lord is the very core of apostolic catechesis (cf., e.g., the discourses of St Peter and St Paul reported in the Acts of the Apostles).

15:3–8. On the verbs "deliver" and "receive" see the note on 1 Cor 11:23–26. St Paul reminds the Corinthians of certain basic points in his preaching—that Jesus Christ died for our sins; "that he was buried, that he was raised on the third day in accordance with the scriptures" (a statement which has passed directly into the Creed) and was seen by many people.

It should be pointed out that the Greek verb translated as "appeared" refers to being seen by the eye. This is relevant to studying the nature of the appearances of the risen Jesus: St Paul is speaking of true, ocular, sight; there seems to be no way this can be identified with imagination or intellectual vision.

The appearances of the risen Christ are a direct proof of the historical fact of his resurrection. This argument gains special force when one remembers that at the time this letter was written many people who had seen the risen Lord were still alive (v. 6). Some of the appearances referred to by St Paul are also mentioned in the Gospels and in Acts—that to Peter (cf. Lk 24:34), those to the Apostles (cf., e.g., Lk 24:36–49; Jn 20:19–29), that to St Paul himself (cf. Acts 9:1–6); others—that to James and to the five hundred brethren—are mentioned only here.

The importance of this passage is enhanced by the fact that it is the earliest documentary record—earlier than the Gospels—of our Lord's resurrection, which had taken place scarcely twenty years earlier.

15:4. "Was buried": in recounting the death of Christ, all four evangelists expressly mention that his body was buried (cf. Mt 27:57–61 and par.). St Paul also confirms the fact in this letter, written very soon after the time, thereby confirming a tradition which had come down from the beginning (v. 3). The fact that Christ's body was buried eliminates any doubt about his death, and underlines the miracle of the Resurrection: Jesus Christ rose by his own power, re-joining his soul with his body, and leaving the tomb with the same human body (not merely the appearance of a body) as died and was buried, although now that body was glorified and had certain special properties (cf. note on 15:42–44). The Resurrection, therefore, is an objective, physical event, witnessed to by the empty tomb (cf. Mt 28:1ff and par.) and by Christ's appearances.

"He was raised on the third day": Jesus died and was buried on the evening of Good Friday; his body lay in the tomb the entire sabbath, and rose on the Sunday. It is correct to say that he rose on the third day after his death, even though it was not a full seventy-two hours later.

"According to the scriptures": St Paul may be referring to certain passages of the Old Testament which—*after* the event—were seen to foreshadow the Resurrection—for example, the episode of Jonah (chaps. 1–2), which Jesus in fact applied to himself (cf. Mt 12:39–40; cf. also Hos 6:1–2 and Ps 16:9–10).

hundred brethren at one time, most of whom are still alive, though
some have fallen asleep. 7Then he appeared to James, then to all Lk 24:50
the apostles. 8Last of all, as to one untimely born, he appeared also Acts 12:17ff
to me. 9For I am the least of the apostles, unfit to be called an Rom 1:1ff
apostle, because I persecuted the church of God. 10But by the 1 Cor 9:1; Mt 5:19; Eph 3:8
grace of God I am what I am, and his grace toward me was not in
vain. On the contrary, I worked harder than any of them, though it 1 Tim 1:15f 2 Cor 11:23
was not I, but the grace of God which is with me. 11Whether then
it was I or they, so we preach and so you believed.

The basis of our faith

12Now if Christ is preached as raised from the dead, how can
some of you say that there is no resurrection of the dead? 13But if
there is no resurrection of the dead, then Christ has not been

---

15:9–10. St Paul's humility, which leads him to think that his past faults render him unworthy of the grace of the apostolate, is precisely what gives God's grace scope to work in him. "Admit outright that you are a servant whose duty it is to perform very many services. Do not pride yourself on being called a son of God: let us recognize grace, yet be mindful of our nature; do not be proud of having rendered good service, of having done what you were supposed to do. The sun fulfils its function; the moon obeys; the angels carry out their charge. The Lord's chosen instrument for the Gentiles says, 'I am unfit to be called an apostle, because I persecuted the church of God' (1 Cor 15:9) […]. Neither should we seek to be praised on our own account" (St Ambrose, *Expositio Evangelii sec. Lucam*, 8, 32).

However, the grace of God is not enough on its own. As in St Paul's case, man's cooperation is needed, because God has chosen to rely on our free response to grace: "God, who created you without you, will not save you without you" (St Augustine, *Sermon,* 169, 13). And, commenting on St Paul's words—"Not I, but the grace of God which is with me"—Augustine points out, "that is, not just me, but God with me; and therefore not the grace of God alone, nor myself alone, but the grace of God *and* myself" (*De gratia et libero arbitrio*, 5, 12).

15:12–19. Paul very forcefully states that the resurrection of Christ is an essential truth of the Christian faith; without it that faith is vain. For, by rising from the dead Christ completes the work of Redemption. Dying on the cross meant victory over sins; but it was necessary also that he should rise from the dead and thereby conquer death, the outcome of sin (cf. Rom 5:12). "It was necessary that Christ should rise again in order to manifest the justice of God; for it was most appropriate that he who through obedience to God was degraded, and loaded with ignominy, should by him be exalted. […] He rose also to confirm our faith, which is necessary for justification; for the resurrection of Christ from the dead by his own power affords an irrefutable proof that he was the Son of God. Again the resurrection nourishes and sustains our hope. As Christ rose again, we rest on an assured hope that we too shall rise again; the members must necessarily

raised; [14]if Christ has not been raised, then our preaching is in vain
Acts 1:22; 5:32 and your faith is in vain. [15]We are even found to be misrepre-
senting God, because we testified of God that he raised Christ,
whom he did not raise if it is true that the dead are not raised.
Rom 4:24–25 / 1 Cor 6:14 [16]For if the dead are not raised, then Christ has not been raised.
[17]If Christ has not been raised, your faith is futile and you are still
in your sins. [18]Then those also who have fallen asleep in Christ
have perished. [19]If for this life only we have hoped in Christ, we
are of all men most to be pitied.

Rom 8:11ff / Col 1:18

The cause of our resurrection

1 Thess 4:14 [20]But in fact Christ has been raised from the dead, the first fruits
Gen 3:16–19 / Rom 5:12, 18, 21 of those who have fallen asleep. [21]For as by a man came death, by
a man has come also the resurrection of the dead. [22]For as in

---

arrive at the condition of their head. […] Finally, the resurrection of our Lord, it should also be taught, was necessary to complete the mystery of our salvation and redemption. By his death Christ liberated us from sin, by his resurrection he restored to us the most important of those privileges which we had forfeited by sin" (*St Pius V Catechism*, 1, 6, 12).

In these verses St Paul is really giving indirect arguments in support of Christ's resurrection, by pointing out what an absurd situation we would be in if Jesus Christ had not risen: our faith would be in vain (vv. 14,17,18), as would our hope (v.19); the Apostles would be false witnesses and their preaching valueless (vv. 14–15); and we would still be in our sins (v. 17). Christians, in other words, would be "of all men most to be pitied" (v. 19).

15:20–28. The Apostle insists on the solidarity that exists between Christ and Christians: as members of one single body, of which Christ is the head, they form as it were one organism (cf. Rom 6:3–11; Gal 3:28). Therefore, once the resurrection of Christ is affirmed, the resurrection of the just necessarily follows. Adam's disobedience brought death for all; Jesus, the new Adam, has merited that all should rise (cf. Rom 5:12–21). "Again, the resurrection of Christ effects for us the resurrection of our bodies not only because it was the efficient cause of this mystery, but also because we all ought to arise after the example of the Lord. For with regard to the resurrection of the body we have this testimony of the Apostle: 'As by a man came death, by a man has come also the resurrection of the dead' (1 Cor 15:21). In all that God did to accomplish the mystery of our redemption he made use of the humanity of Christ as an effective instrument, and hence his resurrection was, as it were, an instrument for the accomplishment of our resurrection" (*St Pius V Catechism*, 1, 6, 13).

Although St Paul here is referring only to the resurrection of the just (v. 23), he does speak elsewhere of the resurrection of all mankind (cf. Acts 24:15). The doctrine of the resurrection of the bodies of all at the end of time, when Jesus will come in glory to judge everyone, has always been part of the faith of the Church; "he [Christ] will come at the end of the world, he will judge the living and the dead; and he will reward all, both the

Adam all die, so also in Christ shall all be made alive. 23But each
in his own order: Christ the first fruits, then at his coming those
who belong to Christ. 24Then comes the end, when he delivers the

Rom 8:9
1 Thess 4:16
Rev 20:5
Dan 2:44

---

lost and the elect, according to their works. And all those will rise with their own bodies which they now have so that they may receive according to their works, whether good or bad; the wicked, a perpetual punishment with the devil; the good, eternal glory with Christ" (Fourth Lateran Council, *De fide catholica*, chap. 1).

15:23–28. St Paul outlines very succinctly the entire messianic and redemptive work of Christ: by decree of the Father, Christ has been made Lord of the universe (cf. Mt 28:18), in fulfilment of Ps 110:1 and Ps 8:7. When it says here that "the Son himself will also be subjected to him who put all things under him", this must be understood as referring to Christ in his capacity of Messiah and head of the Church; not Christ as God, because the Son is "begotten, not created, consubstantial with the Father" (*Nicene-Constantinopolitan Creed*).

Christ's sovereignty over all creation comes about in history, but it will achieve its final, complete, form after the Last Judgment. The Apostle presents that last event—a mystery to us—as a solemn act of homage to the Father. Christ will offer all creation to his Father as a kind of trophy, offering him the Kingdom which up to then had been confided to his care. From that moment on, the sovereignty of God and Christ will be absolute, they will have no enemies, no rivals; the stage of combat will have given way to that of contemplation, as St Augustine puts it (cf. *De Trinitate*, 1, 8).

The Parousia or second coming of Christ in glory at the end of time, when he establishes the new heaven and the new earth (cf. Rev 21:1–2), will mean definitive victory over the devil, over sin, suffering and death. A Christian's hope in this victory is not something passive: rather, it is something that spurs him on to ensure that even in this present life Christ's teaching and spirit imbue all human activies. "Far from diminishing our concern to develop this earth," Vatican II teaches, "the expectancy of a new earth should spur us on, for it is here that the body of a new human family grows, foreshadowing in some way the age which is to come. That is why, although we must be careful to distinguish earthly progress clearly from the increase of the Kingdom of Christ, such progress is of vital concern to the Kingdom of God, insofar as it can contribute to the better ordering of human society.

"When we have spread on earth the fruits of our nature and our enterprise—human dignity, brotherly communion, and freedom—according to the command of the Lord and in his Spirit, we will find them once again, cleansed this time from the stain of sin, illuminated and transfigured, when Christ presents to his Father an eternal and universal kingdom of truth and life, a kingdom of holiness and grace, a kingdom of justice, love and peace (*Roman Missal*, preface for the solemnity of Christ the King). Here on earth the Kingdom is mysteriously present; when the Lord comes it will enter into its perfection" (*Gaudium et spes*, 39).

15:24. "When he delivers the kingdom to God the Father": this does not quite catch the beauty of the Greek which literally means "when he delivers the kingdom to the God and Father". In New Testament Greek, when the word *Theós*

kingdom to God the Father after destroying every rule and every
Ps 110:1 Mt 22:44 authority and power. 25 For he must reign until he has put all his
Rev 20:14; 21:4 enemies under his feet. 26 The last enemy to be destroyed is death.
Ps 8:7 27 "For God[z] has put all things in subjection under his feet." But
when it says, "All things are put in subjection under him," it is
Col 3:11 plain that he is excepted who put all things under him. 28 When all
things are subjected to him, then the Son himself will also be
subjected to him who put all things under him, that God may be
everything to every one.

(God) is preceded by the definite article (*ho Theós*) the first person of the Blessed Trinity is being referred to.

15:25. "He must reign": every year, on the last Sunday of ordinary time, the Church celebrates the solemnity of Christ the King, to acknowledge his absolute sovereignty over all created things. On instituting this feast, Pius XI pointed out that "He must reign in our minds, which should assent with perfect submission and firm belief to revealed truths and to the teachings of Christ. He must reign in our wills, which should obey the laws and precepts of God. He must reign in our hearts, which should spurn natural desires and love God above all things, and cleave to him alone. He must reign in our bodies and in our members, which should serve as instruments for the interior sanctification of our souls, or, to use the words of the Apostle Paul, as instruments of righteousness unto God (Rom 6:13)" (*Quas primas*).

15:27. By "all things" the Apostle clearly means all created beings. In pagan mythology, rivalry and strife occurred among the gods and sometimes led to the son of a god supplanting his father. St Paul wants to make it quite clear that Holy Scripture suggests nothing of that kind. No subjection is possible among the three persons of the Blessed Trinity, because they are one God.

15:28. The subjection of the Son which St Paul speaks of here is in no way opposed to his divinity. He is referring to what will happen when Christ's mission as Redeemer and Messiah comes to an end, that is, once final victory is won over the devil, sin and its consequences. The final victory of Jesus Christ will restore to all creation its original harmony, which sin destroyed.

"Who can realize", St Bernard comments, "the indescribable sweetness contained in these few words: God will be everything to everyone? Not to speak of the body, I see three things in the soul—mind, will and memory; and these three are one and the same. Everyone who lives according to the spirit senses in this present life how far he falls short of wholeness and perfection. Why is this, if not because God is not yet everything to everyone? That is why one's mind is so often mistaken in the judgment it makes, that is why one's will experiences such restlessness, why one's memory is thrown into confusion by many things. The noble person is, without wanting to be, at the mercy of this triple vanity, yet he does not lose hope. For he who responds so generously to the desires of the soul must also provide the mind with fullness and

z. Greek *he*

[29]Otherwise, what do people mean by being baptized on behalf of
the dead? If the dead are not raised at all, why are people baptized on
their behalf? * [30]Why am I in peril every hour? [31]I protest, brethren, Rom 8:36
by my pride in you which I have in Christ Jesus our Lord, I die every 2 Cor 4:10f
day! [32]What do I gain if, humanly speaking, I fought with beasts at Is 22:13
Ephesus? If the dead are not raised, "Let us eat and drink, for
tomorrow we die." [33]Do not be deceived: "Bad company ruins good
morals." [34]Come to your right mind, and sin no more. For some have Acts 26:8 Rom 13:11
no knowledge of God. I say this to your shame. Eph 5:14

The manner of the resurrection of the dead

[35]But some one will ask, "How are the dead raised? With what
kind of body do they come?" [36]You foolish man! What you sow Jn 12:24
does not come to life unless it dies. [37]And what you sow is not the

---

light, the will with abundance of peace, and the memory with visions of eternity. O truth, O charity, O eternity, O blessed and blessing Trinity! This wretched trinity of mine, sighs for thee, for it is unfortunately still far from thee" (*Sermon on the Song of Songs*, 11).

15:29. Verses 23–28 were a type of aside, dealing with Christ as Redeemer. St Paul now returns to the main theme of the chapter. He makes reference to a strange custom which implicitly indicates belief in resurrection. No other source provides information about this custom and therefore it is not possible to say exactly what it involved. Probably some Corinthian Christians baptized their children in the name of Christian relatives in the hope that these relatives might also receive a share in resurrection in Christ. The Apostle is neither approving or condemning this custom; he is simply saying that it demonstrates Christian belief in the resurrection of the dead.

15:33. The quotation is from the Greek poet Menander, *Thais*.

15:35–38. Now that he has shown that the dead will rise, St Paul goes on to deal with what form this resurrection will take. He postulates certain questions (v. 35) and replies to them using comparisons taken from the vegetable, animal and mineral worlds, to help explain what this resurrection involves (vv. 36–41). He goes on to describe the qualities of the risen body (vv. 42–44), referring in particular to one of those qualities, its spiritual nature or "subtility" (vv. 44–50). He then describes the circumstances in which the general resurrection will take place (vv. 51–53), and he ends with a hymn of joy and thanksgiving for all these wonders of God (vv. 54–58).

15:36–41. The Apostle uses the analogy of a seed to explain what resurrection involves: just as a seed has to corrupt in order to yield new life, the body has to die in order to be raised up. In the process of becoming a new plant the seed takes on a new form: the plant is something distinct from the original seed; similarly, risen bodies will be endowed with new qualities which they did not have during their mortal life (cf. note on vv. 42–44).

By referring to the difference in the flesh of different animals and to the way that one star shines differently from

body which is to be, but a bare kernel, perhaps of wheat or of
Gen 1:11 some other grain. 38But God gives it a body as he has chosen, and
to each kind of seed its own body. 39For not all flesh is alike, but
there is one kind for men, another for animals, another for birds,
and another for fish. 40There are celestial bodies and there are
terrestrial bodies; but the glory of the celestial is one, and the
glory of the terrestrial is another. 41There is one glory of the sun,
and another glory of the moon, and another glory of the stars; for
star differs from star in glory.

42So is it with the resurrection of the dead. What is sown is
Phil 3:20f perishable, what is raised is imperishable. 43It is sown in
dishonour, it is raised in glory. It is sown in weakness, it is raised

---

another, St Paul is trying to explain that risen bodies are also differentiated, the differences being a function of charity (cf. *St Pius V Catechism*, 1, 12, 13).

15:42–44. These verses are the basis of the Church's teaching about the qualities of glorified bodies—impassibility or incorruptibility, glory or brightness, power or agility, subtility or spirituality. This is what the *St Pius V Catechism* has to say on the subject: "The bodies of the risen saints will be distinguished by certain transcendent endowments, which will ennoble them far beyond their former condition. Among these endowments four are specially mentioned by the Fathers, which they infer from the doctrine of St Paul and which are called 'gifts'.

"The first endowment or gift is impassibility, which shall place them beyond the reach of suffering anything disagreeable or of being affected by pain or inconvenience of any sort […]. 'What is sown' says the Apostle, 'is perishable, what is raised is imperishable' (1 Cor 15:42) […]. The next quality is brightness, by which the bodies of the saints shall shine like the sun […]. This quality the Apostle sometimes calls 'glory' […]. This brightness is a sort of radiance reflected on the body from the supreme happiness of the soul. It is a participation in that bliss which the soul enjoys, just as the soul itself is rendered happy by a participation in the happiness of God. Unlike the gift of impassibility, this quality is not common to all in the same degree. All the bodies of the saints will be equally impassible; but the brightness of all will not be the same, for, according to the Apostle, 'there is one glory of the sun, and another glory of the moon, and another glory of the stars, for star differs from star in glory' (1 Cor 15:41–42).

"To the preceding quality is united that which is called agility, by which the body will be freed from the heaviness that now presses it down, and will take on a capability of moving with the utmost ease and swiftness, wherever the soul pleases […]. Hence these words of the Apostle: 'It is sown in weakness, it is raised in glory' (1 Cor 15:43). Another quality is that of subtility, which subjects the body to the dominion of the soul, so that the body shall be subject to the soul and ever ready to follow her desires. This quality we learn from these words of the Apostle: 'It is sown a physical body, it is raised a spiritual body' (1 Cor 15:44)" (I, 12, 13).

The bodies of the reprobate do not have these qualities proper to glorified bodies (cf. *St Pius X Catechism*, 246).

in power. 44It is sown a physical body, it is raised a spiritual body. Gen 2:7
If there is a physical body, there is also a spiritual body. 45Thus it Jn 6:63
is written, "The first man Adam became a living being"; the last 2 Cor 3:6, 17
Adam became a life-giving spirit. 46But it is not the spiritual
which is first but the physical, and then the spiritual. 47The first Gen 2:7
man was from the earth, a man of dust; the second man is from
heaven. 48As was the man of dust, so are those who are of the
dust; and as is the man of heaven, so are those who are of heaven. Gen 5:3 Rom 8:29
49Just as we have borne the image of the man of dust, we shall[a] Phil 3:21
also bear the image of the man of heaven. 50I tell you this, Jn 3:5f 1 Cor 6:9
brethren: flesh and blood cannot inherit the kingdom of God, nor
does the perishable inherit the imperishable.

15:44–50. The Apostle develops what he has said about those who rise having spiritual bodies—which might seem to be a self-contradictory notion. Through descent from Adam, whose body was formed from the dust of the earth (cf. Gen 2:7), men receive an earthly animal body which is destined to perish; Christ, the new Adam, when he comes again will give his own a heavenly body, perfect and immortal: "It is called a spiritual body," St Augustine says, "not because it has become a spirit but because it is in such a way subject to the spirit, to fit it for its heavenly abode, that every kind of earthly weakness and imperfection is changed into a heavenly permanence" (*De fide et symbolo*, chap. 6).

Even in this present life the Christian should strive to reflect this image of "the man of heaven", by reproducing in himself the life of Christ: having died to sin through Baptism he has already been raised with Christ to a new life (cf. Col 3:1–4). Christ's resurrection, St Thomas Aquinas explains, "is an exemplary cause with regard to the resurrection of souls, because even in our souls we must be conformed with the risen Christ, the Apostle says (Rom 6:4–11): 'Christ was raised from the dead by the glory of the Father, that we too might walk in newness of life [...]. Christ being raised from the dead shall never die again [...] so you also must consider yourselves dead to sin', so that you 'might live with him' (1 Thess 5:10)" (*Summa theologiae*, 3, 56, 2).

15:45. Commenting on this verse, St John of Avila explains that "God created the first man and blew into his face, he gave him the breath of life, and he became a living being. *Et factus est primus Adam in animam viventem, novissimus Adam in spiritum vivificantem* (1 Cor 15:45). The second Adam was made, Jesus Christ, and not only was he given and did he have life for himself like the first Adam, but he had it for many others. Christ has a living spirit, a life-giving spirit which raises up those of us who desire to live. Let us go to Christ, let us seek Christ, who has the breath of life. No matter how evil you be, how lost, how disorientated, if you go to him, if you seek him, he will make you well, he will win you over and set you right and heal you" *(Sermon on Pentecost Sunday)*.

a. Other ancient authorities read *let us*

1 Thess 4:5–17 51 Lo! I tell you a mystery. We shall not all sleep, but we shall
Num 10:3 all be changed, 52 in a moment, in the twinkling of an eye, at the
Mt 24:31 1 Thess 4:5, 17 last trumpet. For the trumpet will sound, and the dead will be
2 Cor 5:1–5 raised imperishable, and we shall be changed. 53 For this perishable nature must put on the imperishable, and this mortal nature

---

15:51–53. St Paul succinctly describes the moment of the general resurrection, in the same kind of a way as he does in 1 Thessalonians 4:16–17: "For the Lord himself will descend from heaven with a cry of command, with the archangel's call, and with the sound of the trumpet of God. And the dead in Christ will rise first; then we who are alive, who are left, shall be caught up together with them in the clouds to meet the Lord in the air; and so we shall always be with the Lord." His use of the first person plural when speaking of those who are alive at the time of the Lord's coming does not mean that he thinks it will happen in his own lifetime: it is simply a literary device to make his description more vivid. In fact, he says in 1 Thessalonians 5:1–11 that the time of the Parousia is hidden from us, and in the present letter he includes himself among those who will be raised from the dead (cf. 1 Cor 6:14).

"We shall not all sleep, but we shall all be changed": the Vulgate, following certain codexes, had "We shall all be raised, but not all of us shall be changed." However, the New Vulgate translation seems to us to be the sounder; it is in line with the great majority of the ancient codexes and with the Greek Fathers. Also, it seems to be more in keeping with the context, for St Paul here is speaking only of the resurrection of the just (cf. general note on this chapter, above), and the Vulgate reading would be introducing a change by bringing in the resurrection of the damned, whereas it is only the bodies of the just that will be glorified. St Paul's statement that some—the just who are still alive at the time of the Lord's coming—will not die seems difficult to reconcile with the idea that death will affect everyone because it is a consequence of original sin (cf. Rom 5:12ff; 1 Cor 15:22). The *St Pius V Catechism* says that all men will die, and it explains what St Paul says in 1 Thessalonians 4:15–17 by saying that "on being taken up they shall die" [the idea, taken from St Ambrose, is that death will overtake those who are still alive—and then, immediately, the soul will return to the body: trs. note]. Some theologians argue that this is not at odds with the universality of death: God can make an exception to this rule in the case of the just in the very last generation of mankind, in the same kind of way as his exemption of the Blessed Virgin from original sin is not at odds with the universality of original sin. In the last analysis we must realize that all this is part of the whole mystery of what God will do at the end of time, and that the Magisterium of the Church has not pronounced on the matter: it is one that is open to theological research and opinion.

The repetition, four times, of the words "this mortal nature will put on" (cf. vv. 53–54) makes it quite clear that the body that will be raised will be the same body as one had on earth: "Man is to rise again in the same body with which he served God, or was a slave to the devil, that in the same body he may experience rewards and a crown of victory, or endure the severest punishments and torments" (*St Pius V Catechism*, 1, 12, 8).

must put on immortality. 54When the perishable puts on the
imperishable, and the mortal puts on immortality, then shall come
to pass the saying that is written:
"Death is swallowed up in victory."
55 "O death, where is thy victory? Is 25:8 Hos 13:14
O death, where is thy sting?"
56The sting of death is sin, and the power of sin is the law. 57But Rom 7:13
thanks be to God, who gives us the victory through our Lord Jesus
Christ.

15:54–58. The chapter ends with words of joy and thanksgiving to God for the tremendous benefits bought by the death and resurrection of our Lord, benefits which result from his victory over those enemies which had made man their slave—sin, death and the devil. Jesus Christ, by dying on the cross—offering himself to God the Father in atonement for all the offences of mankind—has conquered sin and the devil, who attained power through sin. And his victory was completed by his resurrection, which routed death. This has made it possible for his elect to be raised in glory, and is the cause of their resurrection. "In Christ", Pope John Paul II explains, "justice is done to sin at the price of his sacrifice, of his obedience 'even to death' (Phil 2:8). He who was without sin, 'God made him to be sin for our sake' (2 Cor 5:21). Justice is also brought to bear upon death, which from the beginning of man's history had been allied to sin. Death has justice done to it at the price of the death of the one who was without sin and who alone was able—by means of his own death—to inflict death upon death (cf. 1 Cor 15:54f) [...]. In this way the cross, the Cross of Christ, in fact, makes us understand the deepest roots of evil, which are fixed in sin and death; thus the Cross becomes an eschatological sign. Only in the eschatological fulfilment and definitive renewal of the world will love conquer, in all the elect, the deepest sources of evil, bringing as its fully mature fruit the kingdom of life and holiness and glorious immortality. The foundation of this eschatological fulfilment is already contained in the Cross of Christ and in his death. The fact that Christ 'was raised the third day' (1 Cor 15:4) constitutes the final sign of the messianic mission, a sign that perfects the entire revelation of merciful love in a world that is subject to evil. At the same time it constitutes the sign that foretells 'a new heaven and a new earth' (Rev 21:1) when God 'will wipe away every tear from their eyes and death shall be no more, neither shall there be mourning nor crying nor pain any more, for the former things have passed away' (Rev 21:4)" (*Dives in misericordia*, 8).

15:56–57. The Apostle here summarizes his teaching on the connexions between death, sin and the Mosaic Law, a teaching which is given in a much more elaborate form in chaps. 5–7 of his Letter to the Romans. Sin is the sting of death in the sense that death entered the world through sin (cf. Rom 5:12) to do harm to men. Sin, in its turn, grew as a result of and was reinforced by the Mosaic Law: the Law did not induce people to sin but it was the occasion of increase in sin in the sense that it made it plainer where good lay and yet did not provide the grace to enable man to avoid sin (cf. *Commentary on 1 Cor,* ad loc.).

2 Chron 15:7 58Therefore, my beloved brethren, be steadfast, immovable,
Rev 14:13 always abounding in the work of the Lord, knowing that in the Lord
your labour is not in vain.

10. MESSAGES AND WORDS OF FAREWELL

Gen 2:10 **Collection for the church of Jerusalem**
Acts 11:29 16 1Now concerning the contribution for the saints:* as I
Acts 20:7 directed the churches of Galatia, so you also are to do. 2On
the first day of every week, each of you is to put something aside
and store it up, as he may prosper, so that contributions need not
be made when I come. 3And when I arrive, I will send those
2 Cor 8:20f whom you accredit by letter to carry your gift to Jerusalem. 4If it
seems advisable that I should go also, they will accompany me.

15:58. In these last words of the chapter St Paul exhorts Christians to fight on, full of hope, convinced that work in the ordinary activities of one's day is an offering pleasing to God, a means to holiness and a way to attain final victory with Christ. "Do not ever forget that after death", St Josemaría Escrivá reminds us, "you will be welcomed by Love itself. And in that love of God you will find as well all the noble loves which you had on earth. The Lord has arranged for us to spend this brief day of our earthly existence working and, like his only-begotten Son, 'doing good' (Acts 10:38). Meanwhile we have to be on our guard, alert to the call St Ignatius of Antioch felt within his soul as the hour of his martyrdom approached: 'Come to the Father' (*Epistle to the Romans*, 8); come to your Father, who anxiously awaits you" (*Friends of God*, 221).

16:1–4. This last chapter of messages and greetings opens with a reminder about the duty to give financial help to poorer Christians, specifically those in Jerusalem (cf. 2 Cor 8:1–6; 9:1–5; Rom 15:27). This is a practice that Christians have always kept up and one which the Church does not allow them to forget—"to help the Church" (fifth commandment of the Church: cf. *Pius X Catechism*, 476) and to help those most in need. "Charitable action today can and should reach all men and all needs. Wherever people are to be found who are in want of food and drink, of clothing, housing, medicine, work, education, the means necessary for leading a truly human life, wherever there are people racked by misfortune or illness, people suffering exile or imprisonment, Christian charity should go in search of them and find them out, comfort them with devoted care and give them the help that will relieve their needs. This obligation binds first and foremost the more affluent individuals and nations" (Vatican II, *Apostolicam actuositatem*, 8).

"The first day of the week": that is, Sunday. This remark clearly indicates that from the very beginning Christians celebrated this day with special solemnity, commemorating the Lord's resurrection at liturgical and eucharistic assemblies.

16:5–9. St Paul mentions the journeys he is planning and his intention to spend a

Plans for the months ahead

[5]I will visit you after passing through Macedonia, for I intend to   Acts 19:21
pass through Macedonia, [6]and perhaps I will stay with you or even   Rom 15:24
spend the winter, so that you may speed me on my journey,   Tit 3:12
wherever I go. [7]For I do not want to see you now just in passing; I   Acts 18:21; 20:2
hope to spend some time with you, if the Lord permits. [8]But I will   Acts 19:1, 10
stay in Ephesus until Pentecost, [9]for a wide door for effective   2 Cors 2:12
work has opened to me, and there are many adversaries.   Col 4:3; Rev
[10]When Timothy comes, see that you put him at ease among   3:8; 1 Cor 4:17 Phil 2:20
you, for he is doing the work of the Lord, as I am. [11]So let no one   1 Thess 4:12
despise him. Speed him on his way in peace, that he may return to
me; for I am expecting him with the brethren.
[12]As for our brother Apollos, I strongly urged him to visit you
with the other brethren, but it was not at all his will[b] to come now.
He will come when he has opportunity.

Exhortations and greetings

[13]Be watchful, stand firm in your faith, be courageous, be strong.   Eph 6:10
[14]Let all that you do be done in love.

---

good while in Corinth. The severe warnings the letter contains should not lead us to think that the Corinthians were not devout Christians or that the Apostle did not have high regard for them; on the contrary, he had great affection for this community, which he had founded (cf. Acts 18:1–18), and if he speaks so plainly to them it is because he expects them to yield greater fruit.

16:10–12. Here he speaks of two of his co-workers. Timothy was still a young man (cf. 1 Tim 4:12; 5:1; 2 Tim 1:6–8), which is why St Paul calls on them to respect him on account of his dignity as a minister ("for he is doing the work of the Lord, as I am": v. 10). Christians have always had special regard for their priests and ministers. St Catherine of Siena places these words on Jesus' lips: "I do not wish the reverence which is due to priests to be diminished, for the reverence and respect which is shown them is not directed to them but to me, by virtue of the blood which I have given them to administer. Were it not for that, you need show them the same reverence as is shown lay people—no more [...]. Do nothing to offend them, for if you offend them you offend me, not them. That is why I have forbidden it: I have laid it down that my Christs should not be touched" (*Dialogue*, chap. 116).

Apollos was better known to the Christians of Corinth, because he had spent long periods of time among them (cf. Acts 19:1; note on 1 Cor 1:11–12).

16:13–14. St Paul summarizes the main points he wants to make. Using military language, he reminds them that the Christian life is one of struggle against one's passions and against the temptations of the devil, and that everything a Christian does should be inspired by charity. Far from being opposed virtues, fortitude and charity are perfectly

b. Or *God's will for him*

Rom 16.5 [15]Now, brethren, you know that the household of Stephanas
were the first converts in Achaia, and they have devoted themselves to the service of the saints; [16]I urge you to be subject to
such men and to every fellow worker and labourer. [17]I rejoice at the
coming of Stephanas and Fortunatus and Achaicus, because they
1 Thess 5:12 have made up for your absence; [18]for they refreshed my spirit as well
as yours. Give recognition to such men.

Acts 18:2 [19]The churches of Asia send greetings. Aquila and Prisca,
together with the church in their house, send you hearty greetings
2 Cor 13:12 in the Lord. [20]All the brethren send greetings. Greet one another
with a holy kiss.

---

complementary; a person cannot have one without the other: "If you are really going to love, you have to be strong and loyal; your heart has to be firmly anchored in faith, hope and charity. Only people who are inconstant and superficial change the object of their love from one day to the next: that's not love at all, it's the pursuit of selfishness. When love exists there is a kind of wholeness—a capacity for self-giving, sacrifice and renunciation. In the midst of that self-denial, along with painful difficulties, we find joy and happiness, a joy which nothing and no one can take away from us" (St Josemaría Escrivá, *Christ Is Passing By*, 75).

16:15–20. These personal references to his co-workers (vv. 10–12) and to other Christians, so frequent in St Paul's letters, indicate the strong sense of brother hood which imbued the early Church.

Stephanas had been baptized by St Paul (1:16). Although he was not the first Corinthian christened (cf. Acts 18:8), he receives the honorary title of "first convert of Achaia " (*primitiae* = first fruits), such is his special dedication to the rest of the faithful (v. 15). Fortunatus and Achaicus are not mentioned anywhere else; they may have been members of Stephanas' family or at least have had some special role in the Corinthian church. St Paul shows how much he appreciates their visit.

Aquila and Prisca were a married couple with special links with the Christians of Corinth, as we know from the fact that St Paul stayed at their house during his first visit to that city (Acts 18:1–3). They also made a great contribution to the apostolate in many other places; in Ephesus they furthered Apollos' education in the faith (cf. Acts 18:24–26), and later on we find them in Rome (Rom 16:3). They are an excellent example of the importance of the role of lay people in the Church.

16:20. This custom of the kiss is mentioned three other times in St Paul's letters, always with the adjective "holy" (Rom 16:16; 2 Cor 13:12; 1 Thess 5:26). Kissing was the normal form of greeting in the East (cf. Lk 7:45) but St Paul adds to it a religious significance: it is a sign of supernatural charity and of shared faith. We find it with this meaning in the early liturgy of the Church: "The kiss of peace", Tertullian wrote, "is the seal of prayer" (*De oratione*, 14).

The Roman Missal envisages that when pastoral reasons so advise, a greeting of peace may be given before Communion with some appropriate gesture. It is a sign that our Lord's instruction is being obeyed: "If you are offering your gift on the altar, and there remember that your brother has something against you, leave your gift there before the altar and go; first be

[21]I, Paul, write this greeting with my own hand. [22]If any one Gal 6:11ff
has no love for the Lord, let him be accursed. Our Lord, come![c]
[23]The grace of the Lord Jesus be with you. [24]My love be with you
all in Christ Jesus. Amen.

---

reconciled to your brother, and then come and offer your gift" (Mt 5:23–24).

16:21–24. By writing the last lines of some letters in his own handwriting, St Paul is witnessing to the whole text being his (cf. Gal 6:11; Col 4: 18; 2 Thess 3:17).

"Let him be accursed" (*"anathema sit"*): this formula (cf. Gal 1:8) has a broad meaning: apparently a person "shunned" in this way was excluded from Church meetings; it also meant that the guilty person was deserving of punishment by God (cf. note on Rom 9:3). The Apostle's harsh words are better understood in the light of 1 Cor 12:3: "No one speaking by the Spirit of God ever says, 'Jesus be cursed!'"; in other words, those who offend our Lord, because they do not love him, are deserving of maximum punishment.

"Our Lord, come!" is a translation of an Aramaic ejaculatory prayer, "*Maranatha!*" It can possibly, though not probably, be read as "*Maran atha*", meaning "Our Lord is coming" or "has come". It was such an ancient prayer and so familiar to the first Christians that St Paul did not consider it necessary to translate it. It effectively acknowledges Jesus Christ as Lord and sovereign who reigns over us from heaven and will come at the end of time in majesty and glory (cf. Phil 4:5; Rev 22:20). According to the *Didache* (10, 6) this invocation was used in early Christian times after the Eucharistic Prayer. This ancient custom has been reintroduced in the present Roman Missal as one of the acclamations the people say after the consecration rendered in English as "Christ has died, Christ has risen, Christ will come again."

St Paul's final greeting, which the Liturgy includes at the beginning of the Mass, is a form of blessing that implies a confession of faith in our Lord's presence among Christians. Commenting on these words St John Chrysostom says, "Every good shepherd and every teacher has the duty to help his brethren with advice but, above all, with prayers and entreaty" (*Hom. on 1 Cor*, 44, ad loc.).

c. Greek *Maranatha*

Introduction to the Second Letter to the Corinthians

THE REASON FOR THE LETTER

Between the First Letter to the Corinthians, written in the spring of the year 57, and the Second Letter, a number of events must have occurred which led St Paul to write again to the faithful at Corinth. It is still not clear what actually happened. It would seem that, contrary to his plans (cf. 1 Cor 16:5–9), St Paul had to leave Ephesus before Pentecost 57 (cf. Acts 20:1–2). There are indications that after he left he made a trip to Corinth, because in this second letter he tells the Corinthians he is planning a "third" visit (cf. 2 Cor 12:14; 13:1). From Ephesus he went to Troas and from there to Macedonia; it was from Macedonia that he sent this letter, towards the end of 57, as we have said in the Introduction to the first letter.

During this short visit, St Paul must have been harassed by certain Judaizers who had reached Corinth and undermined his authority. He defends himself against their accusations in chapters 10–13 especially. Apparently someone even attacked the Apostle directly (cf. 2 Cor 2:5f) or else one of his personal representatives, without the community immediately taking steps to discipline the person responsible (cf. 2 Cor 7:12). Paul's visit must have been marred by this incident, which caused much distress (cf. 2 Cor 2:1). St Paul calls on the Corinthians to forgive these offences and to set about rebuilding their community (cf. 2 Cor 2:11).

Because of this troubled visit, the Apostle wrote "out of much affliction and anguish of heart" (2 Cor 2:4) a letter which has not survived. Some scholars claim that this letter is incorporated in 2 Corinthians 10–13, but their arguments are not conclusive.

Titus had been the bearer of the now-lost letter and he managed to get the Corinthians to repent of their behaviour and restore unity (cf. 2 Cor 7:5–7). Due to the unrest caused by the silversmiths of Ephesus (cf. Acts 19:23ff) the Apostle had to leave that city and was unable to meet Titus again until he reached Macedonia: he probably met him at Philippi. Titus brought encouraging news from Corinth; St Paul, much consoled, then responded with this new letter, which the Church acknowledges as inspired.

There are, therefore, good grounds for saying that St Paul wrote four letters to the faithful at Corinth: the first, pre-canonical, which was lost, is mentioned

in 1 Corinthians 5:9; the second, written in Ephesus in spring 57, is inspired and forms part of the canon as the First Letter to the Corinthians; the third, also written in Ephesus, "with many tears" is mentioned in 2 Corinthians 2:4; the fourth was composed in Macedonia in the autumn of 57, and entered the canon as the Second Letter to the Corinthians.

CONTENT

The Second Letter to the Corinthians deals with three points, which cover three large sections:

1. *St Paul's defence against his enemies* (chaps. 1–7). Paul's apologia for himself and his apostolate delineates the role of the apostles as pillars of the Church.

2. *The collection for the church of Jerusalem* (chaps. 8–9). Already in 1 Corinthians, he was encouraging more well-to-do Christians to help their brethren in Jerusalem who were experiencing severe difficulties due to persecution and penury. In this second letter he devotes two chapters to this subject.

3. *Paul justifes his conduct* (chaps. 10–13). Because those who denied his authority were still living in Corinth, the Apostle feels obliged to make a personal apologia. He deals, item by item, with the lies that had been told about him and gives the faithful more than enough arguments to answer his caluminatiors. The apologia also acts as a preparation for his next—third—visit to Corinth, which took place at the beginning of 58.

AUTHENTICITY AND INTEGRITY

There is no doubt about this being a genuine Pauline letter. This is borne out by external evidence—quotations from and references to the letter in the works of the Fathers and ecclesiastical writers, from earliest times; internal evidence also—style, language and form of argument—clearly reflects St Paul's personality.

Some scholars have raised doubts as to whether the text that has come down to us is exactly the same as the original. These doubts refer to three passages:

a) *2 Corinthians 6:14–71.* This passage, which does somewhat break the run of the text, is, it has been argued, out of place and belongs properly to 1 Corinthians; other scholars think it is a fragment from the "pre-canonical", letter mentioned in 1 Corinthians 5:9. It must be pointed out, however, that all the Greek manuscripts and early translations do have this passage, in this place, and there is no evidence of any kind to suggest that it may once have been located elsewhere.

b) *Chapter 9.* According to some, this was not originally a run-on from the previous chapter but rather a short, independent communication addressed to the churches of Achaia. The reason given is that it deals with the same subject as chapter 8 and St Paul does not usually repeat the same ideas in adjacent texts. However, internal evidence (chapter 9 appears, even grammatically, to be a continuation of chapter 8) and, particularly, external evidence (all the manuscripts contain this chapter) argue that these two chapters are a continuity.

c) *Chapters 10–13.* Given the radical change of tone between chapters 1–9, where the Apostle speaks in a very calm and affectionate way, and these last chapters, which are severe and harsh, some scholars have viewed the latter as a separate piece of Pauline writing, quite possibly a large part of the intermediary, lost letter, written "with many tears" (cf. 2 Cor 2:3:9). However, this change of tone can be explained if one bears in mind that in these chapters the Apostle is really speaking against the agitators who wormed their way into the Corinthian community. Besides, the change of tone is not all that sudden, and the last chapters do contain some affectionate remarks (cf. 2 Cor 11:2; 12:15).

THE APOSTOLIC MINISTRY

This is one of the letters in which St Paul writes most eloquently and movingly, and one which most clearly reveals his rich personality.

In view of the circumstances which gave rise to the letter, the main thread that runs through it—except for chapters 8 and 9 which deal with the collection of money—is his defence of his apostolic ministry, providing, in that context, probably the fullest New Testament teaching on the office of apostle.

As in all his letters he begins immediately by expressing his profoujnd conviction of being "by the will of God an apostle of Christ Jesus" (2 Cor 1:1), conscious of the fact that this divine election is not the result of any personal merit: rather, it is by the mercy of God that he was given this ministry (cf. 2 Cor 4:1). God, who called him despite his shortcomings, also equips him to carry out this task (cf. 2 Cor 3:5–6).

Christian apostolate is presented as a participation in the redemptive work of Christ: the apostle is God's co-worker (cf. 2 Cor 6:1), Christ's ambassador (cf. 2 Cor 5:20), a minister of the reconciliation which God brought about through Christ (cf. 2 Cor 5:18–19). Because of this, Paul has to preach Christ faithfully—Christ in whom God's promises have been fulfilled (cf. 2 Cor 1:18–20)—and to spread the fragrance of Christ everywhere (cf. 2 Cor 2:14).

Just as Christ's work of redemption reached its climax in his passion and death, so too the Christian apostle participates in a special way in the sufferings of Christ (cf. 2 Cor 1:5). St Paul was profoundly convinced of this;

it was the motive force of his life—which explains why on occasions he speaks to us about his own experience. Here he first deals with the subject in general terms (cf. 2 Cor 4:7–12), pointing out that God allows his apostles to suffer affliction "to show that the transcendent power belongs to God and not to us" (2 Cor 4:7). A little further on an now speaking in more concrete terms, he lists a series of tribulations he has experienced, to show that in all things he is a servant of God (2 Cor 6:3–10). And towards the end of the letter he gives a long, detailed, and yet surely not a complete, list of what he has done and suffered for Christ (cf. 2 Cor 11:23–33). All of this is summed up in a single sentence: "the love of Christ controls us": "*Caritas Christi urget nos*" (2 Cor 5:14f).

To this he adds his disinterested preaching of the Gospel (cf. 2 Cor 11:7ff): he does not seek his own advantage in anything he does; all that interests him is the glory of God and the salvation of the souls entrusted to him (cf. 2 Cor 12:33ff). A love similar to that between parents and children unites him to the faithful (cf. 2 Cor 6:11–13; 12–14). They are his letter of recommendation, his credentials (cf. 2 Cor 3:2f), and one day they will be his pride before the Lord (cf. 2 Cor 1:14). That is why he is so jealous for them on God's behalf and will not allow anyone to lead them astray (cf. 2 Cor 11:2ff).

Through having to defend his apostolate against the Judaizers who have infiltrated the ranks of the Corinthians, St Paul demostrates the superiority of the New Covenant, of which he is a minister, as compared with the Old; this he does by a series of contrasts: the Old Covenant is the written code which "kills", the New is the spirit which gives life; the former led to death and condemnation, the latter gives life and justifies; the former is transient, the latter lasts forever (cf. 2 Cor 3:6–11).

THE SECOND LETTER OF PAUL TO THE CORINTHIANS

The Revised Standard Version, with notes

INTRODUCTION

Greeting

1 [1]Paul, an apostle of Christ Jesus by the will of God, and Timothy our brother. Acts 16:1ff 1 Cor 1:1f

To the church of God which is at Corinth, with all the saints who are in the whole of Achaia:

[2]Grace to you and peace from God our Father and the Lord Rom 1:7
Jesus Christ.

Thanksgiving

[3]Blessed be the God and Father of our Lord Jesus Christ, the Dan 9:9
Father of mercies and God of all comfort, [4]who comforts us in all Rom 15:5
our affliction, so that we may be able to comfort those who are in 1 Pet 1:3

1:1–11. As in almost all his letters St Paul begins with a greeting (vv. 1–2) and an act of thanksgiving to God (vv. 3–11). See the note on 1 Cor 1:2–9).

St Paul introduces himself in his usual way—"an apostle of Christ Jesus by the will of God"—but his description takes on special significance in this instance, because he will devote a substantial part of the letter to defend his calling as apostle against people who, apparently, have been questioning his credentials (cf. chaps. 10–13).

Timothy was well known to the Corinthians: he had worked with Paul in the early stages of Gospel preaching in Corinth (cf. Acts 18:5) and had visited them on another occasion as the Apostle's envoy (cf. 1 Cor 4:17; 16–10).

1:1–2. The Romans had divided Greece into two provinces—Macedonia in the north and Achaia—(comprising central Greece and the Peloponnese peninsula) in the south. Corinth was the capital of Achaia. Although St Paul had actually preached only in Corinth and Athens, the fact that he is addressing Christians "in the whole of Achaia" says much for the apostolic zeal of those first converts, who had brought the seed of the Gospel to other parts of the region.

St Paul's description of the Christians as "saints" shows that the Christian vocation involves a calling to strive hard for holiness (cf. *Lumen gentium*, 10).

"Grace and peace": "Grace is the first good, because it is the source of all good things […]. The last of all good things is peace, because it is the general goal of the mind. For, whichever way this word 'peace' is used, it is in the sense of a goal or end; in eternal glory, in government and in one's manner of living, peace has the sense of 'end'" (St Thomas Aquinas, *Commentary on 2 Cor,* ad loc.).

1:3–11. St Paul's act of thanksgiving here is rather different from that in other letters, where he gives thanks to God for the favours enjoyed by the Christians to whom he is writing, in order to make them more appreciative of their calling. Here he thanks God for consoling him in his distress.

1:3. "God and Father of our Lord Jesus Christ": the Greek can be interpreted in two ways—a) God [the Father] who is the Father of our Lord Jesus Christ; b) God [the Father] who is the God and the Father of our Lord Jesus Christ. The

Ps 34:20 any affliction, with the comfort with which we ourselves are
Col 1:24 comforted by God. 5For as we share abundantly in Christ's sufferings, so through Christ we share abundantly in comfort too.[a] 6If
we are afflicted, it is for your comfort and salvation; and if we are

---

second version, which is more likely the correct one, may seem odd at first sight: however, any difficulty disappears if one bears in mind that Jesus himself in the Gospel calls the Father "my God": "I am ascending to my Father and your Father, to my God and your God" (Jn 20:17). If one remembers that there are two natures in Christ—the divine and the human—the expression "the God of our Lord Jesus Christ" is referring to Jesus as man; whereas "the Father of our Lord Jesus Christ" refers to Jesus' sonship both as God (the eternal sonship of the Word) and as man (his conception in time in the pure womb of the Blessed Virgin, by the action of the Holy Spirit, without the intervention of man).

"The Father of mercies": a Hebraicism, often used in the Old Testament, to refer to God who has "bowels of mercy".

Mercy, according to St Augustine, is "a certain compassion for another's wretchedness that arises in our heart, whereby we feel impelled to give him every possible help" (*The City of God*, 9, 5). And so, St Thomas explains, mercy is something proper only to God: "Mercy is accounted as being proper to God therein his omnipotence is revealed to the highest degree" (*Summa theologiae*, 2–2, 30, 4), for it is capable of relieving every kind of wretchedness.

God's mercy consoles the Apostle in his sufferings, thereby enabling him to console others. It is this merciful God that is revealed to us by Jesus Christ: "The truth, revealed in Christ, about God the 'Father of mercies' (2 Cor 1:3) enables us to see him as particularly close to man, especially when man is suffering, when he is under threat at the very heart of his existence and dignity" (John Paul II, *Dives in misericordia*, 2).

1:5–11. These verses show the deep solidarity that exists among the members of Christ's mystical body, and between them and their head.

This mutual union and interaction in the members of the Church is what enables them to share spiritual benefits with one another—the communion of saints; and it flows between the three parts of the Church—the Church militant or pilgrim (on earth), the Church suffering (in Purgatory), and the Church triumphant (in heaven); it is what permits those in one part, for example, to help the others by prayer (cf. v. 11): "This is truly a tremendous mystery, upon which we can never meditate enough—that the salvation of many souls depends on the prayers and voluntary mortifications offered for that intention by the members of the mystical body of Jesus Christ" (Pius XII, *Mystici Corporis*). Conscious of this fact, the Christian should offer many prayers, sacrifices and actions for the whole Church—for the Pope, for bishops and priests, and for all the faithful, especially those most in need.

1:6. "Your comfort and salvation": "salvation" also includes spiritual health, which culminates in eternal salvation. Our desire for spiritual health, our hope of salvation, gives us the patience or fortitude we need for the battles of this life; and this patience leads to salvation.

a. Or *For as the suffering of Christ abound for us, so also our comfort abounds through Christ*

comforted, it is for your comfort, which you experience when you
patiently endure the same sufferings that we suffer. [7]Our hope for
you is unshaken; for we know that as you share in our sufferings,
you will also share in our comfort.

[8]For we do not want you to be ignorant, brethren, of the afflic- Acts 19:23
tion* we experienced in Asia; for we were so utterly, unbearably 1 Cor 15:32
crushed that we despaired of life itself. [9]Why, we felt that we had
received the sentence of death; but that was to make us rely not on
ourselves but on God who raises the dead; [10]he delivered us from so 2 Thess 4:18
deadly a peril, and he will deliver us; on him we have set our hope
that he will deliver us again. [11]You also must help us by prayer, so Rom 8:27ff
that many will give thanks on our behalf for the blessing granted us
in answer to many prayers.

PART ONE

St Paul's defence against his enemies

1. HIS SIMPLICITY AND SINCERITY

The evidence of his actions and his letters

[12]For our boast is this, the testimony of our conscience that we 1 Cor 1:17
have behaved in the world, and still more toward you, with Heb 13:18

1:8–9. "We despaired of life itself": this is the most likely reading of the Greek text; the New Vulgate translation—"we no longer had any desire to live"—has a difference nuance which we feel does not really fit in the context.

We do not know exactly what kind of affliction St Paul is referring to. It may be the riot caused by Demetrius the silversmith in Ephesus, which forced the Apostle to leave that city (cf. Acts 19:23–41). Whatever it was, St Paul uses it to stress once again that we should place our confidence in God and not in ourselves (cf., e.g., 1 Cor 1:31; 9:26–27).

1:12–7:16. In this first section of the letter, St Paul explains to the Corinthians the way he has acted in their regard; he takes issue with the criticisms some have levelled against him that his teaching is difficult to understand, that he is inspired by human motives (1:12–2:17), that he is proud and arrogant in the way he claims authority (3:1 –6:10). The last part of this section (6:11 7:16) is an exhortation to the Corinthians to win back their trust and affection.

From the evidence contained in chapters 10–13, the indications are that the people who were laying false accusations against St Paul were Judaizers, that is, people who wanted Christians to adhere to the prescriptions of the Law of Moses; hence their attempt to discredit the Apostle, the defender of the freedom

holiness and godly sincerity, not by earthly wisdom but by the
grace of God. 13For we write you nothing but what you can read
Phil 2:16 and understand; I hope you will understand fully, 14as you have
understood in part, that you can be proud of us as we can be of
you, on the day of the Lord Jesus.

---

from these restrictions which Jesus Christ won by dying on the cross. All through his life St Paul had to contend with doctrinaire attitudes of this type (cf., for example, his Letter to the Galatians).

This entire passage gives a very good idea of St Paul's ardent, passionate character: he opens his heart to the Corinthians, pouring out his affection and apostolic concern for them. This explains the frequent repetitions and digressions and the rather untidy nature of his exposition. It is a further example of the way in which the charism of divine inspiration—under whose influence he is writing—respects and takes account of the personality of the human author of Holy Scripture, the hagiographer.

1:12–14. Before explaining the way he has acted towards them, St Paul wants to make it clear that he has always been sincere and upright: he appeals to the testimony of his conscience—as he does so often (cf. Acts 23:1; 24:16; Heb 13:18)—which confirms that he has acted in line with the will of God. He stresses that this sincerity is also to be found in his letters: his adversaries may have been claiming that in these also he acted in a two-faced way; No, he says, they are perfectly straightforward.

These verses show that one of St Paul's main purposes in writing this letter is to regain the affection and trust of the Corinthians, which possibly was being eroded by the unrelenting defamation and calumny of his opponents.

As he does with other communities he founded (cf. 1 Thess 2:19; Phil 2:16), St Paul indicates that he hopes to be able to boast of them when Jesus Christ comes to judge mankind. On the expression "the day of the Lord Jesus", see the note on 1 Cor 1:8–9.

1:15–2:4. St Paul meets head-on the charge of being "all talk" and of not keeping his word—because he failed to visit to Corinth as he said he would. The itinerary given here (vv. 15–16) seems to conflict with that given in 1 Corinthians 16:5–6, where he said that he would first go to Macedonia. We do not know when he told the Corinthians about this latest projected journey: he may have done so in the letter mentioned in 2:3–4, a letter which has not come down to us (cf. note on 1:23 2:4); or perhaps at the time of a possible visit to Corinth between the first letter and this one (cf. "Introduction to St Paul's Letters to the Corinthians", above).

If this visit did not happen, he explains, it was not because he announced it too hastily or because he failed to keep his word (as his detractors must have been arguing). The main reason was his love for the Corinthians and his desire not to distress them (cf. 1:23; 2:1). It is difficult to say what he is referring to. The most likely explanation is that there had been some unpleasant incidents during his possible second visit to Corinth, incidents which culminated in some particularly serious offence to him personally (cf. note on 2:5–11). For this reason he thought it more prudent to write (2:3–4), in order to fix things up prior to a visit.

Why he has not visited Corinth

15 Because I was sure of this, I wanted to come to you first, so that
you might have a double pleasure;[b] 16 I wanted to visit you on my 1 Cor 16:5f
way to Macedonia, and to come back to you from Macedonia and
have you send me on my way to Judea. 17 Was I vacillating when I Rom 7:5ff
wanted to do this? Do I make my plans like a worldly man, ready
to say Yes and No at once? 18 As surely as God is faithful, our
word to you has not been Yes and No. 19 For the Son of God, Jesus
Christ, whom we preached among you, Silvanus and Timothy and
I, was not Yes and No; but in him it is always Yes. 20 For all the Rev 3:14ff
promises of God find their Yes in him. That is why we utter the
Amen through him, to the glory of God. 21 But it is God who estab- 1 Jn 2:27
lishes us with you in Christ, and has commissioned us; 22 he has put Eph 1:13f
his seal upon us and given us his Spirit in our hearts as a guarantee.

1:15. "A double pleasure": the first would have been their conversion, which came about through St Paul's preaching.

1:17–20. He calls on God to witness to the sincerity of his actions and to his being a man of his word. He cannot act otherwise, he explains, because he preaches Jesus Christ and follows him: and Christ is absolutely faithful and truthful (cf. Jn 14:6) and demanded sincerity in word and in deed (cf. Mt 5:37; Jas 5:12). The faithfullness of Christ—in whom it is always "Yes" (vv. 19–20)—is the model for all Christians, both those who dedicate their lives totally and exclusively to God in celibacy and those who do so through marriage. Referring to this passage, John Paul II teaches that "just as the Lord Jesus is 'the faithful witness' (Rev 3:14), the 'yes' of the promises of God (cf. 2 Cor 1:20), so Christian couples are called to participate truly in the irrevocable indissolubility that binds Christ to the Church, his bride, loved by him to the end (cf. Jn 13:1)" (*Familiaris consortio*, 20).

Relying on Christ's faithfullness the faithful are able to say that "Amen" ("So be it"), by which they adhere fully to the Apostle's teachings. From the very beginning of Christianity, the "Amen" was said at the end of the Church's public prayers (cf. 1 Cor 14:16).

Silvanus, called Silas in the Acts of the Apostles (Acts 15:40), had helped St Paul to found the Church in Corinth (cf. Acts 18:5).

1:18. "As surely as God is faithful": so translated to evoke a form of words used in taking an oath; literally, "Faithful is God."

1:21–22. As in other passages of this letter (cf. 3:3; 13:13), St Paul is here referring explicitly to the promises made of the Blessed Trinity: it is God (the Father) who has given us our "commission" (anointed us with grace), establishing us in the Son, through the gift of the Holy Spirit in our hearts.

Using three different expressions—"commissioned" (anointed), "put his seal upon us", given us his Spirit "as a guarantee"—the Apostle describes the way God acts in the soul: in Baptism the Christian is spiritually anointed with grace and incorporated into Christ; he is

b. Other ancient authorities read *favour*

Rom 1:9; 5:5ff 23But I call God to witness against me—it was to spare you that
1 Pet 5:3 I refrained from coming to Corinth. 24Not that we lord it over your
1 Jn 1:3f faith; we work with you for your joy, for you stand firm in your
1 Cor 4:21 2 faith. 1 I made up my mind not to make you another painful
Acts 20:31 visit. 2For if I cause you pain, who is there to make me glad but
the one whom I have pained? 3And I wrote as I did, so that when
I came I might not suffer pain from those who should have made

---

thereby "sealed", for he no longer belongs to himself but has become the property of Christ; and together with grace, he receives the Holy Spirit as a "guarantee", a pledge of the gifts he will receive in eternal life. All those effects of Baptism are reinforced by the sacrament of Confirmation (St Paul may well have had this sacrament in mind also, when writing these words).

Commenting on this passage St John Chrysostom explains that by this action the Holy Spirit establishes the Christian as prophet, priest and king: "In olden times these three types of people received the unction which confirmed them in their dignity. We Christians have not one of these three dignities but all three, pre-eminently. For, are we not kings, who shall infallibly inherit a kingdom? Are we not priests, if we offer our bodies as a sacrifice, instead of mere animal victims, as the Apostle says: 'I appeal to you … to present your bodies as a living sacrifice, holy and acceptable to God' (Rom 12:1)? And are we not constituted prophets if, thanks to God, secrets have been revealed to us which eye has not seen nor ear heard?" (*Hom. on 2 Cor*, 3).

"He has put his seal on us": the *St Pius V Catechism* uses these words to explain the "character" which the sacraments of Baptism, Confirmation and Order impress on the soul; Paul "not obscurely describes by the word 'sealed' a character, the property of which is to impress a seal or mark. This character is, as it were, a distinctive impression stamped on the soul which perpetually inheres and cannot be blotted out" (2, 1, 30).

1:23–2:4. St Paul gives on oath the true reason why he did not go to Corinth: he did not want to distress them further (cf. note on 2 Cor 1:15 2:4). This passage is another example of the Apostle's warm-heartedness: he rejoices with the joy and suffers with the suffering of his brothers and sisters in the faith (cf. 11:28–29; 1 Thess 2:19–20); his love for them is so great that it can compare only with that of a mother or father (cf. 1 Cor 4:15; Gal 1:19).

The letter written "with many tears" (2:4) between 1 and 2 Corinthians has not survived. It may have caused some people distress (cf. 7:8–12), but it caused him, Paul says, more distress to write it. Here we can see St Paul's fortitude: even though he suffers tremendously to think of the pain his words may cause, he does not on that account refrain from correcting when correction is called for (vv. 2–4). To act otherwise would mean consulting his own comfort. "Keeping quiet when you can and should take someone to task is the same as consenting [in what he had done] and we know that the same punishment is reserved for those who consent as for those who actually do the evil" (St Bernard, *Sermo in nativ. Ioann.*, 9).

2:2. "The one whom I have pained": this is probably no reference to one particular person but to the entire local church of

me rejoice, for I felt sure of all of you, that my joy would be the
joy of you all. [4]For I wrote you out of much affliction and anguish
of heart and with many tears, not to cause you pain but to let you
know the abundant love that I have for you.

Forgiveness for those who offend us

[5]But if any one has caused pain, he has caused it not to me, but in 1 Cor 5:1
some measure —not to put it too severely—to you all. [6]For such a Col 3:13
one this punishment by the majority is enough; [7]so you should
rather turn to forgive and comfort him, or he may be overwhelmed

---

Corinth, which Paul is addressing as a single individual, as is apparent in the following verses.

2:5–11. Here St Paul refers to the main cause of his distress. These words have often been seen as referring to the man guilty of incest whom the Apostle condemned in 1 Corinthians 5:1–5. However, many scholars are of the view that the passage has to do with some grave personal offence against Paul (cf. 7:12) or one of his co-workers, during his second visit to Corinth (cf. note on 1:5 2:4). The offender would have been a Judaizer who had the support of a minority in the Corinthian church.

This offence may have been the main reason for the letter written "with many tears" and for the dispatch of Titus to Corinth (cf. 2:13; 7:6–16) to obtain reparation for that fault (although in v. 9 St Paul makes it clear that he is more interested in testing the community's obedience than in atonement for the offence: cf. also 7:12). Most of the faithful reacted very well, condemning the person responsible and possibly excluding him from the community. Now the Apostle asks them to forgive the man, in case excessive severity lead him to despair.

2:5. The causes of the Apostle's distress are also a cause of distress for the Christians of Corinth. This solidarity of sentiment should always exist between the faithful and their bishops: they should make their bishop's concerns their own and help him to carry out his ministry, especially by daily prayer for his person and intentions. "Nor should they [the laity] fail to commend to God in their prayers those who have been placed over them, who indeed keep watch as having to render an account of our souls, that they may do this with joy and not with grief (cf. Heb 13:17)" (*Lumen gentium*, 37).

2:7. By encouraging the faithful to forgive and console the sinner? St Paul wants to ensure that he is not tempted to despair of God's pardon. The devil can sometimes tempt a person to feel that nothing can be done about his present sins—or to feel his past sins as a dead weight.

Should we find ourselves in this situation, St John of Avila advises, "let us realize that he [the devil] is not the offended party, nor is he the judge who must judge us. It is God we offend when we sin, and he it is who must judge men and devils too. Therefore, let us not be concerned when the accuser accuses us; rather let us be consoled by the thought that he who is the offended party and the judge pardons and absolves us, by means of our repentance and his ministers and sacraments" (*Audi, filia*, chap. 18).

by excessive sorrow. [8]So I beg you to reaffirm your love for him.
[9]For this is why I wrote, that I might test you and know whether
Lk 10:16 you are obedient in everything. [10]Any one whom you forgive, I
also forgive. What I have forgiven, if I have forgiven anything, has
Lk 22:31 been for your sake in the presence of Christ, [11]to keep Satan from
Eph 4:27 gaining the advantage over us; for we are not ignorant of his designs.

Paul's eagerness for news

Acts 14:27 [12]When I came to Troas to preach the gospel of Christ, a door was
1 Cor 16:9 opened for me in the Lord; [13]but my mind could not rest because
I did not find my brother Titus there. So I took leave of them and
went on to Macedonia.

2:10. "In the presence of Christ": that is, seen by Christ and with his approval. It can also be translated, as the New Vulgate does, as "in the person of Christ".

2:11. Satan's aim is clear—to separate people from God and thereby bring about their eternal damnation. He devotes all his energies to this end. "Be sober, be watchful", St Peter warns. "Your adversary the devil prowls around like a roaring lion, seeking some one to devour" (1 Pet 5:8).

And yet, the Christian should not go in fear of the devil. The saints sometimes compare him to a chained dog: he barks a lot, but he can bite only those who go near him. We have many ways of keeping out of his reach, such as, for example, "fleeing from dangerous occasion [of sin], keeping our senses under control, frequent reception of the sacraments, and having recourse to prayer" (*St Pius X Catechism*, 317).

2:12–17. St Paul begins to tell the Corinthians that it was his love and concern for them which led him to go into Macedonia looking for Titus (vv. 12–13) No sooner has he said this—without even mentioning his meeting with Titus—than he pours out his soul in thanksgiving to God (vv. 14–16) for the good reports his co-worker brought him (cf 7:4–16). This exultation leads him on to another subject—defence of himself against new accusations (chaps 3–7) v. 17 is a kind of transition to that theme and he does not go back to his original line of thought until chapter 7 (vv. 4ff).

2:12–13. Troas was a coastal town in Asia Minor, north of Ephesus, on the road to Greece; the Apostle had passed through it in the course of his second missionary journey (cf. Acts 16:8–10). He heads for Troas again when he has to leave Ephesus on account of the silversmiths' riot (cf. Acts 19:23ff), and he begins to preach. Things must have looked very promising: "a door was opened for me in the Lord" (cf. 1 Cor 16:8–9).

However, his concern over the Christians of Corinth was such that he could not wait for Titus, and headed off into Macedonia to find him. Like St Paul, the primary concern of every Christian should be to confirm believers in the faith. This was what our Lord did immediately after his resurrection: he appeared first to the Apostles and to some of the disciples.

14But thanks be to God, who in Christ always leads us in triumph,
and through us spreads the fragrance of the knowledge of him
everywhere. 15For we are the aroma of Christ to God among those 1 Cor 1:18
who are being saved and among those who are perishing, 16to one a Lk 2:34
fragrance from death to death, to the other a fragrance from life to
life. Who is sufficient for these things? 17For we are not, like so 1 Pet 4:11
many, pedlars of God's word; but as men of sincerity, as commissioned by God, in the sight of God we speak in Christ.

2:14–16. Led in triumph by God (v. 14), the Apostle spreads everywhere the sweet fragrance of Christ—a simile taken from the custom of burning incense along the route of a victorious general. Every Christian who tries to live in keeping with the faith he professes also spreads this same fragrance: "Every Christian should make Christ present among men. He ought to act in such a way that those who know him sense 'the aroma of Christ' (2 Cor 2:15). People should be able to recognize the Master in his disciples" (*Christ Is Passing By*, 105).

And, as in the case of the Master—"set for the fall and rising of many in Israel, and for a sign that is spoken against" (Lk 2:34)—this sweet aroma spread by his disciples is a cause of salvation for some and of condemnation for others. "The Gospel", Chrysostom comments, "continues to spread everywhere a sweet and precious savour, even though some be lost who do not believe it. It is not the Gospel but their own perverseness that brings about their perdition; I would even say that the perdition of the wicked is a proof of the sweetness of this spiritual honey. The salvation of the good and the perdition of the wicked declare the efficacy of the Gospel. The sun, because it is especially bright, hurts the eyes of the weak; and Jesus is come 'for the fall and rising of many'" (*Hom. on 2 Cor*, 5).

2:14. "Leads us in triumph": the Apostle seems to be thinking of the "triumphs" or the triumphal processions of great generals in ancient times, when they paraded at the head of their army on returning home from victorious campaigns; similarly, God passes through the world in triumph by means of the Gospel, associating the apostles with his progress.

Referring to the great sufferings which this victory involves, St Jerome comments: "God's triumph is the sufferings the martyrs undergo in Christ's battle, the shedding of their blood, and their joy in the midst of tribulation. For when a person sees the way martyrs are made to suffer, and how steadfastly they hold their ground, and how they glory in their suffering, the aroma of knowledge of God is spread among the Gentiles, and they begin to realize that if the Gospel were not true, no one would defend it at such cost" (*Epist.*, 150, *ad Hedibiam*).

2:16–17. The second part of v. 16—"Who is sufficient for these things?", who is up to them—and v. 17 act as an introduction to the Apostle's defence of his ministry in 3:1–6:10.

Here he contrasts the sincerity of his preaching with the way the false apostles (who are attacking him and trying to undermine his authority) adulterate the word of God being more interested in personal success than in Christ' success "Adulterating the word of God", St Gregory the Great explains, "is either seeing in it something which is not really there, or seeking from it not spiritual fruit

2. THE IMPORTANCE OF APOSTOLIC OFFICE

Paul's letter of recommendation

Acts 18:27
Rom 16:1
1 Cor 5:12
1 Cor 9:2
Ex 24:12; Prov 3:3; 7:3; Jer 31:33; Ezek 11:19; 36:26
Rom 15:16

3 1Are we beginning to commend ourselves again? Or do we
need, as some do, letters of recommendation to you, or from
you? 2You yourselves are our letter of recommendation, written
on your[c] hearts, to be known and read by all men; 3and you show
that you are a letter from Christ delivered by us, written not with
ink but with the Spirit of the living God, not on tablets of stone but
on tablets of human hearts.

---

but the adulterous offspring of human praise. Sincere preaching [of the word of God] means seeking the glory of its author and creator" (*Moralia*, 22 12).

3:1–6:10. St Paul is accused of pride by his opponents, who have misinterpreted his references in letters to his apostolic journeys (cf., e.g., 1 Cor 2:7–16; 4:14–21). Because he realizes that what he said above (cf. 2:14–16) may give rise to further charges, and before going on to confront his adversaries directly—as he does in chapters 10–13 particularly—he begins a long exposition on apostolic ministry. He explains the superiority of his ministry over that of the Old Covenant (3:4–18), the authority and sincerity with which that ministry is carried out (4:1–6), and the trials and sufferings it involves (4:7–5:10); and he goes on to justify his own conduct and the principles which inspire it (cf. 5:11–6:10).

3:1–3. Letters of recommendation were commonly used in St Paul's time (cf., e.g., Acts 9:2; 15:22–30). Given the ironical way he refers to them in v. 1, it would appear that his enemies had arrived in Corinth with some letter of this sort. Paul can present a more eloquent and powerful letter—the Corinthians themselves: it was his preaching that led to their conversion. He says this, St John of Avila comments, "because they were an adequate letter to explain who St Paul was and how beneficial his presence had been. And he says that this letter is one which all can know and read, because anyone, no matter how uncultured he be, even if he does not understand the language of words, can understand the language of good example and virtue, whose results he can see, and so can come greatly to esteem one who has such fine disciples" (*Audi, filia*, chap. 34).

This letter has been written by Christ himself. St Paul and his co-workers have always acted as scribes, and what has been written on the hearts of the Corinthians and on the Apostle's own heart has been written by the Holy Spirit himself.

These references to "tablets of stone" and "human hearts" are connected with the history of the people of Israel. On Sinai God gave Moses tablets of stone containing the Covenant. Centuries later, at the time of the Babylonian exile, which was a punishment from God for the unfaithfullness of the chosen people, God, through his prophets, promised to make a New Covenant—a Law written on their hearts (cf. Jer 31:33), giving them a new heart and new soul, taking away their heart of stone and giving them a heart of flesh (cf. Ezek 11:19; 36:26).

c. Other ancient authorities read *our*

Christian ministry is greater than that of the Old Covenant

4 Such is the confidence that we have through Christ toward God.
5 Not that we are competent of ourselves to claim anything as
coming from us; our competence is from God, 6 who has made us
competent to be ministers of a new covenant, not in a written code
but in the Spirit; for the written code kills, but the Spirit gives life.

Jer 31:31
Jn 6:63
Rom 7:6
1 Cor 11:25

3:4–11. In these verses St Paul deals with a subject which he discusses more fully in his letters to the Romans and the Galatians—the superiority of the New Covenant, through which Christ reconciles men to God their Father, over the Old Covenant which God made with Moses. Here he just outlines the superiority of the apostles' ministry over that of Moses. The latter was a dispensation of death and condemnation (vv. 6, 7, 9) and it was temporary (vv. 7, 11); that of the apostles, on the other hand, is a dispensation of life and salvation (vv. 6–9) and it is permanent (v. 11). So, if the ministry of Moses was splendid, that of the apostles will be all the more splendid.

When St Paul speaks of a ministry of "death" and "condemnation" (vv. 7, 9), this does not mean that the Old Covenant was not something in itself holy and just, but that the Law of Moses—part of that Covenant—although it pointed the way to righteousness, was inadequate because it did not give people the resources to conquer sin. It is in this sense that the Old Law can be said to have involved death and condemnation: for it made the sinner more conscious of the gravity of his sin, thereby increasing his guilt (cf. Romans, chaps. 7–8 and corresponding notes): "For," St Thomas Aquinas explains, "it is more serious to sin against the natural law when that law is written down, than against the natural law on its own" (*Commentary on 2 Cor,* ad loc.).

3:5. The Magisterium of the Church quotes these words when teaching the need for the Holy Spirit to enlighten and inspire man to enable him to accept the truths of faith or choose some good connected with eternal salvation (cf. Second Council of Orange, can. 7). Therefore, anyone is foolish who thinks he can claim as his own the good deeds he does or the apostolic results he obtains: they are in fact a gift from God. As St Alphonsus says, "the spiritual man dominated by pride is the worst kind of a thief because he is stealing not earthly things but the glory that belongs to God [...]. For, as the Apostle tells us, we, on our own, cannot do anything good or even have a good thought (cf. 2 Cor 3:5) [...]. Therefore, whenever we do something good, let us say to the Lord, 'We return to thee, O Lord, what we have received from thee' (cf. 1 Chron 29:14)" (*Treasury of Preaching Material*, 2, 6).

3:6. Taking up again the simile he has used in v. 3, St Paul speaks about the "letter" and the "Spirit" (cf. Rom 2:29; 7:6) to show the difference between the Law of the Old Testament and that of the New. The Law of Moses is the "letter" insofar as it simply publishes the precepts which man must keep, without providing the grace necessary for keeping them. The New Law, on the other hand, is the "Spirit", because it is the Holy Spirit himself who, through grace, spreads charity in the hearts of the faithful (cf. Rom 5:5), and charity is the fullness of the Law (cf. Rom 13:10). "What is predominant in the law of the New Testament," St Thomas Aquinas explains,

Ex 34:30 [7]Now if the dispensation of death, carved in letters on stone,
came with such splendour that the Israelites could not look at
Moses' face because of its brightness, fading as this was, [8]will not
the dispensation of the Spirit be attended with greater splendour?
Deut 27:26 [9]For if there was splendour in the dispensation of condemnation, the
Rom 1:17; 3:21 dispensation of righteousness must far exceed it in splendour.
Ex 34:29ff [10]Indeed, in this case, what once had splendour has come to have
no splendour at all, because of the splendour that surpasses it.
[11]For if what faded away came with splendour, what is permanent
must have much more splendour.

[12]Since we have such a hope, we are very bold, [13]not like
Moses, who put a veil over his face so that the Israelites might not

---

"and whereon all its efficacy is based, is the grace of the Holy Spirit, which is given through faith in Christ. Consequently the New Law is chiefly the grace itself of the Holy Spirit, which is given to those who believe in Christ" (*Summa theologiae*, 1–2, 106, 1). Hence the law of the Gospel can also be called the law of the Spirit (cf. Rom 8:2), the law of grace or the law of charity.

After pointing out how the Law of Moses laid down the death penalty for certain sins, St John Chrysostom comments: "The Law, if it lays hold of a murderer, puts him to death; the Gospel, if it lays hold of a murderer, enlightens him and gives him life [...]. How lofty is the dignity of the Spirit, seeing that his tables are better than those former ones [the "tables" of the Law], for they do even greater things than raising a dead man to life! For the death from which grace delivers us is much more lamentable than physical death" (*Hom. on 2 Cor*, 6).

3:7–10. In the book of Exodus (34:29–35) we are told that the face of Moses, when he came down from Mount Sinai, where he had been speaking to God, was radiant with light. So bright was it—for it reflected the splendour of God—that the Israelites were afraid to go near him.

St Paul here refers to that event to show the superiority of the New Covenant.

3:12–18. In these verses St Paul continues to stress that the apostolic ministry is superior to that of Moses; he recalls the veil with which Moses covered his face after he had been speaking to Yahweh. The Apostle declares that this event was a symbol: the veil served Moses not only to hide the radiance of his face at the start but also to hide the gradual disappearance of this splendour, which was temporary, like the covenant it symbolized. By contrast, the ministers of the New Covenant proclaim it with unveiled face (v. 18); they have no need to hide anything; they speak out clearly and boldly (v. 12) because the light of the Gospel which they irradiate is permanent and everlasting.

Pursuing this comparison, St Paul explains that the Jews who do not believe in Christ still have this veil covering their eyes, and cannot even understand the Old Testament, for that Testament can only be properly understood with the help of the light brought by Jesus Christ, the fullness of revelation. "The economy of the Old Testament was deliberately so orientated," Vatican II teaches, "that it should prepare for and declare in prophecy the coming of Christ, redeemer of all men, and of the

see the end of the fading splendour. [14]But their minds were Rom 10:4; 11:25
hardened; for to this day, when they read the old covenant, that
same veil remains unlifted, because only through Christ is it taken
away. [15]Yes, to this day whenever Moses is read a veil lies over
their minds; [16]but when a man turns to the Lord the veil is removed. Ex 24:34
[17]Now the Lord is the Spirit, and where the Spirit of the Lord is, Rom 11:23–26
there is freedom. [18]And we all, with unveiled face, beholding[d] the Ex 16:7–10 Mt 17:2
glory of the Lord, are being changed into his likeness from one Rom 8:29ff 1 Jn 3:2
degree of glory to another; for this comes from the Lord who is
the Spirit.*

---

messianic kingdom. God, the inspirer and author of the books of both Testaments, in his wisdom has so brought it about that the New should be hidden in the Old and that the Old should be made manifest in the New. For, although Christ founded the New Covenant in his blood (cf. Lk 22:20; 1 Cor 11:25), still the books of the Old Covenant, all of them caught up into the Gospel message, attain and show forth their full meaning in the New Testament (cf. Mt 5:17; Lk 24:27; Rom 16:25–26; 2 Cor 3:14–16) and, in their turn, shed light on it and explain it" (*Dei Verbum*, 15f).

3:17. Various interpretations are given to these words. Some apply them to Christ and say that when St Paul says "the Lord is the Spirit" he is referring to Christ's being the deep, spiritual meaning underlying the letter of the Old Testament, which the Jews cannot grasp because of the veil which covers their minds (cf. vv. 15–16). Many Fathers, on the other hand, apply the verse to the Holy Spirit, making him the subject of the sentence; thus, they would read it as "The Spirit is the Lord." In any event, the presence of Christ, or of the Holy Spirit, in the New Testament, brings with it the freedom of the children of God obtained by Christ, who has freed us from sin and from the Old Law (cf. Rom 8:1–17; Gal 4:21–31).

Christian freedom does not mean ignoring any bond or law; it means accepting God's commandments not in a servile way, out of fear of punishment, but rather as children who strive to do what pleases their Father God. St Augustine explains this as follows: "That person lives under the weight of the law who avoids sin out of fear of the punishment which the law threatens, rather than because of any liking for righteousness [...]. If you let yourselves be led by the Spirit, you will not be under the weight of the law; of that law which is considered to inspire fear and terror, and does not instil charity or a taste for goodness; charity which has been poured into our hearts, not by the letter of the law, but by the Holy Spirit, who has been given us. That is the law of freedom, not the law of slavery, for it is the law of charity, not that of fear" (*De natura et gratia*, 57, 67).

3:18. The teaching expounded in the previous verses leads to this final joyous declaration, in which St Paul sums up the Christian's spiritual itinerary. Just as Moses' face reflected the splendour of Yahweh after he had been speaking to him on Sinai, Christians in their lives reflect the splendour of Christ, whom they contemplate in faith: "The Christian who has been cleansed by the Holy Spirit

d. Or *reflecting*

Paul's sincere conduct

Rom 1:16
1 Cor 7:25
1 Thess 2:4f
2 Thess 1:12

4 [1]Therefore, having this ministry by the mercy of God,[e] we do
not lose heart. [2]We have renounced disgraceful, underhanded

---

in the sacrament of regeneration", St John Chrysostom comments, "is changed, as the Apostle puts it, into the likeness of Jesus Christ himself. Not only does he behold the glory of the Lord but he takes on some of the features of God's glory [...]. The soul who is regenerated by the Holy Spirit receives and radiates the splendour of the heavenly glory that has been given him" (*Hom. on 2 Cor*, 7).

Moreover, whereas the radiance of Moses was a passing thing, that of Christians steadily increases the more they become identified with Christ through docility to the influence of grace on their souls: "Docility, because it is the Holy Spirit who, with his inspirations, gives a supernatural tone to our thoughts, desires and actions. It is he who leads us to receive Christ's teaching and to assimilate it in a profound way. It is he who gives us the light by which we perceive our personal calling and the strength to carry out all that God expects of us. If we are docile to the Holy Spirit, the image of Christ will be formed more and more fully in us, and we will be brought closer every day to God the Father" (St Josemaría Escrivá, *Christ Is Passing By*, 135).

4:1–6. St Paul here stresses one of the main points he makes in this part of the letter—the sincerity and genuineness of his conduct, and therefore his rejection of anything to do with lies or underhand ways (cf. 1:12, 17; 2:17; 3:1). Unlike the false apostles, his own aim in preaching is to teach the truth of Jesus Christ without any dilution or compromise (cf., for example, 1 Cor 1:18–25; Gal 2:11ff). If, in spite of everything, there are still some who cannot see the truth of the Gospel, the reason lies in their bad dispositions, which allow the devil—the god of this world (cf. Jn 12:31; 14:30; Eph 2:2)—to darken their minds. That is why they fail to recognize the divinity of Jesus Christ, who is the perfect image of God the Father (vv. 4–6).

The Apostle's approach to preaching as here described reminds us of the need to speak out clearly, very conscious that we have been entrusted by God with a treasure which we must respect and venerate and pass on in all its fullness. "Every evangelizer", Pope Paul VI teaches, "is expected to have a reverence for truth, especially since the truth that he studies and communicates is none other than revealed truth and hence, more than any other, a sharing in the first truth which is God himself. The preacher of the Gospel will therefore be a person who even at the price of personal renunciation and suffering always seeks the truth that he must transmit to others. He never betrays or hides truth out of a desire to please men or in order to astonish or to shock, nor for the sake of originality or from a desire to make an impression. He does not refuse truth. He does not obscure revealed truth by being too idle to search for it, or for the sake of his own comfort, or out of fear. He does not neglect to study it. He serves it generously, without making it serve him" (*Evangelii nuntiandi*, 78).

4:1. "By the mercy of God": as the RSV note points out, this in Greek reads "as we have received mercy", or "by the

e. Greek *as we have received mercy*

ways; we refuse to practise cunning or to tamper with God's word,
but by the open statement of the truth we would commend ourselves
to every man's conscience in the sight of God. [3]And even if our 1 Cor 1:18
gospel is veiled, it is veiled only to those who are perishing. [4]In their Col 1:15
case the god of this world has blinded the minds of the unbelievers, 2 Thess 2:11
to keep them from seeing the light of the gospel of the glory of
Christ, who is the likeness of God. [5]For what we preach is not 2 Cor 1:24
ourselves, but Jesus Christ as Lord, with ourselves as your servants[f] Gen 1:3
for Jesus' sake. [6]For it is the God who said, "Let light shine out of Is 9:1
darkness," who has shone in our hearts to give the light of the Heb 1:3
knowledge of the glory of God in the face of Christ.

---

mercy which has been done unto us", which goes back to a Jewish turn of phrase designed to avoid mentioning the name of God. St Paul also speaks in the plural, out of modesty.

4:4. "To keep them from seeing the light of the Gospel": this is what the Greek text means. The New Vulgate translation is somewhat different, but it can be interpreted as meaning the same.

Jesus Christ, perfect God and perfect man, is the perfect likeness of God (cf. Col 1:15; Heb 1:3). "For something to be a perfect image of something else," St Thomas explains, "three things are needed, and all three are to be found perfectly in Christ. The first of these is likeness; the second is the origin; and the third, complete equality. For if there were any dissimilarity between the image and him whose image it is, or if the image did not have its origin in the other, or if there were not perfect equality, given that both have the same nature, there would be no perfect image [...]. Since all three are to be found in Christ—he is the likeness of the Father, he proceeds from the Father, and he is equal to the Father—he is called the image of God in the fullest and most perfect sense" (*Commentary on 2 Cor,* ad loc.). Moreover, as perfect man he is the visible likeness of the invisible God: "No one has ever seen God; the only Son, who is in the bosom of the Father, he has made him known" (Jn 1:18).

4:5. St Paul often calls Jesus "Lord" (cf., e.g., Rom 10:9; 1 Cor 5:6;12:3; Phil 2:11). This is a clear assertion of Christ's divinity, for "Lord" is the word the Greeks normally use when translating "Yahweh" (cf. note on 1 Cor 8:4–6).

This faith in Christ's divinity is so basic to Christianity that St Paul can sum up the essence of his preaching in these words: we preach Christ as Lord.

4:6. Contrary to what happens in the case of those who resist belief (v. 4), God has enlightened the hearts of Christians with the light of faith. St Paul recalls the moment when God created light (cf. Gen 1:3), as if to refer to the new creation resulting from the infusion of the light of faith (cf. 2 Cor 5:17), which only happens with God's intervention: for "no one can 'assent to the Gospel preaching as he must in order to be saved without the enlightenment and inspiration of the Holy Spirit, who gives all men their joy in assenting to and believing the truth' (Second Council of Orange). Hence, faith itself [...] is essentially a gift of God; and the act of faith is a work pertaining to salvation. By this act man offers to God

f. Or *slaves*

The trials Paul has experienced

Acts 9:15 2 Cor 5:1 7But we have this treasure* in earthen vessels, to show that the
1 Cor 4:9–13 2 Cor 6:4–10 transcendent power belongs to God and not to us. 8We are
afflicted in every way, but not crushed; perplexed, but not driven
to despair; 9persecuted, but not forsaken; struck down, but not

---

himself a free obedience inasmuch as he concurs and cooperates with God's grace, when he could resist it" (Vatican I, *Dei Filius*, chap. 3).

Commenting on this passage of the letter, St Thomas Aquinas gives a beautiful description of the way faith works in the soul of St Paul, and in that of every Christian: "Previously, that is, before being converted to Christ, we were dark, like you and like those in whom the brightness of Christ's glory does not shine. Now, however, after Christ calling us through his grace, the darkness has been taken away from us, and the power of the glory of the clear light of Christ is shining in us. It shines so powerfully in us that not only are we given light to let us see: we also have light for giving to others" (*Commentary on 2 Cor,* ad loc.). A Christian should not hide the light of his faith but should use it to enlighten those around him.

4:7–5:10. St Paul now describes the sufferings and tribulations which the apostolic ministry involves and which are like those of Jesus Christ himself (4:7–12). He goes on to show that faith and hope in the resurrection and in heaven sustain Christ's ministers in their sufferings (4:13 5–10).

4:7–12. In contrast to the greatness of the Gospel—the "treasure" entrusted to them by God—St Paul emphasizes the limitations of its ministers: they are "earthen vessels" (v. 7). To illustrate this he describes the afflictions and persecution to which he finds himself subjected and in which God's grace always comes to his aid.

In some way these sufferings of the apostles and of all Christians reproduce in their lives the sufferings of Christ in his passion and death. In his case his suffering opened the way to his glorification after the Resurrection; similarly his servants, even in this life, are experiencing an anticipation of the life they will attain in heaven; this helps them overcome every kind of affliction.

4:7. St Paul again stresses that the effectiveness of all his apostolic activity comes from God (cf., e.g., 1 Cor 1:26–31; 2 Cor 3:5); he it is who places his treasures in poor earthenware vessels. The image the Apostle uses—which is reminiscent of the clay which God used to make Adam (cf. Gen 2:7)—helps Christians realize that through grace they bear in their souls a wonderful treasure, God himself; like earthen vessels they are very fragile and they need to be put together again in the sacrament of Confession. As a gloss on these ideas, St Josemaría Escrivá taught that Christians by bearing God in their souls are enabled to live at one and the same time "in heaven and on earth, divinized: but knowing that we are of the world and made of clay, with the frailty that is typical of clay—an earthenware pot which our Lord has deigned to use in his service. And whenever it has been broken, we have gone and riveted the bits together again, like the prodigal son: 'I have sinned against heaven and against you …'" (quoted in Bernal, *Monsignor Josemaría Escrivá de Balaguer*).

4:8–9. The Apostle's words assure the Christian that he or she can always count

destroyed; [10]always carrying in the body the death of Jesus, so that 1 Cor 15:31
the life of Jesus may also be manifested in our bodies. [11]For while
we live we are always being given up to death for Jesus' sake, so
that the life of Jesus may be manifested in our mortal flesh. [12]So
death is at work in us, but life in you.*

Paul is sustained by hope of heaven

[13]Since we have the same spirit of faith as he had who wrote, "I Ps 116:10
believed, and so I spoke," we too believe, and so we speak,

---

on God's help: no matter what trials they have to undergo, victory can be attained with the grace of God as happened in St Paul's case. "God is faithful, and he will not let you be tempted beyond your strength, but with temptation will also provide you the way of escape, that you may be able to endure it" (1 Cor 10:13). Moreover, St Paul's example reminds us that more or less severe suffering and tribulation will be a normal thing in the lives of Christ's followers; theirs will never be a comfortable, trouble-free life. "If it is your ambition to win the esteem of men, if you desire to be well-regarded and seek only a life of ease, you have gone astray [...]. In the city of the saints, entrance is given, and rest and eternal rule with the King, only to those who have made their way along the rough, narrow way of tribulation" (Pseudo-Macarius, *Homilies*, 12, 5).

4:10–11. As happened in St Paul's case, in their daily lives Christians must relive the sufferings of Christ through self-denial and penance: this is part of following Christ and imitating him. "The Christian vocation is one of sacrifice, penance, expiation. We must make reparation for our sins—for the many times we turned our face aside so as to avoid the gaze of God—and all the sins of mankind. We must try to imitate Christ, 'always carrying in the body the death of Christ', his abnegation, his suffering on the cross, 'so that the life of Jesus may also be manifested in our bodies' (2 Cor 4:10). Our way is one of immolation and, in this denial, we find *gaudium cum pace*, both joy and peace" (St Josemaría Escrivá, *Christ Is Passing By*, 9).

Self-denial, mortification, does not have to be something very overt; it should be practised in the ordinary circumstances of life—for example, by being punctual for appointments, carefully fulfilling one's duties, treating everyone with as much charity as possible, accepting little setbacks in a good-humoured way (cf. St Josemaría Escrivá, *Friends of God*, 138).

4:10. "The death of Jesus": more exactly, the "dying" of Christ: the Greek word refers to the situation of someone who is dying.

4:12. In the apostles, and also in other Christians, the paradox of Jesus' life is verified: his death is the cause of life for all men. "Unless a grain of wheat falls into the earth and dies, it remains alone, but if it dies, it bears much fruit" (Jn 12:24). Afflictions and tribulations, physical and moral pain, daily self-denial and penance, cause Christ's disciple to die to himself and, if united to the sufferings of his Master, they become a source of life for others through the communion of saints.

4:13–18. The Apostle explains where he gets the strength to bear all the tribulations

Rom 1:4ff; 8:11ff   14knowing that he who raised the Lord Jesus will raise us also
Rom 3:24ff   with Jesus and bring us with you into his presence. 15For it is all
2 Cor 1:3–6   for your sake, so that as grace extends to more and more people it
may increase thanksgiving, to the glory of God.
16So we do not lose heart. Though our outer nature is wasting
away, our inner nature is being renewed every day. 17For this slight

---

of this life—from his hope in the resurrection and his expectation of being in heaven with those to whom he is writing (v. 14). There is nothing selfish about this desire for heaven: it helps us to stay true to the faith and it enables us to see all the sufferings of this life as something transitory and slight (v. 17), a necessary step to heaven and a way to obtain incomparably greater happiness. "If we wish to enjoy the pleasures of eternity," St Alphonsus reminds us, "we must deprive ourselves of the pleasures of time. 'Whoever would save his life will lose it' (Mt 16:25) [...]. If we wish to be saved, we must all be martyrs, either by the tyrant's sword or through our own mortification. Let us have this conviction—that everything we suffer is nothing compared with the eternal glory that awaits us. 'I consider the sufferings of this present time are not worth comparing with the glory that is to be revealed to us' (Rom 8:18). These momentary afflictions will bring us eternal happiness (cf. 2 Cor 4:17)" (*Treasury of Preaching Material*, 2, 9).

4:13. The Apostle's faith leads him to keep on preaching, despite all the difficulties this may involve. There is nothing else he can do: he is convinced that his faith is what can save the world and he cannot but strive to spread it. If he acted otherwise it would mean his faith was asleep and he did not truly love others. "When you find that something has done you good," St Gregory the Great explains, "try to bring it to the attention of others. You should, therefore, desire others to join you on the ways of the Lord. If you are going to the forum or the baths, and you meet someone who is not doing anything, you invite him to go along with you. Apply this earthly custom to the spiritual sphere, and as you make your way to God, do not do so alone" (*In Evangelia homiliae*, 6, 6).

4:14. What inspires St Paul's apostolic activity and enables him to bear all the difficulties it involves, is his firm belief in resurrection in glory, the basis and cause of which is Christ's resurrection. He also has the hope of sharing this happiness in heaven, in the presence of God, with all the faithful for whose salvation he is working on earth.

4:15. After reminding the Corinthians that all the sufferings he has been speaking about he has borne for their sake (cf. 4:5), St Paul tells them what motivates him most—the greater glory of God, to whom the faithful should turn in deep gratitude (cf. 1:11; 9:12). This should be man's primary attitude to God—one of profound adoration and thanksgiving for all his benefits, as we are daily reminded in the Preface of the Mass.

"If life's purpose were not to give glory to God, how contemptible, how hateful it would be" (St Josemaría Escrivá, *The Way*, 783).

4:16. These words sum up one of the paradoxes of the Christian life. Whereas the outer man—his perishable body—is wasting away due to tribulation and

momentary affliction is preparing for us an eternal weight of glory
beyond all comparison, 18because we look not to the things that are Heb 11:1–3
seen but to the things that are unseen; for the things that are seen are
transient, but the things that are unseen are eternal.

5 1For we know that if the earthly tent we live in is destroyed, we Job 4:19
have a building from God, a house not made with hands, eternal in Rom 8:23
the heavens. 2Here indeed we groan, and long to put on our heavenly Phil 3:20

---

affliction, the inner man—the life of the soul—is growing and being renewed day by day, until the point comes when it reaches its full growth in heaven. This is something which can clearly be seen in the lives of the saints: in the midst of sufferings of every kind, and despite the fact that their life is wasting away, their soul is being rejuvenated, their joy ever on the increase.

"When does this outer nature waste away?", St John Chrysostom asks. "When it is scourged, when it is persecuted time out of number. Yet 'our inner nature is being renewed every day.' How? By faith, by hope and by charity. Therefore, we must brave these dangers which threaten us. In proportion as our body suffers our soul must grow in hope and become brighter, as gold becomes brighter the greater the heat in which it is being refined" (*Hom. on 2 Cor*, 9).

4:17–18. St Paul's attitude is a model for the kind of supernatural way the Christian should look at everything that happens to him; he should try to see events the way God does, and should concentrate his attention on the things that cannot be seen. By doing this he will more easily recognize the difference between the fleetingness and insignificance of the good things of this life, and the solidity and permanence of heaven: "Let us drink to the last drop the chalice of pain in this poor present life. What does it matter to suffer for ten years, twenty, fifty ... if afterwards there is heaven for ever, for ever, ... for ever?

"And above all—rather than because of the reward, *propter retributionem*—what does suffering matter if we suffer to console, to please God our Lord, in a spirit of reparation, united to him on his Cross; in a word: if we suffer for Love? ..." (St Josemaría Escrivá, *The Way*, 182).

The Magisterium of the Church recalls these words of the Apostle to show that the actions of the just man help him attain heaven (cf. Council of Trent, *De iustificatione*, chap. 16).

5:1–10. The Apostle continues to express his hope in the resurrection and in heaven as something which gives him confidence and a sense of security in the midst of his difficulties. He uses various similes to show the contrast between the present life and the future life: now we live as it were in a tent, a flimsy and temporary dwelling, whereas an eternal building awaits us (v. 1); our mortal life will be clothed in immortality (vv. 2–4; cf. 1 Cor 15:42–44); now we make our way by faith: we do not yet see God; later we shall see him face to face (vv. 6–7; cf. 1 Cor 13:12). Yet, although St Paul harbours the hope of these great blessings and desires to be with his Lord (v. 8), he does not lose sight of the fact that he has to strive now to please God, because he must one day appear before Christ his Judge (vv. 9–10).

5:1. In the Bible we often find life on earth being compared to a fragile, impermanent building: here St Paul speaks of it

dwelling, [3]so that by putting it on we may not be found naked. [4]For
while we are still in this tent, we sigh with anxiety; not that we would
be unclothed, but that we would be further clothed, so that what is
Rom 8:16, 23 mortal may be swallowed up by life. [5]He who has prepared us for this
Eph 1:13f 2 Cor 1:22 very thing is God, who has given us the Spirit as a guarantee.
[6]So we are always of good courage; we know that while we are
1 Cor 13:12 at home in the body we are away from the Lord, [7]for we walk by
Phil 1:21–23 faith, not by sight. [8]We are of good courage, and we would rather be

---

as a "tent". This underlines the fact that life is short and temporary (cf., e.g., Is 38:12; 2 Pet 1:13); in heaven, however, our body will be glorified by God, and will then be an enduring mansion for the soul to inhabit.

The Apostle's words have been taken up in one of the prefaces of Masses for the dead: "Lord, for your faithful people life is changed, not ended. When the body of our earthly dwelling lies in death we gain an everlasting dwelling place in heaven" (*Roman Missal*).

5:2–8. St Paul compares the mortal body to a garment; in eternal life it will be further clothed with glory and immortality. The thought of this makes him yearn to be already with Christ. Years later, writing to the Philippians about this, he tells them of the tension he feels in his soul when he remembers that there is still need for his work as an apostle: "I am hard pressed between the two. My desire is to depart and be with Christ, for that is far better. But to remain in the flesh is more necessary on your account" (Phil 1:23–24).

At the same time, he feels a natural repugnance of death and says that he would like not to have to die—to be deprived of his body (vv. 3–4)—so that he would be invested with immortality without having to pass through death, that is, to be alive when Christ comes in glory. But if it means that he can be with his Lord, he is more than ready to have his soul leave his body (v. 8).

5:3. The New Vulgate reads this verse as "if indeed after we are stripped we are not to find ourselves naked." It expresses his hope that once his mortal body has been taken from him he will not find himself without a body (naked) but instead dressed in a glorious body.

The main Greek manuscripts, however as also many early translations (including the Vulgate), literally say "if it is the case that we shall then find ourselves clothed, and not naked".

5:5. The Apostle once again compares the Holy Spirit to a "guarantee" (cf. 1:22), in this case a guarantee of eternal happiness: the Holy Spirit, who dwells in the soul through grace (cf. 1 Cor 3:16; 6:19), is, as it were, the pledge of immortality. in the same way as he played a part in Christ's resurrection, he will also cause our bodies to rise again (cf. Rom. 8:1).

"At the beginning, God created man for this goal [eternal glory]," St John Chrysostom explains. "He has kept and confirmed this purpose by regenerating us in Baptism. And the pledge or guarantee of this which he has given us is an incalculable treasure, for it is the Holy Spirit himself poured into our souls" (*Hom. on 2 Cor*, 10).

5:6. St Alphonsus comments on this verse: "This is not our fatherland; we are here, as it were, passing through, like pilgrims [...]. Our fatherland is heaven,

away from the body and at home with the Lord. [9]So whether we are
at home or away, we make it our aim to please him. [10]For we must
all appear before the judgment seat of Christ, so that each one may
receive good or evil, according to what he has done in the body.

Mt 25:19–31
Jn 5:27
Rom 2:16; 14:10
Heb 11:6ff

The ministry of reconciliation

[11]Therefore, knowing the fear of the Lord, we persuade men; but
what we are is known to God, and I hope it is known also to your

2 Cor 4:2
1 Pet 1:17

---

which we have to merit by God's grace and our own good actions. Our home is not the one we live in at present, which serves only as a temporary dwelling; our home is eternity" (*Shorter Sermons*, 16).

However, as St Paul himself shows elsewhere (cf. Acts 16:16–40; 22:22–29; Rom 13:1–7; 2 Thess 3:6:13), this "being away" from the Lord does not mean that a Christian should not concern himself with the building up of the earthly city. On the contrary, he should do everything he can to build a world which is more and more like what God wants it to be. Vatican II, for example, exhorts "Christians, as citizens of both cities, to perform their duties faithfully in the spirit of the Gospel. It is a mistake to think that, because we have here no lasting city, but seek the city which is to come (cf. Heb 13:14), we are entitled to shirk our responsibilities; this is to forget that, by our faith, we are bound all the more to fulfil these responsibilities according to the vocation of each one (cf. 2 Thess 3:6–13; Eph 4:28) [...]. The Christian who shirks his temporal duties shirks his duties towards his neighbour, neglects God himself and endangers his eternal salvation. Let Christians follow the example of Christ who worked as a craftsman; let them be proud of the opportunity to carry out their earthly activity in such a way as to integrate human, domestic, professional, scientific and technical enterprises with religious values, under whose supreme direction all things are ordered to the glory of God" (*Gaudium et spes*, 43).

5:7. St Paul here speaks of faith as light which shows us the way as we progress towards eternal life. However, when we reach our home in heaven we will no longer need the light of faith, because God himself and Christ will be our light (cf. Rev 21:23).

5:8–10. Here we can see the Apostle's firm conviction that he will meet the Lord the moment he dies. In other passages of Holy Scripture the same truth is stated (cf. Lk 16:22–23; 23:43), and the Magisterium of the Church has defined that souls will receive their eternal reward or punishment immediately after death—or after they pass through purgatory, if they have to do so (cf. Benedict XII, *Benedictus Deus*, *Dz–Sch*, 1000).

This sentence of reward or punishment—given at the particular judgment and ratified at the general judgment at the end of time—is based on the person's merits gained during his life on earth, for once he has died he can no longer merit. In view of this judgment St Paul exhorts us to do everything we can in this life to please the Lord. "Does your soul not burn with the desire to make your Father–God happy when he has to judge you?" (St Josemaría Escrivá, *The Way*, 746).

5:11–21. After outlining the trials of the apostolic ministry and the hope in the

2 Cor 3:1 conscience. [12]We are not commending ourselves to you again but
giving you cause to be proud of us, so that you may be able to
answer those who pride themselves on a man's position and not
on his heart. [13]For if we are beside ourselves, it is for God; if we
Gal 2:20 are in our right mind, it is for you. [14]For the love of Christ controls

---

resurrection which sustains him (cf. 4:7 5:10), St Paul explains that the underlying motive for everything he does is the love of Christ (v. 14); this includes both Christ's love for man and man's love for Christ.

In the course of describing this love, St Paul gives a very brief summary of what Redemption involves. God has reconciled men to himself through Jesus Christ, who bore the sins of the world and died for all men to prevent their sins being imputed to them. Moreover, God has made the apostles ambassadors of Christ to bring men "the message of reconcilation" (v. 19), exhorting them to regain God's friendship.

5:11–12. These verses act as a link with the previous section, where St Paul finished speaking about the judgment of God. He makes it clear that he is not saying all this to convince God, who knows him very well already, but to influence the Corinthians: it is not his own glory he seeks; he wants to give the Corinthians arguments they can use against his detractors, those Judaizers who boasted so much about external things—perhaps their Jewish background or their contacts with the other apostles (cf. chaps. 10–12)—but who had no genuinely virtuous deeds to show.

The "fear of the Lord" which St Paul speaks about is not a servile fear, which forces one to work for God for fear of being punished otherwise. It is a gift of the Holy Spirit, which encourages a person to serve God and work for him, and to avoid sin because it separates him from God his Father. This gift of the Holy Spirit enabled St Teresa of Avila to say, "There could be no worse death for me than to think I had offended God" (*Life*, chap. 34, 9).

5:13. His enemies must have been saying that St Paul was mad because they could not understand his lofty teaching or the zeal with which he preached. Something similar happened to our Lord (cf. Mk 3:21; Jn 10:20) and will recur again in the Apostle's case some years later (cf. Acts 26:24ff). St Paul does not mind people thinking he is out of his mind—he bears it for God—because of the folly of his preaching (cf. 1 Cor 1:18ff), or his zeal for souls (cf. 2 Cor 11): such behaviour obviously does not make sense to someone who has no supernatural outlook. "Take no notice. Madness has always been the term that 'prudent' people apply to God's works. Forward! Without fear!" (*The Way*, 479).

When he speaks of his reasonableness in dealing with the Corinthians, St Paul may be referring to the numerous explanations he has to give them in regard to their way of behaving.

5:14–15. The Apostle briefly describes the effects of Christ's death, a death he underwent out of love for man; elsewhere at greater length (cf. Rom 6:1–11; 14:7–9; Gal 2:19–20; 2 Tim 2:11) he goes into this doctrine which is so closely connected with the solidarity that exists between Jesus Christ and the members of his mystical body. Christ, the head of that body, died for all his members: and they

us, because we are convinced that one has died for all; therefore
all have died. [15]And he died for all, that those who live might live
no longer for themselves but for him who for their sake died and
was raised.

[16]From now on, therefore, we regard no one from a human
point of view; even though we once regarded Christ from a human
point of view, we regard him thus no longer. [17]Therefore, if any
one is in Christ, he is a new creation;[g] the old has passed away,

Rom 14:7f
1 Thess 2:6

Is 43:18; 65:17
Rom 8:1–10
Gal 6:15
Rev 21:5

---

have mystically died to sin with and in him. Christ's death, is moreover, the price paid for men—their ransom which sets them free from the slavery of sin, death and the devil. As a result of it we belong no longer to ourselves but to Christ (cf. 1 Cor 6:19), and the new life—in grace and freedom—which he has won for us we must live for his sake: "None of us lives to himself, and none of us dies to himself. If we live, we live to the Lord, and if we die, we die to the Lord [...]. For to this end Christ died and lived again, that he might be Lord both of the dead and of the living" (Rom 14:7–9).

"What follows from this?", St Francis de Sales asks. "I seem to hear the voice of the Apostle like a peal of thunder startling our heart: It is easy to see, Christians, what Christ desired by dying for us. What did he desire but that we should become like him? 'That those who live might live no longer for themselves but for him who for their sake died and was raised.' How powerful a consequence is this in the matter of love! Jesus Christ died for us; by his death he has given us life; we only live because he died; he died for us, by us, and in us; our life then is no longer ours, but belongs to him who has purchased it for us by his death: we are therefore no more to live to ourselves but to him; not in ourselves but in him; nor for ourselves but for him" (*Treatise on the Love of God*, book 7, chap. 8).

"The love of Christ controls us", urges us: with these words St Paul sums up what motivates his tireless apostolic activity—the love of Jesus, so immense that it impels him to spend every minute of his life bringing this same love to all mankind. The love of Christ should also inspire all other Christians to commit themselves to respond to Christ's love, and it should fill them with a desire to bring to all souls the salvation won by Christ. "We are urged on by the charity of Christ (cf. 2 Cor 5:14) to take upon our shoulders a part of this task of saving souls. Look: the redemption was consummated when Jesus died on the Cross, in shame and glory, 'a stumbling block' to the Jews and folly to the Gentiles (1 Cor 1:23). But the redemption will, by the will of God, be carried out continually until our Lord's time comes. It is impossible to live according to the heart of Jesus Christ and not to know that we are sent, as he was, 'to save sinners' (1 Tim 1:15), with the clear realization that we ourselves need to trust in the mercy of God more and more every day. As a result, we will foster in ourselves a vehement desire to live as co-redeemers with Christ, to save all souls with him" (*Christ Is Passing By*, 120f).

5:16–17. "Even though we once regarded Christ from a human point of view": Paul seems to be referring to knowledge based

g. Or *creature*

Rom 5:10 behold, the new has come. 18All this is from God, who through
Christ reconciled us to himself and gave us the ministry of
reconciliation; 19that is, in Christ God was reconciling[h] the world

only on external appearances and on human criteria. Paul's Judaizing opponents *do* look on things from a human point of view, as Paul himself did before his conversion. Nothing he says here can be taken as implying that St Paul knew Jesus personally during his life on earth (he goes on to say that now he does not know him personally); what he is saying is that previously he judged Christ on the basis of his own Pharisee prejudices; now, on the other hand, he knows him as God and Saviour of men.

In v. 17 he elaborates on this contrast between before and after his conversion, as happens to Christians through Baptism. For through the grace of Baptism a person becomes a member of Christ's body, he lives by and is "in Christ" (cf., e.g., Gal 6:15; Eph 2:10, 15f; Cor 3:9f); the Redemption brings about a new creation. Commenting on this passage St Thomas Aquinas reminds us that creation is the step from non-being to being, and that in the supernatural order, after original sin, "a new creation was necessary, whereby (creatures) would be made with the life of grace; this truly is a creation from nothing, because those without grace are nothing (cf. 1 Cor 13:2) […]. St Augustine says, 'for sin is nothingness, and men become nothingness when they sin'" (*Commentary on 2 Cor,* ad loc.).

"The new has come": St John Chrysostom points out the radical change which the Incarnation of our Lord Jesus Christ has brought about, and the consequent difference between Judaism and Christianity: "Instead of the earthly Jerusalem, we have received that Jerusalem which is above; and instead of a material temple we have seen a spiritual temple; instead of tablets of stone, holding the divine Law, our own bodies have become the sanctuary of the Holy Spirit; instead of circumcision, Baptism; instead of manna, the Lord's body; instead of water from a rock, blood from his side; instead of Moses' or Aaron's rod, the cross of the Saviour; instead of the promised land, the kingdom of heaven" (*Hom on 2 Cor*, 11).

5:18–21. The reconciliation of mankind with God—whose friendship we lost through original sin—has been brought about by Christ's death on the cross. Jesus, who is like men in all things "yet without sinning" (Heb 4:14), bore the sins of men (cf. Is 53:4–12) and offered himself on the cross as an atoning sacrifice for all those sins (cf. 1 Pet 2:22–25), thereby reconciling men to God; through this sacrifice we became the righteousness of God, that is, we are justified, made just in God's sight (cf. Rom 1:17; 3:24–26 and notes). The Church reminds us of this in the rite of sacramental absolution: "God, the Father of mercies, through the death and resurrection of his son has reconciled the world to himself […]."

Our Lord entrusted the apostles with this ministry of reconcilation (v. 18), this "message of reconcilation" (v. 19), to pass it on to all men: elsewhere in the New Testament it is described as the "message of salvation" (Acts 13:26), the "word of grace" (Acts 14:3; 20:32), the "word of life" (1 Jn 1:1). Thus, the apostles were our Lord's ambassadors to

h. Or *in Christ God was reconcilling*

to himself,* not counting their trespasses against them, and
entrusting to us the message of reconciliation. [20]So we are ambassadors for Christ, God making his appeal through us. We beseech
you on behalf of Christ, be reconciled to God. [21]For our sake he
made him to be sin* who knew no sin, so that in him we might
become the righteousness of God.

Jn 8:46
Gal 3:13
1 Cor 1:30
Phil 3:9
1 Pet 2:22, 24

---

men, to whom St Paul addresses a pressing call: "be reconciled to God", that is, apply to yourselves the reconcilation obtained by Jesus Christ—which is done mainly through the sacraments of Baptism and Penance. "The Lord Jesus instituted in his Church the sacrament of Penance, so that those who have committed sins after Baptism might be reconciled with God, whom they have offended, and with the Church itself whom they have injured" (John Paul II, *Aperite portas*, 5).

5:21. "He made him to be sin": obviously St Paul does not mean that Christ was guilty of sin; he does not say "to be a sinner" but "to be sin". "Christ had no sin," St Augustine says; "he bore sins, but he did not commit them" (*Enarrationes in Psalmos*, 68, 1, 10).

According to the rite of atoning sacrifices (cf. Lev 4:24; 5:9; Num 19:9; Mic 6:7; Ps 40:7) the word "sin", corresponding to the Hebrew *ašam*, refers to the actual act of sacrifice or to the victim being offered. Therefore, this phrase means "he made him a victim for sin" or "a sacrifice for sin". It should be remembered that in the Old Testament nothing unclean or blemished could be offered to God; the offering of an unblemished animal obtained God's pardon for the transgression which one wanted to expiate. Since Jesus was the most perfect of victims offered for us, he made full atonement for all sins. In the Letter to the Hebrews, when comparing Christ's sacrifice with that of the priests of the Old Testament, it is expressly stated that "every priest stands daily at his service, offering repeatedly the same sacrifices, which can never take away sins. But when Christ had offered for all time a single sacrifice for sins, he sat down at the right hand of God, then to wait until his enemies should be made a stool for his feet. For by a single offering he has perfected for all time those who are sanctified" (Heb 10:11–14).

This concentrated sentence also echoes the Isaiah prophecy about the sacrifice of the Servant of Yahweh; Christ, the head of the human race, makes men sharers in the grace and glory he achieved through his sufferings: "upon him was the chastisement that made us whole, and with his stripes we are healed" (Is 53:5).

Jesus Christ, burdened with our sins and offering himself on the cross as a sacrifice for them, brought about the Redemption: the Redemption is the supreme example both of God's justice—which requires atonement befitting the offence—and of his mercy, that mercy which makes him love the world so much that "he gave his only Son" (Jn 3:16). "In the Passion and Death of Christ—in the fact that the Father did not spare his own Son, but 'for our sake made him sin'—absolute justice is expressed, for Christ undergoes the Passion and Cross because of the sins of humanity. This constitutes even a 'superabundance' of justice, for the sins of man are 'compensated for' by the sacrifice of the Man-God. Nevertheless, this justice, which is properly justice 'to God's measure', springs completely from

Paul, a true servant of Christ

Is 49:8
Lk 4:19, 21

6 [1]Working together with him, then, we entreat you not to accept
the grace of God in vain. [2]For he says,
"At the acceptable time I have listened to you,
and helped you on the day of salvation."

---

love, from the love of the Father and of the Son, and completely bears fruit in love. Precisely for this reason the divine justice revealed in the Cross of Christ is 'to God's measure', because it springs from love and is accomplished in love, producing fruits of salvation. The *divine dimension of redemption* is put into effect not only by bringing justice to bear upon sin, but also by restoring to love that creative power in man thanks to which he once more has access to the fullness of life and holiness that come from God. In this way, redemption involves the revelation of mercy in its fullness" (John Paul II, *Dives in misericordia*, 7).

6:1–10. St Paul concludes his long defence of his apostolic ministry (cf. 3:1 6:10) by saying that he has always tried to act as a worthy servant of God. First he calls on the Corinthians to have a sense of responsibility so that the grace of God be not ineffective in them (vv. 1–2), and then he briefly describes the afflictions this ministry has meant for him. Earlier, he touched on this subject (cf. 4:7–12), and he will deal with it again in 11:23–33.

6:1–2. St Paul exhorts the faithful not to accept the grace of God in vain—which would happen if they did not cultivate the faith and initial grace they received in Baptism and if they neglected the graces which God continues to send them. This exhortation is valid for all Christians: "We receive the grace of God in vain", St Francis de Sales points out, "when we receive it at the gate of our heart, without allowing it to enter: we receive it without receiving it; we receive it without fruit, since there is no use in feeling the inspiration if one does not consent unto it. And just as the sick man who has the medicine in his hands, if he takes only part of it, will only partially benefit from it, so too, when God sends a great and mighty inspiration to move us to embrace his love, if we do not avail of it in its entirety, we shall benefit from it only partially" (*Treatise on the Love of God*, book 2, chap. 11).

The Apostle urges them to cultivate the grace they have been given, using a quotation from Isaiah (49:8): the right time has come, the day of salvation. His words recall our Lord's preaching in the synagogue of Nazareth (cf. Lk 4:16–21).

The "acceptable time" will last until Christ comes in glory at the end of the world (in the life of the individual, it will last until the hour of his death); until then, every day is "the day of salvation": "*Ecce nunc dies salutis*, the day of salvation is here before us. The call of the good shepherd has reached us: '*ego vocavi te nomine tuo*, I have called you by name' (Is 43:1). Since love repays love, we must reply: '*ecce ego quia vocasti me*, Here I am, for you called me' (1 Sam 3:5) [...]. I will be converted, I will turn again to the Lord and love him as he wants to be loved" (St Josemaría Escrivá, *Christ Is Passing By*, 59).

6:3. St Paul had previously warned the Corinthians of the danger of being a stumbling block for others (cf. 1 Cor 8:8–13). All Christians need to heed this

Behold, now is the acceptable time; behold, now is the day of
salvation. [3]We put no obstacle in any one's way, so that no fault
may be found with our ministry, [4]but as servants of God we
commend ourselves in every way: through great endurance, in
afflictions, hardships, calamities, [5]beatings, imprisonments, tumults,
labours, watching, hunger; [6]by purity, knowledge, forbearance, Rom 12:9

---

warning, especially those who have positions of greater responsibility in the Church. The Apostle feels urged by this duty to live always as a "servant of God", ensuring that his conduct is always in accord with what he preaches and avoiding doing anything which could in any way be misunderstood (cf. 1 Cor 9:12; 10:32f).

6:4–10. In these verses the Apostle outlines what his desire to be a faithful servant of God has involved. First he speaks of the sufferings he has borne with great patience (vv. 4f); then of the virtues which help him overcome these severe trials (vv. 6–7a); then of the weapons which he uses in this difficult spiritual combat (vv. 7b–8a); and finally, in a series of antitheses he contrasts human judgments of himself and his co-workers, with the true facts (vv. 8b–10).

"These words of the Apostle", St Josemaría Escrivá comments, "should make you happy, for they are, as it were, a ratification of your vocation as ordinary Christians in the middle of the world, sharing with others—your equals —the enthusiasms, the sorrows and the joys of human life. All this is a way to God. What God asks of you is that you should, always, act as his children and servants.

"But these ordinary circumstances of life will be a divine way only if we really change ourselves, if we really give ourselves. For St Paul uses hard words. He promises that the Christian will have a hard life, a life of risk and of constant tension. How we disfigure Christianity if we try to turn it into something nice and comfortable! But neither is it correct to think that this deep, serious way of life, which is totally bound up with all the difficulties of human existence, is something full of anguish, oppression or fear.

"The Christian is a realist. His supernatural and human realism helps him appreciate all the aspects of his life—sorrow and joy, his own and other people's suffering, certainty and doubt, generosity and selfishness. The Christian experiences all this, and he confronts it all, with human integrity and with the strength he receives from God" (*Christ Is Passing By*, 60).

6:4–5. Patience, which enables the Apostle to endure all his difficulties, is a virtue necessary for the Christian's life, which helps him endure physical or moral pain with resilence, peace and serenity. St Teresa of Avila has a poem which touches on this: "Let nothing disturb thee; let nothing dismay thee; all things pass; God never changes; patience attains all that it strives for. He who has God finds he lacks nothing: God alone suffices" (*Poems*, 30).

6:6–7. Forbearance is a virtue which helps us to seek a very distant good, one which will take a long time to obtain, and to endure this delay without losing heart. St Paul includes it among the fruits of the Holy Spirit (cf. Gal 5:22).

"By the Holy Spirit": that is, directed in apostolic work by the Holy Spirit, who

Eph 6:11ff kindness, the Holy Spirit, genuine love, 7truthful speech, and the
power of God; with the weapons of righteousness for the right hand
and for the left; 8in honour and dishonour, in ill repute and good
Ps 118:18 2 Cor 4:10f repute. We are treated as impostors, and yet are true; 9as unknown,
and yet well known; as dying, and behold we live; as punished, and
Rom 8:32 Phil 4:12f yet not killed; 10as sorrowful, yet always rejoicing; as poor, yet
making many rich; as having nothing, and yet possessing everything.

---

enlightens him in his preaching and moves the hearts of his hearers, preparing them to accept the Gospel.

"By truthful speech": St Paul has already spoken to the Corinthians about this, by pointing to the sincerity of his preaching, the fact that he does not mislead them or flatter them (cf. 2:17; 4:2). It is not the preacher's skill but the "power of God" that causes his message to be accepted (cf. 1 Cor 2:4f).

6:7–8. "The weapons of righteousness": St Paul also calls these the "armour of light" (Rom 13:12) as opposed to that of iniquity (cf. Rom 6:13) and worldly weapons (cf. 2 Cor 10:4), and he will write further about this, using the metaphor of combatants of his time: "Take the whole armour of God, that you may be able to withstand in the evil day, and having done all, to stand. Stand therefore, having girded your loins with truth, and having put on the breastplate of righteousness, and having shod your feet with the equipment of the gospel of peace; above all taking the shield of faith, with which you can quench all the flaming darts of the evil one. And take the helmet of salvation, and the sword of the Spirit, which is the word of God" (Eph 6:13–17).

This reference in v. 7 to weapons for the right hand and for the left comes from the practice of soldiers, who wielded offensive weapons—lance and sword—with one hand and carried defensive weapons—the shield—in the other.

7:8–10. In seven antitheses the Apostle contrasts his enemies' mistaken opinions about himself and his co-workers, with the true facts. As a faithful follower of our Lord, he bears out what Jesus said would happen: "A disciple is not above his teacher, nor a servant above his master; it is enough for the disciple to be like his teacher, and the servant like his master. If they have called the master of the house Beelzebul, how much more will they malign those of his household" (Mt 10:24f).

It is quite possible for a disciple of Christ to meet up with opposition from people who misread his actions or his intentions, for there are some who "when they discover something which is clearly good, poke at it to see if there is not something bad hidden underneath" (St Gregory the Great, *Moralia*, 6, 22). As in St Paul's case, disciples should keep on working, and not let themselves become disillusioned or bitter: "With me it is a very small thing I should be judged by you" (1 Cor 4:3).

6:10. "Always rejoicing": even in the midst of severe difficulties St Paul always manages to remain cheerful. Joy is a Christian gift, the result of divine filiation—our realization that God is our Father, that he is all-powerful and that he has boundless love for us; it is something we should never lose: "let them be sad who are determined not to recognize that they are children of God" (St Josemaría Escrivá, *Friends of God*, 108).

3. ST PAUL OPENS HIS HEART

His love for the Corinthians

11Our mouth is open to you, Corinthians; our heart is wide. 12You Ps 119:32
are not restricted by us, but you are restricted in your own affections. 13In return—I speak as to children—widen your hearts also. 1 Cor 4:14

Contact with unbelievers

14Do not be mismated with unbelievers. For what partnership have
righteousness and iniquity? Or what fellowship has light with
darkness? 15What accord has Christ with Belial?[i] Or what has a

---

"As having nothing, yet possessing everything": "They have nothing and possess everything who are the lovers of God, for when they lack earthly things, they are content to say, 'My Lord, you alone are enough for me', and that leaves them fully satisfied" (St Alphonsus, *The Love of Our Lord Jesus Christ*, chap. 14).

6:11–7:16. In these verses, which form the end of the first part of the epistle (cf. note on 1:12 7:16), St Paul makes an energetic appeal to the Corinthians in an attempt to win back their trust and affection. Here again we can see his immense affection and concern for his flock, the same as moved him to write elsewhere: "My little children, with whom I am again in turmoil until Christ be formed in you" (Gal 4:19).

This long exhortation consists of two parts, separated by some verses in which he speaks about relations with unbelievers (6:14 7:1).

6:11–13. St Paul has ample room in his heart for the Corinthians; he now asks them to reciprocate this affection (cf. 7:2). His love for God had expanded his heart, enabling him to love all men, which was why he wanted to bring everyone to know Christ. "Charity is a virtue which inflames and consumes", St John Chrysostom explains. "It was this that opened Paul's mouth and enlarged his heart [...]. For nothing is bigger than Paul's heart which loved all the faithful with more ardour than even the most passionate of hearts; his love was not divided and therefore weakened: it abided in him and communicated itself to all equally" (*Hom. on 2 Cor*, 13).

6:14–7:1. In this passage St Paul deals with the Corinthians' relations with pagans. The apparently sudden change of subject, coupled with the continuity between vv. 6:13 and 7:2, has led some scholars to think that this passage may originally have been placed elsewhere: however, all the codexes and early translations carry it here.

The Apostle had already spoken to the Corinthians about this subject (cf. 1 Cor 5:9–13; 10:14–33). What led him to bring it up again may have been his feeling that the Corinthians were on too close terms with pagans and were thereby putting their faith at risk (cf. 6:1) and were keeping his teaching and his affection at bay. He begins by using an image which literally has to do with animals being yoked together; he may have taken this from certain Old Testament passages

i. Greek *Beliar*

Lev 26:12
Ezek 37:27
Jn 14:23
1 Cor 3:16

believer in common with an unbeliever? 16What agreement has
the temple of God with idols? For we are the temple of the living
God; as God said,

"I will live in them and move among them,
"and I will be their God,
"and they shall be my people.

---

which forbade animals of different species being yoked together (cf. Deut 22:10; Lev 19:19). He wants to stress the great difference there is between a Christian and a pagan, a point which he now develops.

As was pointed out in the note on 1 Corinthians 5:9–10, he is not saying that Christians should avoid all contact with unbelievers; if they did that, they would be depriving them of the chance of conversion; what he does want to stress is that they should avoid contacts which put their faith at risk.

"Christian education will always have to remind the student today of his privileged position and of his resultant duty to live in the world but not in the way of the world, according to the prayer of Jesus for his disciples: 'I do not pray that thou shouldst take them out of the world, but that thou shouldst keep them from the evil one. They are not of the world, as I am not of the world' (Jn 17:15–16). And the Church adopts this prayer as its own.

"But this distinction is not a separation. Neither is it indifference or fear or contempt. When the Church distinguishes itself from human nature, it does not oppose itself to human nature, but rather unites itself to it. Just as the doctor who, realizing the danger inherent in a contagious disease, not only tries to protect himself and others from such infection, but also dedicates himself to curing those who have been stricken, so too the Church does not make an exclusive privilege of the mercy which the divine goodness has shown it, nor does it distort its own good fortune into a reason for disinterest in those who have not shared it; but rather in its own salvation it finds an argument for interest in and for love for anyone who is either close to it or can at least be approached through universal effort to share its blessings" (Paul VI, *Ecclesiam suam*, 46f).

6:14. By applying to himself in Baptism the merits obtained by Jesus Christ, the Christian has shed unrighteousness, he has been justified in God's sight; the pagan, on the other hand, is still in the state of "iniquity", that is, has not yet received the fruit of Redemption (cf. 1 Cor 1:30). The light of faith has also taken the Christian out of the darkness in which the person estranged from God is plunged: "once you were darkness, but now you are light" (Eph 5:8).

6:15. "Belial" or "Beliar" is a Hebrew word which literally means "useless", of no value, and which was used with the same meaning as "perverse". St Paul uses it here to refer to Satan, the leader of the evil spirits; this is the sense it is given in Jewish non-bibical literature.

6:16. "We are": the RSV and some Greek manuscipts read thus. The New Vulgate, in the line with another series of Greek manuscripts, reads "you are". Both mean the same.

This teaching about the Christian being the temple of God (also to be found elsewhere: cf. 1 Cor 3:16f; 6:19f) makes it clear that the Blessed Trinity dwells in the soul in grace.

[17]Therefore come out from them,
and be separate from them, says the Lord,
and touch nothing unclean;
then I will welcome you,
[18]and I will be a father to you,
and you shall be my sons and daughters,
says the Lord Almighty."

Is 52:11 Jer 51:45 Ezek 20:34, 41 Rev 18:4

2 Sam 7:8, 14 Is 43:6 Jer 31:9; 32:38 Hos 1:10

7 [1]Since we have these promises, beloved, let us cleanse ourselves from every defilement of body and spirit, and make holiness perfect in the fear of God.

Paul's joy at the news brought by Titus

[2]Open your hearts to us; we have wronged no one, we have Acts 20:33
corrupted no one, we have taken advantage of no one. [3]I do not 2 Cor 6:11–13
say this to condemn you, for I said before that you are in our

---

"What more do you desire, O soul," St John of the Cross asks, quoting this verse, "and what more do you seek outside yourself, for within yourself you have your riches, your delights, your satisfaction, your fullness and your kingdom, which is your Beloved, whom your soul desires and seeks? Rejoice and be glad in your inner recollection with him; for you have him so near. There desire him, there adore him, and do not go to seek him outside yourself, for that will only make you weary and distracted, and you will not find him, or enjoy him more surely or more quickly or more intimately than within yourself" (*Spiritual Canticle*, first stanza).

The Old Testament text quoted by St Paul seems to be taken from Lev 26:11f and Ezek 37:27. Even in the Old Testament God's special familiarity with the chosen people meant that they had to keep away from idols and stay utterly true to God.

6:17–18. These verses are a composite of Old Testament texts (cf. Is 52:11; 2 Sam 7:14; and others).

Divine sonship, in which the people of Israel shared in the Old Testament (cf. Ex 4:22; Deut 7:6; Rom 9:4), has been won by Jesus Christ for those who believe in him: "To all who received him, who believed in his name, he gave power to become children of God" (Jn 1:12; cf. Rom 8:14–17). This fact is something the Christian should reflect on often—that he is a son of almighty God, whom Christ himself has taught us to call "Our Father" (cf. Mt 6:9 and par.). It is a consideration that should fill us with joy and serenity.

"Rest and repose in the fact of being children of God. God is a Father who is full of tenderness, of infinite love. Call him 'Father' many times a day and tell him—alone, in your heart—that you love him, that you adore him, that you feel proud and strong because you are his son" (St Josemaría Escrivá, *Friends of God*, 150).

"Come out from them": "them" refers to the Gentile peoples who are refusing to embrace the true faith.

6:2–16. St Paul now takes up again where he left off in 6:11–13; he wants to regain

Col 1:24 hearts, to die together and to live together. [4]I have great confidence
in you; I have great pride in you; I am filled with comfort. With all
our affliction, I am overjoyed.

Acts 20:1f [5]For even when we came into Macedonia, our bodies had no
rest but we were afflicted at every turn—fighting without and fear
Ps 113:6; 138:6 2 Cor 1:3f; 2:13 within. [6]But God, who comforts the downcast, comforted us by

---

the full confidence and affection of the Corinthians, some of whom may have grown a little cool due to the persistent criticism of the Apostle by his enemies. Opening his heart fully, he tells them how happy he was over the good news Titus brought him (cf. v. 5ff); this links up with what he had begun to tell them in chapter 2 (cf. 2:12f) and which he interrupted to make his long apologia.

7:4. Someone with a purely human outlook will fail to understand how the Apostle can say he is overjoyed despite all his afflictions. But this is just another example of the ongoing paradox of Christianity: Jesus Christ won his victory by dying on the cross; the Christian is able to find joy in suffering and tribulation (cf. Mt 5:11f) because in this experience he finds the Master's cross: "Is it not true that as soon as you cease to be afraid of the Cross, of what people call the cross, when you set your will to accept the Will of God, then you find happiness, and all your worries, all your sufferings, physical or moral, pass away? Truly the Cross of Jesus is gentle and lovable. There, sorrows cease to count; there is only the joy of knowing that we are co-redeemers with him" (St Josemaría Escrivá, *The Way of the Cross*, II).

7:5–16. St Paul shows how tremendously happy he is with the news brought by Titus, whom he had gone to Macedonia to meet rather than wait for him to reach Troas (cf. note on 2 Cor 12f). Titus in fact had been very well received by the faithful of Corinth (v. 15); moreover, they had reacted very well to Paul's previous letter—the letter "written with many tears" (vv. 7, 9, 11; cf. 2:3f). This leads St Paul to say that, even if at first it weighed on him, he now rejoices at the grief it caused them, because it was a holy grief and had led them to repent. His attitude makes it quite clear that fear of hurting people should never be used as an excuse for not reproaching them if reproach is called for: "It can happen," St Augustine points out, "and often does happen, that one's brother is for a while saddened when he is reproached, and resists and argues. But later he reflects in silence, with no other witness than God and his conscience, and he is not afraid of what people think about his being corrected; he is afraid of displeasing God if he does not mend his ways. And then he no longer does the thing he was corrected about; and the more he detests his sin, the more he loves his brother for being the enemy of his sin" (*Letter*, 210, 2).

7:6. The role of comforter is attributed in God to the Holy Spirit; in fact he is given the name of Comforter or Paraclete (cf. Jn 14:16–17 and note). "The Holy Spirit," St John of Avila teaches, "is the Comforter. And how well able he is to comfort: he is given that very name, the Comforter! [...]. Whenever you are sad, be sure that the Holy Spirit will comfort you in your sorrow, if you have him in your soul. The apostle St Paul says this, for if someone were to think, Who could comfort such sadness as mine, such distress, Who would come to my help,

the coming of Titus, [7]and not only by his coming but also by the
comfort with which he was comforted in you, as he told us of your
longing, your mourning, your zeal for me, so that I rejoiced still
more. [8]For even if I made you sorry with my letter, I do not regret
it (though I did regret it), for I see that that letter grieved you,
though only for a while. [9]As it is, I rejoice, not because you were
grieved, but because you were grieved into repenting; for you felt
a godly grief, so that you suffered no loss through us. [10]For godly Mt 27:3–5
grief produces a repentance that leads to salvation and brings no Heb 12:17
regret, but worldly grief produces death. [11]For see what earnestness this godly grief has produced in you, what eagerness to clear

---

there is 'fighting without and fear within', (he should remember that) 'God, who comforts the downcast, comforted us' (2 Cor 7:56). The passion of the Holy Spirit is to comfort those who are in distress [...], to comfort everyone; let us ask him to be good enough to come to our hearts and comfort us" (*Sermon on Sunday within the Octave of the Ascension*).

7:8. See the note on 1:23–24 regarding the letter to which St Paul refers.

7:9–11. St Paul distinguishes "godly grief" from "worldly grief". The former is the same as contrition—"a deep sorrow and detestation for sin committed, with a resolution of sinning no more" (Council of Trent, *De Paenitentia*, chap. 4); it leads a person to repent and do penance, and it is combined with hope, because it involves confidence in being forgiven; for this reason it can be said to contain joy; this is the kind of grief the Corinthians had. "Worldly grief", however, leads to despair: it admits that sin has been committed but, in his pride the sinner thinks that he cannot be forgiven: this was the kind of grief Judas had, which led him to commit suicide (cf. Mt 27:3–10).

"The sadness which healthy repentance produces," Cassian comments, "is proper to the obedient, affable, humble, sweet, gentle and patient man, because it comes from the love of God. He endures physical pain and contrition of spirit, thanks to his lively desire for perfection. He is also cheerful and in some way he feels strengthened by the hope of putting his experience to good use [...]. Diabolical sadness is the very opposite. It is rough, impatient, full of bitterness and disgust, and it also involves a kind of painful despair" (*Institutions*, book 9, chap. 11).

In v. 11 St Paul lists some of the effects their "godly grief" has had on the Corinthians—some relating to their feelings towards himself, others to their attitude to the person guilty of the offence against him (cf. 2:5–11).

7:11–12. On the offence which occasioned that letter, see the note on 2:5–11. The Apostle's remarks about it here seem to support the view that he is not referring to the case of the man guilty of incest.

St Paul clarifies why he wrote that letter—to move them to repentance, the genuineness of which they would prove to God by showing their affection for Paul. The purpose of correction should always be the good of the person corrected. "we should correct out of love," St Augustine teaches, "not out of a desire to hurt them, but with the affectionate intention of getting them to change. If we correct

yourselves, what indignation, what alarm, what longing, what
zeal, what punishment! At every point you have proved yourselves
guiltless in the matter. [12]So although I wrote to you, it was not on
account of the one who did the wrong, nor on account of the one
who suffered the wrong, but in order that your zeal for us might be
revealed to you in the sight of God. [13]Therefore we are comforted.

And besides our own comfort we rejoiced still more at the joy
of Titus, because his mind has been set at rest by you all. [14]For if
I have expressed to him some pride in you, I was not put to
shame; but just as everything we said to you was true, so our
2 Cor 2:9 boasting before Titus has proved true. [15]And his heart goes out all
Eph 6:5 Phil 2:12 the more to you, as he remembers the obedience of you all, and
the fear and trembling with which you received him. [16]I rejoice,
because I have perfect confidence in you.

---

others in that way we shall be keeping very well the precept, 'If your brother sins against you, go and tell him his fault, between you and him alone' (Mt 18:15). Why do you correct him? Because it hurts you to have been offended by him? God forbid! If you do it for self-love you achieve nothing. If it is love that moves you, you do very well. The same passage enables us to see if the love that ought to move you is yours or his: 'If he listens to you', Christ says, 'you have gained your brother.' And so you have to work to win him to God" (*Sermon,* 82, 4).

7:13–16. Such is St Paul's charity that others' joys make him rejoice more than his own. In those verses we can see that he is happy and consoled on two scores —Titus' pleasure at what he found in Corinth, and Paul's legitimate pride over the very good impression the Corinthians made on Titus: Paul is obviously very happy with the good news about those in his pastoral care; it is the kind of happiness a father has when he sees his children are well behaved.

8:1–9:15. Now, taking for granted that the Corinthians trust him once more, the Apostle begins the second part of his letter (chaps. 8–9), which has to do with the collection for the faithful in Jerusalem, a collection which he organized not only in Corinth but also in the other churches he had founded (cf. Rom 15:26; 1 Cor 16:1). This was indeed one of the points about which the apostolic council at Jerusalem (cf. Gal 2:10; Acts 15) reminded the churches—to remember the poor, something St Paul always tried to do, as we can see clearly from these pages.

In addition to alleviating the material needs of the "saints"—that is, the Christians (cf. 1:1)—of the mother church, the Apostle sees this collection as a way of showing the fraternal unity Gentile converts have with that church (cf. 9:12–14).

He had already taken this matter up in 1 Corinthians 16:1–4; in fact, even before that, a year earlier, the Corinthians had indicated that they wanted to help Jerusalem and had begun to collect funds (cf. 8:10; 9:2). He must be bringing it up again—and at length—because the fervour of the Corinthians' first charity must have cooled somewhat due to the crisis in the Corinthian church.

It is interesting to note how delicately the Apostle broaches this subject: in the

PART TWO

The collection for the church of Jerusalem

The Macedonians' good example

8 [1]We want you to know, brethren, about the grace of God which Rom 3:24ff
has been shown in the churches of Macedonia, [2]for in a severe 15:26
test of affliction, their abundance of joy and their extreme poverty
have overflowed in a wealth of liberality on their part. [3]For they

---

original text there is no mention of "money" or "alms". Instead, he uses more a spiritual vocabulary—"grace", "willing gift", "love", "relief of the saints".

St Paul begins by citing the generosity of the Macedonians (8:16), and he then goes on to appeal to the Corinthians (8:7–15). After recommending those whom he is sending to organize the collection (8:16–24), he asks that it be done without delay (9:15) and reminds them of the blessings that almsgiving brings (9:615).

8:1–15. St Paul wants to get the Corinthians to be generous. First, he points to the example given by the Macedonians (vv.1–6). Macedonia was one of the two provinces into which the Romans had divided Greece; Achaia, the other, had Corinth as its capital (cf. note on 1:1–2). In Macedonia, from where the Apostle is writing, there were Christian communities at Philippi, Thessalonica, and Beroea, which he had founded during his second missionary journey (cf. Acts 16:11 17:15). He plays on the natural rivalry between the two provinces, raising it onto a supernatural plane. He also mentions our Lord (v. 9), who, in his incarnation and throughout his life, gave us a wonderful example of generosity and detachment.

The Apostle also appeals directly to the Corinthians, reminding them of their earlier readiness to contribute and encouraging them to complete what they started to do so eagerly.

8:1–6. The Macedonians, he points out, have been remarkably generous; despite their poverty they have regarded it as a grace to be able to help their brothers in the faith (v. 4); and not only did they help materially—and beyond their means (vv. 3, 5)—but they also contributed personnel (v. 5).

These Christians in Macedonia provide us with a fine example of magnanimity: they could easily have felt excused from coming to the aid of their brothers, in view of their own poverty; instead they were more than generous in almsgiving. "Magnanimity", St Josemaría Escrivá teaches, "means greatness of spirit, a largeness of heart wherein many can find refuge. Magnanimity gives us the energy to break out of ourselves and be prepared to undertake generous tasks which will be of benefit to all. Small-mindedness has no home in the magnanimous heart, nor has meanness, nor egoistic calculation, nor selfinterested trickery. The magnanimous person devotes all his strength, unstintingly, to what is worthwhile. As a result he is capable of giving himself. He is not content with merely giving. He gives his very self. He thus comes to understand

gave according to their means, as I can testify, and beyond their
means, of their own free will, 4begging us earnestly for the favour
Acts 11:29 2 Cor 9:1 of taking part in the relief of the saints—5and this, not as we
expected, but first they gave themselves to the Lord and to us by
the will of God. 6Accordingly we have urged Titus that as he had
already made a beginning, he should also complete among you
this gracious work.

Appeal for generosity

1 Cor 1:5; 16:1f 7Now as you excel in everything—in faith, in utterance, in knowledge, in all earnestness, and in your love for us—see that you
excel in this gracious work also.

---

that the greatest expression of magnanimity consists in giving oneself to God" (*Friends of God*, 80).

8:1. "The grace of God which has been shown in the churches of Macedonia": it is not possible to translate this phrase literally. Paul seems to be saying two things: on the one hand, he is referring to the collection, which he calls "grace", made *by* the churches of Macedonia; but this generous work of charity is, at the same time, a grace of God *to* the Macedonians. The Greek preposition translated as "in" has this dual meaning.

The term "grace" appears quite often in chapters 8 and 9, with different nuances: sometimes it refers to God's benevolence and love towards men (cf. 8:9); sometimes to the blessings the Christians enjoy (cf. 9:8, 14); and also to the works of charity which this divine grace helps them to carry out (cf. 8:1, 4, 6, 7, 19: on some occasions the RSV has "favour").

8:2. St Paul stresses the paradox of the Christian life—joy in tribulation, wealth in poverty (cf. 7:4). This point would possibly have been useful for the Corinthians, among whom the pride of some had given rise to considerable dissension (cf. 1 Cor 1:10 4:21; 6:1–11; 8:8–13). The afflictions to which he refers may have gone back to the very earliest days of these communities (cf. Acts 16:20ff; 17:5ff). He also refers to them in 1 Thess 1:6; 2:14ff.

8:5. The wonderful generosity of those early Christians of Macedonia—of Philippi, Thessalonica and Beroea—is borne out by the fact that they gave not only material aid but their very selves, for, comments St Thomas Aquinas, "that is the order that should obtain in giving—that one first be acceptable to God, for if one is not pleasing to God, neither will one's gifts be acceptable" (*Commentary on 2 Cor*, ad loc.).

In referring to the generous dedication of these Christians, St Paul may have in mind some of his most loyal co-workers, who came from these communities—for example, Lydia and Epaphroditus, from Philippi (cf. Acts 16:11ff; Phil 2:25ff); Sopater, from Beroea; Aristarchus and Secundus, from Thessalonica (cf. Acts 20:3–5).

8:7–15. The Apostle now appeals directly to the generosity of the Corinthians and reminds them of our Lord's example (v. 9). They are already noted for other charisms—"in faith, in utterance, in

[8]I say this not as a command, but to prove by the earnestness of
others that your love also is genuine. [9]For you know the grace of our Mt 5:3ff; 8:20 Phil 2:6f
Lord Jesus Christ, that though he was rich, yet for your sake he
became poor, so that by his poverty you might become rich. [10]And in
this matter I give my advice: it is best for you now to complete what
a year ago you began not only to do but to desire, [11]so that your

---

knowledge" (cf. 1 Cor 1:5; 12:8f); now they should be seen to be outstanding in charity. He tells them this is not a command but rather advice (vv. 8, 10) and then encourages them to complete the collection they have begun; it is not designed to impoverish them but to have them help those in need.

8:7. "In your love for us": the New Vulgate, which relies on the best Greek manuscripts, translates this as "in the love that we have given you". St Paul is referring to Christian charity towards others, in which he formed them during the years when he preached to them. The variant, found in the RSV and other versions, is not in our opinion as suitable to the context.

8:8. "By the earnestness of others": this must be a reference to the generosity of the Macedonians, whose example he has just proposed to them.

8:9. Jesus Christ is *the* example of detachment and generosity. Our Lord, because he is God, was in need of nothing; but by becoming man he voluntarily despoiled himself of the splendour of his divinity (cf. Phil 2:6f) and lived on earth as a poor man—from his birth in poverty in Bethlehem to his death on the cross; sometimes he did not even have the bare necessities of life (cf. Lk 9:58).

"If you do not believe that poverty is enriching," St John Chrysostom comments, "picture your Lord and you will doubt me no longer. For had he not become poor, you could not have become rich. By a miracle which men cannot understand, poverty has produced these riches—the knowledge of God and godliness, liberation from sin, justification, sanctification, the countless good things which he has bestowed on us and will bestow on us in the future. All those things have accrued to us through his poverty—through his taking our flesh and becoming man and suffering what he suffered. And yet, unlike us, he did not deserve punishment and suffering" (*Hom. on 2 Cor*, 17).

8:10. "It is best for you": commenting on this advice of the Apostle, St Thomas Aquinas points out the benefits the almsgiver receives: "Mercy is more useful to the person who gives (the alms). For, he who exercises it thereby makes a spiritual gain, whereas the recipient makes only a temporal gain" (*Commentary on 2 Cor,* ad loc.).

More specifially, almsgiving is one of the main ways to cure the wounds of the soul, which is what sins are. Thus, the *St Pius V Catechism*, when commenting on the petition in the Our Father, "Forgive us our trespasses [...]", after mentioning Penance and the Eucharist, puts almsgiving third on the list as "a medicine suited to heal the wounds of the soul; therefore, those who desire to make pious use of this prayer should act kindly to the poor according to their means. Of the great efficacy of alms in effacing the stains of sin, the angel of the Lord in the book of Tobit, St Raphael, is a witness;

readiness in desiring it may be matched by your completing it out of
Prov 3:27f Mk 12:43 what you have. [12]For if the readiness is there, it is acceptable
according to what a man has, not according to what he has not. [13]I do
not mean that others should be eased and you burdened, [14]but that as
a matter of equality your abundance at the present time should supply
their want, so that their abundance may supply your want, that there
Ex 16:18 may be equality. [15]As it is written, "He who gathered much had
nothing over, and he who gathered little had no lack."

Paul praises Titus and Timothy

[16]But thanks be to God who puts the same earnest care for you
into the heart of Titus. [17]For he not only accepted our appeal, but

---

he says, 'Almsgiving delivers from death, and it will purge away every sin' (Tob 6:12:9) and leads to mercy and life everlasting" (4, 14, 23).

8:12. What the Apostle says here recalls how our Lord praised the widow who put her penny in the temple treasury. Even though she gave a minute amount, in God's eyes it was a great deal, because it was all she had (cf. Mk 12:41–44; Lk 21:1–4), and what God principally rewards is the generous intention. "In this connexion," Pope John Paul II comments, "the most eloquent example is that of *the poor widow*, who puts a few small coins in the temple treasury: from the material point of view, it is difficult to compare this offering with those which others gave. Yet Christ said, 'She out of her poverty put in all the living that she had' (Lk 21:3–4). Therefore, what mainly counts is the *interior value of the gift*—the readiness to share everything, promptness in giving oneself.

"Let us recall here what St Paul said: 'If I give away all I have [...] but have not love, I gain nothing' (1 Cor 13:3). Also, St Augustine puts it very well: 'If you put your hand out to give, but do not have pity in your heart, you have done nothing; whereas if you have pity in your heart, even if you have nothing to give with your hand, God accepts your alms'" (John Paul II, *General Audience*, 28 March 1979).

8:14. The spiritual abundance of the Christians of the church of Jerusalem can relieve the spiritual indigence of the new Christians of Corinth (cf. 9:12–14). St Paul also says this in his Letter to the Romans in connexion with this collection: "for if the Gentiles have come to share in their spiritual blessings, they agree also to be of service to them in material blessings" (15:27).

8:15. St Paul supports with the authority of Holy Scripture what he has just been saying about equity (v. 14), by referring to the manna with which God miraculously nourished the people of Israel in the wilderness. Everyone was given an omer (about four litres or a gallon) a day. In the morning, after gathering the manna—some more, others less—"when they measured it with an omer, he who gathered much had nothing over, and he who gathered little had no lack; each gathered according to what he could eat" (Ex 16:18). St Paul is saying something similar: every Christian should have what he needs, and should be helped by his brothers in the faith wherever necessary.

8:16–24. He now recommends the people appointed to take up the collection. In

being himself very earnest he is going to you of his own accord.
[18]With him we are sending the brother who is famous among all
the churches for his preaching of the gospel; [19]and not only that, Gal 2:10
but he has been appointed by the churches to travel with us in this
gracious work which we are carrying on, for the glory of the Lord
and to show our good will. [20]We intend that no one should blame us
about this liberal gift which we are administering, [21]for we aim at Rom 12:17
what is honourable not only in the Lord's sight but also in the sight
of men. [22]And with them we are sending our brother whom we have
often tested and found earnest in many matters, but who is now more Rom 16:7
earnest than ever because of his great confidence in you. [23]As for 2 Cor 7:13; 12:18

---

addition to Titus, who very probably was also the bearer of this letter, two other brethren are referred to, but their names are not given (vv. 18, 19, 22). It is very difficult to say who they might have been.

However, it has often been suggested that the first (vv. 18f) was probably St Luke, who would have been with St Paul in Macedonia when he wrote this letter, and who afterwards joins him on his journey to Jerusalem (cf. Acts 20–21). His fame for preaching the Gospel would refer to his zeal for preaching, for as yet he had not written his Gospel. The third envoy (v. 22) is more difficult to identify; some think that he may have been Apollos, who was well known to the Corinthians (cf. 1 Cor 3:4–6; 16:12).

8:16–17. Titus' attitude is a very good example of the way a Christian should practise obedience: he agrees to St Paul's request and makes it completely his own. This is the way the faithful should react to what their pastors, speaking in God's name, tell them to do: "Like all Christians the laity should promptly accept in Christian obedience what is decided by the pastors who, as teachers and rulers of the Church, represent Christ. In this they will follow Christ's example who, by his obedience unto death, opened to all men the blessed way of the liberty of the sons of God" (*Lumen gentium*, 37).

8:20–21. St Paul's prudence should be noted: he is careful to ensure that his involvement in the collection is above suspicion. What he says here recalls our Lord's warning: "Let your light so shine before men, that they may see your good works and give glory to your Father who is in heaven" (Mt 5:16; cf. Prov 4:3; Rom 12:17). The Apostle's attitude sets an example which those who work in the Lord's service should always keep before their minds. "I don't doubt your good intentions," St Josemaría Escrivá says. "I know that you act in the presence of God. But (and there is a 'but') your actions are witnessed or may be witnessed by men who judge by human standards. … And you must give them good example" (*The Way*, 275).

8:23. "The glory of Christ": the Apostle describes his co-workers in this way because their holiness and concern for their brothers reflect the glory of Jesus Christ.

Pope Paul VI applies these words to priests: "In this way, in our world, which needs God's glory (cf. Rom 3:23), priests, ever more perfectly conformed to

Titus, he is my partner and fellow worker in your service; and as for
our brethren, they are messengers[j] of the churches, the glory of
Christ. [24]So give proof, before the churches, of your love and of our
boasting about you to these men.

Appeal for speediness

2 Cor 8:4, 20 **9** [1]Now it is superfluous* for me to write to you about the
2 Cor 8:19 offering for the saints, [2]for I know your readiness, of which I
boast about you to the people of Macedonia, saying that Achaia
has been ready since last year; and your zeal has stirred up most
2 Cor 8:24 of them. [3]But I am sending the brethren so that our boasting about
you may not prove vain in this case, so that you may be ready, as
I said you would be; [4]lest if some Macedonians come with me and
find that you are not ready, we be humiliated—to say nothing of
you—for being so confident. [5]So I thought it necessary to urge the
brethren to go on to you before me, and arrange in advance for
this gift you have promised, so that it may be ready not as an
exaction but as a willing gift.

---

the one and supreme Priest, will be a real glory to Christ (2 Cor 8:23), and, through them, the glory of the grace of God will be magnified in the world of today (cf. Eph 1:6)" (*Sacerdotalis caelibatus*, 45).

9:1–5. St Paul wants to stay on the subject of the collection, exhorting them to complete it without delay (vv. 1–5), and pointing out what blessings the givers will receive (vv. 6–15).

As before (8:1–5), he avails of the friendly rivalry between the two provinces of Greece, but this time he does it the other way round: he has boasted to the Macedonians about the zeal and readiness of the faithful at Corinth, who were the first to start the collection; but his boasting will be vain if they fail to do what they set about.

The whole purpose of the visit by Titus and his two companions is to organize things so that when St Paul arrives—and possibly some Macedonians with him—everything will be ready.

9:3. "I am sending the brethren": literally, "I sent the brethren to you": Greek uses what is called the epistolary aorist ("I sent"), because when this letter is read in Corinth, the sending of Titus and his companions, who deliver it, will be something that happened in the past.

9:5. These words are a warning that alms, if not given in a spirit of generosity and self-sacrifice, are really a sign of greed and meanness rather than charity.

"A willing gift": literally "a blessing", which is probably a Hebrew way of saying this: for example, in Proverbs 11:25 a generous person is described, literally, as "a soul of blessing"; in Judges 1:15 and 1 Samuel 25:27 a generous and splendid gift is called, literally, a "blessing", hence "in blessings" (v. 6) = bountifully.

"Almsgiving is called a 'blessing'," St Thomas comments, "because it is the cause of eternal blessing. For by the action of giving, the person is blessed by God and by men" (*Commentary on 2 Cor,* ad loc.).

j. Greek *apostles*

Blessings to be expected

6The point is this: he who sows sparingly will also reap sparingly, Prov 11:24f; 19:17
and he who sows bountifully will also reap bountifully. 7Each one 1 Chron 29:17
must do as he has made up his mind, not reluctantly or under
compulsion, for God loves a cheerful giver. 8And God is able to
provide you with every blessing in abundance, so that you may
always have enough of everything and may provide in abundance
for every good work. 9As it is written, Ps 112:9

> "He scatters abroad, he gives to the poor;
> his righteousness[k] endures for ever."

9:6–15. The collection appeal ends with some remarks about the benefits that accrue from it. First, St Paul says that the generous almsgiving of the Corinthians will stand to them in this life and in the next (vv. 6–10), and then he refers to its effects on the faithful in Jerusalem: they will praise God and feel closer to the Christians of Corinth (vv. 11–15).

A person who is generous in almsgiving draws down on himself the blessings of God. St Augustine says: "Your Lord says this to you, '[…] Give to me and receive. In due course I will give back what is due to you. What will I give back? You gave little to me, you will receive a great deal; you gave me earthly things, I will give back heavenly things; you gave me temporal things, you will receive eternal things; you gave me what was mine, you will receive me, myself […].' See whom you lent to. He nourishes (others) and (yet he himself) suffers hunger for your sake; he gives and is needy. When he gives, you wish to receive; when he is needy, you are unwilling to give. Christ is needy when a poor man is needy. He who is disposed to give eternal life to all his own has deigned to receive temporal things in (the person of) anyone who is needy" (*Sermon,* 33, 8).

9:6. This image of sowing and reaping is often used in Holy Scripture to indicate the connexion between one's actions and reward or punishment in the next life (cf. Prov 22:8; Mt 25:24–26; Gal 6:7f). What the Apostle says here reminds us of our Lord's promise: "Give and it will be given to you; good measure, pressed down, shaken together, running over, will be put into your lap" (Lk 6:38). However much we give God in this life, he will reward us with much more in the next.

9:7. "God loves a cheerful giver": a teaching often found in Scripture (cf. Deut 15:10; Ps 100:2; Sir 35:11; Rom 12:8). An alms or a service done reluctantly can never please anyone, particularly God our Lord: "If you give bread and it makes you sad to do so," St Augustine comments, "you lose both the bread and the reward" (St Augustine, *Enarrationes in Psalmos*, 42, 8); whereas the Lord is delighted when a person gives something or gives himself lovingly and spontaneously, not as if he were doing a great favour (cf. *Friends of God*, 140).

9:8–10. St Paul emphasizes the abundant divine blessings—both temporal and spiritual—which generous almsgiving brings. In the Old Testament we read in the book of Tobit: "Give alms from your

k. Or *benevolence*

Is 55:10 Ho 10:12 [10]He who supplies seed to the sower and bread for food will
supply and multiply your resources[l] and increase the harvest of
2 Cor 4:15 your righteousness.[k] [11]You will be enriched in every way for great
generosity, which through us will produce thanksgiving to God;

---

possessions to all who live uprightly, and do not let your eye begrudge the gift when you make it. Do not turn your face away from any poor man, and the face of God will not be turned away from you. If you have many possessions, make your gift from them in proportion; if few, do not be afraid to give according to the little you have. So you will be laying up a good treasure for yourself against the day of necessity. For charity delivers from death and keeps you from entering the darkness; and for all who practise it charity is an excellent offering in the presence of Most High" (4:7–11). To almsgiving can be applied our Lord's promises about the hundredfold in this life and then everlasting life—promises made to all those who give up something in his name (cf. Mt 19:28f).

"Righteousness" is equivalent to holiness. In the Bible the person is described as righteous or "just" who strives to do God's will and serve him to the best of his ability (cf., e.g., notes on Mt 1:19; 5:6).

9:10. "For," comments St John Chrysostom, "if even to those who sow the earth and to those who are concerned about the needs of the body, God gives in great abundance, much more will he give to those who till the soil of heaven and apply themselves to the salvation of their souls, for he wills that we should spare no sacrifice in that regard [...].

"This holy apostle gives these two principles: in temporal things one should limit oneself to what is necessary; but in spiritual things one should seek as much as possible. Therefore he asks that we should not simply give alms, but give alms generously. That is why he calls alms 'seed'. Just as corn cast into the ground produces a crop, so generous alms produces righteousness and abundant harvest" (*Hom. on 2 Cor,* 20).

9:11–15. The collection is designed to relieve the material needs of the brethren in Jerusalem, but St Paul expects it to produce spiritual fruit above all—thanksgiving to God, on the part of those who receive the aid, for the faith and fraternal charity of the Corinthians, and prayer for them; and this will make for greater solidarity between Christians of Jewish origin and those of Gentile origin. This unity of the churches was one of the Apostle's prime objectives (cf., e.g., 1 Cor 1:10ff).

This concern about the needs of others, such as we see among the first Christians (cf. Acts 2:44–47; 4:34–37), which St Paul impresses on the faithful in the new communities he founds, should always stand to us as an example: no Christian can be indifferent to the needs, spiritual or material, of others; he should generously try to meet these needs.

9:11. "Through us": in the sense that it will be Paul and his co-workers who bring the collection to Jerusalem.

9:13–14. "You will glorify": that is, they will give glory to God through their obedience and generosity.

The New Vulgate prefers the alternate reading "they will glorify", meaning that

k. Or *benevolence* **l.** Greek *sowing*

12for the rendering of this service not only supplies the wants of
the saints but also overflows in many thanksgivings to God.
13Under the test of this service, you[m] will glorify God by your — Acts 2:42; 1 Cor 16:1ff
obedience in acknowledging the gospel of Christ, and by the
generosity of your contribution for them and for all others; 14while
they long for you and pray for you, because of the surpassing
grace of God in you. 15Thanks be to God for his inexpressible gift! — 2 Cor 8:9

PART THREE

Paul justifies his conduct

4. A REPLY TO ACCUSATIONS

Paul's readiness to use his apostolic authority

10 1I, Paul, myself entreat you, by the meekness and gentle- — Mt 11:29
ness of Christ—I who am humble when face to face with — Phil 2:1
you, but bold to you when I am away!*—2I beg of you that when — 1 Cor 4:21

---

the Jerusalem Christians, when they receive this generous gift from Corinth, will praise God for the faith and charity of the Corinthians, and will also give him glory through their prayers for the Corinthians.

9:15. Foreseeing all the spiritual blessings the collection will bring, the Apostle burst out into an act of thanksgiving to God. The "inexpressible gift" he speaks of may be both greater unity among Christians (cf. Gal 3:28; Col 3:11) and the grace of God which is producing, in the Corinthians, abundant fruit of charity towards their brethren.

10:1–13:10. In this third section of the letter St Paul makes a personal apologia in which he answers the charges made against him by his enemies in Corinth. These, it would seem, were people who had come to Corinth with letters of introduction (3:1); of Jewish origin (11:22), they were trying to discredit the Apostle in the eyes of the Corinthians.

St Paul's style of writing changes at this point; he is outspoken and vigorous, because he realizes what harm might be done to this young Christian community if they broke with their founder and first Apostle. This explains why he does something he normally would not do (cf. 11:16, 21; 12:1, 11): he launches into justifying his action in order to answer these people who are seeking to discredit him. He does not say who they are—these "superlative apostles", as he sarcastically calls them (cf. 11:5; 12:11)—or what their teaching is: they may have been Judaizers; he had many confrontations with people of that type (cf. note on 1:12 7:16).

m. Or *they*

I am present I may not have to show boldness with such confidence as I count on showing against some who suspect us of
Eph 6:13–17 acting in worldly fashion. 3For though we live in the world we are
not carrying on a worldly war, 4for the weapons of our warfare are

---

He begins by defending himself against the charge of being a weak apostle (10:1–11) and points to the authority with which he worked in Corinth (10:12–18). He then compares his title to boast with his adversaries' (11:1 12:8). And then he explains why he has defended himself in this way—to get the Corinthians to repent of their behaviour before his next visit (12:19 13:10).

10:1–11. In this passage St Paul defends his apostolic authority. Apparently some people had accused him of being faint-hearted in his manner: they said that he was forceful only in writing (vv. 1–10). They misread the Apostle's meekness and gentleness for pusillanimity. St Paul was perfectly aware of the apostolic authority Christ had given him, well aware of the power at work within him. However, following his Master's example (cf. Mt 11:29), he preferred, if at all possible, to use this power only to build up morale, not to criticize. Our Lord, when necessary, also acted and spoke with remarkable severity and energy (cf., e.g., Mt 23:13ff; Mk 11:15ff).

10:1. This verse marks a break with the earlier part of the letter (cf. 1:1). Up to this, it was St Paul and Timothy who were addressing the faithful of Corinth; now the Apostle speaks for himself, to reply to the charges made against him.

10:2–6. St Paul here presents his life as an apostle as a kind of warfare. He often uses this comparison in his letters (cf., e.g., 6:7; Eph 6:13–17; 2 Tim 2:3f); it shows that the Christian life is incompatible with an easy-going, bourgeois approach to things.

In this instance he uses the comparison to explain how he fights with those who denigrate him: he uses God's weapons—which are supernatural and irresistible—to deal with the lies, arrogance and disobedience of his enemies. In this connexion, see the note on 2 Corinthians 6:7–8.

"In a worldly fashion": "according to the flesh". St Paul often uses this language, but it has to be read in context to see exactly what he means. "We live in the world", in the flesh (v. 3), refers to life in the body, the life we live when we are on this earth, whereas "acting in a worldly fashion" (vv. 2–3) clearly has a pejorative meaning; it is the same as acting from purely human motives. "Acting in a worldly fashion applies to people who make worldly things their goal and therefore design their actions so as to obtain worldly things. Since these things can be taken away from them by men, those who have a tendency to be drawn towards worldly things, behave in a deferential and mild way towards others" (*Commentary on 2 Cor,* ad loc.).

"Worldly weapons" (v. 4): as distinct from spiritual weapons, which derive from God and draw their power from him.

10:5. So powerful are these weapons, St Paul explains in military language, that they demolish all the fortresses built by human pride to resist "the knowledge of God"; once these fortresses are demolished, reason is led "captive" to obey Christ: the Apostle may be thinking particularly of the message of the cross,

not worldly but have divine power to destroy strongholds. [5]We
destroy arguments and every proud obstacle to the knowledge of
God, and take every thought captive to obey Christ, [6]being ready 2 Cor 2:9
to punish every disobedience, when your obedience is complete.
[7]Look at what is before your eyes. If any one is confident that
he is Christ's, let him remind himself that as he is Christ's, so are
we. [8]For even if I boast a little too much of our authority, which the Jer 1:10
Lord gave for building you up and not for destroying you, I shall not 1 Cor 5:4f 2 Cor 12:6;
be put to shame. [9]I would not seem to be frightening you with 13:10
letters. [10]For they say, "His letters are weighty and strong, but his

---

which he so rigorously contrasted in his first letter with the wisdom of this world (cf. 1 Cor 1:18ff; 3:18ff). "The believer's mind is said to be made captive", St Thomas Aquinas explains, "in the sense that it is governed by forces foreign to itself, and not according to its natural powers" (*De veritate*, 14, 1), for faith is not the outcome of human reasoning but of that grace which moves the person to trust in God.

Accepting the mysteries of God, submitting one's mind and giving obedience to faith (cf. Rom 1:5; 16:26) is not a humiliation for man; it is in fact very much in keeping with human nature. "Just as the obedience of the will", St John of Avila teaches, "consists in denying itself in order to do God's will, so the service which the mind must render God is to deny itself by *believing* God's word [...] And since man's will is dedicated to God and sanctified by denying itself, his mind should not remain in an unsanctified state by believing itself and not obeying God, since it is destined to be blessed in heaven by seeing him clearly. As St Augustine says, 'the reward of faith is seeing'; therefore, there is no justification for the mind not rendering service on earth: the service it owes is belief" (*Audi, filia*, chap. 38).

10:6. Once the Corinthians' obedience is complete and they are firmly attached to Paul, it will be possible to punish the offenders—both the enemies of the Apostle who are trying to subvert the Corinthians' trust in him, and also unrepentant sinners (cf. 12:20 13:3). The punishment he refers to has a medicinal purpose, that is, it is designed to bring about repentance and atonement for sin.

10:7–8. Here he defends his apostleship briefly; later he will do so at more length and in greater detail (cf. chaps. 11, 12). Here he limits himself to pointing out that he too has been sent by Christ, from whom he received the mission of founding and building up the Christian community in Corinth.

"Look at what is before your eyes": this translation, which is valid, would mean a call to commonsense and realism, for all the work done in Corinth speaks in Paul's favour. The original can also be translated as "you only see the surface": this would mean he accuses the Corinthians of judging by human standards—which would lead them to the conclusion that he is not a genuine apostle.

10:10. This criticism by his enemies that St Paul is "weak" does not seem to refer to his physical appearance; nor can it be deduced that he was short in stature or had a bad physique. When they say "his bodily presence is weak", what they

2 Cor 13:2, 10 bodily presence is weak, and his speech of no account." 11Let such
people understand that what we say by letter when absent, we do
when present.

Paul's province includes Corinth

2 Cor 3:1; 5:12 12Not that we venture to class or compare ourselves with some of
those who commend themselves. But when they measure
themselves by one another, and compare themselves with one
another, they are without understanding.

Rom 12:3; 15:19f 13But we will not boast beyond limit, but will keep to the limits
God has apportioned us, to reach even to you. 14For we are not
overextending ourselves, as though we did not reach you; we were
Rom 5:20 the first to come all the way to you with the gospel of Christ. 15We
do not boast beyond limit, in other men's labours; but our hope is
that as your faith increases, our field among you may be greatly
Acts 19:21 enlarged, 16so that we may preach the gospel in lands beyond you,
without boasting of work already done in another's field. 17"Let

---

seem to be doing is misreading his meekness (cf. 10:1) and his solicitude for all souls (cf. 1 Cor 9:22). When they say that his speech is "of no account", it means that they have failed to realize that he did not want to couch his preaching "in plausible words of wisdom, but in demonstration of the Spirit and power, that your faith might not rest in the wisdom of men but in the power of God" (1 Cor 2:4f; cf. notes on 1 Cor 2:1–3; 2:4f).

10:12–18. Now—in a rather complicated style—he replies to the criticism made of him, by pointing out the rights he has to work as an apostle in Corinth. First, he shows how silly his enemies are to try to set themselves up as the standard in which to glory (v. 12). He, on the contrary, can be assessed by a clear criterion (vv. 13–16)—the area of work God marked out for him (the conversion of the Gentiles: cf. Rom 11:13; Gal 2:7) and the work he has already done in this regard. Corinth comes within his terms of reference, and it was he who founded the Christian community there: he is not, therefore, boasting in someone else's territory. His desire now is to consolidate the faith of the Corinthians, so that he can move on to other regions. He ends by reminding them again (cf. 1 Cor 1:31) that all success must be attributed to God (vv. 17f).

10:15–16. St Paul had imposed upon himself the ambition of preaching "the gospel, not where Christ has already been named, lest I build on another man's foundation" (Rom 15:20). His indefatigable zeal leads him to work incessantly at his apostolate: he wants to establish the faith of the Corinthians so he can bring the Gospel to new places. He may have been thinking of Spain (cf. Rom 15:24, 28), which was then on the western limits of the known world.

10:17–18. The Apostle recalls the words of Jeremiah—"let him who boasts boast of the Lord" (9:22f)—words already quoted in 1 Corinthians 1:31 to show how absurd it is to try to boast about oneself or to push oneself forward, when the only valid recommendation is that made by

him who boasts, boast of the Lord." [18]For it is not the man who commends himself that is accepted, but the man whom the Lord commends.

Jer 9:22f
1 Cor 1:31; 4:5

5. THE APOSTLE'S GROUNDS FOR BOASTING

His zeal

11 [1]I wish you would bear with me in a little foolishness. Do
bear with me! [2]I feel a divine jealousy for you, for I
betrothed you to Christ to present you as a pure bride to her one

Deut 4:24ff
Eph 5:26f

God: and that is a recommendation St Paul can claim to have, borne out as it is by the success of his apostolic work. Inspired by these words of the Apostle, St Bernard shows the very relative value of human judgments: "Why I am so solicitous for the judgment of another, or for my own, if their opprobrium will not condemn me nor their praises save me? My brothers, if I had to present myself before your tribunal, rightly would I be happy to receive your praise. And if I had to be judged by my own conscience and made do with my own opinion of myself, I would be glad of my self-esteem. But since I have to appear, not before your judgment or my own, but before the judgment of God, how foolish, how deluded I would be to take refuge in your testimony or in my own, especially since God is such that everything is bare and open to his gaze, and he has no need of anyone's testimony about man?" (*Sermon on the triple glory*, 2).

11:1–12:18. In spite of what he has just said, St Paul here goes on to provide an elaborate justification of his conduct. He has a profound distaste for this and throughout the apologia he repeatedly excuses himself (cf. 11:1, 16–18, 21, 23; 12:1, 6, 11); but he feels he has to go through with it because it is the only way he can counter the effects of his enemies' criticism. He opens his heart to the Corinthians to show the sufferings his life as an apostle involves and the wonderful revelations God has deigned to give him; this will make them realize who this man is who first preached the Gospel among them, and they can then compare his credentials with those of his attackers.

The whole passage shows very clearly St Paul's passionate temperament and his ardent zeal for souls; he does not mind doing something which costs him a great deal, if that is what has to be done to ensure that souls he has won for Christ are not lost; and he overlooks the fact that the Corinthians have not spoken out on his behalf (as was their duty: cf. 12:11), that they have not responded to his love and vigilance for them (cf. 12:15), or that his words have been misinterpreted (cf. 12:19). His attitude stands as a very good example of upright intention: he devotes his whole life to souls, seeking no human recompense (cf. 12:15).

He begins by asking them to forgive his boasting (11:1–6), and goes on to point out that one of his boasts is that he had no worldly purpose of any kind when preaching in Corinth (11:7–15). Again he asks them to forgive his boasting (11:16–21) and then lists the other points on which he can claim credit—the sufferings in which preaching has involved him (11:22–33) and the visions the Lord

Gen 3:4, 6, 13
Rev 21:2–9

husband. 3But I am afraid that as the serpent deceived Eve by his
cunning, your thoughts will be led astray from a sincere and pure
devotion to Christ. 4For if some one comes and preaches another
Jesus than the one we preached, or if you receive a different spirit
from the one you received, or if you accept a different gospel from
the one you accepted, you submit to it readily enough. 5I think that
I am not in the least inferior to these superlative apostles. 6Even if
I am unskilled in speaking, I am not in knowledge; in every way
we have made this plain to you in all things.

---

has granted him (12:1–10). And at the end of the apologia he again asks them to forgive him (12:11–18).

11:2–3. The simile of the husband and wife is often used in the Old Testament to describe the relationship between God and his people (cf. Is 62:5; Jer 3:6ff; Ezek 16:8ff). God—who says of himself, "I the Lord your God am a jealous God" (Ex 20:5)—tells his people, "You shall love the Lord your God with all your heart, and with all your soul, and with all your might" (Deut 6:5; cf. Mt 22:37). In the New Testament Christ is the husband and the Church his bride (cf. Eph 5:25ff; Rev 21:9; 22:17), "whom he redeemed with his blood, and he gave the Holy Spirit to her as his pledge. He saved her from the slavery of the devil; he gave his life for her sins and he arose for her justification" (St Augustine, *In Ioann. Evang*., 8, 4).

St Paul acts the part of the bridegroom's friend (cf. Jn 3:29) whose duty it is to protect the virginity of the bride, and he sees the danger she is in from the snares of her enemies.

"The Apostle", St Thomas comments, "is saying that the Church is like Eve; the devil sometimes attacks her openly by the actions of tyrants and powers, in which case he is 'like a roaring lion (who) prowls around seeking some one to devour' (1 Pet 5:8). At other times he molests her in a hidden way through heresies which promise the truth and pretend to be sound—in which case he is like the serpent who seduces in an astute way, promising things he cannot give" (*Commentary on 2 Cor,* ad loc.).

11:4. It is not possible to say exactly whether the Apostle is referring to something which actually happened, or whether he is proposing an absurd hypothesis. If the first, he may be referring to the teachings of the Judaizers, who were arguing that in order to be saved it was necessary to keep the prescriptions of the Old Law—which meant substituting the spirit of sons of God for the spirit of slavery, thereby undervaluing the person of Christ and his work of salvation.

If he is proposing a theoretical case, what he means is that if anyone preaches to them a more sublime Gospel than the one he has preached they would do well to listen to that preacher; but that could not happen, because there is only one Jesus and only one Gospel (cf. Gal 1:6–9), and, moreover, as he goes on to tell them in detail, he is in no way inferior to these intruders who are making out that they are apostles.

"Another Jesus": this follows the Greek text. The New Vulgate has "another Christ".

11:5–6. In speaking here of these "superlative apostles" St Paul does not seem to be referring to the apostles chosen by our

Paul accepted no material support in payment for preaching 1 Cor 9:12, 18
7 Did I commit a sin in abasing myself so that you might be Phil 4:10, 15
exalted, because I preached God's gospel without cost to you? 8 I 2 Cor 12:13
robbed other churches by accepting support from them in order to
serve you. 9 And when I was with you and was in want, I did not
burden any one, for my needs were supplied by the brethren who
came from Macedonia. So I refrained and will refrain from
burdening you in any way. 10 As the truth of Christ is in me, this
boast of mine shall not be silenced in the regions of Achaia. 11 And 1 Cor 9:15
why? Because I do not love you? God knows I do!

Lord, but rather to be alluding sarcastically to his opponents. Later on he will refer to them again in the same terms (12:11; cf. 1 Cor 11:12f).

"Unskilled in speaking": this cannot mean that the Apostle had special difficulty in expressing himself: he must mean that he is not a professional orator, that is, someone who, after the style of the time, had been trained in rhetoric. Elsewhere he has spoken at length to the Corinthians (cf. 1 Cor 1:18–34) about his apparent lack of eloquence, and the divine wisdom which he nevertheless communicated.

1:7–15. St Paul made a point of preaching the Gospel without reward, not exercising his right to be financially supported by the faithful but instead earning enough through work to maintain himself: this clearly shows the uprightness of his intention. This he explained previously (cf. 1 Cor 9:4–18 and corresponding notes), and now repeats: he sees this as something praiseworthy and does not intend to alter his practice (v. 10), particularly as it marks him as different from the false apostles who have appeared in Corinth. So, it is not lack of affection for the Corinthians that has led him to act in this way, nor, as he says ironically (v. 1), is he wrong in doing so.

In Corinth, specifically, he worked at tent-making with Aquila and Priscilla (cf. Acts 18:1–3). He experienced want, and had to "rob" others—as he says, by way of exaggeration (v. 8)—in order to be able to keep on serving them: possibly he is referring to Silas and Timothy as those who brought him the wherewithal from Macedonia (Acts 18:5). As we point out in the note on 1 Corinthians 9:15–18, the only exception he made was in the case of the Philippians (Philippi was the capital of Macedonia), whom he allowed to meet his need on occasions (cf. Phil 4:15f).

Once again we can see Paul's remarkable capacity for work and self-sacrifice; in this he sets an example for all Christians. "What did the holy apostles teach us, or what do they teach us?", St Bernard asks himself. "Not the skill of the fisherman, not how to make tents or things like that [...]. They taught us how to live. Do you think that knowing how to live is not much? It is a great deal, or rather the greatest thing of all [...]. The upright life I judge to consist in suffering evils, doing good and persevering like that to death" (*Sermon on the feast of SS. Peter and Paul*, 1, 3).

11:11. "God knows I do": this sentence, in the original, is somewhat ambiguous; but he obviously is calling God to witness how much he loves the Corinthians.

[12]And what I do I will continue to do, in order to undermine the
claim of those who would like to claim that in their boasted mission
2 Cor 2:17 Phil 3:2 they work on the same terms as we do. [13]For such men are false
apostles, deceitful workmen, disguising themselves as apostles of
Christ. [14]And no wonder, for even Satan disguises himself as an
angel of light. [15]So it is not strange if his servants also disguise
themselves as servants of righteousness. Their end will correspond
to their deeds.

Paul apologizes for boasting

2 Cor 12:6 [16]I repeat, let no one think me foolish; but even if you do, accept
me as a fool, so that I too may boast a little. [17](What I am saying
I say not with the Lord's authority but as a fool, in this boastful
confidence; [18]since many boast of worldly things, I too will boast.)
[19]For you gladly bear with fools, being wise yourselves! [20]For you

---

11:13–15. The Apostle here launches a severe attack on his opponents: they say that they are apostles of Christ, but in fact they are servants of the devil. And they behave like Satan—the prince of darkness (cf. Eph 6:12), who projects himself as an angel of light. St Paul's words recall our Lord's warning in the Gospel: "Beware of false prophets, who come to you in sheep's clothing but inwardly are ravenous wolves" (Mt 7:15).

Deception has always been one of the main weapons the devil—the father of lies (cf. Jn 8:44)—uses to lead men astray: "To begin with", St Thomas Aquinas explains, "he does not suggest obvious evil things to us, but rather something which has the appearance of good, his purpose being to divert a person, however slightly, from his basic resolutions, because once someone has been led away even slightly from his course, it is easier for the devil to draw him towards sin. 'Even Satan disguises himself as an angel of light' (2 Cor 11:14). Then, when he has managed to get him to sin, he binds him in such a way that he cannot get up [...]. Thus, the devil moves in two stages: he deceives, and after deceiving he keeps (a person) in sin" (*On the Lord's Prayer*).

11:16–21. The Apostle breaks off once more to excuse his boasting. The only reason why he is making this apologia is to defend his apostolic authority over the Corinthians.

"The Apostle", St John Chrysostom comments, "acts like someone of illustrious race who has chosen to dedicate himself to leading a holy life and who feels compelled to sing the praises of his family in order to take down certain people who are priding themselves on being well-born. Do you think he is acting in a vain way? No, because the only reason he boasts is to humble these vain people" (*Hom. on 2 Cor,* 24).

11:19–20. These words are heavily ironical, caricaturing as they do the foolishness of the Corinthians, who consider themselves to be so sensible. St Paul upbraided them on this score previously (cf. 1 Cor 1:18 4:21). In this instance their foolishness consists in letting themselves be taken advantage of by intruders and doing nothing about it.

bear it if a man makes slaves of you, or preys upon you, or takes
advantage of you, or puts on airs, or strikes you in the face. 21To
my shame, I must say, we were too weak for that!

What Paul has suffered for Christ

But whatever any one dares to boast of—I am speaking as a
fool—I also dare to boast of that. 22Are they Hebrews? So am I.
Are they Israelites? So am I. Are they descendants of Abraham? Phil 3:5
So am I. 23Are they servants of Christ? I am a better one—I am 1 Cor 15:10
talking like a madman—with far greater labours, far more imprison- 2 Cor 10:7
ments, with countless beatings, and often near death. 24Five times Deut 25:3

11:21. "To my shame, I must say": this could also be translated as "To shame you I tell you", for the Greek does not make it clear who feels ashamed. St Paul is still speaking sarcastically: he argues that he showed himself too weak to the Corinthians, for he has not taken advantage of them the way the false apostles have. That may be why, he tells them, they consider him inferior to the latter.

11:23–33. St Paul begins his apologia proper, in which he points out his merits in contrast with those of his opponents. On the score of race, he is their equal (v. 22); on the score of being a minister of Christ, he is much better qualified: as proof of this he offers the physical suffering he has undergone in his apostolate (vv. 23–27, 30–33), and the moral suffering (vv. 28f). One cannot fail to be moved by this outline of his sufferings, an account which provides us with extremely valuable information about his life not contained in the Acts of the Apostles. Although this list is not exhaustive (cf. v. 28), and much suffering still lies ahead of him, we can see that Ananias' prophecy has already come true: "I will show him how much he must suffer for the sake of my name" (Acts 9:16).

It is very revealing that the evidence he provides to show his superiority as a servant of Christ is precisely his sufferings. Our Lord had already said, "If any man would come after me, let him deny himself and take up his cross daily and follow me" (Lk 9:23). Suffering, the cross, is something inseparable from the Christian life, and a sure sign that one is following in the Master's footsteps. St Josemaría Escrivá comments: "When we set out seriously along the 'royal highway', that of following Christ and behaving as children of God, we soon realize what awaits us—the Holy Cross. We must see it as the central point upon which to rest our hope of being united with our Lord.

"Let me warn you that the programme ahead is not an easy one. It takes an effort to lead the kind of life our Lord wants. Listen to the account St Paul gives of the incidents and sufferings he encountered in carrying out the will of Jesus: 'Five times I have received at the hands of the Jews the forty lashes less one' (2 Cor 11:24–28)" (*Friends of God*, 212).

11:22. The Apostle makes it quite clear that he is the equal of his opponents as far as background goes. The three terms used (Hebrew, Israelite, descendant of Abraham), although in a way they all mean the same, have different shades of meaning. "Hebrews" here designates both origin—descendants of Eber (cf.

Acts 14:19; I have received at the hands of the Jews the forty lashes less one.
16:22 [25]Three times I have been beaten with rods; once I was stoned. Three
times I have been shipwrecked; a night and a day I have been adrift
at sea; [26]on frequent journeys, in danger from rivers, danger from
robbers, danger from my own people, danger from Gentiles, danger
2 Cor 6:5 in the city, danger in the wilderness, danger at sea, danger from false
1 Thess 2:9 brethren; [27]in toil and hardship, through many a sleepless night, in
Acts 20:18–21 hunger and thirst, often without food, in cold and exposure. [28]And,
apart from other things, there is the daily pressure upon me of my
Rom 9:1–3 anxiety for all the churches. [29]Who is weak, and I am not weak?
1 Cor 9:22 Who is made to fall, and I am not indignant?

Gen 11:14)—and race. It may be that Paul's enemies questioned his ethnic purity on the grounds that he had been born in Tarsus, a city in Asia Minor; however, he was "a Hebrew born of Hebrews" (Phil 3:5) and spoke Hebrew (cf. Acts 21:40). "Israelites"—descendants of Jacob, whose name Yahweh changed to "Israel" (cf. Gen 32:28)—would indicate that he was a member of the chosen people who had the true religion. Being a "descendant of Abraham" would refer to the fact that he was an heir to the messianic promises.

St Paul often had to make a point of stressing his Jewish origin (cf. Acts 22:3; Rom 11:1; Gal 1:13ff; Phil 3:4ff). Probably his opponents were forever trying to discredit his teaching—about the superiority of the New Law over the Old, about circumcision not being necessary—by saying he was not a Jew. He most certainly is, he says, and he often refers to his immense love for those of his race (cf. Rom 9).

11:24. It is not possible to say exactly when these beatings took place; they are not reported in the Acts of the Apostles. Possibly they occurred in some of the synagogues where he went to preach: synagogues in the diaspora had authority to inflict this form of punishment. Because Jewish law laid down a maximum of forty lashes (cf. Deut 25:2f), usually only thirty-nine were given to avoid going beyond the limit. It was a very severe and demeaning form of punishment.

11:25. The Romans beat people with rods. Though three beatings are mentioned here the Acts of the Apostles only tell us of one instance of Paul's being punished in this way—at Philippi (cf. Acts 16:22–24). On the three occasions he must have been beaten unlawfully, for Roman law prescribed that this punishment could only be imposed on Roman citizens—St Paul was a Roman (cf. Acts 22:25–29)—when they were under sentence of death.

The stoning took place at Lystra, and after it the Apostle was dragged out of the city and left for dead (cf. Acts 14:19f).

The Acts of the Apostles refer to only one instance of shipwreck (cf. Acts 27:9ff).

11:28–29. In addition to the physical sufferings mentioned, others still greater weigh down on the Apostle—who was "all things to all men" (1 Cor 9:22)—those to do with the pastoral care of people who sought his help, and the care of the churches he had founded. The physical evils, St John Chrysostom comments, "no matter how terrible they may have been, passed over quite quickly

30If I must boast, I will boast of the things that show my 2 Cor 12:5
weakness. 31The God and Father of the Lord Jesus, he who is 2 Cor 1:23
blessed for ever, knows that I do not lie. 32At Damascus, the Acts 9:22–25
governor under King Aretas guarded the city of Damascus in
order to seize me, 33but I was let down in a basket through a
window in the wall, and escaped his hands.

Visions and revelations

12 1I must boast; there is nothing to be gained by it, but I will
go on to visions and revelations of the Lord. 2I know a man
in Christ who fourteen years ago was caught up to the third

---

and left behind them a great consolation. But what afflicted Paul, what oppressed his heart and made him so anxious was the pain caused him by the laxity of all the faithful without any distinction. It was not only the behaviour of prominent members that caused him pain; he was indifferent to no one; he ranked all Christians, irrespective of who they were, as his dearly beloved children" (*Hom. on 2 Cor*, 25).

The Apostle, who is identified with Christ (cf. Gal 2:19f), makes his own the words of his Master: "I am the good shepherd. The good shepherd lays down his life for the sheep" (Jn 10:11). He stands as a model for pastors of the Church as regards the solicitude they should have for the souls God has entrusted to them.

11:30. As if by way of summing up what he has said already, St Paul points out that he is really boasting about his "weakness", that is, about things which worldly eyes see as weakness, failure and humiliation. He will go on to explain that it is really in these things that God's power and strength are most clearly to be seen (cf. 12:7:10): this "weakness" makes fruitful the work of his chosen ones.

This is another example of the paradox of the Christian life: Christ won victory on the cross, and his apostles rejoice and are proud to suffer on his account (cf. 7:4; 8:2; Acts 5:41; Gal 6:14).

11:31. On this phrase, "the God and Father of the Lord Jesus", see the note on 2 Cor 1:3.

11:32–33. Just when he seems to have finished listing his sufferings, St Paul suddenly breaks his flow and mentions one very specific event, which the Acts also tell us about (cf. 9:22–25). Probably he decided to refer to it because it was the first time in his apostolic life that his life was seriously at risk.

The king in question was Aretas IV, king of the Nabateans, a people well established to the south and east of Palestine. Herod Antipas repudiated a daughter of Aretas IV when he took the wife of his brother Philip (cf. Mt 14:1–12). The governor had tried to arrest St Paul at the instigation of the Jews.

12:1–10. He continues his apologia by referring to visions and revelations he has received from the Lord. From other letters and from the Acts of the Apostles we know that there were many of these in the course of his life (cf. Acts 9:1–8; 16:9; 18:9f; 17–21; 27:23f; 1 Cor 15:8; Gal 1:12); but he refers to only one of them.

heaven—whether in the body or out of the body I do not know,
God knows. 3And I know that this man was caught up into
Paradise—whether in the body or out of the body I do not know,
Lk 23:43 Rev 2:7 God knows—4and he heard things that cannot be told, which man
2 Cor 11:30 may not utter. 5On behalf of this man I will boast, but on my own

---

The Apostles couches this account in the third person—"a man in Christ"—possibly because he feels embarrassed (vv. 1, 5) to have to reveal these graces God has given him. Therefore, after describing these visions briefly (vv. 1–6), he speaks about the weakness the Lord has allowed him to have, to prevent him from taking pride in these wonderful experiences (vv. 7–10).

"Fourteen years ago": that is, in the period 43–44, possibly during his stay in Tarsus (cf. Acts 9:30), Antioch (Acts 11:25ff; 13:1–3) or Jerusalem (Acts 11:30).

12:2–4. Although he is able to quote the precise time of the vision, he cannot explain how it happened. It may have been an instance of supernatural contemplation in which his physical senses played no part, which would explain why he does not know whether he was in the body or not. St Thomas Aquinas, with St Augustine, is of the view that St Paul was given a vision of the essence of God, as Moses had been (cf. Ex 33:11; Deut 34:10): "The Apostle's very words indicate this. For he says that 'he heard words that cannot be told, which man may not utter', and such would be words pertaining to the vision of the blessed, which transcends the state of the wayfarer" (*Summa theologiae*, 2–2, 175, 3). To help us understand the difficulty St Paul had in explaining himself, we might study what St Catherine of Siena said when God revealed to her some of the mysteries of divine providence: "O eternal Father, fire and depths of love, eternal mercy! O hope! O refuge of sinners, eternal and infinite good! [...] What need have you of your creatures? [...] What more can I say? Shall I act like a baby and say, Ah, ah, ah, for that is all I can say: language cannot express the affection of a soul that infinitely desires you? I seem to be saying what Paul said: 'Words cannot describe, not ear hear, nor eyes see ... what I have seen.' What did you see then? I have seen the mystery of God. But, what is this that I am saying? Not, to be sure, that I have seen them with these lower senses; however, I tell you, my soul, that you have tasted and have seen the very depths of supreme, eternal Providence" (*Dialogue*, 10).

"The third heaven": according to some commentators, this simply refers to the situation in which the blessed dwell, that is, the most sublime level of divine contemplation. Others see in it an echo of Jewish traditions which spoke of a first heaven (the atmosphere of the earth), a second (the heaven of the stars) and a third (the dwelling-place of God). In any event, "Paradise" (v. 4) would have the same meaning.

12:5–6. The Apostle is speaking metaphorically as if there were two people in him—one, who receives supernatural gifts, which he glories in as coming from God; the other, who experiences severe afflictions of different kinds, which he also boasts about because they show forth God's power (cf. 12:9). "In man", St Thomas comments, "two things may be considered—the gift of God, and the human condition. If one glories in some

behalf I will not boast, except of my weaknesses. [6]Though if I wish
to boast, I shall not be a fool, for I shall be speaking the truth. But I
refrain from it, so that no one may think more of me than he sees in
me or hears from me. [7]And to keep me from being too elated by the Job 2:6
abundance of revelations, a thorn* was given me in the flesh, a
messenger of Satan, to harass me, to keep me from being too elated.
[8]Three times I besought the Lord about this, that it should leave me; Lk 1:35
[9]but he said to me, "My grace is sufficient for you, for my power is
made perfect in weakness." I will all the more gladly boast of my
weaknesses, that the power of Christ may rest upon me. [10]For the Phil 4:13 Col 1:24

---

divine gift, as coming from God, that is a good boast, because it is boasting in the Lord [...]. But if one glories in that gift as something coming from oneself, then that is a bad kind of boast" (*Commentary on 2 Cor,* ad loc.).

12:7–10. Displaying admirable humility, St Paul now refers to the weakness God allowed him to experience to ensure his supernatural gifts did not make him proud. It is impossible to say what exactly the "thorn in his flesh" was. Some Fathers—St Augustine, for example—and modern commentators think that it was some particularly painful and humiliating physical ailment, possibly the same one as he refers to in Galatians 4:13f, where he also speaks in general terms. Others, like St John Chrysostom, are of the view that he is referring to the pain which continual persecution caused him. Others—from St Gregory the Great onwards—opt for an ascetical interpretation; they say he is referring to temptations to do with conscience; but the supporters of the two other theses argue, for example, that it is unlikely that St Paul would have mentioned anything of that kind, because it could have given his enemies ammunition for further attacks.

St Paul asked God to take this "thorn" away, but the heavenly answer he received is very revealing: God's grace is enough to enable him to cope with this difficulty—which serves to reveal God's power. And so it is that he boasts of and is content with his weaknesses and the persecution he suffers: in these circumstances he is stronger than ever, thanks to God's supernatural help.

When commenting on this passage, St Thomas explains that God sometimes permits certain kinds of evil in order to draw out greater good: for example, in order to protect people from pride—the root of all vices—he sometimes allows his chosen ones to be humiliated by an illness, or a defect, or even by mortal sin, in order that "the person who is humbled in this way might recognize that he cannot stand firm by his own efforts alone. Hence it is said in Romans 8:28, 'We know that in everything God works for good with those who love him'—not of course that God seeks the sin but [the sinner's] turning to him" (*Commentary on 2 Cor,* ad loc.).

12:7. "A messenger of Satan", an angel of Satan: this is how he describes the humilating "thorn". This suggests that the disability could have been seen as an obstacle to evangelization—which the devil, logically, would have been keen to frustrate (cf. 2:11; 11:14f).

12:8–10. Christians can learn a great deal about the ascetical struggle from

sake of Christ, then, I am content with weaknesses, insults, hardships, persecutions, and calamities; for when I am weak, then I am strong.

Paul again apologizes for boasting

11 I have been a fool! You forced me to it, for I ought to have been commended by you. For I was not at all inferior to these superlative

---

these words. They remind us, on the one hand, of the need to ask the Lord to help us when we experience difficulties, and at the same time to be full of trust and to abandon ourselves to God, who knows what is best for us. "The Lord is good", St Jerome teaches, "because he often does not give us what we desire, in order to give us something we would prefer" (*Epist. ad Paulinum*).

The passage also shows us what attitude we should take to our own weakness: "We have to glory", St Alphonsus says, "in the knowledge of our own weakness in order to acquire the strength of Jesus Christ, which is holy humility", without "giving in to lack of confidence, as the devil wants, and falling into more serious sins" (*Treasury of Preaching Material*, 2, 6).

At the same time this passage teaches us that awareness of our personal shortcomings should lead us to put all our trust in God: "We have to cry out ceaselessly with a strong and humble faith, 'Lord, put not your trust in me. But I, I put my trust in you.' Then, as we sense in our hearts the love, the compassion, the tenderness of Christ's gaze upon us (for he never abandons us) we shall come to understand the full meaning of those words of St Paul, *virtus in infirmitate perficitur* (2 Cor 12:9). If we have faith in our Lord, in spite of our failings—or rather, with our failings—we shall be faithful to our Father, God; his divine power will shine forth in us, sustaining us in our weakness" (St Josemaría Escrivá, *Friends of God*, 194).

12:11–18. St Paul ends this long apologia section of the letter by once more excusing himself: "I have been a fool" (cf. the note on 11:1–6). However, he makes it clear, it was the Corinthians themselves who made him speak of his personal experiences: that would not have been necessary if they had done what they ought—come to his defence (vv. 11f). The only reason why they could possibly have felt less favoured than the other churches, he tells them ironically, is because he was not a burden on them—but he does not plan to change his policy (vv. 13–15). He ends by dealing with something his opponents must have been accusing him of—that he does not exploit the Corinthians directly, but he does so indirectly, through his co-workers.

12:11. Paul accuses the Corinthians of not standing up for him against his accusers: if they had done so, he would not be forced to praise himself. They should have realized this themselves and not made him compare himself with his opponents—the "superlative" apostles, as he ironically calls them (cf. note on 11:5–6)—to none of whom is he inferior.

"Even though I am nothing": he wants to stress once more (cf. 12:7–10) that everything good in him comes from God. This attitude should spur us on to implore heaven to give us the light we need to recognize our own littleness: if we admit to it our Lord will be able all the more to fill our hearts.

apostles, even though I am nothing. [12]The signs of a true apostle Rom 15:19 Heb 2:4
were performed among you in all patience, with signs and
wonders and mighty works. [13]For in what were you less favoured Acts 1:8ff Rom 15:19
than the rest of the churches, except that I myself did not burden 1 Thess 1:5
you? Forgive me this wrong!*

[14]Here for the third time I am ready to come to you. And I will 2 Cor 13:1
not be a burden, for I seek not what is yours but you; for children
ought not to lay up for their parents, but parents for their children.

12:12. Here he says that two distinguishing marks of an apostle are patience and miracles. By patience (cf. 6:4) he may mean the constancy with which he bore contradiction and persecution in Corinth: this may have been why the Lord appeared to him in a vision to comfort him (cf. Acts 18:9f). Applying the reference to "the signs of a true apostle" to Paul himself, St John Chrysostom comments: "What a sea of good works has he traversed in a few words! And notice what he puts first—'patience'. For this is the characteristic of an apostle—to bear all things nobly. This then he expresses in a single word; but upon the miracles, which were not his own doing, he speaks at greater length. Consider how many prisons, how many stripes, how many dangers, how many conspiracies, how many sleet-showers of temptations, how many civil, how many foreign wars, how many pains, how many attacks, he has implied here in that word, 'patience'!" (*Hom. on 2 Cor*, 27).

"Signs and wonders and mighty works": these interchangeable terms are used in the New Testament to refer to all kinds of miraculous events. We do not know what sort of miracles St Paul worked in Corinth—the Acts of the Apostles do not report them—which helped reinforce the authority of his teaching. These words are reminiscent of the summary account of apostolic preaching St Mark gives at the end of his Gospel: "They preached everywhere, while the Lord worked with them and confirmed the message by the signs that attended it" (Mk 16:20).

12:13–15. He once more reminds them of the policy he has followed in his apostolic work—that of not using his right to be supported by the faithful (cf. 1 Cor 9ff; 2 Cor 11:7–15). Here he does so ironically—as if the Corinthians felt injured by this way of acting—and goes on to say that he does not plan to change it (cf. note on 11:7–15).

In this connexion he says that his attitude to the Corinthians is like that of a father who saves up for his children and spends himself for them, careless of whether they appreciate it or not. It is very moving to see once again St Paul's immense love for souls and the disinterestedness with which he works for their salvation; it is something that can be explained only by that spiritual fatherhood—stronger than natural fatherhood—which he feels for the members of his churches: "though you have countless guides in Christ, you do not have many fathers. For I became your father in Christ Jesus through the gospel" (1 Cor 4:15).

12:14. "For the third time": the second visit, which Acts does not mention, may have taken place between the first letter and this one (cf. note on 1:15 2:4).

12:15. Pope Pius XII used this verse to describe the solicitude which priests

Phil 2:17 15I will most gladly spend and be spent for your souls. If I love
you the more, am I to be loved the less? 16But granting that I
myself did not burden you, I was crafty, you say, and got the better
of you by guile. 17Did I take advantage of you through any of
2 Cor 6:16–18 those whom I sent to you? 18I urged Titus to go, and sent the
brother with him. Did Titus take advantage of you? Did we not act
in the same spirit? Did we not take the same steps?

6. THE APOSTLE'S NEXT VISIT

The reason for his apologia

19Have you been thinking all along that we have been defending
Rom 1:29ff ourselves before you? It is in the sight of God that we have been
1 Cor 4:6
2 Cor 10:2 speaking in Christ, and all for your upbuilding, beloved. 20For I fear

---

should have for all souls: "Would that each of you could on the evidence of the faithful attribute to himself in humble sincerity the words of the Apostle: 'I will gladly spend and be spent for your souls' (2 Cor 12:15). Enlighten men's minds with divine truth; guide their consciences in the way of uprightness; strengthen and refresh the souls that are tossed by doubt or tortured with suffering. These are the chief activities of your apostolate. Whatever other activities our times demand, these too you must engage in. But let it be clear that, in all that he does, the priest aims only at the good of souls and that he looks only to Christ, to whom he must dedicate not only his energy but also himself" (*Menti nostrae*).

12:16–18. In a rather contorted style, the Apostle refers here to another calumny spread by his opponents: they were saying that he did not personally demand anything from the faithful, but then he sent in his co-workers to take advantage of them. He simply reminds them of how his envoys in fact acted.

The visit by Titus must have been the one mentioned in 2:13 and 7:6–16. There is no way of knowing who the other envoy was.

12:19–13:10. The Apostle ends this third section of his letter (chaps. 10–13) by once more explaining why he has made this personal apologia—to build up the Corinthians (12:1921)—and by making some suggestions in connexion with his next visit to Corinth (13:1–10).

12:19. He anticipates what he imagines some people will think on reading his letter—that his main purpose is to justify himself in their eyes, in the way an accused makes his case before a tribunal. No, that is not the case: he does not mind what people think; he is speaking to them in the presence of God, who is the true judge (cf. 1 Cor 4:3f); what makes him write as he does is the good of the faithful, their "upbuilding" or edification.

For someone as warmhearted as St Paul, whose only thought is the salvation of souls, his strained relations with the community of Corinth must have been very painful: he had to regain their confidence, for his enemies' attacks had caused some to distrust him; to win them

that perhaps I may come and find you not what I wish, and that you
may find me not what you wish; that perhaps there may be
quarrelling, jealousy, anger, selfishness, slander, gossip, conceit, and
disorder. 21I fear that when I come again my God may humble me 2 Cor 2:1; 13:2
before you, and I may have to mourn over many of those who sinned
before and have not repented of the impurity, immorality, and
licentiousness which they have practised.

Preparation for his next visit

13 1This is the third time I am coming to you. Any charge must Deut 19:15 Mt 18:16 1 Tim 5:19
be sustained by the evidence of two or three witnesses. 2I

---

back he opens his heart (6:11–13) and soul (11:1ff) to them. And yet he senses that his attitude may be misinterpreted, and that he should make it clear that his affection is not lack of fortitude (10:1–6), and that if he does open his heart to them, he is not doing so to excuse himself.

If this was St Paul's experience, no Christian should be surprised to meet misunderstanding and difficulties, great and small, in his apostolate; that only means that a rich harvest is to come: "Unless a grain of wheat falls into the earth and dies, it remains alone; but if it dies, it bears much fruit" (Jn 12:24).

12:20–21. If he seeks to build up the Corinthians (cf. v. 19), it is because he is afraid that on his next visit he may find them immersed in the sins he warned them about in his previous letter. One of these sins is pride (cf. 1 Cor 1:18 4:21), which lies at the root of divisions among the brethren and of the disorders listed in v. 20; another is impurity (cf. 1 Cor 6:12ff): St Paul suspects that this sin—so easy to fall into in Corinth, due to the corrupt atmosphere of that city (cf. note on 1 Cor 6:12–20)—still has a grip on many, because they have not resolved to make a serious effort, with God's help, to escape from it (v. 21).

The profound pain which St Paul feels on account of the sins of others—they make him weep—should make the Christian eager to atone to God our Lord for all the offences offered him. "Don't be content", the founder of Opus Dei advises, "to ask Jesus pardon just for your own faults: don't love him just with your own heart.... Console him for every offence that has been, is, or will be done to him. Love him with all the strength of all the hearts of all those who have most loved him ..." (*The Way*, 402).

13:1–4. He now makes some suggestions connected with his next visit (vv. 1–10), beginning by telling them that he is planning to act energetically, using all his apostolic authority against those who do not want to mend their ways. In an ironic style he says that if this is the proof they want that Christ is acting in him (cf. 10:1–11), they will be able to see it for themselves.

13:1. The Apostle invokes a legal ruling in the Old Testament (Deut 19:15)—which our Lord recalled in the Gospel (Mt 18:16; Jn 8:17) and which St Paul himself will later recommend to Timothy (1 Tim 5:19)—according to which two or three witnesses had to come forward before a person could be condemned. Some commentators apply these words to his visit to Corinth, as if he meant that these words would be enough evidence to

warned those who sinned before and all the others, and I warn
them now while absent, as I did when present on my second visit,
that if I come again I will not spare them—[3]since you desire proof
that Christ is speaking in me. He is not weak in dealing with you,
Rom 1:4ff; but is powerful in you. [4]For he was crucified in weakness, but
8:11ff lives by the power of God. For we are weak in him, but in dealing
Phil 2:7f with you we shall live with him by the power of God.
1 Cor 11:28 [5]Examine yourselves, to see whether you are holding to your
faith. Test yourselves. Do you not realize that Jesus Christ is in
you?—unless indeed you fail to meet the test! [6]I hope you will
find out that we have not failed. [7]But we pray God that you may

---

condemn those who had not mended their ways by the time he arrived. Whether this is so or not, what he means is that—even though he will not be indulgent—he will judge them in a prudent fashion and without any improvisation.

13:3–4. These verses are based on St Paul's doctrine on the identification of the Christian with Jesus Christ (cf., e.g., Rom 6:3–11; Gal 2:20; Phil 1:21). Our Lord, during his life on earth—especially by permitting his passion and death—chose to appear weak; however, by rising from the dead he manifested his divine power, which previously had been hidden from view. In a similar way St Paul, who has appeared to be weak—by bearing with the rebellious types in Corinth—is now considering using his God-given apostolic authority.

13:5–10. He makes it clear that he would prefer not to use his authority, for it has been given him for building up, not tearing down (v. 10). And so he invites the Corinthians to carefully examine their consciences, to put themselves to the test, rather than have him do so: this will tell them whether their conduct is or is not in line with that of Jesus, and by doing that they will also see whether or not St Paul's conduct has been correct (vv. 6ff).

At the same time he prays to God that their conduct may be beyond reproof even if as a consequence of this—and once again he shows his admirable uprightness of intention—some should consider him to be weak or blameworthy, because he fails to act with the severity he said he would use (vv. 8f).

"This is paternal affection," St John Chrysostom comments, "to prefer the salvation of his disciples to his own good name" (*Hom. on 2 Cor*, 29).

13:5. This advice to the Corinthians to make a searching examination of conscience reminds us of the critical importance of the practice of daily examination of conscience in the Christian life. The saints have always recommended this practice: "As a diligent inquirer into your purity of soul," St Bernard used to say, "call your life to account in a daily examination; check carefully where you have gained ground and where you have lost ground [...]. Try to know yourself. Place all your faults before your eyes, look at yourself as if at another; and then bewail what you see" (*Meditationes piissimae*, 5, 14).

13:7. Commenting on this prayer of St Paul's, St Thomas Aquinas reminds us that "in order to avoid sin two things are

not do wrong—not that we may appear to have met the test, but
that you may do what is right, though we may seem to have failed.
8For we cannot do anything against the truth, but only for the 1 Cor 13:6
truth. 9For we are glad when we are weak and you are strong. What Jer 1:10
we pray for is your improvement. 10I write this while I am away 2 Cor 10:4, 8, 11
from you, in order that when I come I may not have to be severe
in my use of the authority which the Lord has given me for
building up and not for tearing down.

7. WORDS OF FAREWELL

11Finally, brethren, farewell. Mend your ways, heed my appeal, Rom 15:33
agree with one another, live in peace, and the God of love and Phil 4:4

---

necessary—free choice and the grace of God. For, if free choice were not necessary, man would not be given precepts, prohibitions or exhortations. And punishments too would serve no purpose. Grace is necessary also, because man could not hold his ground were God not governing all by means of his grace [...]. Therefore, showing that both things are necessary, the Apostle asks God to provide grace, and admonishes them to exercise their free choice to avoid evil and do good" (*Commentary on 2 Cor,* ad loc.).

13:8. If the Corinthians mend their ways, there will no longer be grounds for punishment, and in that case St Paul has no intention of acting unjustly—doing anything against the truth—just to demonstrate his authority.

13:10. The rule St Paul gives for exercising God-given authority—that it be used for building up and not tearing down—is followed by the Hierarchy of the Church, as the Magisterium has often pointed out: "The bishops", Vatican II, for example, says, "as vicars and legates of Christ, govern the particular Churches assigned to them by their counsels, exhortations and example, but over and above that also by the authority and sacred power which indeed they exercise exclusively for the spiritual development of their flock in truth and holiness, keeping in mind that he who is greater should become as the lesser and he who is the leader as the servant (cf. Lk 22:26–27). [...] In virtue of this power bishops have a sacred right and a duty before the Lord of legislating for and of passing judgment on their subjects, as well as of regulating everything that concerns the good order of divine worship and of the apostolate" (*Lumen gentium*, 27).

13:11. In his words of farewell, the Apostle once more shows his great affection for the faithful of Corinth, exhorting them to practise the fraternity proper to Christians and thus live in concord and peace (cf. 1 Cor 1:10–17). And, St John Chrysostom comments, he tells them what this will lead to: "Live in peace, and the God of love and peace will be with you, for God is a God of love and a God of peace, and in these he takes his delight. It is love will give you peace and remove every evil from your church" (*Hom. on 2 Cor*, 30).

1 Cor 16:20 peace will be with you. 12Greet one another with a holy kiss. 13All
the saints greet you.
14The grace of the Lord Jesus Christ and the love of God and
the fellowship of[n] the Holy Spirit be with you all.

St Paul's call to the faithful to be cheerful is particularly significant—"*gaudete*" (rejoice) in the New Vulgate—contains a message he repeats on other occasions: "Rejoice in the Lord always; again I will say, Rejoice" (Phil 4:4; cf. 3:1). Joy is something very characteristic of Christians because their awareness of being children of God tells them that they are in the hands of God, who knows everything and can do everything (cf. note on 6:10). Therefore, we should never be sad; on the contrary: we should go out into the world, St Josemaría Escrivá says, "to be sowers of peace and joy through everything we say and do" (*Christ Is Passing By*, 168).

13:12. On the "holy kiss", see the note on 1 Cor 16:20.

"The saints" who send greetings to the Corinthians are the Christians of Macedonia, from where St Paul is writing. Regarding this description of Christians, see the note on 1 Cor 1:2.

13:14. This final greeting, which has been included in the Liturgy as one of the opening salutations at Mass, is clearly trinitarian. It distinguishes the three divine persons, while also stating their equality: each contributes to the sanctification and salvation of the faithful.

St Thomas points out that this greeting includes reference to all necessary supernatural graces: "The grace of Christ, by which we are justified and saved; the love of God the Father, by which we are united to him; and the fellowship of the Holy Spirit, who distributes the divine gifts to us" (*Commentary on 2 Cor,* ad loc.).

n. Or *and participation in*

New Vulgate Text

EPISTOLA PRIMA AD CORINTHIOS

[1] [1]Paulus, vocatus apostolus Christi Iesu per voluntatem Dei, et Sosthenes frater, [2]ecclesiae Dei, quae
est Corinthi, sanctificatis in Christo Iesu, vocatis sanctis cum omnibus, qui invocant nomen Domini
nostri Iesu Christi in omni loco ipsorum et nostro: [3]gratia vobis et pax a Deo Patre nostro et Domino
Iesu Christo. [4]Gratias ago Deo meo semper pro vobis in gratia Dei, quae data est vobis in Christo Iesu,
[5]quia in omnibus divites facti estis in illo, in omni verbo et in omni scientia, [6]sicut testimonium Christi
confirmatum est in vobis, [7]ita ut nihil vobis desit in ulla donatione, exspectantibus revelationem Domini
nostri Iesu Christi; [8]qui et confirmabit vos usque ad finem sine crimine in die Domini nostri Iesu Christi.
[9]Fidelis Deus, per quem vocati estis in communionem Filii eius Iesu Christi Domini nostri. [10]Obsecro
autem vos, fratres, per nomen Domini nostri Iesu Christi, ut idipsum dicatis omnes, et non sint in vobis
schismata, sitis autem perfecti in eodem sensu et in eadem sententia. [11]Significatum est enim mihi de
vobis, fratres mei, ab his, qui sunt Chloes, quia contentiones inter vos sunt. [12]Hoc autem dico, quod
unusquisque vestrum dicit: «Ego quidem sum Pauli», «Ego autem Apollo», «Ego vero Cephae», «Ego
autem Christi». [13]Divisus est Christus? Numquid Paulus crucifixus est pro vobis, aut in nomine Pauli
baptizati estis? [14]Gratias ago Deo quod neminem vestrum baptizavi nisi Crispum et Gaium, [15]ne quis
dicat quod in nomine meo baptizati sitis. [16]Baptizavi autem et Stephanae domum; ceterum nescio si
quem alium baptizaverim. [17]Non enim misit me Christus baptizare sed evangelizare, non in sapientia
verbi, ut non evacuetur crux Christi. [18]Verbum enim crucis pereuntibus quidem stultitia est, his autem,
qui salvi fiunt, id est nobis, virtus Dei est. [19]Scriptum est enim: «*Perdam sapientiam sapientium / et
prudentiam prudentium reprobabo*». [20]Ubi sapiens? Ubi scriba? Ubi conquisitor huius saeculi? Nonne
stultam fecit Deus sapientiam huius mundi? [21]Nam quia in Dei sapientia non cognovit mundus per
sapientiam Deum, placuit Deo per stultitiam praedicationis salvos facere credentes. [22]Quoniam et Iudaei
signa petunt, et Graeci sapientiam quaerunt, [23]nos autem praedicamus Christum crucifixum, Iudaeis
quidem scandalum, gentibus autem stultitiam; [24]ipsis autem vocatis, Iudaeis atque Graecis, Christum
Dei virtutem et Dei sapientiam, [25]quia quod stultum est Dei, sapientius est hominibus, et quod infirmum
est Dei, fortius est hominibus. [26]Videte enim vocationem vestram, fratres, quia non multi sapientes
secundum carnem, non multi potentes, non multi nobiles; [27]sed, quae stulta sunt mundi elegit Deus, ut
confundat sapientes, et infirma mundi elegit Deus, ut confundat fortia, [28]et ignobilia mundi et
contemptibilia elegit Deus, quae non sunt, ut ea, quae sunt, destrueret, [29]ut non glorietur omnis caro
in conspectu Dei. [30]Ex ipso autem vos estis in Christo Iesu, qui factus est sapientia nobis a Deo et
iustitia et sanctificatio et redemptio, [31]ut quemadmodum scriptum est: «*Qui gloriatur in Domino
glorietur*». **[2]** [1]Et ego, cum venissem ad vos, fratres, veni non per sublimitatem sermonis aut
sapientiae annuntians vobis mysterium Dei. [2]Non enim iudicavi scire me aliquid inter vos nisi Iesum
Christum et hunc crucifixum. [3]Et ego in infirmitate et timore et tremore multo fui apud vos, [4]et sermo
meus et praedicatio mea non in persuasibilibus sapientiae verbis, sed in ostensione Spiritus et virtutis,
[5]ut fides vestra non sit in sapientia hominum sed in virtute Dei. [6]Sapientiam autem loquimur inter
perfectos, sapientiam vero non huius saeculi neque principum huius saeculi, qui destruuntur, [7]sed
loquimur Dei sapientiam in mysterio, quae abscondita est, quam praedestinavit Deus ante saecula in
gloriam nostram, [8]quam nemo principum huius saeculi cognovit; si enim cognovissent, numquam
Dominum gloriae crucifixissent. [9]Sed sicut scriptum est: «*Quod oculus non vidit, nec auris audivit*, nec
in cor hominis ascendit, quae praeparavit Deus his, qui diligunt illum». [10]Nobis autem revelavit Deus
per Spiritum; Spiritus enim omnia scrutatur, etiam profunda Dei. [11]Quis enim scit hominum, quae sint
hominis, nisi spiritus hominis, qui in ipso est? Ita et, quae Dei sunt, nemo cognovit nisi Spiritus Dei.
[12]Nos autem non spiritum mundi accepimus, sed Spiritum, qui ex Deo est, ut sciamus, quae a Deo
donata sunt nobis; [13]quae et loquimur non in doctis humanae sapientiae, sed in doctis Spiritus verbis,
spiritalibus spiritalia comparantes. [14]Animalis autem homo non percipit, quae sunt Spiritus Dei, stultitia
enim sunt illi, et non potest intellegere, quia spiritaliter examinantur; [15]spiritalis autem iudicat omnia,
et ipse a nemine iudicatur. [16]*Quis enim cognovit sensum Domini, / qui instruat eum?* Nos autem sensum

Christi habemus. **[3]** 1Et ego, fratres, non potui vobis loqui quasi spiritalibus, sed quasi carnalibus,
tamquam parvulis in Christo. 2Lac vobis potum dedi, non escam, nondum enim poteratis. Sed ne nunc
quidem potestis, 3adhuc enim estis carnales. Cum enim sit inter vos zelus et contentio, nonne carnales
estis et secundum hominem ambulatis? 4Cum enim quis dicit: «Ego quidem sum Pauli», alius autem:
«Ego Apollo», nonne homines estis? 5Quid igitur est Apollo? Quid vero Paulus? Ministri, per quos
credidistis, et unicuique sicut Dominus dedit. 6Ego plantavi, Apollo rigavit, sed Deus incrementum
dedit; 7itaque neque qui plantat, est aliquid, neque qui rigat, sed qui incrementum dat, Deus. 8Qui plantat
autem et qui rigat unum sunt; unusquisque autem propriam mercedem accipiet secundum suum
laborem. 9Dei enim sumus adiutores: Dei agricultura estis, Dei aedificatio estis. 10Secundum gratiam
Dei, quae data est mihi, ut sapiens architectus fundamentum posui; alius autem superaedificat.
Unusquisque autem videat quomodo superaedificet; 11fundamentum enim aliud nemo potest ponere
praeter id, quod positum est, qui est Iesus Christus. 12Si quis autem superaedificat supra fundamentum
aurum, argentum, lapides pretiosos, ligna, fenum, stipulam, 13uniuscuiusque opus manifestum erit; dies
enim declarabit: quia in igne revelatur, et uniuscuiusque opus quale sit ignis probabit. 14Si cuius opus
manserit, quod superaedificavit, mercedem accipiet; 15si cuius opus arserit, detrimentum patietur, ipse
autem salvus erit, sic tamen quasi per ignem. 16Nescitis quia templum Dei estis et Spiritus Dei habitat
in vobis? 17Si quis autem templum Dei everterit, evertet illum Deus; templum enim Dei sanctum est,
quod estis vos. 18Nemo se seducat; si quis videtur sapiens esse inter vos in hoc saeculo, stultus fiat, ut
sit sapiens. 19Sapientia enim huius mundi stultitia est apud Deum. Scriptum est enim: «*Qui apprehendit
sapientes in astutia eorum*»; 20et iterum: «*Dominus novit cogitationes* sapientium / *quoniam vanae
sunt*». 21Itaque nemo glorietur in hominibus. Omnia enim vestra sunt, 22sive Paulus sive Apollo sive
Cephas sive mundus sive vita sive mors sive praesentia sive futura, omnia enim vestra sunt, 23vos autem
Christi, Christus autem Dei. **[4]** 1Sic nos existimet homo ut ministros Christi et dispensatores
mysteriorum Dei. 2Hic iam quaeritur inter dispensatores, ut fidelis quis inveniatur. 3Mihi autem pro
minimo est, ut a vobis iudicer aut ab humano die. Sed neque meipsum iudico; 4nihil enim mihi conscius
sum, sed non in hoc iustificatus sum. Qui autem iudicat me, Dominus est! 5Itaque nolite ante tempus
quidquam iudicare, quoadusque veniat Dominus, qui et illuminabit abscondita tenebrarum et
manifestabit consilia cordium; et tunc laus erit unicuique a Deo. 6Haec autem, fratres, transfiguravi in
me et Apollo propter vos, ut in nobis discatis illud: «Ne supra quae scripta sunt», ne unus pro alio
inflemini adversus alterum. 7Quis enim te discernit? Quid autem habes, quod non accepisti? Si autem
accepisti, quid gloriaris, quasi non acceperis? 8Iam saturati estis, iam divites facti estis. Sine nobis
regnastis; et utinam regnaretis, ut et nos vobiscum regnaremus. 9Puto enim, Deus nos apostolos
novissimos ostendit tamquam morti destinatos, quia spectaculum facti sumus mundo et angelis et
hominibus. 10Nos stulti propter Christum, vos autem prudentes in Christo; nos infirmi, vos autem fortes;
vos gloriosi, nos autem ignobiles. 11Usque in hanc horam et esurimus et sitimus et nudi sumus et
colaphis caedimur et instabiles sumus 12et laboramus operantes manibus nostris; maledicti benedicimus,
persecutionem passi sustinemus, 13blasphemati obsecramus; tamquam purgamenta mundi facti sumus,
omnium peripsema, usque adhuc. 14Non ut confundam vos, haec scribo, sed ut quasi filios meos
carissimos moneam; 15nam si decem milia paedagogorum habeatis in Christo, sed non multos patres,
nam in Christo Iesu per evangelium ego vos genui. 16Rogo ergo vos: imitatores mei estote! 17Ideo misi
ad vos Timotheum, qui est filius meus carissimus et fidelis in Domino, qui vos commonefaciat vias
meas, quae sunt in Christo, sicut ubique in omni ecclesia doceo. 18Tamquam non venturus sim ad vos,
sic inflati sunt quidam; 19veniam autem cito ad vos, si Dominus voluerit, et cognoscam non sermonem
eorum, qui inflati sunt, sed virtutem; 20non enim in sermone est regnum Dei sed in virtute. 21Quid
vultis? In virga veniam ad vos an in caritate et spiritu mansuetudinis? **[5]** 1Omnino auditur inter vos
fornicatio et talis fornicatio, qualis nec inter gentes, ita ut uxorem patris aliquis habeat. 2Et vos inflati
estis et non magis luctum habuistis, ut tollatur de medio vestrum, qui hoc opus fecit? 3Ego quidem
absens corpore, praesens autem spiritu, iam iudicavi ut praesens eum, qui sic operatus est, 4in nomine
Domini nostri Iesu, congregatis vobis et meo spiritu cum virtute Domini nostri Iesu, 5tradere huiusmodi
Satanae in interitum carnis, ut spiritus salvus sit in die Domini. 6Non bona gloriatio vestra. Nescitis quia
modicum fermentum totam massam corrumpit? 7Expurgate vetus fermentum, ut sitis nova consparsio,
sicut estis azymi. Etenim Pascha nostrum immolatus est Christus! 8Itaque festa celebremus, non in
fermento veteri neque in fermento malitiae et nequitiae, sed in azymis sinceritatis et veritatis. 9Scripsi
vobis in epistula: Ne commisceamini fornicariis. 10Non utique fornicariis huius mundi aut avaris aut
rapacibus aut idolis servientibus, alioquin debueratis de hoc mundo exisse! 11Nunc autem scripsi vobis
non commisceri, si is qui frater nominatur, est fornicator aut avarus aut idolis serviens aut maledicus aut
ebriosus aut rapax; cum eiusmodi nec cibum sumere. 12Quid enim mihi de his, qui foris sunt, iudicare?

Nonne de his, qui intus sunt, vos iudicatis? [13]Nam eos, qui foris sunt, Deus iudicabit. *Auferte malum ex*
vobis ipsis! **[6]** [1]Audet aliquis vestrum habens negotium adversus alterum iudicari apud iniquos et non
apud sanctos? [2]An nescitis quoniam sancti de mundo iudicabunt? Et si in vobis iudicabitur mundus,
indigni estis minimis iudiciis? [3]Nescitis quoniam angelos iudicabimus, quanto magis saecularia?
[4]Saecularia igitur iudicia si habueritis, contemptibiles, qui sunt in ecclesia, illos constituite ad
iudicandum? [5]Ad verecundiam vestram dico! Sic non est inter vos sapiens quisquam, qui possit iudicare
inter fratrem suum? [6]Sed frater cum fratre iudicio contendit, et hoc apud infideles? [7]Iam quidem omnino
defectio est vobis, quod iudicia habetis inter vosmetipsos! Quare non magis iniuriam accipitis, quare
non magis fraudem patimini? [8]Sed vos iniuriam facitis et fraudatis, et hoc fratribus! [9]An nescitis quia
iniqui regnum Dei non possidebunt? Nolite errare: neque fornicarii neque idolis servientes neque
adulteri neque molles neque masculorum concubitores [10]neque fures neque avari, non ebriosi, non
maledici, non rapaces regnum Dei possidebunt. [11]Et haec quidam fuistis. Sed abluti estis, sed sanctificati
estis, sed iustificati estis in nomine Domini Iesu Christi et in Spiritu Dei nostri ! [12]«Omnia mihi licent!».
Sed non omnia expediunt. «Omnia mihi licent!». Sed ego sub nullius redigar potestate. [13]«Esca ventri
et venter escis!». Deus autem et hunc et has destruet. Corpus autem non fornicationi sed Domino, et
Dominus corpori; [14]Deus vero et Dominum suscitavit et nos suscitabit per virtutem suam. [15]Nescitis
quoniam corpora vestra membra Christi sunt? Tollens ergo membra Christi faciam membra meretricis?
Absit! [16]An nescitis quoniam, qui adhaeret meretrici, unum corpus est? «*Erunt* enim, inquit, *duo in*
carne una». [17]Qui autem adhaeret Domino, unus Spiritus est. [18]Fugite fornicationem! Omne peccatum,
quodcumque fecerit homo, extra corpus est; qui autem fornicatur, in corpus suum peccat. [19]An nescitis
quoniam corpus vestrum templum est Spiritus Sancti, qui in vobis est, quem habetis a Deo, et non estis
vestri? [20]Empti enim estis pretio! Glorificate ergo Deum in corpore vestro. **[7]** [1]De quibus autem
scripsistis, bonum est homini mulierem non tangere; [2]propter fornicationes autem unusquisque suam
uxorem habeat, et unaquaeque suum virum habeat. [3]Uxori vir debitum reddat; similiter autem et uxor
viro. [4]Mulier sui corporis potestatem non habet sed vir; similiter autem et vir sui corporis potestatem
non habet sed mulier. [5]Nolite fraudare invicem, nisi forte ex consensu ad tempus, ut vacetis orationi et
iterum sitis in idipsum, ne tentet vos Satanas propter incontinentiam vestram. [6]Hoc autem dico
secundum indulgentiam, non secundum imperium. [7]Volo autem omnes homines esse sicut meipsum;
sed unusquisque proprium habet donum ex Deo: alius quidem sic, alius vero sic. [8]Dico autem innuptis
et viduis: Bonum est illis si sic maneant sicut et ego; [9]quod si non se continent, nubant. Melius est enim
nubere quam uri. [10]His autem, qui matrimonio iuncti sunt, praecipio, non ego sed Dominus, uxorem a
viro non discedere [11]—quod si discesserit, maneat innupta aut viro suo reconcilietur—et virum uxorem
non dimittere. [12]Ceteris autem ego dico, non Dominus: Si quis frater uxorem habet infidelem, et haec
consentit habitare cum illo, non dimittat illam; [13]et si qua mulier habet virum infidelem, et hic consentit
habitare cum illa, non dimittat virum. [14]Sanctificatus est enim vir infidelis in muliere, et sanctificata est
mulier infidelis in fratre. Alioquin filii vestri immundi essent; nunc autem sancti sunt. [15]Quod si infidelis
discedit, discedat. Non est enim servituti subiectus frater aut soror in eiusmodi; in pace autem vocavit
nos Deus. [16]Quid enim scis, mulier, si virum salvum facies? Aut quid scis, vir, si mulierem salvam
facies? [17]Nisi unicuique, sicut divisit Dominus, unumquemque, sicut vocavit Deus, ita ambulet; et sic
in omnibus ecclesiis doceo. [18]Circumcisus aliquis vocatus est? Non adducat praeputium! In praeputio
aliquis vocatus est? Non circumcidatur! [19]Circumcisio nihil est, et praeputium nihil est, sed observatio
mandatorum Dei. [20]Unusquisque, in qua vocatione vocatus est, in ea permaneat. [21]Servus vocatus es?
Non sit tibi curae; sed et si potes liber fieri, magis utere! [22]Qui enim in Domino vocatus est servus,
libertus est Domini; similiter, qui liber vocatus est, servus est Christi! [23]Pretio empti estis! Nolite fieri
servi hominum. [24]Unusquisque, in quo vocatus est, fratres, in hoc maneat apud Deum. [25]De virginibus
autem praeceptum Domini non habeo, consilium autem do, tamquam misericordiam consecutus a
Domino ut sim fidelis. [26]Existimo ergo hoc bonum esse propter instantem necessitatem, quoniam
bonum est homini sic esse. [27]Alligatus es uxori? Noli quaerere solutionem. Solutus es ab uxore? Noli
quaerere uxorem. [28]Si autem acceperis uxorem, non peccasti; et si nupserit virgo, non peccavit.
Tribulationem tamen carnis habebunt huiusmodi, ego autem vobis parco. [29]Hoc itaque dico, fratres,
tempus breviatum est; reliquum est, ut et qui habent uxores, tamquam non habentes sint, [30]et qui flent,
tamquam non flentes, et qui gaudent, tamquam non gaudentes, et qui emunt, tamquam non possidentes,
[31]et qui utuntur hoc mundo, tamquam non abutentes; praeterit enim figura huius mundi. [32]Volo autem
vos sine sollicitudine esse. Qui sine uxore est, sollicitus est, quae Domini sunt, quomodo placeat
Domino; [33]qui autem cum uxore est, sollicitus est, quae sunt mundi, quomodo placeat uxori, [34]et divisus
est. Et mulier innupta et virgo cogitat, quae Domini sunt, ut sit sancta et corpore et spiritu; quae autem
nupta est, cogitat, quae sunt mundi, quomodo placeat viro. [35]Porro hoc ad utilitatem vestram dico, non

ut laqueum vobis iniciam, sed ad id quod honestum est et ut assidue cum Domino sitis sine distractione.
36Si quis autem turpem se videri existimat super virgine sua quod sit superadulta, et ita oportet fieri,
quod vult, faciat; non peccat: nubant. 37Qui autem statuit in corde suo firmus, non habens necessitatem,
potestatem autem habet suae voluntatis, et hoc iudicavit in corde suo servare virginem suam, bene
faciet; 38igitur et, qui matrimonio iungit virginem suam, bene facit; et, qui non iungit, melius faciet.
39Mulier alligata est, quanto tempore vir eius vivit; quod si dormierit vir eius, libera est, cui vult nubere,
tantum in Domino. 40Beatior autem erit, si sic permanserit secundum meum consilium; puto autem quod
et ego Spiritum Dei habeo. **[8]** 1De idolothytis autem, scimus quia omnes scientiam habemus. Scientia
inflat, caritas vero aedificat. 2Si quis se existimat scire aliquid, nondum cognovit, quemadmodum
oporteat eum scire; 3si quis autem diligit Deum, hic cognitus est ab eo. 4De esu igitur idolothytorum,
scimus quia nullum idolum est in mundo et quod nullus deus nisi Unus. 5Nam et si sunt, qui dicantur
dii sive in caelo sive in terra, siquidem sunt dii multi et domini multi, 6nobis tamen unus Deus Pater, ex
quo omnia et nos in illum, et unus Dominus Iesus Christus, per quem omnia et nos per ipsum. 7Sed non
in omnibus est scientia; quidam autem consuetudine usque nunc idoli quasi idolothytum manducant, et
conscientia ipsorum, cum sit infirma, polluitur. 8Esca autem nos non commendat Deo; neque si non
manducaverimus, deficiemus, neque si manducaverimus, abundabimus. 9Videte autem, ne forte haec
licentia vestra offendiculum fiat infirmis. 10Si enim quis viderit eum, qui habet scientiam, in idolio
recumbentem, nonne conscientia eius, cum sit infirma, aedificabitur ad manducandum idolothyta?
11Peribit enim infirmus in tua scientia, frater, propter quem Christus mortuus est! 12Sic autem peccantes
in fratres et percutientes conscientiam eorum infirmam, in Christum peccatis. 13Quapropter si esca
scandalizat fratrem meum, non manducabo carnem in aeternum, ne fratrem meum scandalizem.
[9] 1Non sum liber? Non sum apostolus? Nonne Iesum Dominum nostrum vidi? Non opus meum vos
estis in Domino? 2Si aliis non sum apostolus, sed tamen vobis sum; nam signaculum apostolatus mei
vos estis in Domino. 3Mea defensio apud eos, qui me interrogant, haec est. 4Numquid non habemus
potestatem manducandi et bibendi? 5Numquid non habemus potestatem sororem mulierem
circumducendi sicut et ceteri apostoli et fratres Domini et Cephas? 6Aut solus ego et Barnabas non
habemus potestatem non operandi? 7Quis militat suis stipendiis umquam? Quis plantat vineam et
fructum eius non edit? Aut quis pascit gregem et de lacte gregis non manducat? 8Numquid secundum
hominem haec dico? An et lex haec non dicit? 9Scriptum est enim in Lege Moysis: «*Non alligabis os
bovi trituranti*». Numquid de bobus cura est Deo? 10An propter nos utique dicit? Nam propter nos
scripta sunt, quoniam debet in spe, qui arat, arare et, qui triturat, in spe fructus percipiendi. 11Si nos
vobis spiritalia seminavimus, magnum est, si nos carnalia vestra metamus? 12Si alii potestatis vestrae
participes sunt, non potius nos? Sed non usi sumus hac potestate, sed omnia sustinemus, ne quod
offendiculum demus evangelio Christi. 13Nescitis quoniam, qui sacra operantur, quae de sacrario sunt
edunt; qui altari deserviunt, cum altari participantur? 14Ita et Dominus ordinavit his, qui evangelium
annuntiant, de evangelio vivere. 15Ego autem nullo horum usus sum. Non scripsi autem haec, ut ita fiant
in me; bonum est enim mihi magis mori quam ut gloriam meam quis evacuet. 16Nam si evangelizavero,
non est mihi gloria; necessitas enim mihi incumbit. Vae enim mihi est, si non evangelizavero! 17Si enim
volens hoc ago, mercedem habeo; si autem invitus, dispensatio mihi credita est. 18Quae est ergo merces
mea? Ut evangelium praedicans sine sumptu ponam evangelium, ut non abutar potestate mea in
evangelio. 19Nam cum liber essem ex omnibus, omnium me servum feci, ut plures lucri facerem. 20Et
factus sum Iudaeis tamquam Iudaeus, ut Iudaeos lucrarer; his, qui sub lege sunt, quasi sub lege essem,
cum ipse non essem sub lege, ut eos, qui sub lege erant, lucri facerem; 21his, qui sine lege erant,
tamquam sine lege essem, cum sine lege Dei non essem, sed in lege essem Christi, ut lucri facerem eos,
qui sine lege erant; 22factus sum infirmis infirmus, ut infirmos lucri facerem; omnibus omnia factus sum,
ut aliquos utique facerem salvos. 23Omnia autem facio propter evangelium, ut comparticeps eius efficiar.
24Nescitis quod hi, qui in stadio currunt, omnes quidem currunt, sed unus accipit bravium? Sic currite,
ut comprehendatis. 25Omnis autem, qui in agone contendit, ab omnibus se abstinet, et illi quidem, ut
corruptibilem coronam accipiant, nos autem incorruptam. 26Ego igitur sic curro non quasi in incertum,
sic pugno non quasi aerem verberans; 27sed castigo corpus meum et in servitutem redigo, ne forte, cum
aliis praedicaverim, ipse reprobus efficiar. **[10]** 1Nolo enim vos ignorare, fratres, quoniam patres nostri
omnes sub nube fuerunt et omnes mare transierunt 2et omnes in Moyse baptizati sunt in nube et in mari
3et omnes eandem escam spiritalem manducaverunt 4et omnes eundem potum spiritalem biberunt;
bibebant autem de spiritali, consequente eos petra: petra autem erat Christus 5 Sed non in pluribus
eorum complacuit sibi Deus, nam prostrati sunt in deserto. 6Haec autem figurae fuerunt nostrae, ut non
simus concupiscentes malorum, sicut et illi concupierunt. 7Neque idolorum cultores efficiamini, sicut
quidam ex ipsis; quemadmodum scriptum est: «*Sedit populus manducare et bibere, et surrexerunt*

ludere». 8 Neque fornicemur, sicut quidam ex ipsis fornicati sunt, et ceciderunt una die viginti tria milia.
9 Neque tentemus Christum, sicut quidam eorum tentaverunt, et a serpentibus perierunt. 10 Neque
murmuraveritis, sicut quidam eorum murmuraverunt et perierunt ab exterminatore. 11 Haec autem in
figura contingebant illis; scripta sunt autem ad correptionem nostram, in quos fines saeculorum
devenerunt. 12 Itaque, qui se existimat stare, videat, ne cadat. 13 Tentatio vos non apprehendit nisi
humana; fidelis autem Deus, qui non patietur vos tentari super id quod potestis, sed faciet cum
tentatione etiam proventum, ut possitis sustinere. 14 Propter quod, carissimi mihi, fugite ab idolorum
cultura. 15 Ut prudentibus loquor; vos iudicate, quod dico: 16 Calix benedictionis, cui benedicimus, nonne
communicatio sanguinis Christi est? Et panis, quem frangimus, nonne communicatio corporis Christi
est? 17 Quoniam unus panis, unum corpus multi sumus, omnes enim de uno pane participamur. 18 Videte
Israel secundum carnem: nonne, qui edunt hostias, communicantes sunt altari? 19 Quid ergo dico? Quod
idolothytum sit aliquid? Aut quod idolum sit aliquid? 20 Sed, quae immolant, daemoniis immolant et non
Deo; nolo autem vos communicantes fieri daemoniis. 21 Non potestis calicem Domini bibere et calicem
daemoniorum; non potestis mensae Domini participes esse et mensae daemoniorum. 22 An aemulamur
Dominum? Numquid fortiores illo sumus? 23 «Omnia licent!» Sed non omnia expediunt. «Omnia
licent!». Sed non omnia aedificant. 24 Nemo, quod suum est, quaerat, sed quod alterius. 25 Omnes, quod
in macello venit, manducate, nihil interrogantes propter conscientiam; 26 *Domini enim est terra et
plenitudo eius*. 27 Si quis vocat vos infidelium, et vultis ire, omne, quod vobis apponitur, manducate, nihil
interrogantes propter conscientiam. 28 Si quis autem vobis dixerit: «Hoc immolaticium est idolis», nolite
manducare, propter illum, qui indicavit, et propter conscientiam; 29 conscientiam autem dico non tuam
ipsius, sed alterius. Ut quid enim libertas mea iudicatur ab alia conscientia? 30 Si ego cum gratia
participo, quid blasphemor pro eo, quod gratias ago? 31 Sive ergo manducatis sive bibitis sive aliud quid
facitis, omnia in gloriam Dei facite. 32 Sine offensione estote Iudaeis et Graecis et ecclesiae Dei, 33 sicut
et ego per omnia omnibus placeo, non quaerens, quod mihi utile est, sed quod multis, ut salvi fiant.
[11] 1 Imitatores mei estote sicut et ego Christi. 2 Laudo autem vos quod omnia mei memores estis et,
sicut tradidi vobis, traditiones meas tenetis. 3 Volo autem vos scire quod omnis viri caput Christus est,
caput autem mulieris vir, caput vero Christi Deus. 4 Omnis vir orans aut prophetans velato capite,
deturpat caput suum; 5 omnis autem mulier orans aut prophetans non velato capite, deturpat caput suum:
unum est enim atque si decalvetur. 6 Nam si non velatur mulier, et tondeatur! Si vero turpe est mulieri
tonderi aut decalvari, veletur. 7 Vir quidem non debet velare caput, quoniam imago et gloria est Dei;
mulier autem gloria viri est. 8 Non enim vir ex muliere est, sed mulier ex viro; 9 etenim non est creatus
vir propter mulierem, sed mulier propter virum. 10 Ideo debet mulier potestatem habere supra caput
propter angelos. 11 Verumtamen neque mulier sine viro, neque vir sine muliere in Domino; 12 nam sicut
mulier de viro, ita et vir per mulierem, omnia autem ex Deo. 13 In vobis ipsi iudicate: Decet mulierem
non velatam orare Deum? 14 Nec ipsa natura docet vos quod vir quidem, si comam nutriat, ignominia
est illi, 15 mulier vero, si comam nutriat, gloria est illi? Quoniam coma pro velamine ei data est. 16 Si quis
autem videtur contentiosus esse, nos talem consuetudinem non habemus, neque ecclesiae Dei. 17 Hoc
autem praecipio non laudans quod non in melius sed in deterius convenitis. 18 Primum quidem
convenientibus vobis in ecclesia, audio scissuras inter vos esse et ex parte credo. 19 Nam oportet et
haereses inter vos esse, ut et, qui probati sunt, manifesti fiant in vobis. 20 Convenientibus ergo vobis in
unum, non est dominicam cenam manducare; 21 unusquisque enim suam cenam praesumit in
manducando, et alius quidem esurit, alius autem ebrius est. 22 Numquid domos non habetis ad
manducandum et bibendum? Aut ecclesiam Dei contemnitis et confunditis eos, qui non habent? Quid
dicam vobis? Laudabo vos? In hoc non laudo! 23 Ego enim accepi a Domino, quod et tradidi vobis,
quoniam Dominus Iesus, in qua nocte tradebatur, accepit panem 24 et gratias agens fregit et dixit: «*Hoc
est corpus meum, quod pro vobis est; hoc facite in meam commemorationem*»; 25 similiter et calicem,
postquam cenatum est, dicens: «*Hic calix novum testamentum est in meo sanguine; hoc facite,
quotiescumque bibetis, in meam commemorationem*». 26 Quotiescumque enim manducabitis panem hunc
et calicem bibetis, mortem Domini annuntiatis, donec veniat. 27 Itaque, quicumque manducaverit panem
vel biberit calicem Domini indigne, reus erit corporis et sanguinis Domini. 28 Probet autem seipsum
homo, et sic de pane illo edat et de calice bibat; 29 qui enim manducat et bibit, iudicium sibi manducat
et bibit non diiudicans corpus. 30 Ideo inter vos multi infirmi et imbecilles et dormiunt multi. 31 Quod si
nosmetipsos diiudicaremus, non utique iudicaremur; 32 dum iudicamur autem, a Domino corripimur, ut
non cum hoc mundo damnemur. 33 Itaque, fratres mei, cum convenitis ad manducandum, invicem
exspectate. 34 Si quis esurit, domi manducet, ut non in iudicium conveniatis. Cetera autem, cum venero,
disponam. **[12]** 1 De spiritalibus autem, fratres, nolo vos ignorare. 2 Scitis quoniam, cum gentes essetis,
ad simulacra muta, prout ducebamini, euntes. 3 Ideo notum vobis facio quod nemo in Spiritu Dei loquens

dicit: «Anathema Iesus!», et nemo potest dicere: «Dominus Iesus», nisi in Spiritu Sancto. [4]Divisiones
vero gratiarum sunt, idem autem Spiritus; [5]et divisiones ministrationum sunt, idem autem Dominus; [6]et
divisiones operationum sunt, idem vero Deus, qui operatur omnia in omnibus. [7]Unicuique autem datur
manifestatio Spiritus ad utilitatem. [8]Alii quidem per Spiritum datur sermo sapientiae, alii autem sermo
scientiae secundum eundem Spiritum, [9]alteri fides in eodem Spiritu, alii donationes sanitatum in uno
Spiritu, [10]alii operationes virtutum, alii prophetatio, alii discretio spirituum, alii genera linguarum, alii
interpretatio linguarum; [11]haec autem omnia operatur unus et idem Spiritus, dividens singulis, prout
vult. [12]Sicut enim corpus unum est et membra habet multa, omnia autem membra corporis, cum sint
multa, unum corpus sunt, ita et Christus; [13]etenim in uno Spiritu omnes nos in unum corpus baptizati
sumus, sive Iudaei sive Graeci sive servi sive liberi, et omnes unum Spiritum potati sumus. [14]Nam et
corpus non est unum membrum sed multa. [15]Si dixerit pes: «Non sum manus, non sum de corpore», non
ideo non est de corpore; [16]et si dixerit auris: «Non sum oculus, non sum de corpore», non ideo non est
de corpore. [17]Si totum corpus oculus est, ubi auditus? Si totum auditus, ubi odoratus? [18]Nunc autem
posuit Deus membra, unumquodque eorum in corpore, sicut voluit. [19]Quod si essent omnia unum
membrum, ubi corpus? [20]Nunc autem multa quidem membra, unum autem corpus. [21]Non potest dicere
oculus manui: «Non es mihi necessaria!», aut iterum caput pedibus: «Non estis mihi necessarii!». [22]Sed
multo magis, quae videntur membra corporis infirmiora esse, necessaria sunt; [23]et, quae putamus
ignobiliora membra esse corporis, his honorem abundantiorem circumdamus; et, quae inhonesta sunt
nostra, abundantiorem honestatem habent, [24]honesta autem nostra nullius egent. Sed Deus temperavit
corpus, ei, cui deerat, abundantiorem tribuendo honorem, [25]ut non sit schisma in corpore, sed idipsum
pro invicem sollicita sint membra. [26]Et sive patitur unum membrum, compatiuntur omnia membra; sive
glorificatur unum membrum, congaudent omnia membra. [27]Vos autem estis corpus Christi et membra
ex parte. [28]Et quosdam quidem posuit Deus in ecclesia primum apostolos, secundo prophetas, tertio
doctores, deinde virtutes, exinde donationes curationum, opitulationes, gubernationes, genera
linguarum. [29]Numquid omnes apostoli? Numquid omnes prophetae? Numquid omnes doctores?
Numquid omnes virtutes? [30]Numquid omnes donationes habent curationum? Numquid omnes linguis
loquuntur? Numquid omnes interpretantur? [31]Aemulamini autem charismata maiora. Et adhuc
excellentiorem viam vobis demonstro. **[13]** [1]Si linguis hominum loquar et angelorum, caritatem autem
non habeam, factus sum velut aes sonans aut cymbalum tinniens. [2]Et si habuero prophetiam et noverim
mysteria omnia et omnem scientiam, et si habuero omnem fidem, ita ut montes transferam, caritatem
autem non habuero, nihil sum. [3]Et si distribuero in cibos omnes facultates meas et si tradidero corpus
meum, ut glorier, caritatem autem non habuero, nihil mihi prodest. [4]Caritas patiens est, benigna est
caritas, non aemulatur, non agit superbe, non inflatur, [5]non est ambitiosa, non quaerit, quae sua sunt,
non irritatur, non cogitat malum, [6]non gaudet super iniquitatem, congaudet autem veritati; [7]omnia
suffert, omnia credit, omnia sperat, omnia sustinet. [8]Caritas numquam excidit. Sive prophetiae,
evacuabuntur; sive linguae, cessabunt; sive scientia, destruetur. [9]Ex parte enim cognoscimus et ex parte
prophetamus; [10]cum autem venerit, quod perfectum est, evacuabitur, quod ex parte est. [11]Cum essem
parvulus, loquebar ut parvulus, sapiebam ut parvulus, cogitabam ut parvulus; quando factus sum vir,
evacuavi, quae erant parvuli. [12]Videmus enim nunc per speculum in aenigmate, tunc autem facie ad
faciem; nunc cognosco ex parte, tunc autem cognoscam, sicut et cognitus sum. [13]Nunc autem manet
fides, spes, caritas, tria haec; maior autem ex his est caritas. **[14]** [1]Sectamini caritatem, aemulamini
spiritalia, magis autem, ut prophetetis. [2]Qui enim loquitur lingua, non hominibus loquitur, sed Deo;
nemo enim audit, spiritu autem loquitur mysteria. [3]Qui autem prophetat, hominibus loquitur
aedificationem et exhortationem et consolationes. [4]Qui loquitur lingua, semetipsum aedificat; qui autem
prophetat, ecclesiam aedificat. [5]Volo autem omnes vos loqui linguis, magis autem prophetare; maior
autem est qui prophetat quam qui loquitur linguis, nisi forte interpretetur, ut ecclesia aedificationem
accipiat. [6]Nunc autem, fratres, si venero ad vos linguis loquens, quid vobis prodero, nisi vobis loquar
aut in revelatione aut in scientia aut in prophetia aut in doctrina? [7]Tamen, quae sine anima sunt vocem
dantia, sive tibia sive cithara, nisi distinctionem sonituum dederint, quomodo scietur quod tibia canitur
aut quod citharizatur? [8]Etenim si incertam vocem det tuba, quis parabit se ad bellum? [9]Ita et vos per
linguam nisi manifestum sermonem dederitis, quomodo scietur id, quod dicitur? Eritis enim in aera
loquentes. [10]Tam multa, ut puta, genera linguarum sunt in mundo, et nihil sine voce est. [11]Si ergo
nesciero virtutem vocis, ero ei, qui loquitur, barbarus; et, qui loquitur, mihi, barbarus. [12]Sic et vos,
quoniam aemulatores estis spirituum, ad aedificationem ecclesiae quaerite, ut abundetis. [13]Et ideo, qui
loquitur lingua, oret, ut interpretetur. [14]Nam si orem lingua, spiritus meus orat, mens autem mea sine
fructu est. [15]Quid ergo est? Orabo spiritu, orabo et mente; psallam spiritu, psallam et mente. [16]Ceterum
si benedixeris in spiritu, qui supplet locum idiotae, quomodo dicet «Amen!» super tuam benedictionem,

quoniam quid dicas nescit? [17]Nam tu quidem bene gratias agis, sed alter non aedificatur. [18]Gratias ago
Deo quod omnium vestrum magis linguis loquor; [19]sed in ecclesia volo quinque verba sensu meo loqui,
ut et alios instruam, quam decem milia verborum in lingua. [20]Fratres, nolite pueri effici sensibus, sed
malitia parvuli estote, sensibus autem perfecti estote. [21]In lege scriptum est: «*In aliis linguis et in labiis
aliorum / loquar populo huic, / et nec sic exaudient me*», dicit Dominus. [22]Itaque linguae in signum sunt
non fidelibus sed infidelibus, prophetia autem non infidelibus sed fidelibus. [23]Si ergo conveniat universa
ecclesia in unum, et omnes linguis loquantur, intrent autem idiotae aut infideles, nonne dicent quod
insanitis? [24]Si autem omnes prophetent, intret autem quis infidelis vel idiota, convincitur ab omnibus,
diiudicatur ab omnibus, [25]occulta cordis eius manifesta fiunt, et ita cadens in faciem adorabit Deum
pronuntians: «Vere Deus in vobis est!». [26]Quid ergo est, fratres? Cum convenitis, unusquisque psalmum
habet, doctrinam habet, apocalypsim habet, linguam habet, interpretationem habet: omnia ad
aedificationem fiant. [27]Sive lingua quis loquitur, secundum duos aut ut multum tres, et per partes, et
unus interpretetur; [28]si autem non fuerit interpres, taceat in ecclesia, sibi autem loquatur et Deo.
[29]Prophetae duo aut tres dicant, et ceteri diiudicent; [30]quod si alii revelatum fuerit sedenti, prior taceat.
[31]Potestis enim omnes per singulos prophetare, ut omnes discant et omnes exhortentur, [32]et spiritus
prophetarum prophetis subiecti sunt; [33]non enim est dissensionis Deus sed pacis. Sicut in omnibus
ecclesiis sanctorum, [34]mulieres in ecclesiis taceant, non enim permittitur eis loqui; sed subditae sint,
sicut et lex dicit. [35]Si quid autem volunt discere, domi viros suos interrogent; turpe est enim mulieri
loqui in ecclesia. [36]An a vobis verbum Dei processit aut in vos solos pervenit? [37]Si quis videtur propheta
esse aut spiritalis, cognoscat, quae scribo vobis, quia Domini est mandatum. [38]Si quis autem ignorat,
ignorabitur. [39]Itaque, fratres mei, aemulamini prophetare et loqui linguis nolite prohibere; [40]omnia
autem honeste et secundum ordinem fiant. **[15]** [1]Notum autem vobis facio, fratres, evangelium, quod
evangelizavi vobis, quod et accepistis, in quo et statis, [2]per quod et salvamini, qua ratione
evangelizaverim vobis, si tenetis, nisi si frustra credidistis! [3]Tradidi enim vobis in primis, quod et accepi,
quoniam Christus mortuus est pro peccatis nostris secundum Scripturas [4]et quia sepultus est et quia
suscitatus est tertia die secundum Scripturas [5]et quia visus est Cephae et post haec Duodecim; [6]deinde
visus est plus quam quingentis fratribus simul, ex quibus plures manent usque adhuc, quidam autem
dormierunt; [7]deinde visus est Iacobo, deinde apostolis omnibus; [8]novissime autem omnium, tamquam
abortivo, visus est et mihi. [9]Ego enim sum minimus apostolorum, qui non sum dignus vocari apostolus,
quoniam persecutus sum ecclesiam Dei; [10]gratia autem Dei sum id, quod sum, et gratia eius in me vacua
non fuit, sed abundantius illis omnibus laboravi, non ego autem, sed gratia Dei mecum. [11]Igitur sive ego
sive illi, sic praedicamus, et sic credidistis. [12]Si autem Christus praedicatur quod suscitatus est a mortuis,
quomodo quidam dicunt in vobis quoniam resurrectio mortuorum non est? [13]Si autem resurrectio
mortuorum non est, neque Christus suscitatus est! [14]Si autem Christus non suscitatus est, inanis est ergo
praedicatio nostra, inanis est et fides vestra, [15]invenimur autem et falsi testes Dei, quoniam testimonium
diximus adversus Deum quod suscitaverit Christum, quem non suscitavit, si revera mortui non
resurgunt. [16]Nam si mortui non resurgunt, neque Christus resurrexit; [17]quod si Christus non resurrexit,
stulta est fides vestra, adhuc estis in peccatis vestris [18]Ergo et, qui dormierunt in Christo, perierunt. [19]Si
in hac vita tantum in Christo sperantes sumus, miserabiliores sumus omnibus hominibus. [20]Nunc autem
Christus resurrexit a mortuis, primitiae dormientium. [21]Quoniam enim per hominem mors, et per
hominem resurrectio mortuorum: [22]sicut enim in Adam omnes moriuntur, ita et in Christo omnes
vivificabuntur. [23]Unusquisque autem in suo ordine: primitiae Christus; deinde hi, qui sunt Christi, in
adventu eius; [24]deinde finis, cum tradiderit regnum Deo et Patri, cum evacuaverit omnem principatum
et omnem potestatem et virtutem. [25]Oportet autem illum regnare, *donec ponat* omnes *inimicos sub
pedibus* eius. [26]Novissima autem inimica destruetur mors; [27]*omnia* enim *subiecit sub pedibus eius*. Cum
autem dicat: «Omnia subiecta sunt», sine dubio praeter eum, qui subiecit ei omnia. [28]Cum autem
subiecta fuerint illi omnia, tunc ipse Filius subiectus erit illi, qui sibi subiecit omnia, ut sit Deus omnia
in omnibus. [29]Alioquin quid facient, qui baptizantur pro mortuis? Si omnino mortui non resurgunt, ut
quid et baptizantur pro illis? [30]Ut quid et nos periclitamur omni hora? [31]Cotidie morior, utique per
vestram gloriationem, fratres, quam habeo in Christo Iesu Domino nostro! [32]Si secundum hominem ad
bestias pugnavi Ephesi, quid mihi prodest? Si mortui non resurgunt, *manducemus et bibamus, cras enim
moriemur*. [33]Nolite seduci: «Corrumpunt mores bonos colloquia mala». [34]Evigilate iuste et nolite
peccare! Ignorantiam enim Dei quidam habent; ad reverentiam vobis loquor. [35]Sed dicet aliquis:
«Quomodo resurgunt mortui? Quali autem corpore veniunt?». [36]Insipiens! Tu, quod seminas, non
vivificatur, nisi prius moriatur; [37]et quod seminas, non corpus, quod futurum est, seminas, sed nudum
granum, ut puta tritici aut alicuius ceterorum. [38]Deus autem dat illi corpus sicut voluit, et unicuique
seminum proprium corpus. [39]Non omnis caro eadem caro, sed alia hominum, alia caro pecorum, alia

caro volucrum, alia autem piscium. [40]Et corpora caelestia et corpora terrestria, sed alia quidem caelestium gloria, alia autem terrestrium. [41]Alia claritas solis, alia claritas lunae et alia claritas stellarum; stella enim a stella differt in claritate. [42]Sic et resurrectio mortuorum: seminatur in corruptione, resurgit in incorruptione; [43]seminatur in ignobilitate, resurgit in gloria; seminatur in infirmitate, resurgit in virtute; [44] seminatur corpus animale, resurgit corpus spiritale. Si est corpus animale, est et spiritale. [45]Sic et scriptum est: «*Factus est* primus *homo* Adam *in animam viventem*»; novissimus Adam in Spiritum vivificantem. [46]Sed non prius, quod spiritale est, sed quod animale est; deinde quod spiritale. [47]Primus homo de terra terrenus, secundus homo de caelo. [48]Qualis terrenus, tales et terreni, et qualis caelestis, tales et caelestes; [49]et sicut portavimus imaginem terreni, portabimus et imaginem caelestis. [50]Hoc autem dico, fratres, quoniam caro et sanguis regnum Dei possidere non possunt, neque corruptio incorruptelam possidebit. [51]Ecce mysterium vobis dico: Non omnes quidem dormiemus, sed omnes immutabimur, [52]in momento, in ictu oculi, in novissima tuba; canet enim, et mortui suscitabuntur incorrupti, et nos immutabimur. [53]Oportet enim corruptibile hoc induere incorruptelam, et mortale induere immortalitatem. [54]Cum autem corruptibile hoc induerit incorruptelam, et mortale hoc induerit immortalitatem, tunc fiet sermo, qui scriptus est: «*Absorpta est mors in victoria. /* [55]*Ubi est, mors, victoria tua? / Ubi est, mors, stimulus tuus?*» [56]Stimulus autem mortis peccatum est, virtus vero peccati lex. [57]Deo autem gratias, qui dedit nobis victoriam per Dominum nostrum Iesum Christum. [58]Itaque, fratres mei dilecti, stabiles estote, immobiles, abundantes in opere Domini semper, scientes quod labor vester non est inanis in Domino. **[16]**[1]De collectis autem, quae fiunt in sanctos, sicut ordinavi ecclesiis Galatiae, ita et vos facite. [2]Per primam sabbati unusquisque vestrum apud se ponat recondens, quod ei beneplacuerit, ut non, cum venero, tunc collectae fiant. [3]Cum autem praesens fuero, quos probaveritis, per epistulas hos mittam perferre gratiam vestram in Ierusalem; [4]quod si dignum fuerit, ut et ego eam, mecum ibunt. [5]Veniam autem ad vos, cum Macedoniam pertransiero, nam Macedoniam pertransibo; [6]apud vos autem forsitan manebo vel etiam hiemabo, ut vos me deducatis, quocumque iero. [7]Nolo enim vos modo in transitu videre; spero enim me aliquantum temporis manere apud vos, si Dominus permiserit. [8]Permanebo autem Ephesi usque ad Pentecosten; [9]ostium enim mihi apertum est magnum et efficax, et adversarii multi. [10]Si autem venerit Timotheus, videte, ut sine timore sit apud vos, opus enim Domini operatur sicut et ego; [11]ne quis ergo illum spernat. Deducite autem illum in pace, ut veniat ad me; exspecto enim illum cum fratribus. [12]De Apollo autem fratre, multum rogavi eum, ut veniret ad vos cum fratribus, et utique non fuit voluntas, ut nunc veniret; veniet autem, cum ei opportunum fuerit. [13]Vigilate, state in fide, viriliter agite, confortamini; [14]omnia vestra in caritate fiant. [15]Obsecro autem vos, fratres: nostis domum Stephanae, quoniam sunt primitiae Achaiae et in ministerium sanctorum ordinaverunt seipsos; [16]ut et vos subditi sitis eiusmodi et omni cooperanti et laboranti. [17]Gaudeo autem in praesentia Stephanae et Fortunati et Achaici, quoniam id, quod vobis deerat, ipsi suppleverunt, [18]refecerunt enim et meum spiritum et vestrum. Cognoscite ergo, qui eiusmodi sunt. [19]Salutant vos ecclesiae Asiae. Salutant vos in Domino multum Aquila et Prisca cum domestica sua ecclesia. [20]Salutant vos fratres omnes. Salutate invicem in osculo sancto. [21]Salutatio mea manu Pauli. [22]Si quis non amat Dominum, sit anathema. Marana tha! [23]Gratia Domini Iesu vobiscum. [24]Caritas mea cum omnibus vobis in Christo Iesu.

EPISTOLA SECUNDA AD CORINTHIOS

[1] [1]Paulus apostolus Christi Iesu per voluntatem Dei, et Timotheus frater, ecclesiae Dei, quae est Corinthi, cum sanctis omnibus, qui sunt in universa Achaia: [2]gratia vobis et pax a Deo Patre nostro et Domino Iesu Christo. [3]Benedictus Deus et Pater Domini nostri Iesu Christi, Pater misericordiarum et Deus totius consolationis, [4]qui consolatur nos in omni tribulatione nostra, ut possimus et ipsi consolari eos, qui in omni pressura sunt, per exhortationem, qua exhortamur et ipsi a Deo; [5]quoniam, sicut abundant passiones Christi in nobis, ita per Christum abundat et consolatio nostra. [6]Sive autem tribulamur, pro vestra exhortatione et salute; sive exhortamur, pro vestra exhortatione, quae operatur in tolerantia earundem passionum, quas et nos patimur. [7]Et spes nostra firma pro vobis, scientes quoniam, sicut socii passionum estis, sic eritis et consolationis. [8]Non enim volumus ignorare vos, fratres, de tribulatione nostra, quae facta est in Asia, quoniam supra modum gravati sumus supra virtutem, ita ut taederet nos etiam vivere; [9]sed ipsi in nobis ipsis responsum mortis habuimus, ut non simus fidentes in nobis, sed in Deo, qui suscitat mortuos: [10]qui de tanta morte eripuit nos et eruet, in quem speramus, et adhuc eripiet, [11]adiuvantibus et vobis in oratione pro nobis, ut propter eam, quae ex multis personis in

nos est, donationem per multos gratiae agantur pro nobis. [12]Nam gloria nostra haec est, testimonium
conscientiae nostrae, quod in simplicitate et sinceritate Dei et non in sapientia carnali sed in gratia Dei
conversati sumus in mundo, abundantius autem ad vos. [13]Non enim alia scribimus vobis quam quae
legitis aut etiam cognoscitis; spero autem quod usque in finem cognoscetis, [14]sicut et cognovistis nos
ex parte, quia gloria vestra sumus sicut et vos nostra in die Domini nostri Iesu. [15]Et hac confidentia volui
prius venire ad vos, ut secundam gratiam haberetis, [16]et per vos transire in Macedoniam, et iterum a
Macedonia venire ad vos et a vobis deduci in Iudaeam. [17]Cum hoc ergo voluissem, numquid levitate
usus sum? Aut, quae cogito, secundum carnem cogito, ut sit apud me «Est, est» et «Non, non»?
[18]Fidelis autem Deus, quia sermo noster, qui fit apud vos, non est «Est» et «Non»! [19]Dei enim Filius
Iesus Christus, qui in vobis per nos praedicatus est, per me et Silvanum et Timotheum, non fuit «Est»
et «Non», sed «Est» in illo fuit. [20]Quotquot enim promissiones Dei sunt, in illo «Est»; ideo et per ipsum
«Amen» Deo ad gloriam per nos. [21]Qui autem confirmat nos vobiscum in Christum et qui unxit nos
Deus, [22]et qui signavit nos et dedit arrabonem Spiritus in cordibus nostris. [23]Ego autem testem Deum
invoco in animam meam quod parcens vobis non veni ultra Corinthum. [24]Non quia dominamur fidei
vestrae, sed adiutores sumus gaudii vestri, nam fide stetistis. **[2]** [1]Statui autem hoc ipse apud me, ne
iterum in tristitia venirem ad vos; [2]si enim ego contristo vos, et quis est qui me laetificet, nisi qui
contristatur ex me? [3]Et hoc ipsum scripsi, ut non, cum venero, tristitiam habeam de quibus oportebat
me gaudere, confidens in omnibus vobis, quia meum gaudium omnium vestrum est. [4]Nam ex multa
tribulatione et angustia cordis scripsi vobis per multas lacrimas, non ut contristemini, sed ut sciatis quam
caritatem habeo abundantius in vos. [5]Si quis autem contristavit, non me contristavit, sed ex parte, ut non
onerem, omnes vos. [6]Sufficit illi, qui eiusmodi est, obiurgatio haec, quae fit a pluribus, [7]ita ut e contra
magis donetis et consolemini, ne forte abundantiore tristitia absorbeatur, qui eiusmodi est. [8]Propter quod
obsecro vos, ut confirmetis in illum caritatem; [9]ideo enim et scripsi, ut cognoscam probationem vestram,
an in omnibus oboedientes sitis. [10]Cui autem aliquid donatis, et ego; nam et ego, quod donavi, si quid
donavi, propter vos in persona Christi, [11]ut non circumveniamur a Satana, non enim ignoramus
cogitationes eius. [12]Cum venissem autem Troadem ob evangelium Christi, et ostium mihi apertum esset
in Domino, [13]non habui requiem spiritui meo, eo quod non invenerim Titum fratrem meum, sed
valefaciens eis profectus sum in Macedoniam. [14]Deo autem gratias, qui semper triumphat nos in Christo
et odorem notitiae suae manifestat per nos in omni loco. [15]Quia Christi bonus odor sumus Deo in his,
qui salvi fiunt, et in his, qui pereunt: [16]aliis quidem odor ex morte in mortem, aliis autem odor ex vita
in vitam. Et ad haec quis idoneus? [17]Non enim sumus sicut plurimi adulterantes verbum Dei, sed sicut
ex sinceritate, sed sicut ex Deo coram Deo in Christo loquimur. **[3]**[1]Incipimus iterum nosmetipsos
commendare? Aut numquid egemus sicut quidam commendaticiis epistulis ad vos aut ex vobis?
[2]Epistula nostra vos estis, scripta in cordibus nostris, quae scitur et legitur ab omnibus hominibus;
[3]manifestati quoniam epistula estis Christi ministrata a nobis, scripta non atramento sed Spiritu Dei vivi,
non in tabulis lapideis sed in tabulis cordis carnalibus. [4]Fiduciam autem talem habemus per Christum
ad Deum. [5]Non quod sufficientes simus cogitare aliquid a nobis quasi ex nobis, sed sufficientia nostra
ex Deo est, [6]qui et idoneos nos fecit ministros Novi Testamenti, non litterae sed Spiritus: littera enim
occidit, Spiritus autem vivificat. [7]Quod si ministratio mortis litteris deformata in lapidibus fuit in gloria,
ita ut non possent intendere filii Israel in faciem Moysis propter gloriam vultus eius, quae evacuatur,
[8]quomodo non magis ministratio Spiritus erit in gloria? [9]Nam si ministerium damnationis gloria est,
multo magis abundat ministerium iustitiae in gloria. [10]Nam nec glorificatum est, quod claruit in hac
parte, propter excellentem gloriam; [11]si enim, quod evacuatur, per gloriam est, multo magis, quod
manet, in gloria est. [12]Habentes igitur talem spem multa fiducia utimur, [13]et non sicut Moyses: ponebat
velamen super faciem suam, ut non intenderent filii Israel in finem illus, quod evacuatur. [14]Sed obtusi
sunt sensus eorum. Usque in hodiernum enim diem idipsum velamen in lectione Veteris Testamenti
manet non revelatum, quoniam in Christo evacuatur; [15]sed usque in hodiernum diem, cum legitur
Moyses, velamen est positum super cor eorum. [16]*Quando autem conversus fuerit ad Dominum, aufertur
velamen.* [17]Dominus autem Spiritus est; ubi autem Spiritus Domini, ibi libertas. [18]Nos vero omnes
revelata facie gloriam Domini speculantes, in eandem imaginem transformamur a claritate in claritatem
tamquam a Domini Spiritu. **[4]** [1]Ideo habentes hanc ministrationem, iuxta quod misericordiam
consecuti sumus, non deficimus, [2]sed abdicavimus occulta dedecoris non ambulantes in astutia, neque
adulterantes verbum Dei, sed in manifestatione veritatis commendantes nosmetipsos ad omnem
conscientiam hominum coram Deo. [3]Quod si etiam velatum est evangelium nostrum, in his, qui pereunt,
est velatum, [4]in quibus deus huius saeculi excaecavit mentes infidelium, ut non fulgeat illuminatio
evangelii gloriae Christi, qui est imago Dei. [5]Non enim nosmetipsos praedicamus sed Iesum Christum
Dominum; nos autem servos vestros per Iesum. [6]Quoniam Deus qui dixit: «*De tenebris lux*

splendescat», ipse illuxit in cordibus nostris ad illuminationem scientiae claritatis Dei in facie Iesu
Christi. 7Habemus autem thesaurum istum in vasis fictilibus, ut sublimitas sit virtutis Dei, et non ex
nobis. 8In omnibus tribulationem patimur, sed non angustiamur; aporiamur, sed non destituimur;
9persecutionem patimur, sed non derelinquimur; deicimur, sed non perimus; 10semper mortificationem
Iesu in corpore circumferentes, ut et vita Iesu in corpore nostro manifestetur. 11Semper enim nos, qui
vivimus, in mortem tradimur propter Iesum, ut et vita Iesu manifestetur in carne nostra mortali. 12Ergo
mors in nobis operatur, vita autem in vobis. 13Habentes autem eundem spiritum fidei, sicut scriptum est:
«*Credidi, propter quod locutus sum*», et nos credimus, propter quod et loquimur, 14scientes quoniam,
qui suscitavit Dominum Iesum, et nos cum Iesu suscitabit et constituet vobiscum. 15Omnia enim propter
vos, ut gratia abundans per multos gratiarum actionem abundare faciat in gloriam Dei. 16Propter quod
non deficimus, sed licet is, qui foris est, noster homo corrumpitur, tamen is, qui intus est, noster
renovatur de die in diem. 17Id enim, quod in praesenti est, leve tribulationis nostrae supra modum in
sublimitatem aeternum gloriae pondus operatur nobis, 18non contemplantibus nobis, quae videntur, sed
quae non videntur; quae enim videntur, temporalia sunt, quae autem non videntur, aeterna sunt.
[5] 1Scimus enim quoniam si terrestris domus nostra huius tabernaculi dissolvatur, aedificationem ex
Deo habemus domum non manufactam, aeternam in caelis. 2Nam et in hoc ingemiscimus habitationem
nostram, quae de caelo est, superindui cupientes, 3si tamen et exspoliati, non nudi inveniamur. 4Nam et,
qui sumus in tabernaculo, ingemiscimus gravati, eo quod nolumus exspoliari sed supervestiri, ut
absorbeatur, quod mortale est, a vita. 5Qui autem effecit nos in hoc ipsum, Deus, qui dedit nobis
arrabonem Spiritus. 6Audentes igitur semper et scientes quoniam, dum praesentes sumus in corpore,
peregrinamur a Domino; 7per fidem enim ambulamus et non per speciem. 8Audemus autem et bonam
voluntatem habemus magis peregrinari a corpore et praesentes esse ad Dominum. 9Et ideo contendimus
sive praesentes sive absentes placere illi. 10Omnes enim nos manifestari oportet ante tribunal Christi, ut
referat unusquisque pro eis, quae per corpus gessit, sive bonum sive malum. 11Scientes ergo timorem
Domini hominibus suademus, Deo autem manifesti sumus; spero autem et in conscientiis vestris
manifestos nos esse. 12Non iterum nos commendamus vobis, sed occasionem damus vobis gloriandi pro
nobis, ut habeatis ad eos, qui in facie gloriantur et non in corde. 13Sive enim mente excedimus, Deo;
sive sobrii sumus, vobis. 14Caritas enim Christi urget nos, aestimantes hoc quoniam, si unus pro
omnibus mortuus est, ergo omnes mortui sunt; 15et pro omnibus mortuus est, ut et, qui vivunt, iam non
sibi vivant, sed ei, qui pro ipsis mortuus est et resurrexit. 16Itaque nos ex hoc neminem novimus
secundum carnem; et si cognovimus secundum carnem Christum, sed nunc iam non novimus. 17Si quis
ergo in Christo, nova creatura; vetera transierunt, ecce, facta sunt nova. 18Omnia autem ex Deo, qui
reconciliavit nos sibi per Christum et dedit nobis ministerium reconciliationis, 19quoniam quidem Deus
erat in Christo mundum reconcilians sibi, non reputans illis delicta ipsorum, et posuit in nobis verbum
reconciliationis. 20Pro Christo ergo legatione fungimur tamquam Deo exhortante per nos: obsecramus
pro Christo, reconciliamini Deo. 21Eum, qui non noverat peccatum, pro nobis peccatum fecit, ut nos
efficeremur iustitia Dei in ipso. **[6]** 1Adiuvantes autem et exhortamur, ne in vacuum gratiam. Dei
recipiatis 2—ait enim: «*Tempore accepto exaudivi te / et in die salutis adiuvi te*»; ecce nunc tempus
acceptabile, ecce nunc dies salutis—, 3nemini dantes ullam offensionem, ut non vituperetur
ministerium, 4sed in omnibus exhibentes nosmetipsos sicut Dei ministros in multa patientia, in
tribulationibus, in necessitatibus, in angustiis, 5in plagis, in carceribus, in seditionibus, in laboribus, in
vigiliis, in ieiuniis, 6in castitate, in scientia, in longanimitate, in suavitate, in Spiritu Sancto, in caritate
non ficta, 7in verbo veritatis, in virtute Dei; per arma iustitiae a dextris et sinistris, 8per gloriam et
ignobilitatem, per infamiam et bonam famam; ut seductores et veraces, 9sicut qui ignoti et cogniti, quasi
morientes, et ecce vivimus, ut castigati et non mortificati, 10quasi tristes, semper autem gaudentes, sicut
egentes, multos autem locupletantes, tamquam nihil habentes et omnia possidentes. 11Os nostrum patet
ad vos, o Corinthii, cor nostrum dilatatum est. 12Non angustiamini in nobis, sed angustiamini in
visceribus vestris; 13eandem autem habentes remunerationem, tamquam filiis dico, dilatamini et vos.
14Nolite iugum ducere cum infidelibus! Quae enim participatio iustitiae cum iniquitate? Aut quae
societas luci ad tenebras? 15Quae autem conventio Christi cum Beliar, aut quae pars fideli cum infideli?
16Qui autem consensus templo Dei cum idolis? Vos enim estis templum Dei vivi; sicut dicit Deus:
«*Inhabitabo in illis et inambulabo / et ero illorum Deus, et ipsi erunt mihi populus. /* 17*Propter quod
exite de medio eorum / et separamini, dicit Dominus, / et immundum ne tetigeritis; / et ego recipiam vos
/* 18*et ero vobis in Patrem, / et vos eritis mihi in fi lios et filias, / dicit Dominus omnipotens*». **[7]** 1Has
igitur habentes promissiones, carissimi, mundemus nos ab omni inquinamento carnis et spiritus,
perficientes sanctificationem in timore Dei. 2Capite nos! Neminem laesimus, neminem corrupimus,
neminem circumvenimus. 3Non ad condemnationem dico; praedixi enim quod in cordibus nostris estis

ad commoriendum et ad convivendum. 4Multa mihi fiducia est apud vos, multa mihi gloriatio pro vobis;
repletus sum consolatione, superabundo gaudio in omni tribulatione nostra. 5Nam et cum venissemus
Macedoniam, nullam requiem habuit caro nostra, sed omnem tribulationem passi: foris pugnae, intus
timores. 6Sed qui consolatur humiles, consolatus est nos Deus in adventu Titi; 7non solum autem in
adventu eius sed etiam in solacio, quo consolatus est in vobis, referens nobis vestrum desiderium,
vestrum fletum, vestram aemulationem pro me, ita ut magis gauderem. 8Quoniam etsi contristavi vos in
epistula, non me paenitet; etsi paeniteret—video quod epistula illa, etsi ad horam, vos contristavit—
9nunc gaudeo, non quia contristati estis, sed quia contristati estis ad paenitentiam; contristati enim estis
secundum Deum, ut in nullo detrimentum patiamini ex nobis. 10Quae enim secundum Deum tristitia,
paenitentiam in salutem stabilem operatur; saeculi autem tristitia mortem operatur. 11Ecce enim hoc
ipsum secundum Deum contristari: quantam in vobis operatum est sollicitudinem, sed defensionem, sed
indignationem, sed timorem, sed desiderium, sed aemulationem, sed vindictam! In omnibus exhibuistis
vos incontaminatos esse negotio. 12Igitur etsi scripsi vobis, non propter eum, qui fecit iniuriam, nec
propter eum, qui passus est, sed ad manifestandam sollicitudinem vestram, quam pro nobis habetis, ad
vos coram Deo. 13Ideo consolati sumus. In consolatione autem nostra abundantius magis gavisi sumus
super gaudium Titi, quia refectus est spiritus eius ab omnibus vobis; 14et si quid apud illum de vobis
gloriatus sum, non sum confusus, sed sicut omnia vobis in veritate locuti sumus, ita et gloriatio nostra,
quae fuit ad Titum, veritas facta est. 15Et viscera eius abundantius in vos sunt, reminiscentis omnium
vestrum oboedientiam, quomodo cum timore et tremore excepistis eum. 16Gaudeo quod in omnibus
confido in vobis. **[8]** 1Notam autem facimus vobis, fratres, gratiam Dei, quae data est in ecclesiis
Macedoniae, 2quod in multo experimento tribulationis abundantia gaudii ipsorum et altissima paupertas
eorum abundavit in divitias simplicitatis eorum; 3quia secundum virtutem, testimonium reddo, et supra
virtutem voluntarii fuerunt 4cum multa exhortatione obsecrantes nos gratiam et communicationem
ministerii, quod fit in sanctos. 5Et non sicut speravimus, sed semetipsos dederunt primum Domino,
deinde nobis per voluntatem Dei, 6ita ut rogaremus Titum, ut, quemadmodum coepit, ita et perficiat in
vos etiam gratiam istam. 7Sed sicut in omnibus abundatis, fide et sermone et scientia et omni
sollicitudine et caritate ex nobis in vobis, ut et in hac gratia abundetis. 8Non quasi imperans dico, sed
per aliorum sollicitudinem etiam vestrae caritatis ingenitum bonum comprobans; 9scitis enim gratiam
Domini nostri Iesu Christi, quoniam propter vos egenus factus est, cum esset dives, ut illius inopia vos
divites essetis. 10Et consilium in hoc do. Hoc enim vobis utile est, qui non solum facere sed et velle
coepistis ab anno priore; 11nunc vero et facto perficite, ut, quemadmodum promptus est animus velle,
ita sit et perficere ex eo, quod habetis. 12Si enim voluntas prompta est, secundum id quod habet, accepta
est, non secundum quod non habet. 13Non enim, ut aliis sit remissio, vobis autem tribulatio; sed ex
aequalitate 14in praesenti tempore vestra abundantia illorum inopiam suppleat, ut et illorum abundantia
vestram inopiam suppleat, ut fiat aequalitas, sicut scriptum est: 15*«Qui multum, non abundavit; et, qui
modicum, non minoravit»*. 16Gratias autem Deo, qui dedit eandem sollicitudinem pro vobis in corde Titi,
17quoniam exhortationem quidem suscepit, sed, cum sollicitior esset, sua voluntate profectus est ad vos.
18Misimus etiam cum illo fratrem, cuius laus est in evangelio per omnes ecclesias 19—non solum autem
sed et ordinatus ab ecclesiis comes noster cum hac gratia, quae ministratur a nobis ad Domini gloriam
et destinatam voluntatem nostram—20devitantes hoc, ne quis nos vituperet in hac plenitudine, quae
ministratur a nobis; 21*providemus* enim *bona* non solum *coram Domino* sed *etiam* coram *hominibus*.
22Misimus autem cum illis et fratrem nostrum, quem probavimus in multis saepe sollicitum esse, nunc
autem multo sollicitiorem, confidentia multa in vos. 23Sive pro Tito, est socius meus et in vos adiutor;
sive fratres nostri, apostoli ecclesiarum, gloria Christi. 24Ostensionem ergo, quae est caritatis vestrae et
nostrae gloriationis pro vobis, in illos ostendite in faciem ecclesiarum. **[9]** 1Nam de ministerio, quod
fit in sanctos, superfluum est mihi scribere vobis; 2scio enim promptum animum vestrum, pro quo de
vobis glorior apud Macedonas, quoniam Achaia parata est ab anno praeterito, et vestra aemulatio
provocavit plurimos. 3Misi autem fratres, ut ne, quod gloriamur de vobis, evacuetur in hac parte, ut,
quemadmodum dixi, parati sitis, 4ne, cum venerint mecum Macedones et invenerint vos imparatos,
erubescamus nos, ut non dicam vos, in hac substantia. 5Necessarium ergo existimavi rogare fratres, ut
praeveniant ad vos et praeparent repromissam benedictionem vestram, ut haec sit parata sic quasi
benedictionem, non quasi avaritiam. 6Hoc autem: qui parce seminat, parce et metet; et, qui seminat in
benedictionibus, in benedictionibus et metet. 7Unusquisque prout destinavit corde suo, non ex tristitia
aut ex necessitate, *hilarem* enim *datorem* diligit *Deus*. 8Potens est autem Deus omnem gratiam abundare
facere in vobis, ut, in omnibus semper omnem sufficientiam habentes, abundetis in omne opus bonum,
9sicut scriptum est: *«Dispersit, dedit pauperibus; / iustitia eius manet in aeternum»*. 10Qui autem
administrat semen seminanti, et panem ad manducandum praestabit et multiplicabit semen vestrum et

augebit incrementa frugum iustitiae vestrae. [11]In omnibus locupletati in omnem simplicitatem, quae
operatur per nos gratiarum actionem Deo [12]—quoniam ministerium huius officii non solum supplet ea,
quae desunt sanctis, sed etiam abundat per multas gratiarum actiones Deo—[13]per probationem
ministerii huius glorificantes Deum in oboedientia confessionis vestrae in evangelium Christi et
simplicitate communionis in illos et in omnes, [14]et ipsorum obsecratione pro vobis, desiderantium vos
propter eminentem gratiam Dei in vobis. [15]Gratias Deo super inenarrabili dono eius. **[10]** [1]Ipse autem
ego Paulus obsecro vos per mansuetudinem et modestiam Christi, qui in facie quidem humilis inter vos,
absens autem confido in vobis; [2]rogo autem, ne praesens audeam per eam confidentiam, quae existimo
audere in quosdam, qui arbitrantur nos tamquam secundum carnem ambulemus. [3]In carne enim
ambulantes, non secundum carnem militamus [4]—nam arma militiae nostrae non carnalia sed potentia
Deo ad destructionem munitionum—consilia destruentes [5]et omnem altitudinem extollentem se
adversus scientiam Dei, et in captivitatem redigentes omnem intellectum in obsequium Christi, [6]et in
promptu habentes ulcisci omnem inoboedientiam, cum impleta fuerit vestra oboedientia. [7]Quae
secundum faciem sunt, videte. Si quis confidit sibi Christi se esse, hoc cogitet iterum apud se, quia sicut
ipse Christi est, ita et nos. [8]Nam et si amplius aliquid gloriatus fuero de potestate nostra, quam dedit
Dominus in aedificationem et non in destructionem vestram, non erubescam, [9]ut non existimer tamquam
terrere vos per epistulas; [10]quoniam quidem «Epistulae—inquiunt—graves sunt et fortes, praesentia
autem corporis infirma et sermo contemptibilis». [11]Hoc cogitet, qui eiusmodi est, quia quales sumus
verbo per epistulas absentes, tales et praesentes in facto. [12]Non enim audemus inserere aut comparare
nos quibusdam, qui seipsos commendant; sed ipsi se in semetipsis metientes, et comparantes semetipsos
sibi, non intellegunt. [13]Nos autem non ultra mensuram gloriabimur, sed secundum mensuram regulae,
quam impertitus est nobis Deus, mensuram pertingendi usque ad vos. [14]Non enim quasi non
pertingentes ad vos superextendimus nosmetipsos, usque ad vos enim pervenimus in evangelio Christi;
[15]non ultra mensuram gloriantes in alienis laboribus, spem autem habentes, crescente fide vestra, in
vobis magnificari secundum regulam nostram in abundantiam, [16]ad evangelizandum in iis, quae ultra
vos sunt, et non in aliena regula gloriari in his, quae praeparata sunt. [17]*Qui* autem *gloriatur, in Domino
glorietur*; [18]non enim qui seipsum commendat, ille probatus est, sed quem Dominus commendat.
[11] [1]Utinam sustineretis modicum quid insipientiae meae; sed et supportate me! [2]Aemulor enim vos
Dei aemulatione; despondi enim vos uni viro virginem castam exhibere Christo. [3]Timeo autem, ne, sicut
serpens Evam seduxit astutia sua, ita corrumpantur sensus vestri a simplicitate et castitate, quae est in
Christum. [4]Nam si is qui venit, alium Christum praedicat, quem non praedicavimus, aut alium Spiritum
accipitis, quem non accepistis, aut aliud evangelium, quod non recepistis, recte pateremini. [5]Existimo
enim nihil me minus fecisse magnis apostolis; [6]nam etsi imperitus sermone, sed non scientia, in omni
autem manifestantes in omnibus ad vos. [7]Aut numquid peccatum feci meipsum humilians, ut vos
exaltemini, quoniam gratis evangelium Dei evangelizavi vobis? [8]Alias ecclesias exspoliavi accipiens
stipendium ad ministerium vestrum [9]et, cum essem apud vos et egerem, nulli onerosus fui; nam, quod
mihi deerat, suppleverunt fratres, qui venerunt a Macedonia; et in omnibus sine onere me vobis servavi
et servabo. [10]Est veritas Christi in me, quoniam haec gloria non infringetur in me in regionibus Achaiae.
[11]Quare? Quia non diligo vos? Deus scit! [12]Quod autem facio et faciam, ut amputem occasionem
eorum, qui volunt occasionem, ut in quo gloriantur, inveniantur sicut et nos. [13]Nam eiusmodi
pseudoapostoli, operarii subdoli, transfigurantes se in apostolos Christi. [14]Et non mirum, ipse enim
Satanas transfigurat se in angelum lucis; [15]non est ergo magnum, si et ministri eius transfigurentur velut
ministri iustitiae, quorum finis erit secundum opera ipsorum. [16]Iterum dico, ne quis me putet
insipientem esse; alioquin velut insipientem accipite me, ut et ego modicum quid glorier. [17]Quod loquor,
non loquor secundum Dominum, sed quasi in insipientia in hac substantia gloriationis. [18]Quoniam multi
gloriantur secundum carnem, et ego gloriabor. [19]Libenter enim suffertis insipientes, cum sitis ipsi
sapientes; [20]sustinetis enim, si quis vos in servitutem redigit, si quis devorat, si quis accipit, si quis
extollitur, si quis in faciem vos caedit. [21]Secundum ignobilitatem dico, quasi nos infirmi fuerimus; in
quo quis audet, in insipientia dico, audeo et ego. [22]Hebraei sunt? Et ego. Israelitae sunt? Et ego. Semen
Abrahae sunt? Et ego. [23]Ministri Christi sunt? Minus sapiens dico, plus ego: in laboribus plurimis, in
carceribus abundantius, in plagis supra modum, in mortibus frequenter; [24]a Iudaeis quinquies
quadragenas una minus accepi, [25]ter virgis caesus sum, semel lapidatus sum, ter naufragium feci, nocte
et die in profundo maris fui; [26]in itineribus saepe, periculis fluminum, periculis latronum, periculis ex
genere, periculis ex gentibus, periculis in civitate, periculis in solitudine, periculis in mari, periculis in
falsis fratribus, [27]in labore et aerumna, in vigiliis saepe, in fame et siti, in ieiuniis frequenter, in frigore
et nuditate; [28]praeter illa, quae extrinsecus sunt, instantia mea cotidiana, sollicitudo omnium
ecclesiarum. [29]Quis infirmatur, et non infirmor? Quis scandalizatur, et ego non uror? [30]Si gloriari

oportet, quae infirmitatis meae sunt, gloriabor. [31]Deus, et Pater Domini Iesu scit, qui est benedictus in
saecula, quod non mentior. [32]Damasci praepositus gentis Aretae regis custodiebat civitatem
Damascenorum, ut me comprehenderet, [33]et per fenestram in sporta dimissus sum per murum et effugi
manus eius. **[12]** [1]Gloriari oportet; non expedit quidem, veniam autem ad visiones et revelationes
Domini. [2]Scio hominem in Christo ante annos quattuordecim—sive in corpore nescio, sive extra corpus
nescio, Deus scit—raptum eiusmodi usque ad tertium caelum. [3]Et scio huiusmodi hominem—sive in
corpore sive extra corpus nescio, Deus scit—[4]quoniam raptus est in paradisum et audivit arcana verba,
quae non licet homini loqui. [5]Pro eiusmodi gloriabor, pro me autem nihil gloriabor nisi in infirmitatibus
meis. [6]Nam et si voluero gloriari, non ero insipiens, veritatem enim dicam; parco autem, ne quis in me
existimet supra id, quod videt me aut audit ex me, [7]et ex magnitudine revelationum. Propter quod, ne
extollar, datus est mihi stimulus carni, angelus Satanae, ut me colaphizet, ne extollar. [8]Propter quod ter
Dominum rogavi, ut discederet a me; [9]et dixit mihi: «Sufficit tibi gratia mea, nam virtus in infirmitate
perficitur». Libentissime igitur potius gloriabor in infirmitatibus meis, ut inhabitet in me virtus Christi.
[10]Propter quod placeo mihi in infirmitatibus, in contumeliis, in necessitatibus, in persecutionibus et in
angustiis, pro Christo: cum enim infirmor, tunc potens sum. [11]Factus sum insipiens. Vos me coegistis;
ego enim debui a vobis commendari. Nihil enim minus fui ab his, qui sunt supra modum apostoli,
tametsi nihil sum; [12]signa tamen apostoli facta sunt super vos in omni patientia, signis quoque et
prodigiis et virtutibus. [13]Quid est enim quod minus habuistis prae ceteris ecclesiis, nisi quod ego ipse
non gravavi vos? Donate mihi hanc iniuriam. [14]Ecce tertio hoc paratus sum venire ad vos et non ero
gravis vobis; non enim quaero, quae vestra sunt, sed vos, nec enim debent filii parentibus thesaurizare,
sed parentes filiis. [15]Ego autem libentissime impendam et superimpendar ipse pro animabus vestris. Si
plus vos diligo, minus diligar? [16]Esto quidem, ego vos non gravavi; sed cum essem astutus, dolo vos
cepi. [17]Numquid per aliquem eorum, quos misi ad vos, circumveni vos? [18]Rogavi Titum et misi cum illo
fratrem; numquid Titus vos circumvenit? Nonne eodem spiritu ambulavimus? Nonne iisdem vestigiis?
[19]Olim putatis quod excusemus nos apud vos? Coram Deo in Christo loquimur; omnia autem, carissimi,
propter vestram aedificationem. [20]Timeo enim, ne forte, cum venero, non quales volo, inveniam vos, et
ego inveniar a vobis, qualem non vultis, ne forte contentiones, aemulationes, animositates, dissensiones,
detractiones, susurrationes, inflationes, seditiones sint; [21]ne iterum, cum venero, humiliet me Deus meus
apud vos, et lugeam multos ex his, qui ante peccaverunt et non egerunt paenitentiam super immunditia
et fornicatione et impudicitia, quam gesserunt. **[13]** [1]Ecce tertio hoc venio ad vos: *in ore duorum vel
trium testium stabit omne verbum.* [2]Praedixi et praedico, ut praesens bis et nunc absens his, qui ante
peccaverunt, et ceteris omnibus, quoniam si venero iterum, non parcam, [3]quoniam experimentum
quaeritis eius, qui in me loquitur, Christi, qui in vos non infirmatur, sed potens est in vobis. [4]Nam etsi
crucifixus est ex infirmitate, sed vivit ex virtute Dei. Nam et nos infirmi sumus in illo, sed vivemus cum
eo ex virtute Dei in vos. [5]Vosmetipsos tentate, si estis in fide; ipsi vos probate. An non cognoscitis vos
ipsos quia Iesus Christus in vobis est? Nisi forte reprobi estis. [6]Spero autem quod cognoscetis quia nos
non sumus reprobi. [7]Oramus autem Deum, ut nihil mali faciatis, non ut nos probati pareamus, sed ut
vos, quod bonum est, faciatis, nos autem ut reprobi simus. [8]Non enim possumus aliquid adversus
veritatem, sed pro veritate. [9]Gaudemus enim, quando nos infirmi sumus, vos autem potentes estis; hoc
et oramus, vestram consummationem. [10]Ideo haec absens scribo, ut non praesens durius agam
secundum potestatem, quam Dominus dedit mihi in aedificationem et non in destructionem. [11]De cetero,
fratres, gaudete, perfecti estote, exhortamini invicem, idem sapite, pacem habete, et Deus dilectionis et
pacis erit vobiscum. [12]Salutate invicem in osculo sancto. Salutant vos sancti omnes. [13]Gratia Domini
Iesu Christi et caritas Dei et communicatio Sancti Spiritus cum omnibus vobis.

Explanatory Notes

Asterisks in the text of the New Testament refer to these "Explanatory Notes" in the RSVCE.

THE FIRST LETTER OF PAUL TO THE CORINTHIANS

1:2, *saints*: A word commonly used for Christians in Paul's letters and in Acts.

1:12, *Cephas*: i.e., Peter. It does not follow from this that he had ever been to Corinth, but it does indicate his authority there.

2:1–2: Paul's failure at Athens convinced him that lofty words and worldly wisdom were less effective than Jesus crucified.

3:13, *the Day*: i.e., the day of the Lord, God's searching judgments.

3:16, *God's temple*: The dignity of the Christian.

5:1, *father's wife*: Evidently his stepmother.

5:5, *to Satan*: not only excommunicated, but in some sense given over to suffering, for his own good.

5:9–10, *immoral*: Literally, "fornicators."

5:11, *guilty of immorality*: Literally, "a fornicator."

6:1, *the unrighteous*: i.e., civil courts in which the judges were, of course, pagans.

6:9, *the immoral*: Literally, "fornicators."

homosexuals: Greek has, "effeminate or sodomites." The apostle condemns not the inherent tendencies of such, but the indulgence of them.

6:12: This saying is possibly an exaggeration of the freedom from the Mosaic law which Christians enjoyed. The saying had been applied to sinful practices, as is clear from the following verses.

6:13, 18, *immorality*: i.e., sexual immorality.

7:2: Note Paul's insistence on equality of man and woman in certain aspects of christian marriage, and his recognition that the unmarried state is also a gift from God.

8:1–13: Animals sacrificed to pagan gods were often sold as meat in the market. Could Christians buy such meat? Paul allows it so long as scandal is avoided.

9:3: Paul sets great store by the fact that he has earned his living and waived his right to support by the faithful. He uses this as an authentication of his apostolate.

9:5, *a wife*: Greek, "a woman, or a sister." This could mean either a woman who is a Christian, or a wife who is a Christian. There were pious women who ministered to the apostles (Lk 8:3). As many of the apostles must have been married, they may have been ministered to by their wives; though it is possible they had left their wives in answer to the Lord's command to leave all (Lk 18:28–29). *brethren:* See note on Mt 12:46.

10:20: Paul appears to forbid partaking in sacrificial meals. In verse 27 he says they may eat meat offered to idols if it is at an ordinary meal, unless it would cause scandal to any one present.

11:20: There was apparently a common meal before the Eucharist at which food and drink were to be shared. Paul condemns the abuses that had crept in.

12:1: The spiritual gifts here referred to were common in the first age of the Church and helped to establish it on a firm basis.

12:31: Love, however, is far superior to these gifts.

15:13: Again, the resurrection of the dead is linked with Christ's resurrection; cf. Rom 8:11.

15:29: Apparently a custom of vicarious baptism for those who had died without it. Paul mentions it without approving it.

16:1: The collection to be made everywhere for the poor Christians in Jerusalem.

Explanatory Notes

Changes in the RSV for the Catholic Edition

	TEXT		FOOTNOTES	
	RSV	RSVCE	RSV	RSVCE
1 Cor 3:9	fellow workers for God[f]	God's fellow workers[f]	[f]Or *God's fellow workers*	[f]*Or fellow workers for God*
1 Cor 4:6	to live according to Scripture	not to go beyond what is written		
1 Cor 7:25		the unmarried[x2]		
1 Cor 7:28		a girl[m2]		[x2]Greek *virgins*
1 Cor 7:34		girl[m2]		[m2]Greek *virgin*
1 Cor 7:36		betrothed[m2]		
1 Cor 7:37		betrothed[m2]		
1 Cor 7:38		betrothed[m2]		
1 Cor 9:5			[n]Delete existing note and substitute:	[n]Greek a *woman*, a *sister*
1 Cor 9:5	brothers	brethren		

THE SECOND LETTER OF PAUL TO THE CORINTHIANS

1:8, *affliction*: Possibly the disturbance at Ephesus (Acts 19:23–41), or perhaps a serious illness.
3:18: Cleansed in baptism through the power of the Holy Spirit, our soul shines with the reflected glory of God.
4:7, *this treasure*: i.e., the apostolate.
4:12: i.e., we suffer, if necessary, even unto death, that you may have (spiritual) life.
5:19: Or, "God was reconciling the world to himself through Christ."
5:21, *made him to be sin*: i.e., "Sending his own Son in the likeness of sinful flesh and for sin, he condemned sin in the flesh" (Rom 8:3).
9:1, *superfluous*: Yet Paul goes on to do so at some length, exhorting them to be generous.
10:1: Paul is referring ironically to what some people are saying about him; see verse 10.
12:7, *a thorn*: Perhaps some form of sickness or disability, or the opposition of Israel to his teaching.
12:13: Paul ironically asks forgiveness for not being a charge on them as the other apostles were.

Headings added to the Biblical Text

1 CORINTHIANS

INTRODUCTION
Greeting 1:1
Thanksgiving 1:4

Part One: Correction of abuses

1. DIVISIONS AMONG THE CORINTHIANS
An appeal for unity 1:10
The wisdom of the cross 1:18
Paul's preaching in Corinth 2:1
Divine wisdom 2:6
The Corinthians are still unspiritual 3:1
Apostolic ministry 3:4
Servants of Christ 4:1
Trials experienced by apostles 4:8
Admonishment 4:14

2. A CASE OF INCEST
Punishment of the sinner 5:1
Obstinate sinners are to be shunned 5:9

3. RECOURSE TO PAGAN COURTS

4. FORNICATION, A GRAVE SIN
Respect for the body 6:12
Offence to Christ and the Holy Spirit 6:15

Part Two: Answers to various questions

5. MARRIAGE AND VIRGINITY
Relations between husband and wife 7:1
Indissolubility of marriage 7:10
The Pauline privilege 7:12
Leading the life God has assigned 7:17
Excellence of virginity 7:25
Advice to widows 7:39

6. FOOD OFFERED TO IDOLS
Idols have no real existence 8:1
Not scandalizing the weak 8:7
The right of apostles to receive maintenance from the faithful 9:1
St Paul does not exercise that right 9:15
The need for asceticism 9:24
The lesson of Israel's history 10:1
Idolatry and the Eucharist, incompatible 10:14
Practical solutions to certain questions 10:23

7. THE CELEBRATION OF THE EUCHARIST
Women in church 11:1
Abuses in the celebration of the Eucharist 11:17
The institution of the Eucharist and its worthy reception 11:23

8. GIFTS AND GRACES
Kinds of spiritual gifts 12:1
Unity and variety in the mystical body of Christ 12:12
Hymn to charity 13:1
Prophecy, the gift of tongues, and interpretation of tongues 14:1
Regulation of liturgical assemblies 14:26

9. THE RESURRECTION OF THE DEAD
Christ's resurrection and his appearances 15:1
The basis of our faith 15:12
The cause of our resurrection 15:20
The manner of the resurrection of the dead 15:35

10. MESSAGES AND WORDS OF FAREWELL
Collection for the church of Jerusalem 16:1
Plans for the months ahead 16:5
Exhortations and greetings 16:13

2 CORINTHIANS

INTRODUCTION
Greeting 1:1
Thanksgiving 1:3

Headings added to the Biblical Text

Part One: St Paul's defence against his enemies

1. HIS SIMPLICITY AND SINCERITY
The evidence of his actions and his letters 1:12
Why he has not visited Corinth 1:15
Forgiveness for those who offend us 2:5
Paul's eagerness for news 2:12

2. THE IMPORTANCE OF APOSTOLIC OFFICE
Paul's letter of recommendation 3:12
Christian ministry is greater than that of the Old Covenant 3:4
Paul's sincere conduct 4:1
The trials Paul has experienced 4:7
Paul is sustained by hope of heaven 4:13
The ministry of reconciliation 5:11
Paul, a true servant of Christ 6:1

3. ST PAUL OPENS HIS HEART
His love for the Corinthians 6:11
Contact with unbelievers 6:14
Paul's joy at the news brought by Titus 7:2

Part Two: The collection for the church of Jerusalem

The Macedonians' good example 8:1
Appeal for generosity 8:7
Paul praises Titus and Timothy 8:16
Appeal for speediness 9:1
Blessings to be expected 9:6

Part Three: Paul justifies his conduct

4. A REPLY TO ACCUSATIONS
Paul's readiness to use his apostolic authority 10:1
Paul's province includes Corinth 10:12

5. THE APOSTLE'S GROUNDS FOR BOASTING
His zeal 11:1
Paul accepted no material support in payment for preaching 11:7
Paul apologizes for boasting 11:16
What Paul has suffered for Christ 11:21
Visions and revelations 12:1
Paul again apologizes for boasting 12:11

6. THE APOSTLE'S NEXT VISIT
The reason for his apologia 12:19
Preparation for his next visit 13:1

7. WORDS OF FAREWELL

Sources quoted in the Navarre Bible New Testament Commentary

1. DOCUMENTS OF THE CHURCH AND OF POPES

Benedict XII
Const. *Benedictus Deus*, 29 January 1336
Benedict XV
Enc. *Humani generis redemptionem*, 15 June 1917
Enc. *Spiritus Paraclitus*, 1 September 1920
Clement of Rome, St
Letter to the Corinthians
Constantinople, First Council of
Nicene-Constantinopolitan Creed
Constantinople, Third Council of
Definitio de duabus in Christo voluntatibus et operationibus
Florence, Council of
Decree *Pro Jacobitis*
Laetentur coeli
Decree *Pro Armeniis*
John Paul II
Addresses and homilies
Apos. Exhort. *Catechesi tradendae*, 16 October 1979
Apos. Exhort. *Familiaris consortio*, 22 November 1981
Apos. Exhort. *Reconciliatio et paenitentia*, 2 December 1984
Apos. Letter. *Salvifici doloris*, 11 February 1984
Bull, *Aperite portas*, 6 January 1983
Enc. *Redemptor hominis*, 4 March 1979
Enc. *Dives in misercordia*, 30 November 1980
Enc. *Dominum et Vivificantem*, 30 May 1986
Enc. *Laborem exercens*, 14 September 1981
Letter to all priests, 8 April 1979
Letter to all bishops, 24 February 1980
Gelasius I
Ne forte
Gregory the Great, St
Epistula ad Theodorum medicum contra Fabianum
Exposition on the Seven Penitential
Ne forte
In Evangelia homiliae
In Ezechielem homiliae
Moralia in Job
Regulae pastoralis liber
Innocent III
Letter *Eius exemplo*, 18 December 1208
John XXIII
Pacem in terris, 11 April 1963
Enc. *Ad Petri cathedram*, 29 June 1959
Lateran Council (649)
Canons
Leo the Great, St
Homilies and sermons
Licet per nostros
Promisisse mememeni
Leo IX
Creed
Leo XIII
Enc. *Aeterni Patris*, 4 August 1879
Enc. *Immortale Dei*, 1 November 1885
Enc. *Libertas praestantissimum*, 20 June 1888
Enc. *Sapientiae christianae*, 18 January 1890
Enc. *Rerum novarum*, 15 May 1891
Enc. *Providentissimus Deus*, 18 November 1893
Enc. *Divinum illud munus*, 9 May 1897
Lateran, Fourth Council of (1215)
De fide catholica
Lyons, Second Council of (1274)
Doctrina de gratia
Profession of faith of Michael Palaeologue
Orange, Second Council of (529)
De gratia
Paul IV
Const. *Cum quorumdam*, 7 August 1555
Paul VI
Enc. *Ecclesiam suam*, 6 August 1964
Enc. *Mysterium fidei*, 9 September 1965
Apos. Exhort. *Marialis cultus*, 2 February 1967
Apos. Letter *Petrum et Paulum*, 27 February 1967
Enc. *Populorum progressio*, 26 March 1967
Enc. *Sacerdotalis coelibatus*, 24 June 1967
Creed of the People of God: Solemn Profession of Faith, 30 June 1968
Apos. Letter *Octagesima adveniens*, 14 June 1971

Sources quoted in the Commentary

Apos. Exhort. *Gaudete in Domino*, 9 May 1975
Apos. Exhort. *Evangelii nuntiandi*, 8 Dec. 1975
Homilies and addresses
Pius V, St
Catechism of the Council of Trent for Parish Priests or *Pius V Catechism*
Pius IX, Bl.
Bull *Ineffabilis Deus*, 8 December 1854
Syllabus of Errors
Pius X, St
Enc. *E supreme apostolatus*, 4 October 1903
Enc. *Ad Diem illum*, 2 February 1904
Enc. *Acerbo nimis*, 15 April 1905
Catechism of Christian Doctrine, 15 July 1905
Decree *Lamentabili*, 3 July 1907
Enc. *Haerent animo*, 4 August 1908
Pius XI
Enc. *Quas primas*, 11 December 1925
Enc. *Divini illius magistri*, 31 December 1929
Enc. *Mens nostra*, 20 December 1929
Enc. *Casti connubii*, 31 December 1930
Enc. *Quadragesimo anno*, 15 May 1931
Enc. *Ad catholici sacerdotii*, 20 December 1935
Pius XII
Enc. *Mystici Corporis*, 29 June 1943
Enc. *Mediator Dei*, 20 November 1947
Enc. *Divino afflante Spiritu*, 30 September 1943
Enc. *Humani generis*, 12 August 1950
Apost. Const. *Menti nostrae*, 23 September 1950
Enc. *Sacra virginitas*, 25 March 1954
Enc. *Ad caeli Reginam*, 11 October 1954
Homilies and addresses
Quierzy, Council of (833)
Doctrina de libero arbitrio hominis et de praedestinatione
Trent, Council of (1545–1563)
De sacris imaginibus
De Purgatorio
De reformatione
De sacramento ordinis
De libris sacris
De peccato originale
De SS. Eucharistia
De iustificatione
De SS. Missae sacrificio
De sacramento matrimonio
Doctrina de peccato originali
Doctrina de sacramento extremae unctionis
Doctrina de sacramento paenitentiae
Toledo, Ninth Council of (655)
De Redemptione
Toledo, Eleventh Council of (675)
De Trinitate Creed
Valence, Third Council of (855)
De praedestinatione
Vatican, First Council of the (1869–1870)
Dogm. Const. *Dei Filius*
Dogm. Const. *Pastor aeternus*
Vatican, Second Council of the (1963–1965)
Const. *Sacrosanctum Concilium*
Decree *Christus Dominus*
Decl. *Dignitatis humanae*
Decl. *Gravissimum educationis*
Decl. *Nostrae aetate*
Decree *Optatam totius*
Decree *Ad gentes*
Decree *Apostolicam actuositatem*
Decree *Perfectae caritatis*
Decree *Presbyterorum ordinis*
Decree *Unitatis redintegratio*
Dogm. Const. *Dei Verbum*
Dogm. Const. *Lumen gentium*
Past. Const. *Gaudium et spes*

Liturgical Texts

Roman Missal: Missale Romanum, editio typica altera (Vatican City, 1975)
The Divine Office (London, Sydney, Dublin, 1974)

Other Church Documents

Code of Canon Law
Codex Iuris Canonici (Vatican City, 1983)
Congregation for the Doctrine of the Faith
Declaration concerning Sexual Ethics, December 1975
Instruction on Infant Baptism, 20 October 1980
Inter insigniores, 15 October 1976
Letter on certain questions concerning Eschatology, 17 May 1979
Libertatis conscientia, 22 March 1986
Sacerdotium ministeriale, 6 August 1983
Libertatis nuntius, 6 August 1984
Mysterium Filii Dei, 21 February 1972
Pontifical Biblical Commission
Replies
New Vulgate
Nova Vulgata Bibliorum Sacrorum editio typica altera (Vatican City, 1986)

Sources quoted in the Commentary

2. THE FATHERS, ECCLESIASTICAL WRITERS AND OTHER AUTHORS

Alphonsus Mary Liguori, St
Christmas Novena
The Love of Our Lord Jesus Christ reduced to practice
Meditations for Advent
Thoughts on the Passion
Shorter Sermons
Sunday Sermons
Treasury of Teaching Material
Ambrose, St
De sacramentis
De mysteriis
De officiis ministrorum
Exameron
Expositio Evangelii secundum Lucam
Expositio in Ps 118
Treatise on the Mysteries
Anastasius of Sinai, St
Sermon on the Holy Synaxis
Anon.
Apostolic Constitutions
Didache, or *Teaching of the Twelve Apostles*
Letter to Diognetus
Shepherd of Hermas
Anselm, St
Prayers and Meditations
Aphraates
Demonstratio
Athanasius, St
Adversus Antigonum
De decretis nicaenae synodi
De Incarnatio contra arianos
Historia arianorum
Oratio I contra arianos
Oratio II contra arianos
Oratio contra gentes
Augustine, St
The City of God
Confessions
Contra Adimantum Manichaei discipulum
De Actis cum Felice Manicheo
De agone christiano
De bono matrimonii
De bono viduitatis
De catechizandis rudibus
De civitate Dei
De coniugiis adulterinis
De consensu Evangelistarum
De correptione et gratia
De doctrina christiana
De dono perseverantiae
De fide et operibus
De fide et symbolo
De Genesi ad litteram
De gratia et libero arbitrio
De natura et gratia
De praedestinatione sanctorum
De sermo Domini in monte
De spiritu et littera
De Trinitate
De verbis Domini sermones
Enarrationes in Psalmos
Enchiridion
Expositio epistulae ad Galatas
In I Epist. Ioann. ad Parthos
In Ioannis Evangelium tractatus
Letters
Quaestiones in Heptateuchum
Sermo ad Cassariensis Ecclesiae plebem
Sermo de Nativitate Domini
Sermons
Basil, St
De Spiritu Sancto
Homilia in Julittam martyrem
In Psalmos homiliae
Bede, St
Explanatio Apocalypsis
In Ioannis Evangelium expositio
In Lucae Evangelium expositio
In Marci Evangelium expositio
In primam Epistolam Petri
In primam Epistolam S. Ioanis
Sermon super Qui audientes gavisi sunt
Super Acta Apostolorum expositio
Super divi Iacobi Epistolam
Bernal, Salvador
Monsignor Josemaría Escrivá de Balaguer, Dublin, 1977
Bernard, St
Book of Consideration
De Beata Virgine
De fallacia et brevitate vitae
De laudibus novae militiae
Divine amoris
Meditationes piissimae de cognitionis humanae conditionis
Sermons on Psalm 90
Sermon on Song of Songs
Sermons
Bonaventure, St
In IV Libri sententiarum
Speculum Beatae Virgine
Borromeo, St Charles
Homilies

Sources quoted in the Commentary

Catherine of Siena, St
Dialogue
Cano, Melchor
De locis
Cassian, John
Collationes
De institutis coenobiorum
Clement of Alexandria
Catechesis III, De Baptismo
Commentary on Luke
Quis dives salvetur?
Stromata
Cyprian, St
De bono patientiae
De dominica oratione
De mortalitate
De opere et eleemosynis
De unitate Ecclesiae
De zelo et livore
Epist. ad Fortunatum
Quod idola dii non sint
Cyril of Alexandria, St
Commentarium in Lucam
Explanation of Hebrews
Homilia XXVIII in Mattheum
Cyril of Jerusalem, St
Catecheses
Mystagogical Catechesis
Diadochus of Photike
Chapters on Spiritual Perfection
Ephraem, St
Armenian Commentary on Acts
Commentarium in Epistolam ad Haebreos
Eusebius of Caesarea
Ecclesiastical History
Francis de Sales, St
Introduction to the Devout Life
Treatise on the Love of God
Francis of Assisi, St
Little Flowers
Reflections on Christ's Wounds
Fulgentius of Ruspe
Contra Fabianum libri decem
De fide ad Petrum
Gregory Nazianzen, St
Orationes theologicae
Sermons
Gregory of Nyssa, St
De instituto christiano
De perfecta christiana forma
On the Life of Moses
Oratio catechetica magna
Oratio I in beatitudinibus
Oratio I in Christi resurrectionem
Hippolytus, St
De consummatione saeculi
Ignatius of Antioch, St
Letter to Polycarp
Letters to various churches
Ignatius, Loyola, St
Spiritual Exercises
Irenaeus, St
Against Heresies
Proof of Apostolic Preaching
Jerome, St
Ad Nepotianum
Adversus Helvidium
Comm. in Ionam
Commentary on Galatians
Commentary on St Mark's Gospel
Contra Luciferianos
Dialogus contra pelagianos
Expositio in Evangelium secundum Lucam
Homilies to neophytes on Psalm 41
Letters
On Famous Men
John of Avila, St
Audi, filia
Lecciones sobre Gálatas
Sermons
John Chrysostom, St
Ante exilium homilia
Adversus Iudaeos
Baptismal Catechesis
De coemeterio et de cruce
De incomprehensibile Dei natura
De sacerdotio
De virginitate
Fifth homily on Anna
Hom. De Cruce et latrone
Homilies on St Matthew's Gospel, St John's Gospel, Acts of the Apostles, Romans, Ephesians, 1 and 2 Corinthians, Colossians, 1 and 2 Timothy, 1 and 2 Thessalonians, Philippians, Philemon, Hebrews
II Hom. De proditione Iudae
Paraeneses ad Theodorum lapsum
Second homily in praise of St Paul
Sermon recorded by Metaphrastus
John of the Cross, St
A Prayer of the Soul enkindled by Love
Ascent of Mount Carmel
Dark Night of the Soul
Spiritual Canticle
John Damascene, St
De fide orthodoxa
John Mary Vianney, St
Sermons

Sources quoted in the Commentary

Josemaría Escrivá, St
Christ Is Passing By
Conversations
The Forge
Friends of God
Furrow
Holy Rosary
In Love with the Church
The Way
The Way of the Cross
Josephus, Flavius
Against Apion
Jewish Antiquities
The Jewish War
Justin Martyr, St
Dialogue with Tryphon
First and Second Apologies
à Kempis, Thomas
The Imitation of Christ
Luis de Granada, Fray
Book of Prayer and Meditation
Guide for Sinners
Introduccíon al símbolo de la fe
Life of Jesus Christ
Sermon on Public Sins
Suma de la vida cristiana
Luis de Léon, Fray
Exposición del Libro de Job
Minucius Felix
Octavius
Newman, J.H.
Biglietto Speech
Discourses to Mixed Congregations
Historical Sketches
Origen
Contra Celsum
Homilies on Genesis
Homilies on St John
In Exodum homiliae
Homiliae in Iesu nave
In Leviticum homiliae
In Matth. comm.
In Rom. comm.
Philo of Alexandria
De sacrificio Abel
Photius
Ad Amphilochium
Polycarp, St
Letter to the Philippians
del Portillo, A.
On Priesthood, Chicago, 1974
Primasius
Commentariorum super Apocalypsim B. Ioannis libri quinque
Prosper of Aquitaine, St
De vita contemplativa
Pseudo-Dionysius
De divinis nominibus
Pseudo-Macarius
Homilies
Severian of Gabala
Commentary on 1 Thessalonians
Teresa of Avila, St
Book of Foundations
Exclamations of the Soul to God
Interior Castle
Life
Poems
Way of Perfection
Tertullian
Against Marcion
Apologeticum
De baptismo
De oratione
Theodore the Studite, St
Oratio in adorationis crucis
Theodoret of Cyrus
Interpretatio Ep. ad Haebreos
Theophylact
Enarratio in Evangelium Marci
Thérèse de Lisieux, St
The Autobiography of a Saint
Thomas Aquinas, St
Adoro te devote
Commentary on St John = Super Evangelium S. Ioannis lectura
Commentaries on St Matthew's Gospel, Romans, 1 and 2 Corinthians, Galatians, Ephesians, Colossians, Philippians, 1 and 2 Timothy, 1 and 2 Thessalonians, Titus, Hebrews
De veritate
Expositio quorumdam propositionum ex Epistola ad Romanos
On the Lord's Prayer
On the two commandments of Love and the ten commandments of the Law
Summa contra gentiles
Summa theologiae
Super Symbolum Apostolorum
Thomas More, St
De tristitia Christi
Victorinus of Pettau
Commentary on the Apocalypse
Vincent Ferrer, St
Treatise on the Spiritual Life
Vincent of Lerins, St
Commonitorium
Zosimus, St
Epist. Enc. "Tractoria" ad Ecclesias Orientales